LOOS
1915

ABOUT THE AUTHOR

Nick Lloyd is a lecturer in the Defence Studies Department at King's College, London, based at the Joint Services Command and Staff College in Shrivenham, Wiltshire. He was educated at the University of Birmingham, where he was founding editor of the Journal of the Centre of First World War Studies. He has taught previously at the University of Birmingham and at the Royal Air Force College in Cranwell, Lincolnshire. He lives in Cheltenham.

LOOS 1915

NICK LLOYD

Front cover illustrations: Troops advancing to the attack through chlorine gas: a remarkable private photograph taken by a member of the London Rifle Brigade on the opening day of the battle of Loos, 25 September 1915. *Courtesy of the Imperial War Museum, HU63277B.* German troops in a shallow trench typical of the early years of the First World War. *Courtesy of Jonathan Reeve JR920b62p193 19001950.*
Back cover and spine illustration: Artist's impression of the British infantry assault. *Author's collection.*

This edition first published 2008

The History Press Ltd
The Mill, Brimscombe Port
Stroud, Gloucestershire, GL5 2QG
www.thehistorypress.co.uk

Reprinted 2015, 2018

British Library Cataloguing in Publication Data.
A catalogue record for this book is available from the British Library.

ISBN 978 0 7509 4676 9

Typesetting and origination by The History Press Ltd.
Printed in Great Britain by TJ International Ltd, Padstow, Cornwall

CONTENTS

LIST OF ABBREVIATIONS

AG	Adjutant-General
AAG	Assistant Adjutant-General
ADC	Aide-de-Camp
AMS	Assistant Military Secretary
APM	Assistant Provost Marshal
Bde	Brigade
BEF	British Expeditionary Force
BGGS	Brigadier-General, General Staff
BGRA	Brigadier-General, Royal Artillery
BLL	Brotherton Library, Leeds
BLO	Bodleian Library, Oxford
CAB	Cabinet Papers
CE	Chief Engineer
CIGS	Chief of the Imperial General Staff
CGS	Chief of the General Staff
C-in-C	Commander-in-Chief
CO	Commanding Officer
CRA	Commanding Royal Artillery
CRE	Commanding Royal Engineers
DA	Deputy Adjutant

DAAG	Deputy Assistant Adjutant-General
DMO	Director of Military Operations
DMT	Director of Military Training
DSD	Director of Staff Duties
DSO	Distinguished Service Order
FOO	Forward Observation Officer
FSR	Field Service Regulations
GHQ	General Headquarters
GOC	General Officer Commanding
GQG	Grand Quartier Général (French General Headquarters)
GSO1	General Staff Officer (Grade 1)
GSO2	General Staff Officer (Grade 2)
GSO3	General Staff Officer (Grade 3)
HAR	Heavy Artillery Reserve
HE	High Explosive
HLI	Highland Light Infantry
HMSO	Her Majesty's Stationary Office
HQ	Headquarters
IWM	Imperial War Museum
KIA	Killed in action
KOSB	King's Own Scottish Borders
KOYLI	King's Own Yorkshire Light Infantry
KRRC	King's Royal Rifle Corps
LHCMA	Liddell Hart Centre for Military Archives, King's College London
MGGS	Major-General, General Staff
MGRA	Major-General, Royal Artillery
NAM	National Army Museum
NCO	Non-Commissioned Officer
OC	Officer Commanding
OHL	*Oberste Heersleitung* (German General Headquarters)
OP	Observation Post
OR	Other Ranks
PRO	Public Record Office
QMG	Quartermaster-General
RA	Royal Artillery
RAMC	Royal Army Medical Corps
RE	Royal Engineers
RFA	Royal Field Artillery
RFC	Royal Flying Corps
RGA	Royal Garrison Artillery
RHA	Royal Horse Artillery

TNA	The National Archives of the UK, Kew
VC	Victoria Cross
WO	War Office

ACKNOWLEDGEMENTS

This book is based upon my PhD thesis, 'The British Expeditionary Force and the Battle of Loos', which was completed at the University of Birmingham in July 2005. During the four years that I spent as a postgraduate student at Birmingham my supervisor, Dr John Bourne, became a personal friend. I will always be grateful to him for his constant help, support and wisdom. A special salute should be paid to Professor Peter Simkins who read through most of the drafts and provided penetrating insight, advice and much-needed encouragement. My external examiner, Professor Gary Sheffield, also deserves credit for helping to iron out a number of inconsistencies within the text. All have been a pleasure to work with.

I have learnt much from all those who have given me the benefit of their expertise during the course of this project. I am indebted to Dr Correlli Barnett, Dr Sanders Marble, Dr William Philpott and Andrew Rawson. My sincere thanks also go to Jonathan Reeve, Sophie Bradshaw and all at Tempus for agreeing to publish the manuscript and for always being supportive and helpful. Needless to say, any errors contained within this book, either of interpretation, diction or research, are mine alone.

Financial support for this project was provided by the School of Historical Studies at the University of Birmingham, which paid my tuition fees in the third year of my PhD, and the *Western Front Association*, which kindly awarded me a research grant.

I wish to acknowledge the generous help and assistance that I have received from the staff of the following institutions: the Bodleian Library; the Brotherton Library; the Imperial War Museum; the Liddell Hart Centre for Military Archives at King's College London; The National Archives; the National Army Museum; the Imperial War Museum; and the University of Birmingham's Main Library.

For various acts of kindness and assistance I would like to thank the following: Matt Brosnan; Harry Buglass for the maps; Susan Campbell; Peter Cluderay; Jean Luc Gloriant; Major A.G.D. Gordon of Cape Town; the late Albert 'Smiler' Marshall; Nick Sedlmayr; Dr John Sneddon; Gareth Weedall; Steven Weselby; and Kate Conlin, Antje Pieper and Delia Bettaney for translating various French and German sources.

There are those without whom this book could not have been started, let alone completed. Heartfelt thanks to Tim and Tez, not only for allowing me to sleep on their sofa during my periodic visits to London, but also for watering and feeding me after long days spent in the archives. Another heartfelt dedication goes out to Louise Campbell who has been a wonderful and inspiring companion. Finally, I would like to thank my parents, John and Sue, and my late grandparents, Gladys and George, for their tireless devotion to my education and wellbeing.

Royal Air Force College, Cranwell, Lincolnshire
February 2006

INTRODUCTION

The Battle of Loos (25 September–13 October 1915) occupies a unique place in British military history. When it took place it was the biggest land battle Britain had ever fought. It witnessed the debut on the Western Front of several New Army divisions that had been raised after the outbreak of war and was the first and only British offensive to be preceded by a discharge of cylinder-released chlorine gas and smoke. The battle was also a key moment in the rise of General Sir Douglas Haig, who replaced Field Marshal Sir John French as Commander-in-Chief of the British Expeditionary Force (BEF) after the battle had ended. But while these facts have been widely recognised as marking a significant milestone in the experience of the BEF, apart from the appropriate volume of the British Official History, published in 1928, Loos has failed to attract much scholarly attention.[1] It remains a 'forgotten battle', lost in the mists of rumour, hearsay and myth.

The Battle of Loos is also important in that it defies the usual image of the First World War. It was fought before modern industrialised warfare, with its shattering artillery bombardments, had turned the Western Front into a hellish moonscape of craters and trenches, devoid of any human movement. British troops fought at Loos in flat caps with a rifle and bayonet. Although certain areas of the battlefield, particularly in the north, saw close-fought bombing actions of the type that would become so familiar to the British later on in the war, there was also fighting in woodland, on slag heaps and in built-up areas, as well as large-scale manoeuvres across the open. Many books deal with the experience of the British Army on the Western Front, but very few have concentrated on this early part of the war, with most British commentators preferring to focus on either 1916, the year of the Somme, or the Third Battle of Ypres ('Passchendaele') in 1917. However, the early battles of the war, particularly during 1915, defined what would happen later on as experience was gained, lessons were learnt and soldiers and politicians gradually came to terms with the revolution in warfare that they were witnessing.

Details of Loos can be found in numerous books and in various individual chapters scattered through more general pieces on the Western Front.[2] Its haunting presence can also be found in a wide variety of memoirs and personal histories.[3] Opinions on the battle have tended to range between the two extremes that generally characterise writing about the British Army during the First World War. The most common view is that Loos was a prime example of 'bungling' on the part of British High Command. Indeed, it may have initially been heralded as a great victory, but as the long-desired war of movement failed to materialise and as the huge casualty returns sank in, disillusionment and disappointment were swift to emerge. Around Loos there lingers a bitter sense of futility and slaughter, only redeemed by tales of astonishing courage. While Robert Graves called the battle a 'bloody balls-up', the experience of another young subaltern distilled down to a feeling of utter helplessness, 'cannon fodder' as he called it.[4] To David Lloyd George, the poor results of the battle – what he called 'futile carnage' – could be blamed squarely upon internal problems within the BEF, particularly the blinkered 'military minds' that so frustrated him.[5] Captain Basil Liddell Hart agreed, calling it 'the unwanted battle', and Alan Clark, whose *The Donkeys* (1961) has perhaps been the most influential account of the fighting, wrote a bitter, if unreliable, polemic against the butchery of the British High Command and the scandalous squandering of the lives of their own men.[6]

This view has not gone unchallenged, however. The British Official Historian, Sir James Edmonds, saw Loos in different terms. In sharp contrast to Lloyd George and Alan Clark, Edmonds's account emphasised the external factors that plagued the BEF during this period, such as the restrictions of coalition warfare, the lack of artillery ammunition, poorly trained officers and men, and the excellence of the Imperial Germany Army. Although Edmonds did not shrink from criticising a number of senior British commanders, most notably Sir John French, he was mainly concerned with other matters. According to him, Loos was the inevitable result of 'using inexperienced and partly trained officers and men to do the work of soldiers, and do it with wholly insufficient material and technical equipment'. He also believed that had 'bad luck' and a 'succession of accidents' not occurred, much more could have been accomplished.[7] Despite the heavy casualties and bitter disappointment, Loos was not futile. For example, Brigadier-General John Charteris, who served on the staff of First Army during the battle, emphasised its role in the 'hard experience' of the Western Front.[8] Another staff officer, Lieutenant-Colonel J.T. Burnett-Stuart, agreed. He felt that the battle had 'taught many lessons', including the importance of 'limited objective' attacks, the movement of reserves and the handling of artillery.[9] In more recent times, John Terraine has defended the capability of British High Command and stressed the 'lack of anything approaching strategic independence', which forced Britain to take part in a battle for which she was ill prepared and which her generals had counselled against.[10] The continuing influence of these ideas can be found in two recent popular accounts: Gordon Corrigan's *The Unwanted Battle* (2006) and Niall Cherry's *Most Unfavourable Ground* (2005), both of which echo the conclusions first made in the British Official History.[11]

Which of these opposing views is correct? While the more vitriolic attacks of the 'lions led by donkeys' school can be safely dismissed,[12] an explanation for the problems experienced by the British at Loos that relies totally upon external factors is not satisfactory, however. Indeed, not all historians have been persuaded by this line of argument. One of the most influential critics is the Canadian historian Tim Travers. Travers occupies something of a middle position between those who see the problems experienced by the BEF as primarily caused by internal problems – for example, poor command and leadership – and those who blame external factors, such as the lack of pre-war preparation, the quality of the enemy and the constrictions of coalition warfare. While agreeing that a 'learning curve' took place and the BEF certainly improved and developed during the war, Travers is critical of the structure and ethos of the pre-war Regular Army. According to Travers, it was rigid, dominated by factions, cliques and class, and was also curiously backward-looking. In a number of books and articles, Travers has criticised the British High Command for its reluctance to abandon an established, but out-of-date and even dangerous, mental paradigm of the 'cult of the offensive', which elevated the importance of character and morale in warfare above firepower and technology, with devastating consequences.[13]

Travers is not without his critics, however. A consistent concern is his reliance upon several 'court gossips' – including the correspondence of the military theorist Basil Liddell Hart – and his failure to explain the massive improvement in the BEF's battlefield performance in 1917–18.[14]

Nevertheless, Travers's findings on 1914–16 remain valid. External problems, such as lack of equipment and shells there may have been, but as numerous historians have pointed out, these were not helped by some of the curious decisions made by British High Command itself. Several examples from 1915 will suffice. The vindictive dismissal of Sir Horace Smith-Dorrien, the repeated, unnecessary and fruitless counter-attacks at the Second Battle of Ypres, and the debacle over the reserve divisions (XI Corps) at Loos point to structural failings in command and leadership within the BEF that had little to do with shell shortages or political pressure. This cannot be ignored. In 1915 the BEF was far from being the hardened meritocracy of later years, but on the other hand, it was not an army of stupid amateurs, welded to optimistic and out-of-date pre-war ideas either. It is clear that only by seeing both external and internal factors together can a true picture of events emerge.

This book will examine both how the BEF came to fight the Battle of Loos, and how it planned and executed the subsequent operation with reference to both internal and external factors. It aims to place the experience of the British at Loos firmly in the context of much recent research, including the 'learning curve' and 'revolution in military affairs',[15] and seeks to shed fresh light upon some of the controversies of the battle, such as the employment of poison gas and the contentious issue of the reserve divisions. It is based mainly upon unpublished archive material, most of which is contained in archives scattered around London, such as The National Archives, the Imperial War Museum, the National Army Museum and the Liddell Hart Centre for Military Archives. The personal papers of many of the key actors have been consulted at length, including those of Herbert Asquith, Sir John French and Lord Kitchener. A host of other personal papers, diaries and eyewitness accounts have been also been used. Most of the operational and tactical details from the battle stem from the army papers held in The National Archives. These sources include unit war diaries, operation orders and draft plans, and allow a close analysis of the events of the battlefield to emerge, which is untainted by later arguments and controversies. The correspondence between Sir James Edmonds and numerous veterans of Loos has also been extensively mined. These letters provide useful information on command, especially the relationships between senior officers, the 'feel' of the battlefield and the impact of Loos upon subsequent British offensives.

Although many of these sources have been available for nearly forty years and have been quoted briefly in some recent studies, the vast majority of the material used in this account has never been consulted previously in the context of a complete operational history of the Battle of Loos. They can, therefore, provide important and often 'fresh' information about the strategic complexities of the war, how the battle was planned and executed, the wider development of the BEF on the Western Front, the response of Britain's wartime volunteers to battle, and the nature of combat during the First World War. Admittedly these sources can have drawbacks. For example, unit reports and war diaries can range in detail – from the concise to the very poor – and some tend to exaggerate the heroism of the rank and file, but they often provide an unparalleled glimpse into the operational and tactical realities of the Western Front. This study will concentrate primarily on the planning and execution of the attack at Loos from the British perspective, while the German side of operations will only be summarised briefly. Analysing the tactical performance of German units on the Western Front can be difficult because many of the battalion and brigade war diaries were destroyed in Allied bombing raids during the Second World War. However, from a consultation of the relevant regimental histories and the German Official History, both written in the 1920s, important details can be gleaned, which can aid understanding of how the British attacks progressed and why there was no decisive breakthrough.

1

THE ORIGINS OF THE BATTLE OF LOOS: MAY–AUGUST 1915

The Battle of the Marne in September 1914 cast a long shadow over the events of the following four years. The collapse of Germany's bold bid for victory in the west, and the failure of France's efforts to take the war to the enemy in Alsace-Lorraine, left both sides in uncharted territory. With the creation of a trench stalemate stretching from the North Sea to Switzerland, Germany and France were forced to rethink their strategies in the winter of 1914–15. After fevered debates over whether to concentrate her strength against France or Russia, Germany sanctioned increased efforts in the east and the Balkans during 1915. France, meanwhile, was left to face the devastating consequences of the loss of much of her industrial heartland and the presence of the enemy a mere five days' march from Paris. With inactivity a politically unacceptable strategy, the French Army conducted a series of major offensives on the Western Front throughout 1915, determined to drive the invaders from the soil of France.

Beginning in late December and continuing until the end of March, the First Battle of Champagne raged on the wooded slopes between Rheims and Verdun. The French infantry, floundering heroically against the prepared German positions, desperately tried to open a big enough breach in the enemy lines to win a major strategic victory. But although much blood and ammunition was spent, the German line stubbornly refused to crack. The fighting then flickered further north. Between May and June the Second Battle of Artois was fought, and while the nature of trench warfare was beginning to become depressingly familiar, with its heavy casualties and limited gains of ground, tantalising success was achieved around Souchez and Vimy Ridge. One French corps almost reached the battle-scarred summit, before ammunition supplies dwindled, troops became exhausted and the suffocating cloak of stalemate descended once again upon the opposing positions.

The French High Command, known as *Grand Quartier Général* (GQG), was not, however, unduly disturbed by the events of the winter and spring. The autumn would see the culmination of France's offensive efforts in 1915 with huge sequenced attacks in both Artois and Champagne. Aimed at striking the flanks of the German line, which bulged out around Noyon, it was hoped that these attacks would cause the collapse of the entire enemy position and restore the war of movement. This great effort required the application of not only every man and gun in the French Army, but also the assistance of her allies on the Western Front. The Belgian Army, largely locked up in the last remaining free corner of Belgium around the Yser, would be unable to help, but the British Expeditionary Force (BEF), holding a line of ever-increasing length from Ypres to Lens, would prove a valuable ally. Britain's contribution to the autumn offensive would take the form of the Battle of Loos, a subsidiary operation fought around the northern outskirts of Lens, on the left of the French attack in Artois.

The failure of the Schlieffen Plan had profound consequences for Germany's strategy during the First World War.[1] Haunted by the prospect of a war on two fronts, which it was believed Germany could not win, it had been an article of faith for Count Alfred von Schlieffen and his successors that only by an annihilating victory in the west (*Vernichtung*) could victory be achieved. With France regarded as the most dangerous of the Reich's foes, the vast bulk of Germany's strength would be deployed in an ambitious flanking march through Belgium and northern France. It was calculated that by bringing such overwhelming strength to bear, France's numerically weaker forces would succumb in six weeks, leaving Germany to deal with Russia's more ponderous masses at leisure. But events had not conformed to Schlieffen's grand design. This forced a dramatic revision in Germany's traditional orientation. The decision in the winter of 1914–15 by the German High Command, in effect, to reverse the tenets of the Schlieffen Plan and attempt to gain victory in the east, had not been taken lightly.[2] The breakdown and subsequent retirement of Colonel-General Helmuth von Moltke, Chief of the General Staff, in mid-September 1914 had brought the then War Minister, General Erich von Falkenhayn, to the fore. Falkenhayn was 54 years-old in 1915, a cold, calculating, but thoroughly modern soldier.[3] Although he despaired that Germany's failure to win a short war meant that she was now condemned to lose a long one, Falkenhayn still believed in the primacy of the Western Front. But this position was becoming under increasing criticism, especially from those officers who had experienced a different war in the east. With the spectacular tactical success of the Battle of Tannenburg (26–31 August 1914) already approaching near mythical status, the views of its chief architects, the duo of General Paul von Hindenburg and General Erich Ludendorff, could not be ignored. They believed that Russia was now Germany's weaker foe and massive pincer movements in the east could retrieve the decisive victory lost on the Marne.[4]

While the backroom intrigues that surrounded the reorientation of German strategy in this period do not concern us, suffice to say Falkenhayn was extremely reluctant to divert his gaze from the west. Haunted by Napoleon's doomed campaign against Russia in 1812, Falkenhayn dreaded his armies being sucked into the endless expanses of Poland and Ukraine. As he recorded in his memoirs, 'Napoleon's experiences did not invite an imitation of his example.'[5] But under pressure Falkenhayn eventually gave in and agreed to renewed offensive operations in the east. The performance of German troops versus the Russians had been cause for celebration, but the weakness of Austria-Hungary had been palpable, with defeats in Galicia and Serbia sharpening the ethnic divisions in her armed forces. German reinforcements were duly dispatched eastwards. Although Falkenhayn tried to temper the grand plans of Hindenburg and Ludendorff, their operations were spectacularly successful. On 2 May 1915 the booming of a four-hour German bombardment signalled the beginning of the Gorlice-Tarnow offensive. What one historian has described as the 'greatest single campaign of the whole war',[6] Gorlice-Tarnow precipitated the great Russian retreat of the summer. The Russian Army, crippled by unrest at home and shortages of even the most basic war materiel, could offer only spasmodic resistance. By the end of the summer, the Central Powers had advanced over 300 miles and inflicted around two million casualties on their enemy. This success then filtered down to the Balkans. On 7 October, assault troops crossed the Danube and forced the Serbs south through Montenegro and Albania. Bulgaria joined the Central Powers the same month, helping to complete the conquest of Serbia.

1915 was a year of repeated German success, but it was a bleak year for the Allies, and not only on the Western Front. Although buoyed by Italy's declaration of war against Austria on 23 May, it soon became clear that she would not be able to achieve decisive results. The following month she began the first of eleven bloody, but inconclusive, battles of the Isonzo. Stalemate had also spread to the Mediterranean. While the oceans had long been swept of German raiders, and command of the sea was firmly back in the hands of the British Admiralty, there were some who wanted the Royal Navy to be doing more. Winston Churchill, the energetic First Lord of the Admiralty, was one of them. By the close of 1914 he had become the leading proponent of an ambitious scheme to clear the Dardanelles Straits. Strategically daring, even reckless, it imagined a swift, surgical naval strike that would clear the way to Constantinople and defeat Turkey, Germany's main ally in the region. If a way through to the Black Sea could be made, Russia could be supplied and her surplus stores of grain exported to the west. But, as has been recounted numerous times, the Gallipoli expedition, far from being a decisive operation using 'spare' British naval strength, became an open, running sore that devoured ships and precious infantry divisions throughout the year. The belated Anglo-French landing at Salonika, and its swift bottling-up, only served to underline Allied powerlessness.

Debate in Germany over how the war should be won was confined to a small clique of high-ranking officers and statesmen, but the more unstable political situation in France made such a closed debate unlikely. The French Parliament, after being evacuated to Bordeaux in early September 1914, returned to Paris on 20 December, beginning ordinary sessions of parliament the following month.[7] With this return to something approaching normality, French political life regained much of its zest and character. Criticism of the war effort, especially the role of the Commander-in-Chief, which had been silenced after the *Union Sacrée* of August 1914, gradually resurfaced as 1915 wore on. The lack of any real progress in the war, despite heavy fighting – and the catastrophic French casualties – unsettled the country and made the increasing rumours of mismanagement and incompetence, which emanated from the various sections of the war effort, intolerable. Although bitterly resented by the army, a number of parliamentary commissions were set up in 1915 and began to investigate the alleged errors and mistakes that had been made.

As it was difficult to criticise the Commander-in-Chief – most of the French newspapers were solidly pro-army – much of the discontent was directed at the Minister of War, the 56 year-old Socialist, Alexandre Millerand.[8] Widely admired as a calm and determined patriot, Millerand had great political experience. During his time as War Minister in 1912–13 he had worked tirelessly to prepare the nation and her army for a war that he regarded as inevitable. Millerand believed that his primary task was to let the generals get on with the war and keep political interference to a minimum. Others, however, did not share these views. As 1915 continued, criticism of Millerand, and pressure on him to yield some of his power, gradually increased. At a meeting of the Cabinet on 27 May, Raymond

Poincaré, the President of the Republic, accused Millerand of not only giving GQG too much leeway, but also 'of ceaselessly abdicating the rights of civilian power'.[9] That Millerand was too authoritarian, independent and unaccountable was also the opinion of the powerful Senate Army Commission, and with the lack of any tangible Allied victory, Millerand's time was running out.

The Second Battle of Artois ground to a bloody halt in June; the French Tenth Army suffering over 4,000 casualties for every square kilometre it had advanced.[10] Despite its failure and the unsettled political situation at home, the French Commander-in-Chief, General Joseph Jacques Cesaire Joffre, was determined that a renewed offensive in July could prove decisive. Joffre was a big man. Physically intimidating, 'the Victor of the Marne' was a stubborn, phlegmatic engineer, direct and intolerant, yet surprisingly calm. After making his reputation in Africa and the Far East he rose rapidly. Untouched by any trace of scandal that had so damaged the pre-war army, he became Chief of the General Staff in 1911. By the outbreak of war Joffre's imprint was firmly upon the French Army. While purging his command of officers that he did not regard as having sufficient 'offensive spirit', Joffre had adopted Plan XVII, a series of mobilisation orders to be followed once war broke out.[11]

Why did Joffre believe that a new offensive could succeed where previous ones had failed? An analysis of French strategy in this period lies beyond the scope of this study, but it is necessary to understand the principles upon which it was based. Unlike Falkenhayn, Joffre did not have the luxury of deciding where his army would fight. As Correlli Barnett has observed, the German occupation of Belgium and northern France in 1914 presented the Allies with an 'inescapable political compulsion' to drive the invaders out.[12] Joffre recorded in his memoirs how:

> The best and largest portion of the German army was on our soil, with its line of battle jutting out a mere five days' march from the heart of France. The situation made it clear to every Frenchman that our task consisted in defeating this enemy, and driving him out of our country.[13]

This had been the rationale behind the heavy fighting of the winter and the larger efforts in the spring. It would again be the chief motivation for the autumn offensive. Joffre was impatient to achieve decision on the battlefield. He was aware that France's waxing strength would reach its numerical and material peak in the autumn of 1915. If the enemy forces at present occupying northern France could not be defeated, how would the French Army be able to outfight the ten or fifteen corps that Germany could (conceivably) bring from the east in the event of a Russian collapse?

Criticism of this aggressive strategy was not long in arriving. As in Britain, there were serious misgivings in France about letting her soldiers – in Churchill's stinging phrase – 'chew barbed wire' in the west. An increasing number of politicians would have preferred to defer attacking the German lines, at least until Britain's New Armies were ready and fully equipped. On 6 August 1915, Poincaré stated in Parliament that he did not look forward to a new offensive in France and believed that the best policy to pursue was 'active defence'. Joffre was disgusted by such an attitude. He once remarked how 'he had certainly never dreamt of such a thing', and that because it was 'a form of war which was entirely negative… he was therefore wholly opposed to it'.[14] It was also 'unfair' to France's allies, especially Russia, then being pummelled into defeat. According to Joffre, it was 'morally impossible not to pay heed to the appeals of our unfortunate allies'.[15] Joffre was also buttressed by the sheer size of his planned operations. By early June he had sketched out plans for a much larger offensive to take place sometime in July. Instead of singular attacks either in Artois or Champagne, a concept of 'sequenced concentric attacks' was developed.[16] Joffre's plan was a simple extension of his thoughts behind the earlier attempts to break the enemy line in the winter and spring. The flanks of the great German salient between Arras and Rheims were to be struck. A preparatory attack would initially draw off enemy reserves, before the main attack broke through the German lines, causing the collapse of the entire enemy position. Joffre believed that once this had been achieved, a war of movement would resume and Germany's armies could be defeated in detail. As was communicated to the British, it was hoped that 'an attack by upwards of 40 divisions on a front extending from the present left of the Tenth Army to a point some 10 kilometres South of Arras [and] an attack by some 10 divisions in Champagne' could be arranged.[17]

Would this attack achieve its ambitious objectives? Considering both the strength of the German defensive positions and the weaknesses afflicting the French Army, historians have not been slow to criticise Joffre's aggressive strategy.[18] Indeed, although Millerand's tenure as War Minister oversaw vast improvements in the production of war materiel, it could not compensate for a number of serious faults at all levels within the French Army.[19] Confronted by humiliating defeat in 1870, political disarray and demoralisation over the Dreyfus Affair, and a whole series of funding crises and doctrinal confusions, by the turn of the century the French Army was suffering from a crisis of confidence. Fortified by a unifying belief in the importance of 'offensive spirit' and 'moral force', however, a considerable revival had occurred by 1914. Although the extent of its pre-war 'cult of the offensive' has perhaps been overstated, there is little doubt that a belief in the power of the tactical attack, even into the teeth of unsuppressed enemy rifle and machine gun fire, was an important pillar of French military thought before the war.[20] The Commandant of the *École Supérieure de la Guerre*, Colonel Ferdinand Foch (later to command *Groupe d'Armées du Nord* during 1915) was one of the most forceful proponents of the need to inculcate troops with sufficient 'offensive spirit'. Although Foch and his fellow thinkers – notably the influential 'High Priest' of the offensive, Colonel Louis Loizeau de Grandmaison – recognised the strength of modern firepower, they believed that the most important factor in warfare was morale and having an unshakeable will to victory. If troops were imbued with such élan, which echoed an earlier, Napoleonic concept of war, it was believed that they could cross the fire-swept zone between opposing armies and take the fight to the enemy with the 'cold steel'. Such an emphasis on the power of the offensive and morale in warfare proved resistant to change. Joffre's communiqué to his generals on the eve of the autumn offensive remained consistent with this pre-war thought. While admitting that heavy artillery was the 'principal weapon of attack', he explained that the 'dash and devotion of the troops are the principle factors which make for the success of the attack'.[21]

The problem with such 'offensive spirit' was the power of modern weaponry. The great, almost exponential, increase in firepower that had occurred in the second half of the nineteenth century made closely packed infantry formations and bayonet charges extremely hazardous, even verging on the suicidal. Steady troops in entrenched positions, using breech-loading rifles, machine guns, and backed up by quick-firing artillery, were almost impossible to dislodge, without at least crippling casualties amongst the attacking troops. Indeed, the changed nature of warfare had been brutally unmasked as the French pushed into the 'lost provinces' of Alsace and Lorraine in the opening weeks of the war. 'Offensive spirit' had proved a poor substitute for adequate training, tactical skill and material superiority. A recent account records how the French Army was riddled with:

> Incompetent, often elderly commanders, regimental officers too few in number for effective command and with inadequate maps, combat intelligence unreliable or incorrectly evaluated, cavalry steeped in a doctrine of sabre charges rather than reconnaissance, and infantry of reckless bravery but low tactical competence.[22]

Little wonder casualties were so heavy, reaching 200,000 by the end of August alone.[23] The French were also seriously outgunned. Their famed 75mm quick-firing field gun was ill-suited to a war of position – the weight of shell it fired was too small to demolish fortifications or blow up enemy guns – and Germany had nearly double the number of field guns with 'an almost total monopoly in heavy artillery'.[24]

The weaknesses of the French Army meant that it was simply unable to fulfil the role Joffre allocated to it. The repeated efforts throughout the year to appeal against the verdict of stalemate only served to weaken France further. While the French Army suffered over 1,430,000 casualties during 1915 and never again showed the same élan and willingness to sacrifice, the political divides in French society were put under increasing strain as the war dragged on.[25] It was becoming increasingly clear that France could not win the war single-handedly. But what of France's leading allies on the Western Front, the British?

The strategic dilemma faced by Britain during 1915, especially the debate between 'westerners' and 'easterners', has been discussed at length.[26] By the close of 1914 serious and long-term decisions had to be made about Britain's war effort. It was becoming increasingly clear that 'business as usual', the rather loose ethic that Britain had adopted since the outbreak of war, was not going to bring about victory. But what strategy would replace this was not immediately obvious. Would all of Britain's strength be deployed in France in support of General Joffre, or could she still operate a historically independent strategy outside the confines of the Western Front? Because a General Staff had only been created in 1904, Britain was ill equipped with either the personnel or the administrative machinery for an informed choice to be made. The lack of detailed and precise information had the unfortunate result in a profusion of amateur strategy, personified by the meddling figure of Winston Churchill. British strategy was, therefore, often made as a response to current events and vague theories, rather than to a sober appreciation of the strength of the nation and where best this could be brought to bear.

Matters were complicated by the collapse of Prime Minister Herbert Asquith's embattled Liberal Government in May. The formation of the Coalition on 26 May 1915, following the dual blows of the 'Shells Scandal' and the resignation of the First Sea Lord, Admiral Lord Fisher, reflected a growing public uneasiness over the direction of the war. The new government, still led by Asquith, may have promised a firmer, more committed prosecution of the war, but as A.J.P. Taylor acidly commented, only 'appearances were changed'.[27] The new coalition was 'from the outset a suspicious and divided body'.[28] The meetings of the War Cabinet (now called the Dardanelles Committee) were more regular than they had previously been and contained more members than ever, but the decentralisation of power hampered firm decision-making. Different opinions prevailed on every matter; every matter took hours to decide. Maurice Hankey, the amiable Secretary of the Dardanelles Committee, complained that although, individually, 'a more capable set of men could not have been got together,' they were collectively 'never a good team'.[29]

Perhaps the most outstanding member of the Cabinet was the Secretary of State for War, Field-Marshal Earl Kitchener of Khartoum.[30] Kitchener was Britain's most experienced serving soldier. An imposing, gruff, taciturn man, Kitchener had a solid bank of combat experience, organisational expertise and administrative success behind him. From the opening days of the war Kitchener believed it would last at least three years – rank heresy to the popular 'over by Christmas' view – and necessitate the raising of substantial reinforcements to bolster the regular army.[31] Despite desiring to spend the war in Egypt, Kitchener accepted the position of Secretary of State for War on 5 August. Until his death at sea off Scapa Flow in June 1916, Kitchener worked tirelessly in the War Office, organising and administering Britain's growing role in the war. Yet this was not without difficulty. His method of work was notoriously authoritarian and 'oriental'. He tended to shoulder too heavy a burden, being chronically unable to delegate simpler tasks to his aides. And although he oversaw the rapid, and admittedly chaotic, expansion of the British Army and provided a vast increase in guns and shells throughout 1914–15, this was not enough to supply both the BEF and the New Armies.[32]

Kitchener's strategic view of the war was always global and long-term. He wanted French and Russian forces to bear the brunt of the war in the first two years of the conflict, while Britain's New Armies were readied and equipped. Sometime in 1916–17 – in theory – Kitchener's forces would be ready to strike the *coup de grace*, thus winning the war and dominating the peace. As early as 2 January 1915, Kitchener had expressed severe doubts as to the feasibility of breaking the German lines in the west.

> I suppose we must now recognise that the French Army cannot make a sufficient break through the German lines of defence to cause a complete change of the situation and bring about the retreat of German forces from northern Belgium. If that is so, then the German lines in France may be looked upon as a fortress that cannot be carried by assault and also cannot be completely invested.[33]

His views had changed little by the summer. In a paper called 'An Appreciation of the Military Situation in the Future' (dated 26 June), Kitchener recognised that the war would probably last into 1916. Until then, the only area where the Allies could secure an important success was in the Dardanelles. Kitchener was therefore of the opinion that the Allies should adopt a policy of 'active defence' in France. He was adamant that 'French resources in men must not be exhausted by continuous offensive operations which lead to nothing, and which possibly cause the enemy fewer casualties than those incurred by us.'[34] But this caused friction. Although most of Britain's senior politicians agreed with Kitchener (including Asquith, Churchill and Lloyd George), he was forced to balance this evident preference for operations against Turkey with continual pressure from not only the French, but also from the senior officers of the BEF, who urgently requested more drafts and equipment.

Nevertheless, from March 1915, when Britain began the operations to clear the Dardanelles Straits, events on the Western Front assumed a secondary importance. Frustrated at the uneasy stalemate persisting in France, Kitchener, supported by his Cabinet colleagues, gave priority to the attempts to knock out Turkey. The failures in Artois and the BEF's shambolic performance at Aubers Ridge in May only served to underline the impossibility of progress in the west in the near future.[35] The first meeting of the Dardanelles Committee took place on 7 June.[36] It was eventually agreed that a further effort should be made in the Dardanelles. General Sir Ian Hamilton, Commander-in-Chief of the Mediterranean Expeditionary Force (MEF), was to be reinforced with three New Army divisions. It would allow him, given the time taken to ship the reinforcements into position, to make another big attack sometime early in August.

But what would Britain's allies make of this? Relations between Britain and France since August 1914 had undoubtedly been close, but they were strained by mutual incomprehension and the frictions of war. Not only were the British and French bitterly split between themselves, but they also had differing wider agendas. The French were not intrinsically opposed to the Dardanelles expedition, but were never terribly enthusiastic and continually pressed for every ounce of British strength to be deployed on the Western Front. But the British shied away from such a drastic step, preferring to retain some strategic independence. The Allies were also separated by a considerable linguistic barrier; few British could speak good French and many senior French officials refused to speak English.[37] These differences of opinion and temperament were clearly illustrated at the first Anglo-French conference of the war, held at Calais on 6 July 1915. Asquith's later remark that he had 'never heard so much bad French... in his life' highlighted the difficulties of inter-allied co-operation during 1915.[38]

The Calais Conference was one of the most important British strategic milestones of the war. Unfortunately, because no minutes were taken, what was discussed has been the subject of some confusion. It has been generally accepted that with his fluent French Lord Kitchener dominated the proceedings. In line with a Cabinet paper of 2 July, Kitchener made it clear that while the British Government was keen to sanction a renewed summer offensive in the Dardanelles, it would look gravely upon a new attack on the Western Front, preferring instead a policy of 'active defence'.[39] Although some evidence conflicts with the generally accepted version of events – notably the diary of Sir John French[40] – most British accounts agree with Asquith, who believed that 'the man who came out best, not only linguistically, but altogether, out of the thing was K[itchener]'.[41] In his journal Viscount Esher, the Liberal politician, recorded how Lord Kitchener 'delivered a most excellent oration at the meeting; so excellent that the French have wavered and are wavering'.[42] Similarly, although not present at the meeting, Hankey believed Kitchener 'was splendid and dominated the whole show'. According to him, after three hours of discussion, eight points were agreed upon.

1. To continue the war of attrition.
2. No great offensive on a scale which, if unsuccessful, would paralyse us for further offensives later on.
3. Local offensives on a considerable scale.
4. Very heavy entrenchments everywhere.
5. The British to hold a longer front.
6. The new armies to be sent when ready, though the Government to keep their hands free in this respect.
7. The Dardanelles operation to continue.
8. Diplomatic efforts to be concentrated on Romania rather than Bulgaria.[43]

Although most of the French Ministers had apparently been persuaded by Kitchener's performance, Joffre's plans for another large-scale offensive had evidently not been derailed. While most of the British delegation went away well pleased, believing that future offensives in France had been shelved, this was rejected, or at least subtly ignored, at an International Military Conference that took place at Chantilly the following day.

The International Military Conference took place at Chantilly on 7 July. Apart from Sir John French most of the British delegation was not present. Joffre dominated the meeting, saying that the war could only be decided in the large theatres and it was in the interests of the Allies that they should 'prepare to launch a powerful offensive at the earliest possible moment'.[44] Curiously, French agreed with Joffre's sentiments – they had been discussed on 24 June[45] – adding that he 'quite agreed with General Joffre' and would 'assist as far he can any attack of [the] French army'.[46] This startling divergence has attracted considerable attention. Why did Joffre continue to work towards a new offensive and why did Sir John ignore the expressed opinion of his government? One of Kitchener's biographers, Philip Magnus, has suggested that the crucial event was an unofficial interview between the Secretary of State and Joffre before the Calais Conference opened. It is virtually certain that such a meeting occurred; it appears in several reliable accounts, but there is little precise information on what was discussed.[47] According to Magnus, this meeting resulted in a 'private agreement' whereby, in order to gain Joffre's blessing for a renewed effort in the Dardanelles, Kitchener agreed to support his offensive in France if Hamilton failed to clear a way to Constantinople.[48]

Kitchener and Joffre never mentioned the existence of such a pact, and it has been disputed. According to George Cassar, although a pact was not reached, a compromise was. While the BEF would be heavily reinforced, it would be spared participation in a major offensive. After an interview with Henry Wilson (Chief Liaison Officer to GQG) in late June, Kitchener had asked him whether the French would agree to support a new effort at Gallipoli. Wilson had replied that they would do so *only* if a large number of New Army divisions were in France by the winter.[49] On this basis, therefore, Kitchener promised to send his New Armies to France, beginning with six divisions in July, to be succeeded by six more every month. If Joffre still believed that his attack must take place, it must be undertaken by the French *alone*.[50] This view has generally been accepted but it remains problematic.[51] It seems that the answer to why Calais and Chantilly were so different lies in the nature and purpose of both conferences. While Calais was the first Anglo-French conference of the war, Chantilly was merely a meeting of staffs; what David French has called 'little more than an expression of mutual goodwill'.[52] It seems that although he was firmly opposed to any new offensive on the Western Front, Kitchener agreed to let the staff discussions at Chantilly go ahead.[53] After all, what harm was there in planning?

Contrary to what most historians have found, what exactly would happen in the late summer of 1915 was never explicitly decided upon. And although the New Armies would be sent to France, this was not a 'blank cheque', and marked only a halfway stage in a total British commitment to the Western Front. Indeed, a striking feature that emerges from the records of two conferences is the vagueness of the proceedings. British and French Governments took what they wanted from the discussions. As Maurice Hankey found out several days later, the understandings arrived at were being 'interpreted differently in Paris to what they were in London'.[54] Sir William Robertson (CGS GHQ) even informed the King's Private Secretary, Clive Wigram, that 'nothing very definite may be settled or can be settled between the Allies at these meetings', but they did give a good opportunity 'for comparing notes'.[55] Similarly, at Chantilly Millerand had concluded that the conference 'only confirms the ideas of the various commanders in chief and in no way modifies plans'.[56] Allied strategy would wait upon the march of events.

The BEF may have been Britain's most well-organised, equipped and trained army to ever set foot on foreign shores, but by the time the First Battle of Ypres had died down in November 1914, it was a pale shadow of its former glory. Largely gone were its hardened veterans; the victims of the murderous conditions of modern warfare. They had been replaced by a mixture of territorials, reservists, 'dugouts', the Indian Corps and individual volunteers, hurriedly trained and rushed to the front. As might have been expected, the BEF struggled to adapt to a war of unprecedented destruction. The battles it undertook in 1914–15 consumed men and munitions on a scale unimaginable before the war. A shortage of ammunition, particularly artillery shells, was the most noticeable deficit, but an array of equipment, such as shovels, sandbags and grenades, was also required for the new science of trench warfare. These shortages were not helped by the haphazard expansion of the BEF. It had gone to war in August 1914 consisting of two corps, but had grown into six corps, divided into two armies, barely five months later. During 1915 the BEF again trebled in size.[57]

Yet the war still had to be won. German forces were camped across most of Belgium and large expanses of northern France, and with major operations underway in the east, were going nowhere. The French were initially unimpressed by the offensive capability of the BEF, and preferred to use the British to hold stretches of the front. But they were forced to rethink this during 1915. The BEF began the first of its attempts to break through the German lines alone in March 1915 at Neuve Chapelle. The rest of its engagements (until 1917) were all conducted as part of bigger Anglo-French operations.[58] During 1915 General Sir Douglas Haig's First Army, which held the southern sector of the BEF, conducted these attacks. All were unsuccessful in that they did not break cleanly through the German lines and reach the designated objectives. An initial break-in was achieved at Neuve Chapelle (10–12 March), but German reserves skilfully stopped any further progress. Aubers Ridge (9 May) was a disaster with the infantry attack being halted on strengthened German defences, although the limited success at Festubert (15–27 May) did augur well for the future. By the end of 1915 the BEF had suffered nearly 380,000 casualties.

Nothing had prepared Field-Marshal Sir John Denton Pinkstone French, the Commander-in-Chief of the BEF, for the devastating effects of prolonged contact with the Imperial German Army.[59] A soldier of immense experience and proven courage, French was widely seen as one of the greatest cavalry commanders in British history. He had been one of the few British soldiers to emerge from the South African War (1899–1902) with his reputation enhanced. His daring leadership of the Cavalry Division, especially his epic ride at Klip Drift and the subsequent relief of Kimberley, had been one of the most famous actions of the war.

His post-war service was equally impressive. Between 1902 and 1907 he was GOC Aldershot, and following that he became Inspector-General of the Forces. Although he was forced to resign his appointment as Chief of the General Staff in 1914 over the Curragh incident,[60] he was ideally placed to take charge of the BEF when war broke out.

Sir John was not alone in finding the strain of war difficult to cope with. By the spring of 1915 he was 62-years old and in failing health. The limitations in his character and personality were magnified by the stress of war. French was fiery, emotional and temperamental, hardly ideal qualities for a complex war in which the ability to deal with the higher demands of politics and strategy, and to co-ordinate operations alongside Britain's allies, was of far greater importance than personal bravery or 'dash'. His intellectual qualities were also in doubt. Although Sir John had gained a reputation after the South African War for being one of the most modern and forward-looking cavalry thinkers in the British Army, his views remained traditional. He had always been a believer in the continued relevance of traditional shock tactics for the *arme blanche*. He had never attended the Staff College, disliked intellectual pursuits and did not look upon 'book-learning' with much sympathy. French found it particularly taxing having to deal with both his political masters in London and with his allies in France. As Richard Holmes has written, 'Sir John was chronically unsure of his position'.[61] He disliked Lord Kitchener intensely, waged an on-off feud with General Sir Horace Smith-Dorrien (GOC II Corps 1914 and GOC Second Army 1915), which ended with the latter's dismissal in May 1915, and helped to engineer the 'Shells Scandal' that was a contributing factor in the collapse of Asquith's Liberal Government. Sir John's relations with officers of the French Army were equally unstable. After he had discovered that Kitchener had consulted Joffre over whether to replace him in November 1914, Sir John felt understandably eager to cultivate French support. This resulted in considerable tension when Sir John was pressed to conduct operations that he thought either dangerous or unsuitable. French's relations with the fire-eating General Ferdinand Foch (Commander *Groupe d'Armées du Nord*) were little better. Foch possessed a considerable influence over Sir John, often moving him from dire premonitions of disaster to wild flights of optimism.

The staff that surrounded Sir John at GHQ (based at St Omer) did their best to temper the excesses of his character, but with mixed results. French's CGS, the blunt, straight-talking Lieutenant-General Sir William Robertson, was a soldier of rare skill and competence. His excellent performance as QMG of the BEF during 1914 has been recognised by almost all authorities.[62] Although he would waver during the dark days of 1917, Robertson was always an advocate of the war on the Western Front, believing that only by 'the defeat or exhaustion of the predominant partner in the Central Alliance', namely Germany, could victory be achieved.[63] He was suspicious of the strategic ideas of 'easterners' and always regarded the Western Front as the decisive theatre. But Robertson was no blind supporter of Joffre's offensives and would have preferred more modest, 'wearing out' attacks on favourable parts of the German line, at least until Britain's New Armies were fully ready to take to the field.

While Robertson was a staff officer of the first rank, who did much for the smooth running of GHQ, his relationship with Sir John was never warm, and his influence was accordingly limited. Indeed, GHQ may have contained several officers of outstanding competence – such as Brigadier-General F.B. Maurice (BGGS Operations) and Brigadier-General G.M.W. Macdonogh (BGGS Intelligence) – but its 'diverse and often contentious mix of personalities and ideas' meant that there were a number of mutual feuds and jealousies.[64] The poisonous influence of Major-General Henry Wilson (Chief Liaison Officer to GQG) over Sir John was a continual problem. Although he had been manoeuvred out of his rather vague position of 'sub-chief' of the General Staff in January 1915, Wilson still possessed an intellectual dominance at GHQ. He occupied a unique position in the history of the BEF, having taken a leading role in staff discussions over the possible deployment of a British force on the left of the French Army in the event of war.[65] An ardent Francophile, Wilson was widely distrusted by his own army and his murky role in the Curragh 'Mutiny' of March 1914 only added to his reputation as a disloyal intriguer. Robertson voiced a widely felt concern when he accused Wilson 'of leaning too much to the side of the French and not sufficiently to the side of the army to which he belongs'.[66] Vain yet ugly, awkward but confident, Wilson always remained something of an outsider within his own army.

French's command was dictated by the brief set of instructions he had been issued with by Kitchener before embarking for France in August 1914.[67] They enshrined a paradox that Sir John would feel between supporting the French and protecting the interests of the BEF. He was assured that the 'special motive' of the BEF was to 'support and co-operate with the French Army against our common enemies'. Kitchener, naturally cautious and hardly thrilled at the prospect of major continental engagements, warned Sir John that because the size of his army was strictly limited, he was to look gravely upon risking his troops in forward movements, especially when large French forces were not involved. It was evident that Sir John would have to tread a thin line. While making every effort to coincide with plans of their allies, Kitchener stressed that Sir John's command was 'an entirely independent one' and that under no circumstances would he come under the orders of an Allied general.

Kitchener's orders had been vague enough in August 1914, but in the changed circumstances of spring 1915 they were beginning to look badly dated. What were Sir John's thoughts on the situation? His views were mixed. While favouring an independent northern flank operation (the 'Zeebrugge Plan') to free the Channel Coast from German occupation, this was vetoed by the War Cabinet in January 1915.[68] Aware that he had only kept his position because of Joffre's support, Sir John was left with little option but to support the former's plans for large-scale offensive operations in France. And while his moods sometimes bordered on depression, French did believe that a breakthrough in the west was possible. He had disagreed with the views expressed in Kitchener's letter of 2 January, believing that with good weather and ample stocks of ammunition, it was possible to pierce the German lines.[69] Indeed, the initial success at Neuve Chapelle had lent weight to this idea. Although French was desirous to prevent operations in the eastern Mediterranean from eclipsing his command, he was not blind to the strategic opportunities in the Dardanelles.[70] But he did resent the continual diversion of troops, ammunition and other resources from France.

The immediate origins of the Battle of Loos can be traced back to a series of unofficial meetings between Major Sidney Clive (Head of the British Mission at GQG) and various French liaison officers on 3 and 4 June 1915.[71] When the possibility of further offensive operations was floated by Joffre, Sir John's reaction was consistent with his earlier opinions. Although he disagreed with certain requests for the relief of French troops and the evacuation of the Ypres Salient, because the French Army was now reaching its probable maximum, Sir John believed the Allies should strike as soon as possible, adding that a decisive success in recent operations had only been thwarted by of a shortage of ammunition and reserve troops. He utterly rejected a strategy of passive defence. As he told Lord Kitchener, 'such a course can only have a disastrous effect upon the moral and offensive spirit of our troops'.[72]

Although the Calais Conference had tentatively agreed that no large-scale offensives would take place on the Western Front in the foreseeable future, French met General Foch on 19 June and they mulled over Joffre's offensive, then scheduled for 10 July.[73] Foch wanted the British to aid the attack by taking over twenty-two miles of front south of Arras (to be held by Third Army, then forming in England) and by attacking alongside the French Tenth Army, which held the front from Lens to Arras. Sir John was initially enthusiastic and authorised the reliefs. He told General Foch that 'I entirely agree with the French Commanders as to the necessity of attacking on the broadest front', and promised to launch 'the most powerful attack I could between south of the Béthune canal' and the left of the

French Tenth Army. Following his interview with Foch, French wrote to the commander of First Army and asked for a detailed report to be drafted on the feasibility of the proposed operation.

The report that General Sir Douglas Haig submitted to GHQ on 23 June was a model of clarity and sound military reasoning.[74] Later events would prove it mostly correct in its appreciation of the difficulties of the proposed ground. After riding around the lines, trying to find suitable viewing points, and then consulting some of his divisional commanders, Haig's thoughts gradually coalesced. The ground, littered with miners' houses and slag heaps, was 'very difficult'.[75] Although it might have been 'possible to capture the enemy's first line of trenches… it would not be possible to advance beyond because our own artillery could not support us'. According to Haig 'the enemy's defences are now so strong that they [have to] be taken [*sic*] by siege methods – by using bombs and by hand to hand fighting in the trenches!' Yet trench fighting was the only feasible way to advance, the ground above being 'so swept by gun and machine gun and rifle fire that an advance in the open except by night is impossible'.[76] Not only were the enemy's defences 'very carefully sited', but also the whole area from Violaines to Lens was dominated by their artillery.[77] Although extra forming up and supporting trenches could be constructed, because of the white, chalky soil, they would be virtually impossible to conceal from enemy observation. And even if the German front line positions were taken and the advance pressed eastwards, it would not be easy to support the forward troops.

Haig's report introduced a frosty breath of realism into the planning process and was to have a considerable impact upon how the proposed offensive was seen at GHQ. When combined with the findings of the Allied Munitions Conference, held at Boulogne on 19 June, Sir John's clear horizon began to fill with clouds. The conference concluded that for an offensive on the Western Front to have 'a reasonable chance of success', it would have to be delivered on a front of twenty-five miles by over thirty divisions and supported by 1,150 heavy guns.[78] Not until the spring of 1916 could such a mass of offensive power be gathered. Previously, Sir John had been very keen to support Joffre in his offensive, but the combined effects of Haig's report and Boulogne produced a crisis of confidence at GHQ. It marked an important turning point in the planning of the Loos offensive.

The situation that faced Sir John French in late June 1915 was a difficult one. While given a little breathing space – the first of several postponements to the date of the attack had been sanctioned by Joffre (which was now pencilled in for the end of August) – French was beginning to have doubts. Although he remained robustly optimistic, believing that Haig had exaggerated the difficulties of the ground, he concluded, rather gloomily, that he would now have to consider 'the whole subject very carefully'.[79] He still believed in the strategic necessity of Joffre's large-scale offensive, but henceforth displayed a growing reluctance to attack in the suggested location. Strategic optimism was thus combined with tactical pessimism. So concerned did Sir John eventually become that he proposed to drastically curtail British involvement. As might have been expected, the French were resolved to resist this at all costs.

Joffre's plans had also changed. It was gradually becoming clear to Sir John, despite Joffre's best efforts to disguise the fact, that the main effort was now going to be made, not in Artois, but in far-away Champagne.[80] French was now effectively being asked to mount a subsidiary operation (on very unfavourable terrain) to *another* subsidiary operation, rather than being part of a major offensive. This rankled with Sir John. He began to complain frequently of French duplicity.[81] His attitude hardened. When Joffre told him on 11 July that 'we *must* all take the offensive', Sir John curtly replied that 'he always supported Joffre but Joffre appeared to have changed his plans'.[82] He was correct, there had been major disagreements in the French camp. Even Foch, one of the 'High Priests' of the offensive before the war, had now come to the conclusion that a major breakthrough operation in Champagne was no longer feasible.[83] French tried to ease himself from Joffre's grip by offering to take over more line around Ypres, but this was refused.

The ground was the problem. In desperation Sir John decided that he must see it for himself. When he visited the hill of Notre Dame de Lorette, which overlooked the mining area north of Lens, he was not too disheartened.[84] But any remaining optimism Sir John still had now rapidly began to drain away. Foch had written to Wilson on 15 July asking for the British attack to be delivered by ten divisions and a maximum number of guns and ammunition.[85] This was greeted with little enthusiasm. Sir John asked Clive on 20 July to 'remind Joffre of the difficult nature of the country occupied by the Germans in front of the First Army' and that he could only make a strong holding attack.[86] By 22 July French was 'doubtful' about the proposed operation. 'To have any prospect of success', he grumbled, 'such an attack would have to be supported by an almost unlimited expenditure of artillery ammunition.'[87] But, as French well knew, nothing remotely approaching this was available.

While Wilson raved at the pessimism now reigning at GHQ – Clive found him 'much depressed'[88] – Robertson wrote to Haig and asked whether his views on the proposed ground had changed.[89] The commander of First Army replied that they had not.[90] For Haig, the resources at his disposal simply did not:

> permit of an offensive being undertaken on a large scale, such as might lead at once to freedom of manoeuvre, and it is therefore necessary, whilst being prepared for any eventuality in case of success, to limit the offensive to a definite operation within the scope of the forces.

While the area north of Lens was unsuitable, Haig did believe that a 'very definite advantage' would be gained if his forces could push forward and occupy the crest of Aubers Ridge, the distant goal First Army had been vainly trying to reach all spring. French agreed, confiding in his diary that the ground offered 'the least tactical advantages'.[91] He also suggested that the Messines–Wytschaete Ridge could be attacked instead.

Sir John's misgivings were shared by most of the senior officers of the BEF, with the usual exception of Wilson.[92] According to Clive 'everyone who knows the ground has made up his mind that… it is impossible to make progress'.[93] This found no sympathy with the French. At Frévent on 27 July Foch was insistent that the British fight on the left of Tenth Army in order to magnify the effect of both attacks.[94] Sir John's remarks about the difficulty of the ground did find some grudging agreement, but Foch could offer little succour. His fatalistic comment that 'the enemy's lines are strong everywhere, and therefore an attack on some other part of the line would perhaps not be much easier and would certainly give greatly inferior results' was hardly reassuring. The meeting ended with no clear resolution in sight, only French promising to 'consider' Foch's points.

Sir John took two days to 'consider' the results of Frévent. By now he was deeply upset at the details of the proposed offensive and became more so with every passing day. He was evidently still unable to reconcile the dilemma enshrined in Kitchener's instructions of August 1914. The twin aims of supporting the French and of not endangering the BEF now seemed mutually exclusive. Indeed, they were beginning to tear Sir John's command apart. His haphazard relationship with Foch and his dependence on Joffre only complicated matters. French replied on 29 July. After reassuring Joffre of his loyalty and support, Sir John confirmed that his opinions had not changed.[95] Any attack south of the La Bassée canal, he explained, 'as would culminate in the seizure and possession of the hills which command LENS is very improbable'. Even if the enemy's front line trenches were successfully captured, the assault troops would 'find themselves held up by a mass of fortified houses, buildings, slack heaps [*sic*] extending over many square miles of country'. Sir John was understandably averse to sending his men into this morass.

If Sir John had expected any concessions from Joffre he was to be disappointed. Joffre replied on 5 August.[96] He was unmoved by French's concerns, commenting that 'it seems to me that no more favourable ground than that which extends north of Angres to the canal de La Bassée can be found'. If an attack were pressed, in conjunction with Tenth Army, a gigantic pincer movement would be conducted around the enemy's fortified positions in Lens and Lievin. Joffre, either in complete ignorance of the tactical difficulties of the ground or believing that only there could the BEF give practical help to his operations, concluded that 'I cannot suggest a better direction of attack than the line Loos–Hulluch'. As might have been expected, Sir John read Joffre's letter with dismay, taking five days to reply. He repeated that his opinions had not changed. While still believing that attacks north of the La Bassée canal would offer more valuable results, he did add that he would direct his forces 'in accordance with the wishes which you, as Generalissimo expressed'.[97] Yet Sir John had not completely acquiesced. In the last paragraph he explained how:

> I am reinforcing my First Army, which I have directed to assist the attack of your Tenth Army by neutralizing the enemy's artillery and by holding the infantry on its front.[98]

This was French's 'artillery plan', the logical synthesis of his dilemma between supporting the French and not hazarding his army. It would allow him to take part in Joffre's offensive, but not risk an infantry battle over such difficult ground. First Army's guns would simply endeavour to knock out enemy batteries around Lens in support of the French attacks further south.

It is clear that in 1915 British artillery did not have the technical skill, the ammunition or even the number of heavy guns necessary to perform counter-battery fire effectively.[99] This would not have overtly concerned French. He had not adopted the 'artillery plan' because it was a valid and effective way of supporting Tenth Army, but simply because it allowed First Army to keep its infantry in their trenches.[100] The 'artillery plan' was, of course, anathema to Joffre who read French's letter with alarm. After consulting Wilson (who was seemingly working against the wishes of his own Commander-in-Chief), Joffre replied two days later.[101] After reminding French of his promise to support the operations of Tenth Army, Joffre felt that:

> This support can only be effective if it takes the form of a large and powerful attack composed of the maximum force you have available, executed with the hope of success and carried through to the end…

Joffre added, with perhaps a touch of menace, that 'you are aware of the importance of the effort which the French Army is preparing'.

So where did all this wrangling leave future operations on the Western Front? Joffre's irresistible force had met French's immovable object. Sir John's stubborn resistance to the details of the proposed offensive had now become a considerable stumbling block. Yet Joffre's determination had not wavered, especially following his dismissal of one of his army commanders, General Maurice Sarrail, on 22 July. Sarrail had long been a favourite of the Republicans and the left in France, and his dismissal, probably the result of both being perceived as a threat to Joffre and of middling ability, only added fuel to the fires of civilian–military conflict. Inevitably Millerand bore the brunt of the criticism. Amid these new storms, Joffre contacted the embattled War Minister and asked him to talk to Lord Kitchener about the intransigence of the British. As early as 30 July Joffre had written to Millerand about a scheme for putting the British temporarily under French authority, to ensure the planned attacks were properly co-ordinated.[102] By mid-August it was evident to the French that unless Sir John was ordered by his own government to attack, the participation of the BEF would be at best half-hearted. But how would the British react?

By mid-August 1915 the international situation had deteriorated markedly for the Allies. Although the summer had passed quietly for the BEF – hoarding shells and absorbing the first of the New Army divisions – momentous events had taken place on other fronts. Beginning on 2 May, Gorlice-Tarnow had only been the first in a grand series of Austro-German blows that shattered the Russian armies and resulted in the virtual evacuation of Poland. Events had also turned irrevocably against the British on other fronts. By the second week of August it was clear that Hamilton's daring attempt to outflank the Turkish positions at Suvla Bay had failed. Asquith was devastated, writing to a confidant that 'in the whole 12 months of the war, nothing has happened comparable to this'.[103] Others were equally upset. Churchill, in his typically flamboyant prose, recorded how 'the long and varied annals of the British Army contain no more heart-breaking episode than the Battle of Suvla Bay'.[104]

Suvla Bay marked the final straw in the whole series of mistakes and missed opportunities that marred the entire Dardanelles campaign. With the autumn drawing nearer, which would make it more difficult to supply Hamilton's army by sea, the Allied forces at Gallipoli had finally run out of time. As the dim echoes of Suvla reverberated around the War Office, Millerand's request for a firm British commitment to a new offensive arrived on Kitchener's desk. Reluctantly, therefore, the Secretary of State travelled to France on 16 August and spent three days discussing the proposed operations with both the French authorities and the BEF. When he returned to England late on the evening of 19 August, British participation in Joffre's offensive had been guaranteed and Sir John French had been told that, whatever his previous objections, he must now 'co-operate vigorously' in the plans.[105]

Why had Kitchener abandoned his deeply held aversion to offensives on the Western Front and ordered Sir John to attack? Things seemed to have come full circle since Kitchener's apparent triumph at Calais on 6 July. This has been the subject of some speculation. In a recent article, Rhodri Williams has written that British politicians, especially Lord Kitchener, 'acted on the basis of an exaggerated estimate of the extent of defeatism in France'.[106] Central to Williams's thesis is the role that Viscount Esher, and a number of leading French politicians, played in feeding their British contacts with information about how fragile French commitment to the war had become. French politicians and soldiers (plus most of the senior officers of the BEF, notably Robertson, Haig and Wilson) were all of the opinion that the more strength Britain deployed in France, the sooner the German armies would be defeated. In order to convince the wavering British Government 'to concentrate its expanding military resources on the Western Front', a 'myth' of French war-weariness was manufactured, which proved remarkably successful.[107] Yet, as Williams and a number of other historians have made clear, public support for the war in France was actually solid and unyielding, only beginning to waver during 1917.[108]

While Williams's article is a welcome study of the difficulties of Anglo-French relations during this period, it is limited. In particular, it takes too little account of the great influence and importance that Lord Kitchener placed on Russia, and neglects the more global view of the war that Britain and her Empire always had. A less Franco-centric interpretation can be found in Keith Neilson's *Strategy and Supply* (1984), which offers a different view of where British strategic priorities lay. Neilson suggests an 'alliance' theory of British strategy, 'one which takes into consideration the impact of Russia and the Eastern Front in particular on British planning'.[109] This is largely absent from Williams's article, but it is clear that Russia was a key cornerstone in the strategic view of Lord Kitchener.[110] Although concern about French war-weariness was undoubtedly important, it seems that the crumbling state of the Russian war effort and the shock of Suvla Bay prompted Kitchener to make a renewed commitment to the Western Front. As he explained to Haig on 19 August, the Russians 'had been severely handled and it was doubtful how much longer their armies could withstand the German blows'.[111]

Kitchener's biographers are generally split over the exact reasons for his startling decision, reversing as it did his stated desire for an active defence in France during the rest of 1915. Philip Magnus's 1958 biography stated that Kitchener was merely honouring a 'private understanding' reached with Joffre at Calais on 6 July.[112] George Cassar's *Architect of Victory* (1977) offers a more detailed portrait of Kitchener's strategic dilemma, albeit without giving the importance of Russia much prominence. According to Cassar, Kitchener gave his support to Joffre's offensive because, as he later informed the Dardanelles Committee, 'he saw no other way of avoiding a fatal rupture with the French'.[113] Philip Warner admits a number of possibilities, including the rather dubious assertion that Kitchener was supporting Joffre because he wished to be elevated to the position of Supreme Allied Commander, a prospect then being discussed.[114] Warner's other conclusion, that Kitchener felt Joffre's offensive 'offered a chance of winning a war which the British might otherwise lose', is also doubtful. Kitchener's statement to the Dardanelles Committee on 20 August that 'the odds were against a great success' throws considerable doubt upon Warner's assertions.[115] Trevor Royle's *The Kitchener Enigma* (1985) supports the 'alliance' viewpoint, commenting that his decision was 'due mainly to his interpretation of events on the eastern front and the Russian reaction to them'.[116]

The sudden reverses at Tannenberg and the Masurian Lakes in August 1914, and the heavy fighting of the following spring, had confirmed that the Russian 'steamroller' had most definitely been stopped. The idea that Russia might conceivably withdraw from the war was the stuff of nightmares. If Russia went, so did the Allies' numerical superiority, and the German forces would be able to bring reinforcements back to the Western Front. Simultaneously, thousands of Austrian and Turkish forces would be free to move against the Serbians, Italians or British. Although the dramatic events on the Eastern Front may have been taking place over nine hundred miles from the corridors of Whitehall, the gravity of the situation was not lost on the Secretary of State for War. Kitchener had always been aware of Russian military might – often from the hazy view of India's north-west frontier – and to see it so lightly torn apart was deeply distressing.[117] Kitchener echoed the fear of a Russian collapse to French, telling him that 'the Russian news is very serious. I fear we cannot rely on them for much more.'[118]

In order to understand what impact this 'Russian news' had on Kitchener, it is necessary to examine the reports he received from a handful of British officers serving as attachés in the east. Arguably the most important, but certainly the most well-informed officer was the British Military Attaché in Russia, Lieutenant-Colonel Alfred Knox.[119] Knox possessed an extensive knowledge of the Russian armed forces and chronicled, in some detail, how serious the problems within the Tsar's army had become.[120] On 26 May, commenting on the Austro-German drive on the south-west front, Knox gloomily reported that 'the Russians have been driven off a line, which they had sat for four to five months, after two days' fighting', and noted the 'slackness and fatalism' of the officer corps.[121] As the retreat continued the situation deteriorated further.[122] By 6 June the Russian Third Army was described as a 'harmless mob', and in his despatch of 18 June, Knox was warning that the situation on the Eastern Front was 'less favourable than it has been since the commencement of the war'.[123] As well as severe shortages both of artillery and rifle ammunition,[124] casualties had been heavy, especially among officers, for which there was a constant demand.[125]

With these disasters came the understandable sense of betrayal and abandonment within Russia. 'The Russians feel', wrote Knox, 'that their army is being made to bear more than its fair share.'[126] This sentiment only increased as the summer wore on and the inactivity of the Allies in the west became more noticeable. These misunderstandings bred ill feeling. So bad had things got that the Grand Duke Nicholas personally lectured Lieutenant-General Sir John Hanbury-Williams (Head of the British Military Mission to Russia) on 'broken [British] promises and disappointed [Russian] expectations' in June.[127] Colonel Knox and his colleagues were also sometimes subjected to 'unpleasant' verbal attacks by their Russian counterparts.[128] This attitude was repeatedly commented upon by Sir George Buchanan, the British Ambassador in Petrograd. On 24 July he had warned Sir Edward Grey at the Foreign Office of a severe shortage of rifles and that 'the [Russian] public is accusing France and Great Britain of not making more pronounced effort to relieve pressure on this front'.[129] 'Until we are in a position to take a serious offensive in the west,' Buchanan wrote on 7 August, 'nothing will convince [the] Russian public that we are rendering Russia the assistance on which she had counted in her hour of trial.'[130] Hanbury-Williams agreed, lamenting on 11 August that certain rumours and messages had been circulating, which hinted 'that delayed action in taking the offensive there [Western Front] tended to increase the difficulties here'.[131] Particularly troublesome was Russian disappointment with British arms contracts, especially with the Vickers firm, which repeatedly failed to meet targets and deadlines during this period.

Kitchener also had other sources of information. On 19 July 1915, Count Benckendorff, the Russian Ambassador in London, handed Kitchener a letter from the Russian Commander-in-Chief, the Grand Duke Nicholas Nicholaevich. The letter, one of only two from the Grand Duke – both from 1915 – revealed how serious the situation had become. After detailing the various directions of the German advance, the Grand Duke added that:

> In view of these circumstances each action of the Allied armies which prevents the possibilities of new transports of German troops to the Eastern Front is of prime importance.[132]

The Duke was pressing for action on the Western Front. If the Allies had not done all they could to relieve German pressure, it was not inconceivable that peace could be made; indeed Kitchener had been warned by Brigadier-General Hon. H. Yarde-Buller (British Mission with GQG *des Armées Françaises*) on 24 July that if Warsaw fell, the Germans would offer peace.[133] The spectre of a separate German-Russian peace haunted the Allies throughout 1915. As violence, strikes and rioting flared across Russia, vivid echoes of the revolution in 1905 resurfaced. The Acting Vice Consul in Moscow, Robert Bruce Lockhart, could offer no comfort, recording 'a great increase of pessimism and peace talk' in early August.[134] Buchanan's letter of 18 August only added to the gloom. As well as worrying about the general depression of the people, Buchanan commented on rumours of revolution and of a separate peace. There was also 'a good deal of criticism' over the inaction of the armies in the West.[135]

By early August, as the British were finalising plans for a renewed attack in the Dardanelles, the battered Russian forces were in crisis. The fall of Warsaw on 5 August was, in the words of one commentator, the 'culminating tragedy' of the whole summer campaign.[136] Captain James Blair (Assistant Military Attaché) believed that the Austro-Germans could penetrate as far as they wanted into Russia, because 'there is nothing to stop them'.[137] Blair's subsequent despatch three days later echoed this, warning that the Germans could even advance as far as Petrograd.[138] Knox was equally as concerned, recording 'terrible' Russian losses during the fighting around Warsaw and how 5th (Siberian) Division had been 'practically annihilated'.[139] On 15 August, just before Kitchener set sail for France to see Joffre and French, another despatch from Blair arrived, commenting upon the 'growing' feeling that the Allies 'were not doing all they could to assist Russia in her misfortunes'.[140] But with these grim reports often came thinly veiled ideas and advice about what could be done to arrest the situation. Blair argued on 7 August that 'a successful advance on the part of the Allies on the west would immediately alter the whole situation', and he was not alone in this view.[141] Sir William Robertson's 'General Staff Note on the General Military Situation', issued in early August, also made a powerful case for attacking in the west to relieve the pressure on Russia. He concluded that the Allies must 'take the offensive at the earliest possible opportunity'.[142]

These then were the reasons why Kitchener agreed to fight in France. Yet if the situation in France was not unimportant, it seems that French moral weakness did not have such a great impact on Kitchener, but rather a desire to avoid a diplomatic and military row when the international situation was so bad. At the Dardanelles Committee meeting of 3 September, Churchill pressed Kitchener 'to discourage, by every means, the idea of the prosecution of a violent offensive in France'.[143] Kitchener had simply replied that 'if he attempted to do that it would break the Anglo-French Alliance', adding that 'it was not in his power to force that view'. Kitchener's correspondence with Millerand also casts further doubt on Williams's assertion that fear of French defeatism was the *primary reason* British support had been given. Kitchener wrote that:

> The fine attitude of the French troops, and their excellent morale, have made a deep impression on me and I am convinced that under the skilful direction of their commanders, they will go on to victory.[144]

He added, tellingly, that 'the Russian situation is making me anxious. It must be given our full consideration and I think it would be as well to reassure the Russian government, in order to prevent certain harmful influences from striving to push matters to the very worst and to bring about disunity between the Allies.'

Before the BEF could begin detailed preparations for the offensive, Kitchener's decision had to be ratified by the Cabinet. This was done at the meeting of the Dardanelles Committee on 20 August. It was one of the saddest, yet most important conferences of the war.[145] It took the first step in limiting, and then winding down, the operation to clear the Dardanelles Straits, and yet another step towards a total British commitment to the Western Front. As Rhodri Williams noted, a 'further step had been taken towards the Somme'.[146] After discussing the present operations in the Dardanelles at some length, Lord Kitchener pointed out that 'owing to the situation which now existed in Russia he could no longer maintain his attitude, which was agreed upon in conjunction with the French at Calais [in July], viz., that a *real* serious offensive in the West should be postponed until all the Allies were quite ready.'[147] Kitchener then added that:

> There was another point unconnected with the actual strategy, and that was that trench work was becoming very irksome to the French troops, and that an offensive was necessary for the *moral* [*sic*] of the French army, amongst the members of which there was a good deal of discussion about peace.

Whether Kitchener truly believed this is unclear, but it was certainly another reason for action.[148] Kitchener's remarks were understandably unwelcome – indeed many ministers were shocked – and Churchill seems to have secured a kind of personal victory during the meeting, with his forceful and compelling arguments for a passive defence in the west. Asquith was equally disheartened, but although he was possibly the only minister with sufficient stature to stand up to Kitchener, he seems to have meekly acquiesced in the new arrangements, having too high an opinion of the Secretary of State to contradict him.[149] Kitchener's sad comment that 'unfortunately we had to make war as we must, and not as we should like to' summed up the British war effort in 1915. The relevant parties were subsequently informed.[150]

Much ink has been spilled in recent years over the origins of the Somme campaign of 1916, particularly over the extent to which British strategy was subordinated to, or independent of, the French Army.[151] Regarding the Battle of Loos there is little doubt over this matter. The pressure that Britain's allies placed upon the BEF during this period was undeniable. However much politicians in London may have agonised over where to send Britain's New Armies and what type of operation they should be involved in, by the late summer of 1915 the worsening international situation meant that such a debate was becoming increasingly irrelevant. As has been shown, the Battle of Loos emerged as a military gesture designed to appease the fraught nerves of the French and Russian Governments, which by the summer of 1915 were beginning to falter under the stress of total war. As Basil Liddell Hart gloomily noted, Loos was an 'unwanted battle',[152] fought against the opinions of those British officers on the ground, and originally designed more for the political balm it would give to Britain's allies than for any tangible military gains that might result. Nevertheless, as shall be discussed in the following chapter, there were those in the BEF who felt that the coming offensive could do real damage to the German Army and, just possibly, end the war on favourable terms for the Allies.

For the British, the summer of 1915 had seen vacillation, disagreement and meagre resources stretched too thinly. As the disaster that would occur in France now began to unfold, the final vestiges of 'business as usual' were dismantled. Within a month of the autumn offensive in France, the first steps towards compulsory military service had been taken with the Derby Scheme, and Asquith had also successfully pressured Kitchener into instituting a proper General Staff in London, headed by Lieutenant-General Sir Archibald Murray, a committed 'westerner'.[153] And although the debate over where the British armies should fight was still bitter and divisive, it was now largely academic. British strength in France gradually increased as 1915 drew to a close. By the end of the year, with three armies in the trenches, what would become the Somme offensive of the summer had been agreed upon. But the situation for the Allies was still unsettled, and by October, with the new Briand Government in France,

Alexandre Millerand – the War Minister who had worked so hard to free the army from political interference – had been outmanoeuvred and replaced. Joffre's time was now surely running out. The great irony of the long, winding origins of the Battle of Loos was that to have been of most assistance to Russia, the battle should have taken place in late July or early August. Owing to the serious delays and political machinations the grand offensive did not actually take place until late September, when the main damage to Russia's armed forces had already occurred.[154] By this time the great retreat had ended, numerous Russian armies had reformed and the Austro-German forces were too weak to mount further attacks. As early as 31 August 1915 – barely eleven days after the British had finally decided to mount an offensive to take some pressure off Russia – Falkenhayn had begun to divert his gaze back to the west.[155] Allied action had never been so badly co-ordinated or so ill conceived.

2

OPERATIONAL PLANNING: AUGUST–SEPTEMBER 1915

On 6 September 1915 General Sir Douglas Haig gave the main pre-battle conference at the Chateau of Hinges, First Army's headquarters.[1] All the senior First Army officers were present at this gathering, at which Haig expressed his thoughts on the coming attack and repeated the reason why the British and French must launch a new offensive: to take some pressure off Russia. First Army would, therefore, support the French to the 'full extent' of its power. But this was not to be the limited artillery action mooted in early August. Haig was now confident of not only securing the line Loos–Hulluch, but also of taking Hill 70 and then pushing onto the Haute Deule canal, over five miles from the British front line. Anticipating a 'rapid' advance, Haig told the officers that 'it is not enough to gain a tactical success. The direction of our advance', he believed, 'must be such as will bring us upon the enemy's rear so that we will cut his communications and force him to retreat.'

Haig's apologists have tended to see Loos as a tragic example of what happens when politicians go against the professional opinions of soldiers – and to some extent it was – but the tactical arrangements for the battle, as John Terraine has explained, were 'Haig's responsibility'.[2] In contrast to his earlier concerns about an attack between the La Bassée canal and Loos, the commander of First Army had now, seemingly, changed his mind. With an army that, as he fully recognised, was short of guns, shells and trained officers and men – literally everything that modern war required – Haig was planning not merely a limited subsidiary operation, but a high-risk breakthrough aimed at securing a *strategic* victory over the German *Sixth Army*. How Haig came to anticipate this rapid and decisive advance, when all previous experience of First Army during 1915 had been of limited, sometimes non-existent, gains with correspondingly heavy casualties, must be understood if one is to appreciate how the Battle of Loos was planned and fought.

This striking development, from the earlier pessimism to the ambitious and far-reaching plan subsequently adopted, is perhaps the greatest question concerning the planning of the Battle of Loos. Traditional interpretations have tended to stress that this was simply because the orders Sir John French received from Lord Kitchener called for a major 'all-out' attack to be pressed to support Britain's allies. On closer inspection it can be seen that this 'all-out' attack emerged, not so much from Kitchener's orders – which allowed considerable operational scope – but out of the conflicting opinions (and subsequent confusion) between French and Haig as to how the battle would be fought. This stemmed from a number of factors, including Sir John's waning interest in the battle and his recurrent ill health, which did much to hamper GHQ's control of operations. There is also the role of Sir Douglas Haig to reassess, especially in the development of the 'all-out' attack, his thoughts on the theoretical nature of warfare and his attitude to technology, particularly gas.

On the afternoon of 5 August 1915 – the anniversary of British mobilisation the previous year – the sleepy village of Hinges, set amongst open fields two miles north of Béthune, became the base for the headquarters of First Army. After spending most of the summer at the chateau of Aire, Haig had transferred to Hinges to be closer to the front for the coming, *decisive* battle. From the quiet grounds of his headquarters, Haig commanded an army that consisted of over 260,000 men, supported by around 70,000 horses and mules, and split more or less evenly into four corps. Ever since its inception on 26 December 1914, First Army had held the southern sector of the British line. By September 1915 this was twenty-one miles in length. It stretched from the town of Armentières in the north, where it joined General Sir Herbert Plumer's Second Army, to Lens in the south, where the left flank of the French Tenth Army was deployed.[3]

A stocky, dour Presbyterian Scot, Haig was 54-years old, and a waxing power within the British Army.[4] Although they had worked closely together for many years, and held similar views on the continued relevance and importance of cavalry, the cold, inarticulate Haig could not have been less like the emotional Sir John French. While the latter was at his happiest when galloping across the veldt, Haig was more accustomed to working behind the scenes as a staff officer. He was more of an 'educated soldier' than Sir John and had been the author of several military manuals, including *Cavalry Training* (1907) and *Field Service Regulations* (1909). But there were flaws in Haig's character. He may have been a quiet, urbane officer of determination, focus and strict professionalism, but in some respects, he was curiously backward looking; a traditionalist who found it difficult to make the mental leap necessary to understand the warfare that would develop on the Western Front. He was also an incurable optimist, whose glass was always half full. And when this was buttressed by his powerful sense of religious destiny, it was to prove a formidable combination.

While Haig's ability as a commander has been endlessly debated, in order to understand the operations First Army conducted in this period, it is necessary to examine those subordinate officers who were tasked with turning Haig's initial ideas into a workable plan. Corps was the key level of command. First Army consisted of four corps, each containing around 60,000 men.[5] By the summer of 1915 they were deployed as follows. On the extreme left was III Corps, commanded by Lieutenant-General Sir William Pulteney. III Corps was deployed from Armentières to a point opposite the Aubers Ridge. Here it linked up with Indian Corps north of the village of Neuve Chapelle, the scene of much bitter fighting earlier in the year.[6] At the village of Givenchy, just north of the La Bassée canal, Indian Corps met Lieutenant-General Hubert Gough's I Corps. Gough's sector crossed the canal, eventually drawing up on the left of IV Corps on the Vermelles–Hulluch road. IV Corps was commanded by Lieutenant-General Sir Henry Rawlinson and completed First Army's lines.

It was in the days after Sir John French had first proposed his limited 'artillery plan' that Haig began seriously to consider offensive operations in the La Bassée–Loos area. Although only required to neutralise enemy artillery batteries on its front, if the French made major gains south of Lens, First Army would be required to advance and complete the defeat of the enemy. This operation would be made by I and IV Corps, deployed on the southern half of First Army's front. At a meeting with his corps commanders on 13 August, Haig asked Gough to draft plans for the capture of a massive German earthwork (known as the Hohenzollern Redoubt), while Rawlinson was to take the village of Loos and possibly look to an advance towards Hill 70.[7] From the plans the two commanders subsequently drafted it is possible to see a divergence in approach. This seems to have stemmed largely from their differing characters and ideas about war. While Gough's plan was relatively simple – a division would 'rush' the German positions at dawn, following a preliminary bombardment and a gas discharge – Rawlinson's was much more cautious. He was sceptical about the use of gas and offered a three-step operation, using heavy bombardments while slowly sapping forward; a task that he admitted could take up to a week. Haig's reaction to these plans would determine, to a great extent, how First Army would fight the Battle of Loos.

Hailing from an illustrious military family from Ireland – his father, uncle and brother had all received the Victoria Cross – Hubert de la Poer Gough (GOC I Corps) was, by 1915, one of the 'bright young things' of the British Army.[8] A cavalry officer, renowned for his drive and aggression, although somewhat prone to arrogance, Gough was primarily famous before the war for his role in the Curragh 'mutiny' of March 1914, where as GOC 3 Cavalry Brigade, he (supported by his officers) refused to be part of any move to coerce Ulster into accepting Irish Home Rule. Although the resulting political scandal forced the resignation of the then CIGS, Sir John French, Gough survived and went to war with 3 Cavalry Brigade in August 1914. Once at the front Gough was successively promoted, eventually becoming GOC I Corps at age of forty-five in July 1915; something that he admitted brought with it 'special difficulties'.[9] As well as arousing an understandable jealousy among some on account of his meteoric rise, Gough did not shirk controversy and gained a reputation as a ruthless 'thruster' with a habit of sacking subordinates who were less offensively minded than he felt desirable.[10] Gough was also one of Haig's protégés, sharing the latter's views on the continued importance and relevance of cavalry and providing the commander of First Army with a 'spirited, direct and witty' confidant, particularly after the death of his brother 'Johnnie' Gough (MGGS First Army) in February 1915.[11]

At fifty-one years of age, Sir Henry Rawlinson (GOC IV Corps) could not compete with either Gough's youth or his closeness to Haig, but he was an infantryman of great experience and competence. Although not involved in the BEF from August 1914, Rawlinson took part in the abortive operations around Antwerp with IV Corps, before finally arriving on the Western Front in time for the First Battle of Ypres in mid-October. Rawlinson, the subject of arguably the most important biography of a senior British commander in *Command on the Western Front* (1992), seems to have been a curiously frustrating general.[12] Although by as early as March 1915 he had correctly perceived that the key to success on the Western Front was the density of artillery fire and the application of small 'bite and hold' attacks, he was sometimes incapable (or unwilling) of acting upon this knowledge. Throughout 1915 and 1916, Rawlinson was torn between his personal belief in the necessity for limited, artillery-heavy operations aimed at conquering local points of tactical importance and the calls for wider and deeper breakthrough operations that came from more optimistic officers, particularly Haig. But Rawlinson could also not fail to realise how fragile his position would become if he incurred the wrath of his army commander. Indeed, Rawlinson had barely survived a collision with one of his subordinates following the Battle of Neuve Chapelle in March 1915. In the days following the closure of operations, Rawlinson had wanted to send home Major-General F.J. Davies (GOC 8th Division) for apparently 'dissipating' his reserves around the battlefield. In fact, on further investigation, it was revealed that Davies was innocent and Rawlinson had been at fault.[13] The Commander of IV Corps had only survived because of Haig's personal intervention.

Within nine days both corps commanders had drafted plans for the capture of the relevant enemy positions. After making a reconnaissance and visiting Haig to discuss the extent of his attack, Gough completed his plan.[14] With the village of Hulluch as his final objective, Gough proposed initially to secure and consolidate the cluttered mining area around Fosse 8 and the Hohenzollern Redoubt. This would form the left flank for a further assault on the German front line between the Redoubt and the Vermelles–Hulluch road, with a subsequent advance being made in the direction of the Quarries if events proved favourable. So bad were the ground conditions further north that Gough did not consider an attack in this sector practicable. Even if attacks were successful in taking the German front line, they would only then 'run into the labyrinth of houses of Auchy and Haisnes' and so were to be avoided.

While admitting that 'it is impossible to put forward very definitive proposals', Gough felt that the main attack on the Hohenzollern Redoubt should be conducted by 9th (Scottish) Division.[15] While the right brigade would push on towards Fosse 8 and the miners' houses of Corons de Maroc and Corons de Pekin, the left brigade would secure its flank by taking and holding the German front line up to the Vermelles railway. The attack would take place at dawn – 4a.m. in mid-September – when the light was 'poor', thus allowing the whole of the day for consolidation. If the attack was a success, Gough proposed that 7th Division, then deployed on the right of 9th Division, would move forward to take advantage of the favourable situation. Once it had taken the German front line, 7th Division would push on through the Quarries towards Cité St Elie. But this, Gough warned, would be difficult, and 'owing to the great distance that any assault by 7th Division against the line must cover', the attack would be conducted the following night. The ground was 'open, free from obstacles and favourable to a night attack'. As regards the use of asphyxiating gas, Gough believed that it would not alter his plans, but it 'should be used before or at dawn, when [the] enemy [was] tired and panicky'.

Like Gough, Rawlinson spent a great deal of time looking over the proposed ground, and despite actually having a more favourable sector than that occupied by I Corps, he was not happy, recording in his diary that it was 'no easy task to get Hill 70'.[16] As he spent more time working on his plans, Rawlinson's gloom increased. By 20 August he was lamenting that 'it will cost us dear and we shall not get far'.[17] The plan he submitted was, therefore, not surprisingly, notable for its 'extreme caution'.[18] 'After a very careful personal reconnaissance of the ground,' Rawlinson explained, 'I am strongly of opinion that the capture of Hill 70 cannot be undertaken successfully in one rush, but in two or three stages.'[19] The first step would be an attack on the German front line between the Vermelles–Loos road and the La Bassée–Lens road. As the opposing trenches were relatively close together – between 150 and 200 yards – once the wire had been cleared away, the German lines could be 'successfully assaulted without serious loss'. And again like Gough, Rawlinson handed the main attack to a New Army division with which he had been favourably impressed. Sometime between 7 and 9a.m., 15th (Scottish) Division would move forward in two columns and attack the German line.[20] Getting the enemy wire cut was vital therefore, and to achieve this Rawlinson advocated a lengthy seven to ten day bombardment along the whole front of IV Corps.

Once the German defences had been sufficiently softened up, the second stage of Rawlinson's plan could begin. He believed that this would offer a much more serious obstacle. The 'formidable' German second line, known in this sector as the *Loos Defence Line*, was 'well-constructed and strongly wired'. It ran closely in front of the village of Loos, about 500 yards from the German first line, and was built at the bottom of an open slope. To take Loos, Rawlinson recommended two simultaneous attacks, one by 15th Division against Loos, and another by 47th (London) Division further to the south. This latter attack would capture the Double Crassier (a slag heap that enfiladed any advance upon Loos) and the mining buildings of Puits 16, thus both securing the flank and offering something of a diversion. But this would take time. Rawlinson wanted to sap forward from the German first line, down the slope towards Loos – possibly taking a week or more – and then make further attacks, well-supported by artillery and large discharges of gas. A subsequent advance would then, presumably, take place towards Hill 70, although this was not explicitly mentioned in Rawlinson's report.[21]

Haig's response was mixed. Whereas after visiting Gough and his BGRA, Brigadier-General J.F.N. Birch, Haig thought their bombardment plans were 'very good' and was impressed by the two 'keen, energetic officers',[22] he was apparently disappointed with Rawlinson's cautious plan, especially the role he allocated to gas. Because the British and German front line trenches were so close, Rawlinson believed there was no need to use it for the first stage of his operations, preferring instead to reserve it for the attack on Loos itself. Alongside the report, Haig wrote that 'gas must be used by I Corps, and the element of surprise will disappear after its first use!' These remarks revealed much about both Haig and the relationships he had with his two senior corps commanders. Although Gough had admitted that the use, or not, of gas did not materially affect his plans, Haig seems to have read Gough's report first and instinctively taken his side. It would have been relatively simple to alter I Corps' arrangements to suit Rawlinson's plans, but this did not occur. Haig's instinctive preference for Gough, his 'uncertain' attitude towards Rawlinson,[23] and his grand hopes for the gas, meant that the assault at Loos would follow the 'rush' tactics favoured by Gough, rather than Rawlinson's 'bite and hold' operation.

Following Lord Kitchener's visit to France between 16 and 19 August, GHQ informed Haig that the 'artillery plan' was no longer viable.[24] Instead of conducting an artillery battle and not hazarding its infantry, First Army had now to prepare for a major action in which they would 'co-operate vigorously' with the French. Haig's exact orders regarding the battle have not often been consulted, but they deserve to be analysed in some detail. First Army was to launch an attack in concert with the French, scheduled at this point for 8 September. Haig was ordered to 'support the French attack to the full extent of your available resources, and not to limit your action in the manner indicted in the above quoted letter [i.e., the "artillery" plan]'.[25] Sir John's order did, however, give Haig some room to manoeuvre, something that all commentators have missed.

> This instruction is not, however, to be taken as preventing you from developing your attack deliberately and progressively, should you be of the opinion that the nature of the enemy's defences makes such a course desirable.

In other words, as long as First Army attacked with commitment and power, it was Haig's battle. Yet the commander of First Army seems to have either ignored or misunderstood this latter sentence, and this interpretation contained the seeds of the problems that would bear fruit both during the planning and execution of the battle.

Haig seems to have taken the 'full extent of your available resources' to mean an *all-out infantry attack*, and in many of the subsequent conferences and in his correspondence, he always quoted Sir John on this matter. It is clear that that Haig confused the *strategic* need for a 'full' attack with the *tactical* arrangements for the battle.[26] Indeed, a phrase that had begun life as a strategic order from Lord Kitchener to French, now began to appear in the tactical arrangements for the coming offensive. Instead of using all of First Army's resources to effect a strong, supporting attack, Haig simply passed down, without modification, the phrase 'to the full extent of your power' to corps and division, from where it reached brigades and battalions. For example, Brigadier-General M.G. Wilkinson's 44 Brigade 'Preliminary Operation Order' of 13 September, urged that 'the attack of the brigade must be pushed home to the *full extent* of its power',[27] and likewise on 4 September, Haig arranged with Rawlinson that 1st Division's attack would be conducted with 'full power'.[28] When he received a pessimistic letter from Lieutenant-General Sir J. Willcocks (GOC Indian Corps) regarding the coming operations, Haig was exasperated, noting that First Army had been ordered to support the French attack 'to the full extent of its resources'. 'The Indian Corps', Haig added, 'must do it, I have!'[29] This confusion was undoubtedly down to Haig and would have a considerable impact on how the battle was planned and executed lower down the chain of command.

Was an 'all-out' tactical assault what Sir John French wanted? It seems that he desired First Army to attack with commitment and power, but would have preferred a slower, more progressive attack. And although it was not the case that Sir John did not know what type of attack Haig was planning – he himself had urged Haig to attack on 'as wide a front as possible'[30] – it seems that French rapidly lost interest in the whole operation once the decision to embark on an autumn offensive had been taken. A major reason for this seems to have been Sir John's health. During this period it was noticeably in decline. Between the end of August and mid-September, Sir John spent much of his time in bed, suffering from a series of fevers and heavy head colds. This may well have increased the isolation of GHQ and allowed issues, which should have been sorted out earlier – such as the matter of the General Reserve – to continue unresolved.[31] It certainly meant that Sir John exercised a much looser control over operations than he previously had done. Sir William Robertson, French's CGS, had apparently complained that 'he can't get Sir John to do anything', and that 'he is not well'.[32] Similarly, on 29 August, French was 'not at all well' according to his Private Secretary, Lieutenant-Colonel Brinsley Fitzgerald. He did improve over the following days, but his high temperature was worrying, with Sir John being 'very feverish and excitable'.[33] This continued into the following month. By 19 September, Major Sidney Clive (Head of the British Mission at GQG) thought Sir John was 'certainly not well',[34] and it was evidently becoming a serious problem; three days earlier Haig had written to his wife about French's illness, commenting that it was 'unsatisfactory having him laid up at this time'.[35] It was in this 'command vacuum' that Haig planned his battle.

The breezy First Army conference of 6 September was a far cry from the pessimism of the summer.[36] Indeed, grave doubts had now turned to considerable optimism. In concert with the powerful French attacks from Arras and Rheims, First Army would secure the line Loos–Hulluch and the ground extending to the La Bassée canal. The ultimate objectives, Haig pointed out, were Hill 70 and the crossings over the Haute Deule canal at Pont à Vendin. In response to both Gough's and Rawlinson's concerns about enfilade fire, Haig agreed that the central portion of the German line, opposite 7th and 1st Divisions, would also be attacked.[37] Now all six divisions of I and IV Corps, containing over 75,000 men, were to attack simultaneously; from 2nd Division astride the La Bassée canal, to 47th (London) Division, dug in around the mining village of Maroc. This gave the British a considerable numerical superiority. Intelligence indicated, with some accuracy, that there were only 13,000 enemy troops within five miles of the battlefield. There were roughly 6,000 in the front and support lines with 4,000 in local reserve and 3,000 resting in billets.

But even given a similar superiority of men First Army had signally failed to dent the German defences at Aubers Ridge in May. What now would be different? In order to understand how First Army planned the Battle of Loos it is necessary to examine Haig's military education and his thoughts on the nature of warfare. It is clear that the plan subsequently adopted had less to do with the harsh realities of either the ground or the state of the BEF, and more with Haig's belief in what a *proper* offensive should be like. Haig's ideas contained a curious mix of the old and new. While counting, somewhat optimistically, on a 'lavish' discharge of gas – the most recent addition to the British Army's arsenal – the offensive itself was structured within a paradigm of 'classic' nineteenth-century warfare. Tim Travers has shown how the lessons Haig learnt during his time at the Staff College between 1896–7 had a direct influence on the planning and execution of the battles of 1916–17, but the same was evidently true of 1915.[38] So dominant were the ideas of the 1890s that Haig actually mentioned them during the conference. After explaining the orders First Army had received, Haig added that:

> Anything I now say regarding the scope of the forthcoming operations is based on a study of the map, and on the principles which were taught by the late Colonel Henderson at Camberley.[39]

Evidently, the experience of total war in 1914–15 did not compare with the lessons that Henderson had inculcated into his students *before* the South African War of 1899–1902.

The officer of whom Haig had spoken was Colonel G.F.R. Henderson, author of numerous works of military history and, by all accounts, inspirational lecturer at the Staff College.[40] Henderson's forte was the campaigns of the American Civil War. He had published a celebrated life of 'Stonewall' Jackson and a study of the Battle of Fredericksburg, both designed to educate the British officer.[41] Like many of his contemporary military writers, Henderson was keen to stress the importance and power of the offensive and of the absolute necessity to achieve decision on the battlefield. Henderson's influence on the strategic and tactical thought of the British Army has often been investigated and it clearly lingered on into the early years of the Great War. At the conference on 6 September, Haig had announced that it was 'not enough to gain a tactical success', but First Army must advance upon the enemy's rear, cut his communications and 'force him to retreat'. This was a typically Henderson-like ambition; in *The Science of War* (1905), he had written that one of the great secrets of victory was 'by threatening or cutting his [the enemy's] line of communications'.[42] 'Briefly then,' Haig added, 'the question is how to turn our tactical success into a strategical victory.' The seeming confusion of the strategic with the tactical arrangements for the battle was again in evidence. 'All corps on my front,' Haig told the assembled officers, 'must co-operate to the full extent of their power.'[43] Haig repeatedly stressed four key points: secrecy, rapidity, initiative and a vigorous pursuit, as well as urging his corps to attack with the utmost energy.[44]

Haig was therefore very familiar with the importance of gaining a swift, irresistible and decisive victory on the battlefield. These ideas had been stressed both in his *Cavalry Studies*, a discussion of Staff Rides and tactical exercises from his time in India, and in *Field Service Regulations*, the first British Army manual on war organisation and administration that he had co-authored in his capacity as Director of Staff Duties at the War Office between 1907–9.[45] While Haig declared in 1907 that 'the real object in war is a decisive battle',[46] part I of *Field Service Regulations* also contained numerous references to vigorous and decisive offensives.[47] And although *Field Service Regulations* proved capable of considerable flexibility and interpretation,[48] Haig's stamp was clearly upon it. 'Decisive success in battle', it maintained, 'can be gained only by a vigorous offensive'.[49] In Chapter Ten, 'War Against an Uncivilised Enemy', this stress on the offensive was even more apparent. 'A vigorous offensive, strategical as well as tactical, is always the safest method of conducting operations.'[50] There was also a considerable emphasis on the power of morale in military operations: 'success in war depends more on moral than on physical qualities' was a not untypical remark.[51]

Secure both in the continued relevance of the lessons he had first encountered at the Staff College and in the principles he had held ever since, Haig formulated his plans for Loos. But instead of a limited, subsidiary operation on very unfavourable terrain, Haig believed this was to be a *decisive* offensive, which would unfold in clear-cut stages and end in the total defeat of the enemy. The German defenders would be engaged on a wide front, their reserves drawn in and then exhausted, before the decisive blow was struck by one's own reserves. A cavalry pursuit would then scatter the enemy.[52] It is clear that by the summer of 1915, Haig still thought of battle in these rather traditional, almost Napoleonic, terms. In a letter to the Prime Minister in late June, Haig explained that:

> With such changed conditions it might be thought that the old principles of war had also changed. But I do not think that is so. On the contrary the values of surprise and of concentration on the decisive point, is as great as ever. The difficulty is to apply these great principles under the changed conditions.[53]

'And so I feel sure,' Haig added, 'that we ought to aim at engaging the enemy on a *very wide* front, 25 miles say, with many divisions, and [the] aim of wearing him down – the "bataille d'usure" of Napoleon – at the same a large reserve should be retained in a central position in readiness to strike at that point.' Barely a month later Haig's ideal frontage had *quadrupled*. While dining at St Omer with Sir John French and Lord Haldane, the conversation turned onto how to win the war, and Haig apparently told one of the guests that only by 'applying the old principles to the present conditions', could victory be achieved. 'Engage the enemy on a wide front, the wider the better, 100 miles or more, then after five or six days, bring up a strong reserve of all arms, attack by surprise and break through where the enemy had shown he was weak.'[54] But this was not mere fantasy and Haig genuinely seems to have believed that such a decisive victory was possible. His letters to his wife in the run-up to the battle betrayed this optimism. On 15 August he explained to her that it would not be many months 'before the Germans are reduced to make peace on our terms'.[55] Likewise, on 24 August he talked of imminent German bankruptcy and of his hopes that 'the end may come by the *direct result of a victory on this front* – and I have great expectations from our next effort'.[56] As the battle crept ever closer, Haig's confidence seemed to increase, admitting on 22 September to feeling 'pretty confident of some success' and how by October, 'we may be a good distance on the road to Brussels'.[57] Haig's confidence in the coming battle did not, however, merely rest upon abstract theories, but on the expected devastating effect of a new weapon: poison gas.

As well as witnessing the debut of a number of New Army divisions, the Battle of Loos was also unique in that it was the only offensive in British military history to be preceded by a discharge of cylinder-released chlorine gas. The gas attack at Loos has been much criticised, with lurid tales of the gas being blown back onto the attackers tending to overshadow the considerable logistical feats that allowed it to take place.[58] In that over 150 tons of gas could be manufactured and then delivered to the front, barely five months after the German gas attack at Ypres in April, was nothing short of miraculous. But the gas attack was largely a failure; a fact that had less to do with the unfavourable weather conditions that have usually been blamed, and more with the over-optimism and ambition that pervaded all aspects of Haig's plan.

The decision to equip the BEF with a form of gas retaliation and the forming of the Special Brigade – the unit that would put this into effect – has been covered elsewhere,[59] but suffice to say, it was one of the most unique formations in the British Army.[60] It was also led by a suitably eccentric officer, Lieutenant-Colonel Charles Howard Foulkes. Although Foulkes had cheerfully admitted his complete ignorance of either chemistry or gas on taking up his position on 26 May, he was, in many ways, an ideal choice. A 40 year-old sapper with extensive experience in West Africa, India and the West Indies, Foulkes was possessed of a tough, athletic build and a burning determination in everything he did. He took to his task with characteristic single-mindedness and by late summer, through a mixture of voluntary recruitment and sometimes less-than-legal transfers, four companies (numbered 186 to 189) of the Special Brigade had been formed, each split into ten sections and based at Helfaut, six miles south of St Omer.

There were few officers in the BEF who worked harder than Foulkes during the summer of 1915.[61] Within a week of being appointed, he had worked out a detailed scheme for future offensive and defensive gas warfare, which – somewhat understandably – drew heavily from the German gas attack earlier in the year.[62] Chlorine gas was the preferred weapon, to be carried in metal cylinders, three feet in length and between eight and twelve inches in diameter. Clusters of cylinders, or batteries as they were known, were to be placed all along the front trenches in secure, sandbagged bays at 25 yard intervals. When a discharge was to be made, rubber pipes, about ten feet in length, would be connected to the cylinders and thrown over the parapet into no-man's-land.[63] The valves would then be turned on and, given the correct weather conditions, a cloud of gas would form and drift towards the enemy positions.

What then was expected from a chlorine gas attack? Foulkes had told Sir William Robertson (CGS GHQ) that for the first time in which gas was successfully employed 'important results may be achieved'[64] and it was hoped that the gas would enter the German trenches, sink into the deep dugouts and either incapacitate its garrison or force them to the surface where they would suffer from an accompanying bombardment. With this in mind, Foulkes organised a major demonstration of chlorine at Helfaut on 22 August and invited all the senior officers of First Army to attend. By all accounts it was a most successful operation, and although many officers found the use of such a weapon deeply disquieting, not to mention problematic, it was a revelation to Haig. He was deeply impressed by Foulkes's arrangements and was immediately drawn to the new weapon with all the fervour of a religious convert.[65] Haig's views on what a gas discharge could achieve have rarely been explored, but they are vital to understanding what subsequently occurred. The seeming success of the demonstration on 22 August may have reflected well on Foulkes's organisational ability, but it was ironically perhaps 'too successful' and far from being regarded as a novel, double-edged and limited weapon – a 'boomerang ally'[66] as Gough later called it – Haig saw gas as a panacea that would solve all of First Army's problems.[67] It seems that, as had (partly) happened at Ypres in April, Haig believed 'one whiff of the gas'[68] would cause a panic, clear out large sections of the enemy line and allow the attackers to get through the first and second German positions without heavy casualties[69]. Alongside Rawlinson's report of 22 August, Haig had written that:

> The moral effect of the gas on the foremost hostile troops may be such that the defenders of Loos may be affected as was the case North of Ypres after a distance of near five miles.[70]

As this was to be a decisive offensive, gas would be the decisive weapon that would allow this to occur. 'Under certain conditions,' Haig had told the assembled officers on 6 September, 'the gas is effective up to two miles, and it is practically certain that it will be quite effective in many places, if not everywhere along the whole front attacked.'[71] These sentiments undoubtedly had a great impact on Haig's decision to plan for a major 'all-out' attack at Loos.

How valid were these assumptions? Haig's attitude to technology has been much discussed and he was certainly not the technophobe of legend.[72] On the contrary, as regards gas, it must be stressed that Haig was simply too keen, letting his natural optimism get the better of him and believing it could work wonders on the battlefield. There were certainly some senior officers who were not as sanguine as Haig and had grave reservations about the great reliance placed upon a new and untested weapon.[73] Rawlinson was one of them. He regretted (as he saw it) the abandonment of lessons revealed by earlier engagements, believing that too much reliance had been placed on the gas and 'not enough on the artillery'.[74] Lieutenant-General Sir William Pulteney (GOC III Corps) was also less than enthusiastic, and raised his concerns at the conference on 6 September. In order to maximise the terrific shock against the German lines, Haig wanted gas to be released at the same time for both First Army's main and subsidiary attacks. In reply, Pulteney made the point that for the successful use of gas on his front, the wind would have to blow in a different direction for that required further to the south.[75] Pulteney may not have been known for his brilliant insights, but his interjection was a sensible one and brought up serious concerns about the feasibility of what Haig was proposing. Yet, as with much unpalatable information, Haig simply ignored or dismissed it. Haig's reply is not recorded, but from what Lieutenant-Colonel John Charteris (First Army Intelligence Officer) remembered, Haig was in no mood for 'difficulties'.[76]

In Haig's mind, then, the gas attack was a possibly never-to-be-repeated opportunity – a single, one-shot weapon, capable of winning a battle in one bloody stroke. Little was allowed to interfere with this. But even given that gas was still a new, untested and, to a certain extent, unknown weapon, Haig was being not only optimistic, but also unrealistically ambitious. Even Sir James Edmonds, who thought Haig's plan was 'sound', noted that the First Army's attacks were based on the assumption that the gas would be one hundred percent successful![77] This was simply never a possibility and Haig either did not consider, or he dismissed, two very real concerns and, in this case at least, it is difficult to disagree with Travers's thesis that Haig 'sometimes asked technology to adapt to his plans rather than setting plans that made the best use of the available technology'.[78] Given the problems then being experienced in Britain in producing enough chlorine, there was the possibility that not enough gas would be available to drench the German positions. There was also the knowledge that whereas at Ypres in April, Allied troops had very little protection – nothing but damp socks and handkerchiefs – German defenders now had access to two types of respirator.[79] Infantrymen were equipped with cloth pads, which when tied around the nose and mouth and dipped into an anti-gas solution, could neutralise poisonous fumes for around fifteen minutes. To continue working, the pads would then have been re-soaked. The German machine gun crews, however, had been issued with sturdier mine-rescue breathing apparatus with an attached supply of around thirty minutes of oxygen. It was therefore decided that a gas discharge of forty minutes would suffice to exhaust both the cloth pads, even if re-dipped, and the air supply of the machine gunners. It is clear that Haig knew this to be the case,[80] although rather curiously, Charteris recorded on 7 September that the 'Germans opposite us have no respirators'.[81]

By 21 August, the day before Foulkes's demonstration at Helfaut, Haig's plans called for a relatively modest gas attack on a frontage of 6,300 yards.[82] As each cylinder took over average two minutes to empty, a forty-minute discharge would require at least twenty cylinders per battery.[83] Foulkes saw Haig the same day and promised to supply the required amount of gas by the date of the attack, then scheduled for 15 September. He also confidently assured Haig that he would probably be able to supply First Army with a 'good deal' more by the date mentioned.[84] This was to prove a hollow promise, however, and having been misled by over-optimistic reports from the War Office, Foulkes was forced to see Haig five days later and tell him that owing to manufacturing delays, only half the total gas could be delivered on time.[85] Haig was crestfallen, recording that this 'seriously' affected his plans. Foulkes was told to let him know as soon as possible what realistic amount of gas could be furnished on time. 'As matters stand at present', Haig subsequently informed GHQ, 'unless immediate steps are taken to ensure the necessary supply of gas, either the date of our operations will have to be postponed or my plan of operations will have to be modified.'[86]

Haig and Foulkes worked reasonably well together, but tensions lay beneath the surface of their relationship. Foulkes was, and always remained, a great advocate of gas warfare (particularly cylinder discharge), but Haig's grand expectations about what gas could do, and how much would be available, sometimes unsettled him and led to friction. More than once Foulkes tried to steer Haig's thoughts in a more modest direction. When the commander of First Army 'perhaps chaffingly' told him that 'I understand that you guarantee that your gas [will] put the whole of the Germans [*sic*] out of action, and that no artillery preparation will be necessary,' Foulkes quickly countered this, assuring Haig that wire-cutting was absolutely essential.[87] But relations between the two men were not always so good-natured and on 4 September Foulkes recorded a 'slight contretemps' with Haig in his diary over delays in cylinder arrival.[88] He also later complained of how he 'had to bear the brunt of the dissatisfaction felt at the headquarters of the First Army' when supplies failed to meet demand.[89]

It would be inaccurate, however, to say that First Army was misled over the amount of gas that would be available for Loos. GHQ replied to Haig's request on 28 August.[90] 4,440 cylinders would be available for 6 September, with possibly an additional 800 by that date. It was also hoped that by mid-September a further 1,500 cylinders could be supplied, alongside 9,000 smoke candles and twenty-four Stokes mortars and 5,000 smoke shells. This forecast proved surprisingly accurate. The War Office had predicted that 5,240 cylinders would be available and on 25 September I and IV

Corps used 5,028 cylinders between them.[91] Indeed, it seems that the shortage of gas at Loos was not as crippling as has been generally assumed. On the contrary, had Haig's earlier plan for modest attack on a frontage of 6,300 yards been adopted, First Army would have had more than enough gas.[92] But this was jettisoned after Sir John had told Haig to attack to the 'full extent' of his power and between 22 August and 6 September, the frontage of attack was gradually increased, initially to 10,400 yards and finally to 14,500 yards.[93] This created problems. It was simply not true, as Haig had told his officers on 6 September, that the main attacks would be preceded by a 'lavish' discharge of gas. Nowhere on the entire front would a full forty-minute discharge take place; even on the most favourable fronts only twenty-four minutes of gas were available. The amount of cylinders then arriving in France simply could not compete with the expansion in First Army's front. And instead of curtailing the attack, the number of cylinders in each battery was simply reduced and the attack was, in effect, diluted with the addition of smoke candles, in between short bursts of gas. On 17 September batteries that had previously contained fifteen cylinders, which in itself could only create a discharge of half an hour, were reduced to twelve cylinders. North of the canal, batteries now only contained three cylinders.[94]

Historians have sometimes criticised Haig for assuming that smoke would complement the gas attack, claiming that as long as only twenty-four minutes of gas were being released, the German defenders would not fall victim to gas poisoning.[95] Although this is largely correct, perfectly illustrating the problems inherent in the gas plan, it does not entirely make sense. German padded respirators could only last around fifteen minutes before having to be re-dipped in the anti-gas solution. More importantly, for the German machine gunners and their oxygen helmets, as long as the gunners were breathing from them during the gas/smoke discharge, it was irrelevant what atmosphere they were in. After thirty minutes their oxygen supply would be empty, thus leaving them susceptible to poisoning during the last ten minutes of the discharge, two minutes of which contained gas. This was, of course, still far from ideal. Haig was probably hoping that after half an hour of wearing masks (or pads) the German defenders would be tired, confused and unable to function properly. In 1915 gas masks were far from pleasant to wear.

The planning of the gas attack was, as shown, deeply affected by both Haig's over-optimistic appreciation of the likely effectiveness of gas and of the amount required for success. And although it may be argued that Haig was forced to attack over such a wide front, thus compelling the dilution of the gas, this is problematic. The orders Sir John gave to Haig left considerable room to manoeuvre. It seems that on 22 August Haig thought he had stumbled upon a 'wonder weapon', and because he believed gas would prove extremely lethal, Haig did not feel under such pressure to make sure cylinder batteries were capable of delivering a sustained gas attack for forty minutes. As Brigadier-General R.D. Whigham (Deputy CGS) noted, there was 'a strong feeling that if only we could use gas all would be well'.[96] So instead of making it clear to Sir John that gas resources only permitted a limited, relatively narrow attack, Haig 'fudged' it and spread his resources thinly over a wide area, hoping for the best. But, as shall be seen, this was not the only difference of opinion between Sir John and Haig.

Nothing has caused more controversy regarding the Battle of Loos than the fate of the two reserve divisions that saw action on the second day of fighting. 21st and 24th Divisions of XI Corps, inexperienced and worn out after a tiring approach march, were fed into the fighting and suffered over 8,000 casualties between them. By mid-afternoon the bewildered battalions, having run into German reinforcements, were streaming back towards the British lines in some disorder. It was only with the arrival of the third and final division of XI Corps, the Guards Division, that the gaping hole in First Army's southern sector was plugged and the line steadied. This action was to have far-reaching results, being the *prima facie* reason for the dismissal of Sir John French as Commander-in-Chief in December 1915, and of his replacement by Haig. Much has been written about the debacle of the reserves. Most accounts do, however, tend to take a similar line. Sir John French has generally been blamed both for holding the reserve divisions too far back, and of only then handing them over to First Army when it was too late.[97] Admittedly, much of this story is true, but previous accounts have failed to give adequate weight to Sir Douglas Haig's role in the affair, particularly when considering the over-optimism of his plan and the importance this placed on the reserves. XI Corps' fate must therefore be seen, not just as a local difficulty over reserves, but symptomatic of the confusion about what exactly First Army was preparing. For while French wanted a more limited attack, with the reserves being employed *once* success had been achieved, Haig's 'all-out' plan called for the reserves to be used to *ensure* this initial success.

How did this confusion emerge? Five days after being ordered to attack 'to the full extent of his available resources', Haig issued a tentative plan of operations. The role of any reserves in the forthcoming attack was to be as 'detailed by GHQ'.[98] By the late summer of 1915, what was known as Sir John's General Reserve consisted of the newly-formed XI Corps,[99] Cavalry Corps and Indian Cavalry Corps, although the later was stationed behind Third Army in the region of the Somme and would not be available to support Haig's attack. The key element of the reserve forces was undoubtedly XI Corps.[100] On 1 September Robertson visited Hinges and discussed with Haig who should be placed in charge. Haig was anxious that a reputable 'thruster' be appointed and believed that Major-General R.C.B. Haking (GOC 1st Division) was the ideal choice. Robertson apparently agreed and promised to see Sir John about the matter, once 'The Chief' was out of bed and feeling better.[101]

Haig's choice for command of XI Corps was an understandable one. Because First Army was making such a major attack, reserves were vital to its success, and it was essential, as Haig saw it, that they be commanded by someone with proven aggression and commitment to the offensive. This was something that Haking did not lack. Although he may have been one of the foremost 'educated soldiers' of the pre-war British Army, having lectured at the Staff College (1901–6) and been the author of *Company Training* (1913), he is widely seen as the archetypical 'butcher'.[102] Although Haking was an infantryman, he was one of Haig's protégés, whose infamous handling of 1st Division at Aubers Ridge in May, when the attacking brigades lost sixty percent of their fighting strength in little over an hour, only added to his notoriety.[103] While Haking settled into his new position – his promotion had been confirmed on 4 September – and Haig completed his plans, GHQ was curiously silent over the reserves. What was the matter? As has been noted previously, during this period, Sir John French fell ill and was confined to his bed for days; not even his closest staff could stir much activity from him. Sir John caught another 'nasty cold' on 12 September.[104] Haig's note was left unanswered and he was forced to use a meeting at St Omer on 18 September, barely a week before the attack was to go in, to try and settle the matter. After giving a short talk about the operations he had planned, Haig urged the importance of 'having the General Reserve with the lead divisions at Nouex Les Mines and Verquin respectively by the morning of the 25'.[105] According to Haig, Sir John's only reply was to state that 'he did not agree'; evidently not wanting the reserves so far forward.[106]

What then were Sir John's thoughts on the role of the reserve divisions in the coming offensive? They seem to have been somewhat mixed; a matter only clouded by a number of post-battle claims. According to his *Loos Despatch* of 15 October, Sir John believed that a strong central reserve under his own control was necessary, 'in view of the great length of line along which the British troops were operating'.

> This reserve was the more necessary [French added] owing to the fact that the Tenth French Army had to postpone its attack until one o'clock in the day; and, further, that the corps operating on the French left had to be

> directed in a more or less south-easterly direction, involving, in case of our success, a considerable gap in our line.[107]

But these seemingly straightforward reasons were only made *after* the battle had ended, and it is more difficult to assess accurately what Sir John's thoughts were *before* it. In the numerous discussions and conferences in the run-up to Loos, French remained unclear and inconsistent. Most of those at GHQ recorded different versions of Sir John's motives.[108] While the gossipy Chief Liaison Officer, Wilson, recorded that XI Corps was kept under GHQ control because French wanted 'to have some control', was 'jealous of Haig' and 'wanted to fight an action on his own!',[109] Edmonds's memoirs included a rumour that Sir John personally wanted to lead the reserve divisions forward, 'sword in hand'.[110]

On the contrary, it does appear that although Sir John may have dreamt of leading his men forward, this remained in the realms of fantasy. French's thoughts were darkened by his strategic pessimism and far from wanting to 'huroosh' the reserves forward, he remained fearful of what would happen to XI Corps if he gave in to First Army's demands. Sir John was concerned that if the reserves were placed too far forward, they would prove too big a temptation to Haig, who would push them forward in unfavourable circumstances.[111] But there were certainly other reasons. The Deputy-Chief GS remembered that Sir John had claimed that because it was possible the French attack might be repulsed, it was therefore wise to have some troops under his own control for emergencies.[112] Robertson also noted Sir John's lack of faith in a French victory.[113]

Whatever Sir John's reasons for wanting to keep the reserves back and under his own hand, there was no excuse for what subsequently occurred. It was a prime example of how French lacked an effective grip on his subordinates.[114] During this period a dual process of persuasion seems to have occurred between French and Haig over the reserves. Because of their different opinions about the nature of the planned assault, their understanding of the reserves also diverged. Although not comfortable getting involved in the intricacies of Haig's plan, Sir John effectively tried to use the reserves to influence the scope of First Army's operation; by keeping them back, French, in effect, tried to rein Haig in and limit the attack.[115] Instead of, as Rawlinson's Chief of Staff later wrote, 'insisting on Haig carrying out his plan, Sir John tried to compel him to do so by keeping back the infantry reserve'.[116]

Rather curiously, Haig seems not to have realised this was going on. Instead of modifying his plans to take account of this, he cheerfully carried on with his arrangements, putting it all down to, as he saw it, the stupidity and timidity of GHQ.[117] And this was surely not Haig's fault.

It was certainly Sir John's responsibility to make sure Haig was clear on exactly what he was to do and if any confusion existed, French was to blame. While this was occurring, however, Haig was – as he admitted to Edmonds – simultaneously doing his 'utmost to get outside influence to bear on Sir John', including appeals by Kitchener and Foch, to place the reserves under First Army control.[118] The sullen response to his appeals at St Omer on 18 September only sharpened Haig's temper. When Robertson confirmed Sir John's deployment of XI Corps, some 20,000 yards from the front trenches, in the fields and villages surrounding Lillers, Haig was incensed, recording in his diary that this was 'too late!'[119] Haig's MGGS, R.H.K. Butler, was immediately despatched to St Omer, carrying a letter repeating these demands.

> I wish again to draw attention [Haig wrote] to the fact that the whole of the disposable troops of the First Army are being employed in the attack of 25 September from its commencement, that there are no Army reserves, and that, as stated in my memorandum, dated 28 August, the only troops in General Reserve are those detailed by GHQ.
> *The whole plan of the First Army is based on the assumption that the troops in the General Reserve will be close at hand*, and I consider it essential that the heads of the two leading divisions of the XI Corps should be on the line Nouex Les Mines – Beuvry by daylight on 25 September.[120]

This caused one final twist in the month-long struggle over the reserves. Butler returned at 3p.m. bearing a reply from Robertson. 'The Chief' had apparently given in. Robertson was able to confirm that XI Corps would be where Haig desired them – between 5,000 and 7,000 yards from the front line on the morning of 25 September.[121] As Haig explained to Brigadier-General Philip Howell (ex-BGGS Cavalry Corps), 'I had difficulty in getting reserves out of the authorities and in pushing them close enough up,' adding that 'all goes well here and I have every confidence'.[122] All that was required was for them to march into place.

Why then had Sir John seemingly given in at this late stage? A definitive answer eludes the historian, although it may well have been down to the efforts of those Haig enlisted on his side; it seems that the change of heart did not originate within GHQ.[123] It must be stressed that this was, however, not as clear-cut as it may have seemed. The reserves divisions may have been (in theory) closer to the front, but they remained firmly under GHQ control. Sir John explained to his mistress, Mrs Winifred Bennett, that 'I've got several cavalry and infantry divisions in reserve ready to push in where they are wanted'.[124] As was repeatedly explained to the eager men of XI Corps, they would only be pushed forward after the enemy had been 'absolutely smashed and retiring in disorder'.[125] Unfortunately this did not occur and the final settlement of the reserves – if indeed it can be called such – was like so much in the planning prior to Loos, an uneasy compromise between French and Haig, with neither party being totally satisfied. While Sir John still believed the reserves were too far forward, Haig still wanted them to be placed directly under his command. It was clearly unsatisfactory.

As the issue of the reserves rumbled on throughout September, other plans were taking shape. If the gas discharge was to fulfil Haig's 'lavish' expectations, favourable weather conditions were required. Captain Ernest Gold, First Army's meteorological officer, had calculated that for a successful discharge, the wind needed to blow between north-west and south-west, with a speed of at least four miles per hour.[126] Gold did warn, however, that the wind must not be too strong, because that would dissipate the gas too quickly. In other words, First Army needed a flexibility when to strike to ensure the correct weather conditions. But this was to be denied. On 4 September the assault was delayed for ten days and on 15 September, the day initially pencilled in, Haig attended a conference at Chantilly presided over by Joffre and Foch.[127] Various matters of small detail, such as the exact boundaries between the French and the British advances, and more importantly, the use of gas, were discussed. As the French attacks were not reliant upon gas, both Joffre and Foch made it clear that all attacks must go in on 25 September, regardless of weather conditions. Haig protested but without success. The following day, and evidently in some alarm, Haig complained to Robertson.[128] 'As regards the gas question,' he explained, 'I cannot see where the difficulty lies in deciding!' 'On the one hand,' Haig added, 'with the *very extensive* gas and smoke arrangements which have been prepared, decisive results are almost certain to be obtained. On the other hand, without gas, the fronts of our attack must be reduced to what our guns can satisfactorily prepare, with the results normally attendant on small fronts; namely, concentration of hostile guns on point of attack, large losses, small progress!' Haig was unequivocal that in his opinion, 'under no circumstances should our forthcoming attack be launched without the aid of gas'.

Despite Haig's unwillingness to change his plans, he met Gough and Rawlinson on 16 September and asked them to furnish proposals as soon as possible for 'carrying out the attack on as broad as front as possible without the use of gas'.[129] Gough's alternative plans offered no radical revision on his draft of 22 August.[130] He proposed two schemes. The first (A) ran 'a greater risk of failure', but 'greater results' were to be obtained should it be successful. Because artillery was now the most important weapon – which in itself was limited – Gough wanted to curtail the frontage of attack. He recommended that unless gas could be used or an 'overwhelming mass of heavy artillery' brought up, the attack of 2nd Division should be jettisoned. Instead, I Corps should deploy its main strength further south. After a preliminary bombardment lasting four days, 9th and 7th Divisions would attack the enemy positions between the Vermelles railway and the Vermelles–Hulluch road. This would take place an hour before dawn. Gough promised 'a moderately good chance of success if there is an element of surprise'. The 'suddenness and size of the force employed', he hoped, would enable the capture of the German second line 'in practically one rush'. The second scheme (B) was more cautious, which although not offering such 'far-reaching' objectives, did give a greater chance of success. Gough believed the operation would probably take between two and seven days. I Corps' artillery would concentrate its fire for two hours on three separate areas of the battlefield in turn. This was intended to deceive the enemy as to the target area and hopefully draw attention elsewhere. At midday the guns would fire on Fosse 8, and at 2p.m. 9th Division would attack. The guns would then turn against the enemy trenches opposite 7th Division and continue firing until nightfall. 7th Division would attack under the cover of darkness.

If gas was not to be used, wrote Rawlinson, 'it appears to me most undesirable to attack the enemy on as wide a front as is present contemplated'.[131] The Commander of IV Corps was emphatic that the front of attack must be reduced. He bluntly informed Haig that the 'number of guns and the ammunition at our disposal will not permit of a front of nearly 5,000 yards being adequately and simultaneously bombarded'. Rawlinson offered three alternative schemes. Plan A was for a simultaneous dawn attack by 1st and 15th Divisions, aimed at securing Hulluch and Loos respectively. But Rawlinson was not keen, lamenting that the number of guns 'available to support the attack of IV Corps are, in my opinion, not sufficient to cover the attack of both 1st and 15th Divisions simultaneously'. He was, however, more positive about his second and third ideas. Plans B and C were both similar, being based on two staggered attacks stretched over two days. Covered by an intense 'hurricane' bombardment, 15th Division would attack Loos on the afternoon of 25 September. All available artillery would then be switched to support 1st Division's assault on Hulluch, to take place either the following morning, or under the cover of nightfall. Like Gough, Rawlinson admitted that it may have been possible to surprise the enemy by attacking with both divisions at the same time, but this did entail a 'greater risk', albeit with 'more far-reaching results' if successful.

Armed with his corps commanders' reports, Haig considered his response. He felt that the only option available, as he had told Robertson on 16 September, was to delay the assault.[132] If the weather on the morning of

25 September was unsuitable for the gas to be released, a smaller, two division attack would be staged. 9th Division would take the Hohenzollern Redoubt, while 15th Division attacked the Loos salient. The subsidiary attacks scheduled north of the canal would also take place. The main attack would be postponed until the following morning, by which time it was hoped the weather would have improved. If the wind was blowing in the desired direction on the morning of 26 September, the gas would be released and the remaining divisions of I and IV Corps would attack. If, however, the weather was still proving obstinate, the positions gained the previous day would be consolidated and the main attacks would go in on 27 September. Haig added that 'it seems improbable that the weather conditions on one of these days will not be suitable for the use of gas'. It is almost certain that Haig knew his remarks would be unwelcome. Five days earlier Robertson had told him that 'although no objection is likely to be raised to our waiting a few hours, we shall most probably be expected to attack sometime during the day [25 September]'.[133] Also when considering Haig's earlier opposition to using gas once his attacks had begun, it is clear that the smaller two-division plan was never regarded as being feasible. Nevertheless, Robertson did speak to Sir John about Haig's plans, but to no avail. French remained inflexible. 'The Commander-in-Chief desires me in order to avoid any possibility of error', wrote Robertson, 'to repeat his instructions as to the date of the infantry attack, namely, that it will take place on the 25 September.'[134] It was Haig's battle – irrespective of gas or reserves. If the weather was unsuitable, Sir John expected Haig to revert to the two-division assault.

Although Sir John's previous orders regarding the attack First Army had been the subject of some confusion, it was clear from the letter of 18 September what type of attack he wished Haig to prepare. 'With regard to your suggested postponement of the remainder of your attacks until the 27,' Robertson continued, 'the Field-Marshal desires me to say that as our operations are to be carried out in cooperation with those of the French Tenth Army, such a postponement may be highly undesirable. Should the attack of the French Tenth Army be successful, it will be of the utmost importance that your offensive should be continued at the earliest possible moment and in the greatest possible strength.' Haig was ordered to make sure the 'remainder' of his attacks took place either later on 25 September or whenever directed. The final paragraph of Robertson's letter confirmed that Sir John wanted First Army's operation to be more limited (and clearly subsidiary to the French) than it perhaps was:

> You will realise that the Commander-in-Chief attaches primary importance to pressing the attack south of the La Bassée canal immediately *if the French attack is successful*,[135] and therefore if your plans for giving effect to this

> are dependent upon the use of gas, which in the nature of things must be uncertain, they should be altered, if necessary, at the expense of the subsidiary attacks north of the canal.

Barely a week before the battle was to begin, Sir John was only just beginning to tamper with Haig's tactical arrangements. So loud had Haig's persistent demands become – for reserves, gas and now a flexibility when to strike – that French was forced to clear up some ground rules: Haig was simply to attack on 25 September with commitment and power. Anything that interfered with this was unacceptable. After a summer-long saga of trying to escape from Joffre's clutches, Sir John had been given clear and unambiguous orders by the British Government to support the offensive operations. He had thus ordered First Army to make a 'full power' attack, but, at the same time, made it clear that the arrangements for this were to be left to Haig's discretion. If First Army had not attacked on 25 September – for essentially a tactical reason (the gas and the weather) – it would have had repercussions not only on the strict instructions Sir John had been given, but also on the strategic rationale behind the battle. He was understandably unable to contemplate this. But French cannot, however, escape severe censure. Although feeling far from well, he should have made it clear early on what type of attack Haig was to make and what he was to use. Instead, matters that should have been cleared up were either left unresolved or simply 'fudged' to the complete satisfaction of neither party. Perhaps the greatest flaw in Haig's plan was that it was not capable of execution without the gas; something General Foch had apparently warned against.[136] What would happen on 25 September if the weather was unsuitable was never truly resolved. The order left Haig waiting for the wind.

As has been shown, the ambitious attack adopted by First Army emerged from a number of factors: Sir John French's ill health and his virtual abdication of responsibility for the coming attack after 19 August; Haig's over-optimistic appreciation of the effectiveness of the chlorine gas discharge; his adherence to a view of warfare that emphasised 'decisive' battles and was uneasy with anything that diverted from this; and a fundamental misunderstanding concerning the orders he had been given by Sir John. Finally, the poor state of communication between GHQ and First Army should also be noted; something that prevented an open and honest discussion about the aims and objectives of the coming offensive from taking place. The final operations orders were issued on the evening of 19 September.[137] All six divisions of I and IV Corps would attack the German lines between the La Bassée canal and Lens on the morning of 25

September after a forty-minute discharge of chlorine gas and smoke, and a preliminary bombardment that had lasted for over four days. III, Indian and V Corps, the latter from Second Army, would also make subsidiary assaults. Plans had greatly mutated since late August when Haig originally had asked Gough and Rawlinson to plan for a short advance in the wake of French successes south of Lens. Instead of a minor push forward, First Army was now to make the biggest and most ambitious British offensive of the war to date. It was to do this in spite of general agreement about the unsuitability of the ground, untrained troops, lack of ammunition and heroic but rushed gas preparations. But how was the battle planned closer to the front?

3

PRE-BATTLE PREPARATION: SEPTEMBER 1915

During September 1915, while all at GHQ and First Army worked feverishly on operational plans and deployment orders, things were taking shape closer to the front. The build-up of assault troops required more communication, support and reserve trenches to be dug, while existing ones had to be drained, deepened and in places widened. Stores had to be moved up, dugouts constructed and saps pushed out towards the German positions. The unsavoury task of transporting thousands of bulky gas cylinders up to the front line fell in many cases to the infantry, who also had to be given their orders and trained in their respective roles. Detailed preparations for the offensive began in late August, and in the following four weeks, a 'vast and methodical' operation took place that transformed First Army's lines.[1] Watching the columns of lorries, guns and ammunition wagons moving up to the front 'in an endless procession day and night', Major E.S.B Hamilton, a medical officer with 15th (Scottish) Division, recorded in his diary that 'there was never anything like this'.[2]

The preparations that preceded the Battle of Loos were unprecedented, being the largest and most complex logistical operation that had been conducted by the BEF up to that time. These preparations were, however, still inadequate for the scale of the attack that First Army was planning. Admittedly the poor ground conditions caused a number of insurmountable difficulties, but the preparations were plagued by poor staff work, confusion and muddle. As well as the problems that were experienced in pushing the British trenches closer to the German lines, adding extra communication and support trenches, and bringing the required materials to the battlefield, there was also a growing conflict over the tactical plans for the attack. It seems that there was an unresolved tension between those senior British officers at corps and division tasked with fulfilling General Sir Douglas Haig's grand ideas, and a number of subordinates closer to the front line who were in many cases either confused or unhappy about what they were being asked to do. These disagreements, which mirrored the confusion about the aims and objectives of the attack between GHQ and First Army, were never resolved and had important implications for the coming assault. This was especially evident when considering the contested march of the reserve divisions (XI Corps) to the battlefield in the days before the assault; an episode that reveals much about the poor pre-battle preparation, staff work and logistics within First Army.

Once General Sir Douglas Haig and his corps commanders had agreed upon the basic outline of the main assault, tactical planning could go ahead. As has been explained in Chapter 2, First Army's plans for the Battle of Loos were highly ambitious, being based on the infantry conducting an 'all-out' assault that would dislocate the German defences north of Lens and win a major strategic victory. But how were these ambitious plans received lower down the chain of command? While there was a concentration, especially at corps and divisional headquarters (except in one notable case), on far-off 'unlimited' objectives, this was not shared by those closer to the front who were understandably preoccupied with the task of actually cracking the German front line. Because it was 'not enough to gain a tactical success',[3] units had to plan for an 'all-out' attack, which placed a great deal of pressure on subordinates who were faced, on the one hand, with unfavourable ground, and on the other, with the call for a major victory.

As was to be expected, the orders emanating from British divisions echoed those given by Haig in the run-up to the battle and were noticeable for their aggression. Major-General A.E.A. Holland (GOC 1st Division) emphasised the scale of the attack in his pre-battle orders, telling his brigadiers that 'a small tactical success such as the taking of the enemy's front line trenches will in no way meet the requirements of the case'.[4] Similarly, Major-General F.W.N. McCracken (GOC 15th Division) stressed that the attack should be pressed 'with all the offensive power of the division'[5] and Major-General Sir T. Capper (GOC 7th Division) added even *more* emphasis onto the objectives he had been given. Capper, a fiery martinet with a deep and lasting commitment to the offensive,[6] told his subordinates, a week before the battle, that:

> We must abandon all narrow or limited ideas, and keep our eyes fixed on the large object in view. Large reserves are in position behind, ready to support us as soon as we have achieved a certain amount of success... boldness and clarity are to be the keywords of our action. We do not want to "huroosh" forward, but to advance rapidly and in good order.[7]

How were these pronouncements received and what impact did they have on those actually doing the fighting? Far from being equally enthusiastic, those closer to the front were much less sanguine about the prospects of the attack. The difficulty of the ground seems to have been a key factor. Contemporary descriptions of the Loos battlefield are similar in tone and content. As French and Haig had already realised, the proposed ground was unsuitable for a major offensive. Sir John French found Loos 'a veritable shell trap,' while Haig grimly noted that the area was 'covered with coal pits and houses'.[8] To Philip Gibbs, the war reporter, it was quite simply 'hideous territory'.[9] Similarly, according to Paul Maze, a French staff officer with I Corps, it was 'a drab district of coal mines, where even the summer could bring no joy'.[10] The ground bore the scars of many years of intense mining activity. Slagheaps and pitheads dotted the landscape. Although the battlefield was littered with small villages and criss-crossed with roads and tracks, it was generally flat and exposed, only broken by the Grenay–Hulluch ridge and Hill 70 to the east of Loos. These gentle rises, somewhat like soft waves across a calm sea, may not have been of great strategic importance, but they were of immense tactical value and were to be bitterly contested.

The mining buildings themselves were split into two types: *puits* and *fosses*. A *puits* was a small mine of less permanent construction than its bigger cousin, the *fosse,* and usually only consisted of several ramshackle sheds and small brick buildings. A *fosse*, on the other hand, was a large, principal mine, characterised by its steel winding gear that could rise up to one hundred feet into the air. Inevitably, these sturdy metal giants were the stations of precariously seated observers. Although observing from a *fosse* was a risky and nerve-wracking task, the benefits from occupying a commanding position in such a flat landscape were obvious to all. The most famous *fosse* on the battlefield was undoubtedly 'Tower Bridge' in Loos village, which proved impossible for British gunners to hit, but only too easy for a German howitzer battery that felled it in the months after Loos had been taken.[11] The main enemy observation stations south of the La Bassée canal were at Fosse 8 and 'Tower Bridge' and gave the

German *Sixth Army* extensive views over British preparation in the area, thus rendering forlorn any hope of surprise. As the soil in this part of France consisted mainly of chalk and flint, the extra forming up and support trenches that the British would require were easily visible and the 'excavated chalk subsoil' gave them, in the words of one commentator, 'the appearance of lines of sea-foam on a beach'.[12] Alongside a *fosse* was usually a *crassier*. These were piles of waste mining material heaped into ugly pyramids that towered over the surrounding countryside and gave the Loos battlefield its own unique panorama. As well as being useful for artillery observation, these dusty, somewhat treacherous, slagheaps could also be converted into virtually indestructible fortresses, which housed nests of machine guns. The Double Crassier (south-west of Loos) and the Dump (near the Hohenzollern Redoubt) were of particular importance, given their size and location, being effectively able to enfilade any advance upon Loos or Cité St Elie respectively. Most of the *crassiers* on the Loos battlefield were 'cool', and positions could therefore be dug into them, but some, such as Fosse 3 near the village of Philosophe, were hot and proved extremely difficult to burrow into.[13]

Moving eastwards across the ground, as Haig's report of 23 June had made clear, would not be easy.[14] Between the British lines and the Haute Deule canal – First Army's final objective – there were only three main roads leading eastwards.[15] The infantry would be able to make reasonable progress marching across the grass, but getting guns and other supplies forward would take time and cause great congestion on the rudimentary transport network. Even the existing roads tended to be concentrated in the northern half of the British line, with the Vermelles–Hulluch road, which continued onto Vendin le Vieil, being the southernmost route going directly eastwards. The lack of suitable roads *behind* the British line was even more of a problem. Lieutenant-Colonel Hon. M.A. Wingfield (AA&QMG 7th Division) complained that the 'roads here were most inconvenient, practically none of them running straight from west to east, and it was most difficult to effect a traffic circuit at all, without encroaching on the areas of other divisions'.[16]

There were major concerns not only about the ground itself, but also the labyrinth of German defences that had been constructed upon it. Facing Haig's First Army was the German *Sixth Army*, commanded by Crown Prince Rupprecht of Bavaria.[17] A calm and competent commander, Rupprecht was arguably the best royal general in the German Army. The defences in the *Sixth Army* sector were very strong and consisted of two separate lines of defence protected by barbed wire and studded with machine guns. Numerous communication trenches joined the two. There were also several fortified villages situated behind the German front trenches, which provided accommodation and storage facilities. From the La Bassée canal to Lens, the German second line ran closely in front of six mining villages between one and two miles from the front trenches. Stretching from La Bassée, past Haisnes, Cité St Elie, Hulluch, Cité St Auguste to Cité St Laurent, the second line was very similar to its front line counterpart. Strongly wired and deeply dug, the trench system contained a number of *Stützpunkt*, heavily defended 'keeps' that could be defended from all sides, and were still able to resist even if its supporting trench lines were overrun. These keeps were especially important in holding the wide, arching 'D' shaped line that covered open fields from Hulluch to Cité St Laurent.[18]

The concept behind the second line was a simple one. In response to the heavy fighting of the winter and spring, it had proved virtually impossible for assaults to be repulsed along *every* sector of attack, and with the waxing Allied material resources being brought to bear, sooner or later, one line of defences would break. On 13 May 1915 the German Chief of Staff, General Erich von Falkenhayn, issued a memorandum to his armies that discussed the basic offensive methods that had been employed by the French during the previous winter. Offensive operations tended to be characterised by considerable artillery preparation before the infantry were committed. The report admitted that 'the morale of everybody behind the front line was affected by the noise, the clouds of smoke and dust rising like a gigantic wall above the battle line and the shower of splinters raining in every direction'. After the preliminary bombardment had smashed the German lines, an attack would materialise on a narrow frontage and be pressed home by large numbers of soldiers. In order to defeat these attacks:

> What was required was not one or even several lines of fixed defences, but rather a fortified zone which permitted a certain liberty of action, so that the best use could be made of all the advantages offered by the configuration of the ground, and all disadvantages could as far as possible be overcome.[19]

Although the concept of 'defence in depth' would not be fully employed for at least another two years, it is clear that German tactical thought was already developing at considerable speed.[20] With merciless efficiency and using soldiers, engineers and legions of forced labour, a second line was begun in the summer of 1915. By the time the Anglo-French attacks commenced in late September, such a system had not been completed fully, although it was strong in parts, especially against the southern end of the British line. It would prove a considerable asset.

Such matters were not lost on those British officers surveying the battlefield from the front line and there seems to have been a general scepticism about the feasibility of conducting an 'unlimited' operation over such difficult ground. In particular, there were persistent queries about the rather vague 'into the blue' orders that had been issued and greater clarity was often sought. Whereas in later years, British attacks would be split into a number of carefully planned stages – often a series of coloured lines – this was not the case at Loos, and no definite timetable of movements was issued.[21] Indeed, tactical orders seem to have been terribly rushed. This was particularly noticeable in 15th (Scottish) Division, which was to make the main attack of IV Corps. Lieutenant-Colonel J. Rainsford-Hannay (Brigade Major 44 Brigade) complained that his brigade was only given its final objectives – 'into the blue', as he put it – to head off 'beyond Cité St Auguste' 48 hours before the attack.[22] Lieutenant-Colonel J.H. Purvis (CO 12/Highland Light Infantry, 46 Brigade) was also given similar information. He had been told to 'push on as long as you can as you are going to be backed up all the way!'[23]

But no detailed series of objectives came from higher authority. This caused concern. Brigadier-General M.G. Wilkinson (GOC 44 Brigade) evidently did not want his men to make such an ambitious operation and would have preferred a more limited series of attacks. He had told his corps commander (Lieutenant-General Sir Henry Rawlinson) that once Hill 70 had been taken, his men must be allowed to consolidate their positions and await reinforcements before carrying on. This was curtly rejected. Despite his own concerns, Rawlinson urged Wilkinson to 'push ahead as you will have plenty of support'.[24] Even 45 Brigade, the divisional reserve, experienced a similar pressure and again a corresponding reluctance from subordinate officers. After the brigade commander (Brigadier-General F.E. Wallerstein) had urged his officers to get their men over Hill 70, Lieutenant-Colonel J.W. Sandilands (CO 7/Cameron Highlanders) had queried this. 'Can you give us some objective there?' he had asked. 'You have got your objective which is Hill 70,' replied Wallerstein, 'But if you get that and you find there is no opposition push on to Cité St Auguste.'[25]

Such confusion was not, however, unique to 15th Division. Both 1st and 7th Divisions, straddling the Vermelles–Hulluch road in the centre of the British attack, experienced a similar unease. Colonel W.C. Walton (CO 8/Berkshire, 1 Brigade) admitted that he had very little idea of what to do. His commanding officer, Brigadier-General A.J. Reddie (GOC 1 Brigade), had simply told him that 'we were to go as far as we could'. The confusion between operational and tactical attacks was again in evidence. There were apparently no specific objectives, 'except that each battalion was to be exploited to its utmost limit'.[26] The AA&QMG of 7th Division complained that Capper 'never looked at the German front line system' and instead 'fixed his gaze on the second line'.[27] In an interview with him shortly before the battle regarding engineer requirements, Colonel G.H. Boileau (CRE 7th Division) was apparently told to 'never mind about forward RE dumps or tools and wire, your chief job will be to get the division over the canal'.[28] But even so, the orders given to 7th Division were only to secure the *crossings* over the Haute Deule canal, not to cross it.

Interestingly one divisional commander was notable for his absence of aggression. Major-General G.H. Thesiger, GOC 9th (Scottish) Division, so disliked the plan that he disassociated himself from it, and seems to have had relatively little to do with 9th Division's preparations. This may well have been due to his recent arrival; he had only taken charge of the division on 9 September, but there seems to have been some interference in the details of the attack by the commander of I Corps, Lieutenant-General Hubert Gough. In particular, there had been considerable discussion about the attack of 26 Brigade. It was supposed to take Fosse 8 and then undertake a complete right wheel (alongside 28 Brigade), before moving onto further objectives. Within the divisions this was regarded as being unfeasible and Thesiger subsequently made it clear that these orders were not his own, rather Gough's. Major J.G. Collins (8/Black Watch), bitterly upset by this interference in brigade orders, complained that, 'The Corps Commander seems to forget the infantry don't gallop!' Colonel Cameron of Lochiel (CO 5/Cameron Highlanders) subsequently told Lord Sempill (CO 8/Black Watch) that he would take Fosse 8, the first objective, but did not expect to 'get a yard further'.[29]

Things could not have been more different on the extreme right of the British line. Indeed, the experience of 47th (London) Division shows an alternative to the tensions inherent in making such a far-reaching attack. Because it was to undertake only a limited, flank-guarding operation – and in stark contrast to Capper's canal-crossing fantasies – Major-General C. St. L. Barter (GOC 47th Division) was able to place a much greater emphasis on the initial assault on the German front line. As a result there were no 'into the blue' orders issued to his men, and there seems to have been very little unease in his division. For example, one soldier remembered how 'full and elaborate orders were issued'.[30] Because exact, achievable objectives were drawn up, 47th Division was able to construct a flagged course of the terrain, which proved very useful for training purposes. The war diary subsequently recorded that 'every man knew exactly what he had to do: and consequently… the whole assault went like clockwork'.[31] But the success of the assault would depend not only on the tactical plans for the attack, then being drafted at battalion, brigade and divisional headquarters, but also upon what kind of logistical preparation had been made in British divisions scheduled to go 'over the top' on 25 September.

It is often lamented among historians that relatively little attention has been paid to the vital, albeit unglamorous, role that logistics played in British operations during the First World War. And while I.M. Brown's *British Logistics on the Western Front* (1989) is a valuable account of the higher end of logistical preparation, there is much work to be done on the movement, management and use of supplies closer to the front line.[32] How effective were the preparations First Army made for the coming battle? Although certainly impressive in scale, the results seemed to have been mixed. While a number of divisions were able to prepare very effectively for the coming battle, others were hampered by a lack of equipment, supplies and men. Poor staff work was also a constant problem all along the front. First Army (and the BEF more generally) simply did not have the capacity to provide the support that such a massive battle required. There were also worrying problems concerning a lack of communication between senior members of First Army and a confusion over the type of battle that First Army was attempting to conduct.

Given the great reliance placed upon the discharge of chlorine gas, the successful delivery and installation of over 5,000 cylinders into the front trenches of I and IV Corps was perhaps the most pressing concern in the weeks before the battle. And although the arrangements were to some extent miraculous, they were flawed. Lieutenant-Colonel C.H. Foulkes's Special Brigade was not only desperately short of officers and men (most sections were five or six men under establishment), but also in equipment such as slings and poles to carry the cylinders into the trenches.[33] When, on the evening of 17 September, the first cylinders arrived at the railhead behind First Army lines, problems were almost immediately encountered. The lids of the boxes in which the cylinders were stored were difficult to open. Some cylinders were empty or leaking on arrival, while others contained more gas and were heavier than expected. Once the cylinders had been packed into trucks and delivered to the divisional dumps, fatigue parties took over. Accounts of the journey from the dumps to the front trenches are similar in content. It usually took at least four hours (some parties took over *nine* hours[34]) and was of a most exhausting and trying nature.[35] As well as the cylinders – which could weigh up to 160lbs – the connecting pipes were very heavy and difficult to carry through the twisting communication and support trenches. But in what was a feat of considerable labour, the cylinders were installed on time by working-parties, sent from each division (often up to 2,000 men strong), which went into the trenches every night with their dangerous, lumpy burdens.[36]

The installation of gas cylinders must be seen as a major logistical success. It was, however, far from perfect. Despite Haig's best efforts trying to keep the gas preparations a secret, he seems to have failed. Although he had returned a cargo of gas cylinders which had mistakenly arrived at Béthune station back to Boulogne and ordered Foulkes's Special Companies not to mix with other troops,[37] by as early as 5 September surprisingly accurate stories were circulating amongst the British at the front that 'there is to be a very big advance in which we shall use gas all along the line after a four days [*sic*] bombardment'.[38] This was even more worrying because the use of the term 'gas' had been forbidden, instead it was called 'accessory' or 'roger'.[39] Given the flat, open ground and excellent observation possessed by *Sixth Army* over most of the British front, moving vast amounts of guns, troops and stores up unnoticed was virtually impossible, but there seems to have been a carelessness about First Army in its staff work that was repeated across many different areas of the pre-battle preparation. Captain J.C. Dunn (2/Royal Welsh Fusiliers, 19 Brigade) complained on 4 September that all 'Troop, train, and wagon movements were unconcealed' and although 'strict observance' had been maintained at the front in not discussing the coming attack, at the regimental base 'everything was open and public; for weeks beforehand the offensive was the general topic among all ranks'.[40] But rumours were not only reaching the British front line. One German account also recorded how they were not 'caught napping'.

> In mounting the gas batteries they [the British] could not help to make some noise and our patrols reported that unusual hammering on metal. In the following nights I convinced myself of the correctness of their reports and passed them on to my superiors. Only my regimental commander and the surgeon believed in those reports and immediately took action. We had to prepare 20 inches square wooden boxes filled with straw and tar and in the rear they ordered several thousand emergency masks to protect mouth and nose.[41]

It is certain that this was not a unique occurrence, although it seems that the German formation (*14th Division*) opposite 2nd Division, where the front lines were very close together, had a far clearer idea of British preparations than those units further south.[42]

As well as bringing up the gas cylinders, it was essential that First Army construct the necessary positions from which to launch the assault. How effective were these efforts? Results were again mixed. On certain sectors of the front a great deal of work was undertaken. While 15th Division's war diary lists twelve separate tasks that were completed before the attack and the divisional history fifteen, 9th Division also made a major logistical effort.[43] In the weeks leading up to the attack over 12,000 yards of trench were dug, including a number of saps that were pushed out into no-man's-land and then joined together to form a new fire trench within 150 yards of the German positions.[44] Although 7th Division was not making one of the main attacks, its sector had also been transformed.[45] By 4 September no-man's-land was around 500 yards in depth (it had been over 700 yards in places) and a considerable number of new communication trenches had been dug, while existing ones had been strengthened and widened.[46] Progress was evidently pleasing and Brigadier-General Hon. J.F.H.S.F. Trefusis (GOC 20 Brigade) recorded in his diary that 'we are further forward than any other division in everything that is being done'.[47] 47th Division's preparation, for its limited attack south-west of Loos, was almost faultless. It moved into its positions on 26 August and dug over 1,450 yards of new front line, about 200 yards in advance of the old position, in the following four weeks.[48] As well as building a new front line, there were many scarcely smaller tasks including the construction of large ration and equipment dumps, a functioning water-supply system and the laying of miles of telegraph and telephone cables in and around the trenches. By 25 September, 47th Division had dug over two miles of new communication trenches, deepened and widened existing ones and prepared positions for three machine gun batteries on the forward slope of the Maroc Ridge.

The sheer scale of the operation did, however, stretch resources thinly. As a staff officer with 7th Division commented, it was difficult to meet all the requirements not only for an attack on the first and second German lines, but also to 'prepare to carry on onto open warfare'.[49] Indeed, both 9th and 7th Divisions had been materially assisted by the labour of 1st Division, which was one of the most overworked formations within First Army. Because it had originally not been intended that 1st Division would be involved in the main attack, it had spent most of August pushing out a number of saps in I Corps' sector, building keeps in and around Vermelles, and constructing a new front line for 7th Division.[50] When the decision to attack 'all-out' with the six divisions of I and IV Corps had been taken, 1st Division returned hurriedly to its own sector, one vital month having already passed. Deployed on unfavourable ground 1st Division struggled to make adequate preparation. By the first week of September not only was there a shortage of 'jumping off' points and latrines, but there were also too few main communication trenches. Brigadier-General Reddie warned Major-General Holland on 7 September that the 'trenches will be very crowded and there will be no means of communication along the lines, when occupied, owing to their being so narrow'.[51] Reddie was, however, assured the following day that 3 Brigade would help widen the front trenches and dig the required latrines.[52] But these assurances were not kept. What evidence that exists points to a simple lack of time and labour. On 1 August, 3 Brigade complained that owing to the 'great extent of line, and the weakness of the battalions the amount of work required is very heavy'.[53] There were too many tasks and not enough men, a situation only aggravated by heavy enemy shelling.[54]

Major-General H.S. Horne's 2nd Division also experienced a great many problems. Strung out along the La Bassée canal on what was certainly the longest, and arguably the most unfavourable sector of the British line, 2nd Division's front stretched from Givenchy to a point north-west of the Hohenzollern Redoubt. No-man's-land was a sinister, topsy-turvy landscape of huge craters, coarse grass, half-buried skeletons and rotting corpses; the product of months of trench warfare. Along this sector the British trenches ran in close parallel to the German positions and all three of Horne's brigades were in the line, occupied with a constant diet of working-parties and fatigues.[55] The front trenches were drained, deepened and wired, their traverses repaired, fire-steps improved and numerous shellproof shelters constructed. A number of saps were opened up into no-man's-land and a scale model of the ground was constructed and installed around its billets. The front was also one of the most active in First Army. September may have been a quiet month from the other British sectors south of the La Bassée canal, but for 2nd Division, it was a constant battle for supremacy with German tunnellers. According to one observer, nowhere on the Western Front 'was mining so active as here'.[56]

The preparations that British divisions made for the coming offensive were clearly different from each other. Because the operational plans for the battle were so loose and the attacking units had only been given rough objectives, much was left to individual divisions and their commanders. And in the absence of a clear, guiding hand from corps or army about how to prepare for the coming battle and how resources should be managed, divisions went their own ways. This independence was also noticeable in the attacking formations that battalions adopted when crossing no-man's-land on 25 September. It seems that no set tactics were laid down and battalion commanders were left, to a great extent, free to adopt whatever formation they preferred.[57] This confusion was compounded by the remarkable lack of communication between units. This can be illustrated by comparing the construction of flagged course and scale models of the ground. While 2nd, 9th and 47th Divisions made such models, the three other attacking divisions did not place such an emphasis on them.[58] Although this had proven to be of some use earlier in the year, and would later become a staple training technique within the BEF, the lack of a unified logistical plan ensured that this was not enforced.

The medical arrangements for Loos mirrored its other preparations: on a vast scale, but still inadequate. Major-General W.G. Macpherson (DMS First Army) had estimated that several days fighting would produce around 39,000 British casualties,[59] but between 25 September and 1 October,

29,720 wounded were admitted into field ambulances and another 22,315 were treated in casualty clearing stations.[60] Such strain produced severe problems. One medical officer recorded that by the morning of 25 September 'stretchers began to run out',[61] and another remembered how the 'whole thing was a sort of long nightmare with the only thing clear being the necessity for dressing more and more people every minute'.[62] Although Macpherson believed that his medical arrangements were about as good as they could have been, and 'worked well and smoothly', they broke down completely in some parts of the battlefield.[63] The area around the Hohenzollern Redoubt was a particularly ghastly example of how difficult swift evacuation and treatment of casualties could become,[64] but it was not a unique occurrence. There were not enough medical personnel, not enough casualty clearing stations and ambulances, stretchers were a constant problem and hundreds of wounded simply stacked up in the exposed fields behind the lines. Treatment techniques were, however, clearly improving. Abdominal wounds were one of the most feared injuries among fighting soldiers, and in response to surgical advances, it became possible to operate on such wounds successfully if they were treated quickly. Before the battle, it was arranged that men with abdominal wounds should be moved from the battlefield as swiftly as possible to two specialist casualty clearing stations behind the line.[65] Two other special advanced operating centres were also set up to deal with such wounds. According to Macpherson, this procedure was successful and 'the formation of specially staffed advanced operating centres, for early operative treatment of wounds of the abdomen became the rule'.[66]

Across the whole logistical spectrum, therefore, it can be seen that similar experiences were had. The resources at First Army's disposal were bigger than ever, but the amount was still inadequate for the size of the battle Haig was planning. Why was this so? Loos may have been the biggest land battle in British military history to date, but its logistical base was *too small*. Too much was being asked of subordinates, there were too many jobs to complete, and all with limited resources that were being stretched to breaking point. The harassed staff of First Army may have worked wonders of improvisation, particularly with the gas cylinders, but it was surely inevitable that the chronic shortage of experienced and well-trained staff officers would cause difficulties. As I.M. Brown has explained, 'The BEF did not have the capability to provide the support that Loos demanded'.[67] But it should not be assumed that this was simply a consequence of a lack of men or materials. On 29 August Major-General P.E.F. Hobbs (DA&QMG First Army) was recorded as being 'in some doubt both as to the object which the 1st Army has in view, and to the means proposed for carrying it out'.[68] This comment sheds light not only on the ambitious scale of the attack at Loos, but also the poor state of communication within First Army. It seems that these concerns were never really ironed out. Apart from the gas, Haig was not terribly interested in logistics in 1915, and he underrated its importance. Although weaponry and technology feature heavily in Haig's diary, logistical and supply matters do not seem to have made the same impression.[69] There was only one mention of this in Haig's main pre-battle conference on 6 September.[70] It seems that Haig did not realise what demands his offensive would make on supplies and logistics, and in any case, in line with the British Army's doctrine of 'umpiring', it was up to the commander to issue general instructions, and to subordinates to sort it out for themselves.[71]

A key component of the British logistical plan was ensuring that communication was maintained between the assaulting troops and the headquarters in the rear. Many of the inherent difficulties in battlefield communication that would become so familiar to the British on the Western Front were cruelly exposed during the Battle of Neuve Chapelle (10–12 March 1915), when First Army attempted to batter a way through the German defences and sweep up to the Aubers Ridge, a low-lying spur about two miles into the enemy position. Although the initial assault met with some success, a number of undamaged strongpoints on the flanks of the attack caused heavy casualties and the attack bogged down. One of the chief features of the battle was the almost complete loss of control at corps and divisional level soon after the troops went 'over the top'. The British Official History noted that:

> The breaking of all communications with the front line battalions by the German artillery bombardment and the time (two to three hours) taken by runners to get back with reports, made it difficult for the corps and divisional commanders to take any action during the morning. Their task was further complicated by the inaccuracy of some of the reports received, due chiefly to the difficulty of picking up landmarks in this flat featureless district.[72]

It was no surprise that a significant number of commanders, used to personal leadership and frustrated by the dearth of battlefield information, simply left their command posts and went forward to find out for themselves what was happening. The lethality of the modern battlefield meant that a considerable number of them never returned.

What communication methods did the BEF employ in this period? The most widely used device was the telephone. 1915 had seen a rapid growth in its use on the Western Front. By the summer demand for telephone and cable equipment was staggering.[73] It was estimated that for each divisional artillery group around 300 miles of cable were required. On this scale, each corps would use over 1,200 miles of it![74] But such heavy reliance on the telephone system was not without its problems as the understaffed and overworked signal service struggled to cope with the almost exponential expansion in its use. As the telephone system grew in popularity, it gradually became more inefficient and inflexible as the indiscriminate laying of wires caused confusion, expense and much extra work. According to the *History of the Signal Service* (1921), one of the great lessons of the battles of 1915 was the 'development of supplementary means of communication' to take some weight off the telephone system.[75] Various visual signals were available, but none of these was perfect. All were heavily dependent on good weather. A First Army note on communication methods complained on 24 September that flags and discs could only be used for short distances, helios were dependent on the sun, electric lamps had very limited visibility, especially in daytime, while smoke balls were simply not effective.[76] A measure of how serious the BEF considered this communication 'gap' to be was the employment of carrier pigeons on the battlefield. They had been in service as early as September 1914 and were well-established on the Western Front by the following summer.[77]

New wireless technology did threaten to solve some of these problems, but much research and development was still required. Wireless communication was not a new invention in 1914, but the sets that were available were few in number, heavy, bulky and unreliable. It was only with the arrival of a new field set in mid-August 1915, specially designed with an inbuilt receiver and transmitter, and built to stand up to the rigours of active service, that wireless became a viable alternative to visual and telegraphic communication. Loos witnessed the first tactical employment of these short-range (up to 5 miles) wireless sets in military history and by all accounts they did 'excellent' service. But they were still few in number and very expensive.[78] Almost inevitably, when considering the multiple communication difficulties the BEF was experiencing at this time, the burden of carrying messages from the front during battle inevitably fell on the humble runner.

Solving the command and communication riddle on the Western Front was not just a matter of amassing the necessary tools, but of using them correctly. This was especially evident with airpower. Major-General H.M. Trenchard was appointed GOC Royal Flying Corps (RFC) on 25 August 1915 and worked well with Haig for the next three years.[79] By the summer of 1915, the war in the skies above the Western Front was evolving at considerable pace, both in its scale and complexity. Between January and August the RFC doubled in size, with over 170 aircraft being available for the autumn offensive.[80] As well as increasing in size, the range of the operations undertaken by the RFC had also developed. Whereas during 1914 the role of aircraft remained firmly one of reconnaissance, by as early as March 1915, British planes had photographed enemy trenches (and produced maps from them), undertaken bombing operations in the enemy hinterland and engaged in – albeit fledgling – air-to-air combat.[81]

For the coming attack the RFC would conduct its biggest and most ambitious operation to date. All three Wings (each attached to an army) were to be involved.[82] The most important part of the air operation centred on First Wing (Lieutenant-Colonel E.B. Ashmore), which was to be used entirely for artillery spotting, including trench bombardment and counter-battery work. Second and Third Wings (Lieutenant-Colonel J.M. Salmond and Lieutenant-Colonel W.S. Brancker respectively) were also active. Their squadrons were to conduct bombing operations on enemy rail and communication targets (the vital railway junctions of Lille–Douai–Valenciennes) and to protect First Wing from enemy air activity, which with the arrival of the Fokker *Eindecker* and its revolutionary ability to fire synchronised blasts of machine gun fire through its propeller arc, was becoming an increasing menace.[83] As might have been expected, the RFC's bombing operations were inaccurate and did relatively little damage to enemy infrastructure.[84] Aerial bombardment in 1915 was no more than a nuisance weapon and between 1 March and 20 June, out of 141 attempts at bombing enemy targets (mostly at railways and troop columns) only three had definitely been successful.[85] Indeed, even the offensively-minded Trenchard could not have failed to recognise the considerable limitations the RFC was operating under during this period. Although the numbers of aircraft had steadily increased throughout the year, there were still too few planes and many of those were the reliable but increasingly obsolescent B.E.2c.

The most important role of the RFC in the coming offensive would be the vital air–artillery co-operation missions. These operations were fraught with difficulty, not only with technology, but also with poor liaison and staff work. One of the most persistent problems was finding an effective (and accurate) way of communicating detailed information – particularly map references – to those on the ground. The arrival of lightweight and effective wireless transmitters in the autumn of 1915 did much to help,[86] but for those squadrons not equipped with such devices, recourse had to be made to more traditional methods, including *Very* lights, flares, wing-flapping and the dropping of messages. Indeed, it was not unknown for pilots to land near batteries and verbally inform their commanders of what they had seen! But quick and accurate air–artillery co-operation rested not only on technology, but also upon finding an effective vocabulary for these exchanges. Various methods were developed, including the clock code (first used at Neuve Chapelle in March) and zone calls.[87] But difficulties were not just encountered in the air and there was considerable 'cap-badge' resistance from the Royal Artillery about so-called 'interference' from the RFC.[88] Although the first artillery-air co-operation missions had been flown early in the war, the idea of using planes to correct the fire of artillery batteries was still something of a novelty. According to one pilot, 'all arrangements for co-operation including the actual methods of ranging depended at this time upon personal arrangement[s] between battery commander and air observer'.[89] As well as using aircraft to spot for the artillery, First Wing also contained two Kite Balloon sections,[90] which were used to observe the enemy lines and were especially useful for counter-battery work.[91]

1915 had witnessed a spasmodic growth in infantry–air co-operation, but like the artillery missions, the inherent difficulties were considerable. In response to the confusion encountered at Neuve Chapelle once the initial attack had ground to a halt, it had been decided for the Battle of Aubers Ridge in May that the attacking battalions would carry large flags and markers. This would enable RFC aircraft, circling the battlefield, to help identify what progress had been made. But these markers were never really given an opportunity to perform as most of the attacks were stopped by unsuppressed enemy machine guns and devastating artillery fire. The scheme was not abandoned, however, and for the Battle of Loos, infantry battalions were not only given markers, but also large, cloth arrows to help them direct artillery fire upon hostile positions. Measuring fifteen feet in length and about one foot in width, the arrows were to be placed upon the ground, with the arrowhead in the direction of the target. This would hopefully be spotted by friendly aircraft, which would then direct artillery fire onto it.[92] It is not known whether any soldiers during the battle actually used the arrows to try and attract aerial attention, or whether any targets were neutralised by this type of fire. There is no mention of the use of such arrows either in the war diaries, personal memoirs or after-action reports.[93]

The patchy logistical organisation within First Army was especially evident during the march of the reserve divisions to the battlefield. The pre-battle confusion over the role of XI Corps, the main part of GHQ's General Reserve, has already been mentioned, but the circumstances of their actual march to the battlefield needs to be assessed. It is generally accepted this took too long and that they arrived late on the battlefield. But the reason why this occurred was the subject of great scrutiny in the aftermath of the debacle. Nobody wanted to be associated with the horrifying events of 26 September when the reserve divisions were repulsed from the battlefield and it became a subject of fierce debate within the BEF as to who had been responsible.[94] While Sir John French and GHQ wanted to highlight an allegedly poor level of staff work within First Army that had led to unnecessary delays, Haig and his staff, on the other hand, naturally wanted to show how the late release of XI Corps had been the cause of the trouble. First Army also complained about the poor march discipline of the inexperienced divisions.

Who was telling the truth? In the initial aftermath of the attack on the German second line, Haig believed that the delay of the reserve divisions had been due to 'bad march discipline and inexperience of the divisions'.[95] After consulting GOC XI Corps (Lieutenant-General R.C.B. Haking), his earlier opinions were confirmed. Haking, using almost the exact phrases that Haig had uttered, wrote that 'the delay was caused chiefly by their own indifferent march discipline, especially as regards first line transport'.[96] But the reply did, however, contain one rather uncomfortable comment. Haking referred to an earlier letter of 10 October 1915 in which he had said that XI Corps 'was advancing through the administrative area of IV and I Corps who were heavily engaged, [and as a result] the progress was slow'.[97] Since Haking's previous letter, the debate over the march of the reserves had reached crisis point with a growing rift between Sir John and Haig. His comments could have been used to support GHQ's accusation that bad staff-work in First Army, and *not the late release of XI Corps*, was to blame for its late arrival on the battlefield. Haking therefore changed his mind. He excused his previous report by saying that his remarks were based on the 'memory of verbal statements made to me by the GOC 21st and 24th Divisions on the night of 25 [September] at Vermelles', before writing that 'the most careful arrangements were made by First Army to ensure that the two roads were kept clear'. In the final paragraph Haking made it clear as to where his sympathies lay: 'there is none to blame except GHQ and they know it'.

On reflection it is hard to avoid the conclusion that Haking was deliberately falsifying or 'cooking' his evidence to make it more palatable to his army commander. This interpretation is further underlined by a brief note in a copy of the telephone conversations of IV Corps on 25 September 1915. At 12.20p.m. Rawlinson telephoned Haking, urging him to get his corps onto the battlefield as soon as possible. The brief reply that 'Haking says traffic is troubling him' casts great doubt on Haking's assertion that it was bad march discipline and *not* road congestion that caused the delays.[98] Although, according to Tim Travers, Haking was 'perhaps under pressure', his motives are not difficult to fathom.[99] He was one of Haig's protégés and owed his command of XI Corps to the personal influence of the First

Army Commander. Haking could also perhaps sense that the tide of army opinion was now finally pulling against Sir John French and a replacement was required. After further enquiries, and as the arguments between First Army and GHQ rumbled on, Haig defended the preparation his army had made. 'The arrangements made in the First Army for securing a free passage for these divisions', Haig explained to GHQ, 'could not have been improved upon. The staffs and control officers again report that such delay and blocking that did occur was due to the inexperience and faulty march discipline of the divisions themselves.'[100]

The 'bad march discipline' slur was bitterly resented within 21st and 24th Divisions and there was a widespread feeling that they had been treated harshly, which lingered on into the post-war years. Major-General G.T. Forestier-Walker (GOC 21st Division) was deeply upset about how his division had been handled and forcefully defended his role in the affair. He believed that the march discipline of his divisions was 'extraordinarily good' and the cause of the delays was the 'constant blocking of the road at the level crossings'.[101] Major R.B. Johnson (15/Durham Light Infantry, 64 Brigade) went even further.

> Traffic congestion, ignorance of the country, loss of direction in the dark, uncut (or insufficiently cut) wire, deep and wide trench obstacles and full equipment all added to the fatigue in the latter part of the day, and delayed the arrival of some units at their positions more than 'indifferent march discipline'.[102]

Major J. Vaughan (8/Buffs, 72 Brigade) felt that Haking's report was 'exceedingly severe' and blamed the 'enormous amount of traffic on the road' for their late arrival.[103] This was echoed by Brigadier-General B.R. Mitford (GOC 72 Brigade) who lamented the terrible road congestion, especially at a number of level crossings. To compound his frustration, he was held up outside Béthune for five minutes by a rather overzealous military policeman. Because Mitford did not have the correct entry pass, the whole brigade was halted until the matter could be sorted out.[104] This complete lack of liaison was evident to Lieutenant-Colonel H.J.C. Piers (8/Queen's, 72 Brigade) who wrote that 'there were no traffic police – no guide marks – troops of cavalry crossing our route'.[105] Major T.G.F. Paget (7/Northamptonshire, 73 Brigade) remarked that his battalion led the march of 24th Division, and as only five men fell out, he reasoned that there could not have been a great deal of bad marching.[106]

So how difficult was the march to the battlefield and what were the arrangements in First Army like? In order to conceal XI Corps from enemy air observation, it had been decided to move them at night between the hours of 6p.m. and 5a.m. As they arrived on the Western Front, 21st and 24th Divisions were stationed south of St Omer. They had not been long in France before being called into action.[107] The march of XI Corps began on the evening of 20 September and the men reached their appointed destinations in good time and without too many problems.[108] Lieutenant-Colonel Cosmo Stewart (GSO1 24th Division) noted in his diary that the road surface was 'good but hilly' and the weather was fine for the first night of the march. He did believe, however, that the troops 'did not rest properly owing to the men wandering about, chiefly out of curiosity'.[109] This resulted in some battalions being more exhausted than others. But traffic was a more persistent problem. Lieutenant-Colonel A. de S. Hadow (CO 10/Yorkshire, 62 Brigade) wrote to his wife on the evening of 21 September. His battalion had covered eighteen miles, but even so, he complained that the 'progress is not rapid, there are so many checks'.[110] The following night's march, however, was completed on time.

On 23 September XI Corps halted and its divisions rested. 21st Division remained around the village of Ferfay, while 24th Division bivouacked south of the railway at Lambres station. The Guards Division, bringing up the rear, was clustered around Norrent Fontes. Up to this point the divisions had not had a particularly taxing time; they were well used to long route marches with their full packs and had the whole of 23 September to rest. As they neared the battlefield, however, progress slowed. The march that evening was a trying one for all involved. The weather broke and showered the long columns of troops in heavy and 'continuous rain'.[111] As they edged ever closer, progress became increasingly difficult. The war diary of 21st Division noted that its march was 'retarded by motor traffic both ways and at various level crossings'.[112] At 6p.m. on the evening of 24 September 24th Division moved off and marched to Beuvry, with its tail units finishing up around Béthune.[113] 21st Division began marching at 7p.m. and found it extremely tiring carrying their full equipment as well as extra ammunition and three days' rations. It had been hoped that with only three or four miles to go before they reached their allotted areas, the men would have a reasonable night's rest, but unfortunately, the delays on the roads prevented this. By the time the last unit had straggled into its concentration area around Nouex-Les-Mines and Labusieirre, it was 6a.m.[114] As had been confirmed by Sir William Robertson (CGS GHQ) two days earlier, the leading divisions of XI Corps were on the line Nouex-Les-Mines-Beuvry by daylight on 25 September.[115] Unfortunately, they had only just arrived. As the day dawned the reserve divisions were needed on the battlefield.

Reviewing the march of XI Corps, it seems reasonable to assume that although its march discipline could perhaps have been better, contrary to Haig's opinion, it was generally acceptable. As Tim Travers has written, the affair of the reserves 'begins to look as if Haig was at best mistaken in his allegations or, at worst, was engineering a cover-up of 1st Army errors'.[116] The problem was not one of march discipline, but as Gary Sheffield has written, 'bad staff work'.[117] There was a complete lack of coordination and liaison between XI Corps and First Army. The issue of maps perfectly illustrates this lacklustre, sometimes non-existent, liaison. While the six assaulting divisions were well-supplied with adequate maps (for example, they were issued 'lavishly' to one battalion of 47th Division)[118], there seems to have been very little sense of urgency in sending them to XI Corps. For example, Brigadier-General C.E Pereira (GOC 85 Brigade, 28th Division) was only given a single map on entering the battlefield,[119] Lieutenant-Colonel C. Coffin (CRE 21st Division) complained that only *three* maps had been issued to 21st Division,[120] and evidently none whatsoever reached 63 Brigade.[121] Often, even those maps that found their way to XI Corps were of 'no use for finding the way across unknown country at night',[122] and one officer remembered how his map gave special attention to the area around Wingles, nearly three miles from the British front line![123] The problem was not a shortage of maps, but a simple lack of liaison between First Army and its reserves. This simply need not have occurred. Indeed Captain E.H. Smythe (GSO3 Intelligence I Corps) believed that *had the staff known maps were required*, a 'considerable number' of them could have been drawn from stores and given to the divisions moving up.[124] As for maps of IV Corps' sector, XI Corps had been promised them on 14 September, but it is unknown whether any were actually delivered.[125]

It is clear that this situation was, in part, a result of the confusion between French and Haig over who had control of XI Corps, which stemmed back to their differing conceptions of what type of attack First Army was to make. But even if Haig can be forgiven for not knowing exactly what Sir John wanted to do with XI Corps, it was understood that it would have *some* role in the coming attack. Haig must therefore take some of the blame. Why was First Army's staff work so poor? In part it was undoubtedly a reflection of the massive, dislocating growth undertaken by the BEF throughout 1915, and the difficulty of finding suitably trained staff officers for the myriad of new positions created. The ground was also to blame. The roads behind the front ran either south-east or north-east, not east–west, and these were hardly sufficient for the six assaulting divisions, let alone another corps. The arrival of XI Corps behind First Army when a major engagement was going on caused these fragile arrangements to collapse. One staff officer lamented that 'blocks did occur, very bad ones, especially at night when transport came to a standstill for over an hour at a time. A good deal of this might have been avoided.'[126] Yet external factors cannot totally explain the misfortunes of XI Corps, and human error also played its part. The arrangements for the march of the reserve divisions were careless. There was simply no appreciation at First Army Headquarters of the space and infrastructure that would be required if a reserve corps was to march through the back areas of I and IV Corps without serious delay. For example, while huge numbers of wires had been laid in the rear areas of I and IV Corps for communication, *none* had been laid for XI Corps and they had to be 'improvised' on the day; probably a reflection of Haig's neglect of logistical matters as well as Hobbs's confusion about what First Army was doing.[127]

Nevertheless, GHQ cannot be absolved of all blame. As the deployment of XI Corps had been a point of bitter debate in the run-up to the battle, and the matter was never fully cleared up, most subordinates did not exactly know what was going on. If clear orders had been issued earlier, it is likely that better arrangements would have been prepared. Brigadier-General F.B. Maurice (BGGS Operations GHQ) was reflective about what had happened. In a candid letter to Sir James Edmonds, he believed that:

> GHQ should have made arrangements for assisting the march of [the] newly-formed divisions. I think now this was a bad oversight on my part. The reason or excuse for it was that we were pressing Sir John up to the last to hand those divisions over to Haig as soon as they came into his area and we didn't know from hour to hour what the decision would be.[128]

Maurice went over the march orders for XI Corps with Haking and told him that problems could be experienced on the night of 24/25 when his corps would be passing through the rear areas of First Army. But by that time XI Corps would probably be under First Army control and therefore out of Maurice's hands. Maurice admitted that this was a bad mistake and concluded that 'I ought either to have insisted in the First Army making arrangements for clearing the roads or seen to it myself.' Yet even this seemingly simple decision was one of great political importance because Maurice was placed in the grey area between GHQ and First Army, and it would be unfair to blame him for a lack of thoroughness. There was a simple lack of decision about the reserves, and for this Sir John French must take primary responsibility. Things should have been made clearer, earlier. But whatever the later arguments about how XI Corps should be employed, by the morning of 25 September its men were worn-out, hungry and appallingly ignorant of the situation that lay ahead of them.

The march of XI Corps to the battlefield in the days preceding the attack highlighted many of the problems in First Army's pre-battle preparation. Although vast amounts of stores and supplies had been gathered and First

Army conducted a massive digging and engineering operation south of the La Bassée canal, the preparations were marred by confusion and muddle. These problems stemmed in part from the inexperience of the BEF in conducting such large-scale operations, particularly the lack of trained staff officers who would have smoothed out matters on the ground, but they also reflected the higher confusion over the attack between GHQ and First Army. Because the operation was so ambitious and because battalions and brigades were to attack 'all-out', trusting in weight of numbers and the 'offensive spirit', little attempt was made to structure the advance and a number of questions were left unanswered, such as whether there were any intermediate objectives and what units were to do when they reached them. Again, because it was expected that XI Corps would face a fleeing, broken enemy, there seems to have been remarkably little sense of urgency within First Army at instituting a properly organised system of reinforcement that would have enabled XI Corps to reach the battle quickly and without confusion. These inconsistencies that had proved so noticeable in both the planning and tactical preparation for the attack at Loos would continue to plague the battle in the coming days.

While the divisions had been marching, they were aware of an ominous rumbling ahead. Between 21 and 24 September, First Army had been conducting the preliminary bombardment on the German defences. This is the subject to which the next chapter turns.

4

THE PRELIMINARY BOMBARDMENT: 21–24 SEPTEMBER 1915

The preliminary bombardment began between 7 and 8a.m. on 21 September 1915. Shells continued falling on the German lines in varying intensity until the morning of the attack, four days later. It was of vital importance. If the infantry were not to be 'hung up' in no-man's-land, the thick belts of wire and the numerous dugouts and machine gun posts that protected the enemy trenches would have to be cleared away. The German artillery, lurking somewhere behind their defences, would also have to be engaged vigorously, or its efforts to hamper British troops and support counter-attacks could prove devastating. But these tasks were not all completed and the results of the bombardment were disappointing. Although considerable damage was inflicted on certain parts of the German line, enough of their defences were left intact, including most of their artillery, to pose a serious threat to the plans drafted by General Sir Douglas Haig.

Little of any real worth has ever been written about the preliminary bombardment at Loos, the accounts in the British Official History and Robin Prior and Trevor Wilson's *Command on the Western Front* (1992) being the most useful.[1] This lack of attention is understandable, given the reliance placed upon gas and the well-known shortage of ammunition, but it is not altogether excusable and it underrates the importance of the bombardment. It was not an event separate from the infantry attack, but the first act of the fighting, which had a great effect on what would subsequently occur once the infantry left their trenches. Why did the preliminary bombardment fail to achieve its objectives? The shortages in artillery ammunition that dogged the BEF throughout 1915 have been well documented.[2] Less well explored has been how the British used the meagre resources they did have, and despite the technological limitations that the artillery was operating under, it is clear that, as had happened with the gas, the preliminary bombardment was spread not only over a wide length of front, but also to a considerable depth into the German position. This meant that although many more guns and a much greater quantity of ammunition were available at Loos than had been the case earlier in the year, its effect was not proportionally greater. The bombardment was dilute and hampered by poor staff work and bad weather.

By the first week of September the basic outline of what form the bombardment would take had been established. First Army issued its 'General Principles for the Attack' on 6 September.[3] After discussing the role of the infantry and its reserves, the paper listed the aims and objectives of the preliminary bombardment. Spread over several days, it was to be a 'deliberate and carefully observed' shoot that would cut the German wire along the whole front of First Army and destroy not only the enemy's observation posts, but also his strongpoints situated immediately behind the front line. The destruction of enemy batteries and the placement of barrages on German communication trenches in order to prevent, or at least hinder, the movement of reliefs and supplies, were further aims. Once the attack was launched, British guns were expected to support the infantry and to 'gain superiority of fire over the hostile artillery'.

Although 'General Principles for the Attack' must, to some extent, be seen as a 'wish-list' of what, given favourable conditions, needed to have been achieved, it was remarkable for its ambition and optimism, and had little relevance to the poor state of British artillery during 1915. Why was this so? It seems that the type of bombardment chosen at Loos stemmed from a number of sources, including the lessons divined from British attacks earlier in the year, Haig's attitude to artillery and the continuing influence of pre-war gunnery techniques. The former was probably the most pressing influence on the bombardment plans for the battle. During 1915 First Army had embarked upon three major offensive operations: the Battle of Neuve Chapelle (10–12 March), the Battle of Aubers Ridge (9 May) and the Battle of Festubert (15–27 May). They had all been preceded by artillery preparation of varying lengths and effectiveness. While short, intensive bombardments had been fired at both Neuve Chapelle and Aubers Ridge, Festubert had witnessed a much less intensive, more methodical shoot that had been spread over several days.

How effective were these bombardments and what conclusions did the British High Command draw from them? Prior and Wilson have examined Neuve Chapelle and Aubers Ridge in some detail, so it will sufficient to summarise their conclusions.[4] The fierce thirty-five-minute bombardment prior to the attack at Neuve Chapelle had been the most effective. Even though the amount of ammunition and the number of guns used were minuscule when compared with those employed later in the war, First Army managed to achieve a density of fire upon the German front line that was not surpassed or even equalled until 1917. Although fire support was poorer on the flanks, the effects of the shelling in the central section of the German line were devastating, with trenches and wire being completely pulverised. But the subsequent break-in could not be converted into a break-out. Isolated enemy strongpoints held up repeated, albeit clumsy, British attempts to get forward. Because British infantry were not yet equipped with the array of equipment and fire-support weapons that would be placed at their disposal during 1917 and 1918, they found it virtually impossible to work their own way forward into the German defences without close artillery support. This secondary stage of the battle, however, seems to have obscured the success achieved during the initial shelling. Thus any future preliminary bombardment would now not only have to smash the enemy front line, but also eliminate those strongpoints deeper into the defences that had proved so stubborn at Neuve Chapelle.

That the next attack at Aubers Ridge was a 'serious disappointment' was clear to everyone concerned.[5] Despite a bombardment five minutes longer than at Neuve Chapelle, it was weak in comparison. This had a devastating effect on the initial attack against the German front line. It seems that with a greater emphasis on the destruction of those strongpoints and defences further into the German position, combined with the deadening effects of wear on artillery barrels and limited stocks of ammunition, the intensity of the bombardment reached only a fifth of that deployed at Neuve Chapelle.[6] The infantry suffered accordingly. Against strengthened German defences, only small groups were able to effect temporary lodgements into the enemy line. So bad was the congestion and confusion in the British front trenches that the attack was called off the following morning. Casualties numbered over 11,000. From the failure at Aubers a number of conclusions were drawn. According to Martin Samuels, Aubers Ridge marks 'the turning point in British tactical development… in favour of a separation of firepower and assault powers'.[7] Still not perceiving the importance of obtaining a sufficient weight of fire, both Haig and Lieutenant-General Sir Henry Rawlinson (GOC IV Corps) now rejected the short, intensive bombardments they had previously employed. Given adequate amounts of artillery and shells, they now believed that only a long and methodical bombardment could do enough damage to the German defences to make them practicable to infantry.[8] Accordingly, First Army carried out the first lengthy bombardment (spread over three days) at Festubert between 13 and 15 May. With relatively modest objectives and a much more deliberate approach, the results of the battle were promising. Benefiting from good weather and innovative infantry tactics, First Army managed to get considerably further forward than they had at Aubers Ridge.

The success, albeit limited, of the Festubert operation seems to have had a considerable impact on Haig and his staff. At a conference on 24 August, it was unanimously agreed that only a longer bombardment should be employed for the coming battle. Such a bombardment would, it was believed, 'tend to destroy the enemy's morale, his observations… it could be spread along an extensive front, and the gas would probably penetrate to his dugouts, and the enemy's artillery would have no indication of the exact point of attack, and his fire would have to be distributed and not concentrated at the real point of attack.'[9] On the other hand, it was agreed that if an 'intensive bombardment took place on any particular part of the front, it would be a sure indication that we were going to attack there, and the German artillery would become active in this locality at once'. There were other reasons against the adoption of a short bombardment. Brigadier-General A.A. Montgomery (BGGS IV Corps) stated that there were not enough guns and ammunition for an intensive shoot.[10] Given the length of frontage to be attacked, this was a point of vital importance, but it does not seem to have been the main reason why it was not adopted.[11]

Gas was another factor in the decision to opt for a slower, more methodical bombardment. Barely two days after he had witnessed Lieutenant-Colonel C.H. Foulkes's demonstration of chlorine gas at Helfaut, Haig was already incorporating it into his plans. He told the assembled officers at the conference on 24 August that he was aiming at a 'lavish use of gas'. It was hoped this would deal with one of the key elements of the German defences: the deep concrete dugouts. Brigadier-General J.F.N. Birch (BGRA I Corps) was pessimistic about the feasibility of destroying them, about ten or twelve of which would prove problematic to any infantry advance. So well protected were they that 'it would be scarcely worth while trying to destroy them'. Gas, however, could help to *neutralise* them, by either incapacitating the defenders, or forcing them to the surface where they would suffer from the accompanying shrapnel bombardment.

The abandonment of 'hurricane' bombardments and the adoption of the French concept of '*L'artillerie conquiert, l'infanterie occupe*' was not without its problems, however. As John Bourne has written, the 'pre-war tactic of fire *and* manoeuvre was replaced by the concept of fire *then* manoeuvre'.[12] A more methodical shoot would abandon any hope of surprise, and allow the enemy defenders the chance to repair any damage to parapets and wire at night. It would also prove a great strain on both the guns and their crews. But perhaps the most serious problem was Haig's chronic optimism, which infected all aspects of the plans. It seems that he either did not recognise, or simply ignored, the grave limitations British artillery was suffering from in this period. The scale and effectiveness of the bombardment would depend on what implements Haig had at his disposal. But when compared with the ambition of 'General Principles for the Attack', they were woefully inadequate. A lack both of guns, particularly heavier varieties, and ammunition were the most pressing concerns. And while the creation of a Ministry of Munitions and the readjustment of British (and American) industry throughout 1915 would eventually allow bountiful supplies of guns and shells to be delivered to France, not until the summer of 1917 would the necessary equipment be in place, and the techniques that had been devised and refined during 'many a doubtful battle' between 1914–16 finally come of age.[13]

It has sometimes been assumed by historians that the British fought the Battle of Loos 'with little increase in artillery' than had been employed at Neuve Chapelle.[14] This is incorrect. A much greater amount of field and heavy artillery was available for the Battle of Loos than had been the case earlier in the year, but it was still not enough (see Table 1). First Army managed to gather a total of 919 guns, with 238 going to I Corps and 225 to IV Corps.[15]

Table 1. Number of guns involved during the Battles of Neuve Chapelle (10–12 March 1915), Aubers Ridge and Festubert (9–18 May 1915) and Loos (21–27 September 1915)[16]

	Neuve Chapelle	Aubers Ridge and Festubert	Loos
Field guns	400	456	594
Field howitzers	54	78	132
Counter-battery	48	44	76
Heavy howitzers	33	47	69
TOTAL	535	623	871

This may have seemed impressive, but it masked serious limitations when compared with the length of the bombardment frontage. Whereas this had been a mere 1,450 yards at Neuve Chapelle, it had swelled to 11,200 yards for Loos (see Table 2).

Table 2. Length of bombardment frontage (yards) of the Battles of Neuve Chapelle (10–12 March 1915), Aubers Ridge and Festubert (9–18 May 1915) and Loos (21–27 September 1915)[17]

Neuve Chapelle	1,450
Aubers Ridge and Festubert	5,080
Loos	11,200

Was the ammunition situation able to help? First Army had access to a considerable amount of ammunition, far more than has generally been recognised, but again it was not enough. First Army received 650,000 shells for the field artillery (about 1,000 rounds per gun), with 100,000 shells for the howitzers and heavy guns (about 400 rounds per gun).[18]

Shortages of guns and ammunition were not the only concerns. Indeed, the bombardment was littered with technical problems. Because a large number of the guns First Army was employing had been under constant stress all year, mechanical breakdown was not uncommon. On 23 September, LI Brigade RFA (9th Division) recorded that one gun had been put out of action because of a broken trigger, and the buffer springs had failed on another gun. No spares were available until the following day.[18] Similarly, VI (London) Brigade RFA (47th Division) reported one defective gun on 23 September.[20] According to the war diary of VIII (London) Brigade RFA, 'a large number of misfires occurred' during the bombardment owing to mechanical failure.[21] The quality of the ammunition the BEF was receiving was also far from perfect; a result of the rapid, haphazard expansion in the British munitions industry that was currently underway. Historians have estimated that around 30 percent of the ammunition fired before the launching of the Somme offensive on 1 July 1916 did not explode. It is probable that a similar percentage of shells at Loos were 'duds'.[22] While Robert Graves (2/Royal Welsh Fusiliers, 19 Brigade) complained that American ammunition 'contained a high percentage of duds; their driving bands were always coming off',[23] Lieutenant-Colonel A.G. Prothero (CO 2/Welsh, 3 Brigade) estimated that around 100 unexploded shells littered no-man's-land in his sector.[24] Even those shells that *did* explode were not without their problems. On 18 September Rawlinson asked First Army to replace certain stocks of 15-pounder ammunition. He complained that these shells were 'absolutely unreliable and a serious source of danger to our own infantry'.[25] Unfortunately, owing to the chronic shortage of replacement ammunition, First Army refused two days later.[26]

All along the front the enemy machine gun posts were recognised as a key cornerstone of the German defence. If these were put out of action an attack would stand a much better chance of getting through. Brigadier-General Hon. J.F.H.S.F. Trefusis (GOC 20 Brigade) knew as much and told Colonel H.H. Tudor (CO XIV Brigade RHA) about his problem.

> Unless we could knock out the enemy machine-guns, our attack may fail. But it is not possible to knock them out, as they can be shifted and the best way to deal with them is to blind them and without smoke I don't see how we can.[27]

Tudor subsequently pestered Brigadier-General Birch for smoke shells. Birch sent an officer back to England to try and get some. Unfortunately, all Birch received was a number of smoke candles. Tudor was furious, lamenting that 'it quite missed the point' and only shells could effectively blind enemy machine gunners. He noted that 'these candles could not do [this] unless the wind was ideal, blowing straight across the enemy and not too strong'.[28] This episode amply illustrates how seriously hampered the British were in trying to pierce the enemy defences. The equipment they needed (guns, smoke shells and high explosive ammunition) was simply not available.

The lack of heavy guns and quality ammunition was of great importance, but there were more intractable problems that needed to be solved. By September 1915 British artillery was undergoing a rapid and frequently painful process of growth and development, part of what has been termed a 'revolution in military affairs'.[29] The type of war that emerged on the Western Front was simply not foreseen, and if a few bright thinkers had appreciated that the next war would involve barbed wire, entrenchments and the decline in traditional artillery techniques, they were firmly in a minority.[30] Because the front line now stretched for over 400 miles and to an ever-increasing depth, it was no longer safe to rely on old methods. Whereas in the pre-war Royal Artillery, under the dominance of the RHA and RFA, the speed and efficiency with which guns could be drawn into position and fired was a matter of professional pride, the techniques of accurate, long-range 'scientific' gunnery were little understood and only practised in the 'ghetto' of the RGA. But these were exactly the skills now demanded on the Western Front.

While traditional direct fire over open sights had occurred since the start of the war, by as early as the Battle of Le Cateau (26 August 1914), when II Corps lost thirty-eight guns to accurate enemy counter-battery fire, it was found necessary to pull artillery back and conceal it wherever possible.[31] The resulting decline in direct fire had profound results. Now indirect fire, or the shooting at a target which could not be seen (often because it was on the other side of a terrain feature), had to be employed. This may not have been as glamorous, it required much less 'dash' than firing over open sights at visible targets did, but it depended upon greater technical knowledge, which took time to learn and experience to perfect. For a shell to be effective, it had to land on, or near to, its target. But by early 1915, as Prior and Wilson have aptly explained, British artillery 'was not likely to hit, with any certainty or regularity, a target that could not be seen'.[32] Why was this so? It seems that a combination of factors prevented the artillery from being the effective weapon it would later become. Merely finding a target presented great difficulties, let alone hitting it. Although FOOs were used, good observation posts in the flat districts of northern France and Belgium were rare, and while aerial reconnaissance was becoming ever more reliable, its technological difficulties, as well as survey problems, hampered these efforts.[33] There was also a lack of understanding of the effects of wind, air temperature and wear on gun barrels, and the calibration that was needed to combat this.

Technological limitations there certainly were. Most of the field guns available at Loos were 18-pounders, the workhouse of British artillery during the Great War.[34] Entering service in 1904, the quick-firing 18-pounder was primarily designed as an infantry support weapon. Although available in reasonable numbers and very reliable, its weaknesses echoed those of the French 75mm. It was issued mainly with shrapnel, which although lethal against infantry in the open, was decidedly limited in trench warfare. Wire-cutting with shrapnel fired from 18-pounders had first been tried at Neuve Chapelle and would again be employed at Loos. Although recent work has shown that shrapnel shells were preferred during wire-cutting operations, the results of firing were often not terribly clear.[35] And even when equipped with high explosive, which was only available in limited quantities by the time Loos was fought, the shell was too small to demolish sections of enemy trenches, especially the hardened concrete dugouts.[36] The 18-pounder's low angle of fire also meant that its range was limited, with shells rarely landing on top of German trenches, where they would do the most damage.[37] Howitzers, on the other hand, were ideal for positional warfare. Because of their steeper angle of fire they could both engage targets at much greater distances than field artillery, and land on top of trenches. But howitzers and their high-explosive ammunition were in short supply, and only 96 of the vital 6" and 4.5" howitzers were available for the main attacks. Various other types of heavy artillery were used at Loos – including 15", 9.2", 8" and 6" howitzers – but they were small in number (totalling 29 guns), with scarce ammunition and added little to the overall weight of the bombardment.[38]

But why was there so much difference between what British guns could *realistically* achieve and what Haig *wanted* them to achieve? Although it is clear that at least some of these deficiencies were recognised at First Army HQ – indeed Haig had been grumbling about ammunition shortages all year – too little account was taken of the poor performance of British artillery. Although it would be inaccurate to say that Haig did not understand artillery, he was not a terribly great or original thinker about gunnery, and his views remained traditional. Haig believed artillery was primarily there to assist the advance of the infantry and lower the enemy's morale.[39] This was made clear by *Field Artillery Training 1914*:

> Artillery cannot ensure decisive success in battle by its own destructive action. It is the advance of the infantry that alone is capable of producing this result... To help the infantry to maintain its mobility and offensive power by all means at its disposal should be the underlying principle of all artillery tactics.[40]

Haig, therefore, seems to have shoehorned his artillery into his wider ideas on the structured battle, in particular the importance of engaging the enemy on a wide front, wearing down his forces, and then delivering the decisive blow. First Army's artillery was to do a similar thing. They were to be spread over a wide area, wear down the enemy defences and morale, before the final blow was struck by the release of the gas and the infantry assault.

The wide front of attack was of particular importance. There was simply no way, as was recognised, that First Army's artillery could adequately cover the required length of front. Whereas the bombardment frontage had been a mere 1,450 yards at Neuve Chapelle, this had swelled to 11,200 yards for Loos (see Table 2). It does seem that Brigadier-General Birch's later comment, referring to the Somme bombardment of the following year, that 'poor Haig – as he was always inclined to do – spread his guns',[41] was not too unfair, because the same process of 'spreading' artillery occurred at Loos. Why was this so? Much of the answer seems to lie in the particular nature of the plan First Army adopted for the Battle of Loos, particularly the great reliance placed upon the use of poison gas. Because it was believed, especially by Haig, that gas would prove utterly devastating, the artillery bombardment lost much of its *raison d'être*, and its importance was lowered as a result.

Throughout September artillery was assembled for the battle. South of the canal the ground was flat and under direct enemy observation so that the heavy batteries could only be assembled between 3,000 and 4,000 yards from the front line. The field batteries were a little further ahead.[42] The guns were hidden as far as possible in the clusters of mining buildings or any folds in the ground. In some sectors of the battlefield this was not too difficult. For example, North and South Maroc, Vermelles and Grenay all offered 'good cover' and excellent observation posts.[43] The batteries then had to construct gun-pits and dugouts, arrange their communications and register shots on the German lines. The battlefield was divided into an inner and an outer zone. Field artillery firing shrapnel would concentrate on wire-cutting within the inner zone, while heavier calibres fired high-explosive shells at various selected targets in the outer zone.

How were the guns organised? As the British Official History proclaimed, Loos was a 'landmark' in the history of artillery development.[44] The most notable change was the creation of a formal corps artillery headquarters in early September. The idea of centralising all divisional artillery under corps control seems to have been an idea that had been milling around the BEF for some time, but as has been pointed out, the critical shortage in ammunition all year meant that there had been 'little need' for such a change until September.[45] Whereas BGRAs had previously only been advisers without any authority to actually command batteries, they were now able to direct all the field and heavy artillery (except those allotted to counter-battery fire) within each corps. This allowed a much greater level of co-operation to be achieved between batteries, and while there still remained some persistent problems that would not be ironed out until the thorough reorganisation of British artillery in the winter of 1916–17,[46] it was a considerable improvement.

The centralisation of corps artillery may have helped to standardise gunnery practices and clear up some lingering anomalies *within* corps, but organisation *between* corps could still differ widely. Whereas Brigadier-General Birch organised the guns of I Corps into a number of clearly defined sections, the system devised by Brigadier-General C.E.D. Budworth (formally appointed BGRA IV Corps, 10 October 1915) proved 'a most untidy grouping, with an excessive use of groups of sub-groups'.[47] I Corps' artillery was split into five parts. The artillery of each division contained three brigades of 18-pounders and another of 4.5" howitzers, while No. 5 Group HAR and a Siege Group, containing two brigades of RGA, completed the line-up. The organisation within IV Corps was much less straightforward, with 1st Divisional artillery being split into different northern and a southern sub-sections and 47th Division organised into the MacNaughten Group, the Massey Group, as well as a Divisional Reserve Group.

The organisation of artillery was not the only difference between I and IV Corps. Considerable differences existed in their respective 'fireplans'. Birch wrote a simple step-by-step, unified plan, but Budworth's 'fireplan', if it can be called such, was simply to break the bombardment down into five different tasks (ranging from wire-cutting to 'special tasks') and ask his group commanders to 'discuss' these with their divisional commanders. Why were Budworth's plans so different from Birch's, and why was he so reluctant to impose his will on his fellow artillery commanders? The answer seems to lie in the confusing situation that existed within IV Corps HQ during the late summer of 1915. According to Sanders Marble, Rawlinson lacked confidence in his BGRA (Brigadier-General A.H. Hussey) and had asked for his replacement on the same day that a formal corps artillery headquarters was created.[48] Approving of the new arrangements, but without the will to get rid of Hussey – perhaps the memories of the Davies affair were still sharp[49] – Rawlinson played a strange game of delegating all responsibility to Budworth (then BGRA 1st Division), with the formation of the various groups and sub-groups, and avoiding giving Hussey anything to do. Budworth could therefore never actually impose his will on his fellow artillery commanders even if he had been possessed of such a desire.

The only artillery remaining within First Army were those heavy batteries allocated to counter-battery work, which had been retained under First Army control. This task was given to the HAR groups, but was hampered by a confusing chain of command.[50] While No. 5 Group HAR (Brigadier-General T.A. Tancred) was assigned to I Corps, and No. 1 Group HAR (Brigadier-General G. McK. Franks) supported IV Corps, they were not under corps control and were placed directly under Major-General H.F. Mercer at First Army headquarters. To compound matters further Franks was placed in charge of all counter-batteries within First Army.[51] This system proved to be unhelpful and reflected the low priority given to counter-battery fire. Despite Sir John French's promise that 'particular attention' would be paid to this task, relatively few guns were involved.[52] Whereas at Neuve Chapelle just over 10 per cent of the total number of guns were assigned to counter-battery work, at Loos this had fallen to just under 7 percent. On the front of First Army, out of a total of over 900 guns, only sixty-one (split between 60-pounders and 4.7" guns) were set-aside for counter-battery work, with a mere thirty-four guns being available for I and IV Corps.[53] Whether this was the result of a lack of communication between Sir John and Haig is not known, although considering how stretched the artillery was in the crucial matters of wire-cutting and trench-bombardment, it is perhaps not surprising that it was relegated to a lower importance.

During the bombardment south of the canal a number of feint attacks were conducted. These were intended to confuse the enemy as to the time and date of the real attack, and compel him to man his front line and suffer casualties from doing so.[54] The feints all followed the same format.

On the points of enemy trench that had been selected for demonstration, the divisional artillery would open an intense fire for five minutes. After this the guns would lift onto the second line and shell it for a further five minutes. During this lift the infantry in the front trenches would show their bayonets over the parapet, manhandle dummies into position and cheer loudly.[55] It was hoped that this would force the enemy garrison to man their trenches in order to repel the suspected attack. Infantry on adjacent fronts would then open an intense burst of rifle and machine gun fire towards the enemy positions. Finally, the enemy front line would be deluged with fierce shrapnel fire for three minutes. These feints were of some importance, but it was essential that the German defences were badly damaged before they would be practicable to infantry. But was this achieved?

Measuring the success of the preliminary bombardment is not easy. Although the available accounts, war diaries and eyewitness reports are all useful, they can be problematic. It is often impossible to give more than a rough idea of where the reporter was situated and which part of the front he was observing. Even if the location is accurately known, the observer could often only see only a small portion of the front being shelled, thus increasing the chance of misleading or inaccurate reports. It can also be assumed that the gunners of I and IV Corps only had a very rudimentary idea of what was going on at the time. The frontage of the main attack must also be considered. It totalled nearly six miles in length and was not uniform in terrain. While some parts of the German line were clearly visible from the British trenches, others were difficult to observe or covered with long grass. Attempts by the defenders to repair their trenches and wire entanglements further add to the difficulties of accurately assessing what progress was being made. Differences such as these could have a great impact on the local effect of the bombardment. These considerations make it extremely difficult to give a precise overview of the progress of the preliminary bombardment, but they do allow, however, general trends to be perceived.

The first day of the bombardment seems to have opened promisingly, even on those sectors where observation was difficult. 2nd Division occupied what was possibly the worst sector within First Army. As its front was longer than any other division involved in the main assault, there was much more wire to cut. One senior officer later complained of 'an enormous front – few, too few, batteries to cover us'.[56] Its guns had to bombard Mine Trench, Brickstack Trench, the German Ducks Bill, Embankment Redoubt and the Tortoise Redoubt. One battery in 2nd Division reported that the 'wire is not very thick and wouldn't stop anyone'.[57] Two lanes were cut in the wire around the Brickstacks and 'a good deal of damage' was done to some entanglements north of the La Bassée road. Similar success was achieved by the guns of 9th (Scottish) Division.[58] Deployed on the right of 2nd Division, with its front dominated by the imposing shape of the Hohenzollern Redoubt, 9th Division had much to achieve. Its artillery was to cut 'a great mass of black wire' on the west face of the redoubt,[59] in front of the connecting trench (Little Willie), Fosse Trench and around Mad Point. Unfortunately, the wire around this latter stronghold (opposite 28 Brigade) was largely invisible from the British lines.[60]

The ground conditions in the central sector of the British line also presented considerable difficulties. Between the Vermelles–Hulluch and Loos Roads the ground was open and devoid of cover. Observation was hampered by wide stretches of long grass.[61] On the left of this sector was 7th Division. Its artillery was split into two groups and one given to support 9th Division. This latter group was to enfilade the north and south sides of the Hohenzollern Redoubt, which although not part of 7th Division's objectives, could only be observed from certain areas outside 9th Division's zone of operations. Accordingly, two batteries were sandwiched in between 9th and 2nd Division and were to cut the wire in front of Madagascar Trench, Railway Trench and the wire around the formidable Railway Redoubt. The remaining artillery of 7th Division was to bombard Breslau Trench, Quarry Trench, the south-eastern edge of Big Willie and various communication trenches that led to the German second position around Cité St Elie. It seems that the results of the first day's shelling in this area were hardly spectacular. Although some observers recorded that the wire was 'cut to some extent',[62] others were much less sanguine. According to XXXV Brigade RFA (7th Division) wire-cutting was 'indifferent', and 'very little headway seems to have been made'.[63]

Similar unfavourable ground conditions were experienced on the front of 1st Division. Because the ground was so open, the field artillery had to be placed further to the rear. While favourable range was between 1,800 and 2,500 yards, 1st Division's artillery had to shoot at over 3,000 yards. There were, however, more serious deficiencies. Because it had not originally been intended that 1st Division would take part in the main attack, much of its artillery had been distributed to the other divisions in IV Corps. When 1st Division was belatedly ordered to take part, only three batteries of its own artillery were restored to it. As a result, the division had to make do with two batteries from 15th Division, one 6" howitzer battery and some inexperienced batteries from 24th Division.[64] With these meagre resources 1st Division's guns had to clear the wire from the main German frontline as well as two important communication trenches (known as Alley 3 and 4) leading to Hulluch.

The final two British divisions, deployed on the right of the line, seem to have had a good day on 21 September and benefited from the elevated ground conditions they occupied. The main attack had been entrusted to 15th (Scottish) Division, but before any advance could be made, two heavily wired strongpoints, known as the Loos Road and Lens Road Redoubts, would have to be demolished. Although much of the German wire was invisible on the left of 15th Division, visibility did improve further south,[65] and 'satisfactory' progress was achieved against the Loos Road Redoubt.[66] With a view comparable 'to that obtainable over the stage of a theatre from a corner seat in the dress circle', 47th Division formed the hinge of the entire attack.[67] With 'distinctly favourable' ground, its guns were able to enfilade parts of the German line that faced away from the British trenches, giving a distinct advantage not possessed by those divisions situated further north. Its field artillery had to cut the front line wire from the Lens Road Redoubt to the mining buildings of Puits 16 and its howitzers were to shell selected communication trenches. The imposing Double Crassier, a large slagheap bristling with machine guns situated in the centre of the German line, was also to be shelled with howitzers. The first day was reasonably successful. Major Hon. R.G.A. Hamilton (CVIII Brigade RFA, 24th Division) recorded the 'almost unlimited allowance of ammunition' and the 'tremendous rate' of fire, which 'must be fairly drowning him [the Germans] in shells'.[68] Wire-cutting was carried out with 'very satisfactory' results.[69] The Macnaghten Group (firing at the wire in the second German line) also believed that its shooting was accurate.[70]

It was, however, a day of mixed fortunes. While the weather was clear and fine, an easterly wind interfered with the observation of falling shot and blew clouds of dust towards the British trenches. Nearly all the war diaries and operation reports written about 21 September (and the following three days) mention the difficult weather conditions the artillery had to cope with.[71] 2nd Division complained that 'no bombardment results [were] visible from our observation stations' and 7th Division admitted that its heavy guns were 'firing long and the damage to parapets was not extensive'.[72] But these were not the only problems. The repeated firing of the 9.2" howitzers proved too much for their platforms and a number of them broke. The guns then had to be moved.[73] Major-General Mercer (MGRA First Army) also highlighted a number of gunnery accidents, some involving barrels that had become clogged and shells that had not been rammed home.[74] The infantry were not the only ones who were inexperienced.

The weather conditions stubbornly refused to improve throughout the second day and the familiar complaints about poor observation were repeated.[75] But progress was being made. One observer recorded how the German trenches were 'simply one line of busting shells and smoke'.[76] On the front of 2nd Division, a gap of 15–20 yards was reported on the Tortoise Redoubt, the Towpath was cleared and much wire was destroyed in front of the Brickstacks.[77] Indeed, XXXIV Brigade RFA (2nd Division) believed that by the end of the day the wire 'had nearly all been cut sufficiently to form no obstacle to an infantry assault'.[78] Further south, the wire around Mad Point was reported to be completely destroyed and about two thirds of the wire protecting Fosse Trench was 'gone'. The west face of the Hohenzollern Redoubt was cleared and very little wire remained around Little Willie.[79] North of the Hohenzollern Redoubt, the 104th and 12th Batteries from 7th Division had an encouraging day cutting the wire in front of Madagascar and Railway Trenches, but the Railway Redoubt, however, remained undisturbed. It was still protected by thick coils of 'unusually strong' wire.[80] On the more favourable terrain west of Loos, 47th Division was doing well. German wire was significantly thinner than it had been and it was noted how effective 6" howitzer fire on machine gun emplacements was.[81] The Fraser Group, bombarding the German line south of the Double Crassier, reported that the trenches covering it were 'thoroughly smashed'.[82]

On the more unfavourable fronts the bombardment was still struggling to make enough progress. After spending over four hours in the trenches watching the bombardment with Brigadier-General Trefusis, Colonel Tudor remarked that the wire 'seems to require a lot of cutting yet'.[83] Trefusis was of the same opinion and spoke to his divisional commander (Major-General Sir T. Capper) about the possibility of getting more guns for the following day.[84] Trefusis's request seems to have had some effect as both 104th and 12th Batteries, which had been bombarding Madagascar Trench in 9th Division's sector, were moved back to support 7th Division that day.[85] Further south, on the front of 1st Division, it was difficult to improve the rather meagre results of the previous day. Wire-cutting was 'slow', observation 'difficult' and the whole day extremely demoralising.[86] Problems were not confined to Grenay Ridge. Despite cutting large gaps in the German wire, 15th Division's artillery was experiencing trouble knocking out a number of *chevaux de frise* placed in front of the German trenches by its occupants. These were large and difficult to destroy.[87]

Meanwhile what had the RFC being doing? Attached to each corps artillery headquarters was a squadron of aircraft, which would spot targets for the artillery and help correct the fall of shot. While No. 3 Squadron was attached to I Corps, No. 2 Squadron was assigned to work with IV Corps, as well as No. 1 Group HAR for counter-battery work. The task of spotting targets and registering artillery fire was also given to No. 6 Kite Balloon section, attached to First Army. The balloon was deployed near Béthune, and as well as helping to co-ordinate the fire of I and IV Corps, it was to make observations on the strength and direction of the wind and transmit the results to General Haig's headquarters.[88] During the first two days of the bombardment the aircraft of First Wing had been busy spotting for the artillery, and had been fortunate because of the relatively clear weather.[89] Their operations seem to have been reasonably successful. H.A. Jones recorded that 'the squadrons were able to work to their full artillery programmes: our batteries were registered on the first and second line trenches, gun positions and dugouts'.[90] 21 September was 'a good flying day', with No. 2 Squadron engaging (and apparently silencing) four enemy batteries, while No. 3 Squadron did 'much successful trench work', including the taking of numerous photographs of the battlefield.[91] So pleased was the Siege Group with the progress that No. 3 Squadron was congratulated on the 'excellent work' done. Air operations during the following two days 'proceeded satisfactorily' and on 23 September it was reported that the wire-cutting by heavy batteries attached to No. 2 Squadron was 'apparently successful'.[92]

Although the weather on 23 September was not bad enough to prevent artillery observation flights from taking off, the wind changed to the west and it started raining. Light and observation remained poor all day.[93] The volume of artillery fire did, however, increase substantially. Major Hamilton recorded the 'simply appalling' sound and according to Captain J.C. Dunn (2/Royal Welsh Fusiliers, 19 Brigade), the day's gunfire was the 'heaviest there has been'.[94] Enemy artillery, which had been noticeable by its absence, was also showing increasing signs of activity. Haig noted in his diary that First Army had received 170 casualties that day as compared with the usual number of 90 or 100 within the same twenty-four hour period.[95] Although XXII Brigade RFA (7th Division) continued to make progress in its wire-cutting, its war diary records the 'persistent shelling' of its OP.[96] 2nd Division's artillery managed to clear another path south of the Embankment Redoubt.[97] Progress was, however, patchy. An officer in Robert Graves's platoon complained about the resilience of the German wire, remarking that 'our guns don't seem to be cutting it'.[98] Indeed, according to XXXIV Brigade RFA, 'much new wire had been thrown out during the night in front of the parapet, in loose coils'.[99] XXXVI Brigade RFA also complained about the 'very poor attempts' by the infantry to prevent the enemy rewiring its trenches.[100] But it was not all bad news. In front of the Hohenzollern Redoubt, 9th Division continued to make definite progress. Reports indicated that the west face was clear and 250 yards of wire had been destroyed along Madagascar Trench.[101] By the end of the day LII Brigade RFA (9th Division) recorded that 'practically the entire wire to be cut was cut'.[102]

During the day a number of patrols reported that on 1st Division's front 'favourable' and 'satisfactory' progress had been made with wire-cutting.[103]

The regimental history of *157 Infantry Regiment* gloomily noted how its troops were 'under heavy artillery fire'.[104] On the front of 15th Division the enemy wire was by now 'severely damaged', and a number of *chevaux de frise* were destroyed by 6" howitzer fire.[105] By now the enemy wire was 'sufficiently cut' to give an attack a reasonable chance of success, although on the left of 46 Brigade, hostile fire prevented a patrol from examining the German wire. In the south of the battlefield on the front of 47th Division, the important task of wire-cutting continued in earnest. Two large gaps had been blown in the German front line south of the Double Crassier, but north of it, things were not as satisfactory.[106] Reports during the night found that, contrary to earlier patrols, the wire around the Double Crassier remained impassable.[107]

The second part of the aerial operation began on 23 September with a number of long-range bombing flights. The busy railway lines between Lille–Douai–Valenciennes were the targets for both Second and Third Wings.[108] Their efforts were greeted with some success and the German Official History noted that 'considerable military damage' was done.[109] Twenty-three planes of Third Wing bombed the line Douai–Valenciennes, destroying one goods train near Somain. The track near Wallers and the engine sheds north of Valenciennes were also hit. Eight planes from Second Wing and three from No. 12 Squadron (attached to GHQ) attacked the Lille–Valenciennes line, but the only damage recorded was to a signal box between Orchies and Templeuve. The attacks on the communications network did receive a boost, however, when British artillery fire destroyed the railway station at Pont à Vendin.

Rain greeted the final day of the bombardment. First Wing was able to continue spotting for the artillery, and although visibility improved during the afternoon, the low cloud and mist grounded aerial bombing flights. Despite the bad weather 'a great deal of work was done' with 'numerous hostile batteries' located and fire directed upon them.[110] But more generally, 24 September seems to have been a mixed day. Some observers reported significant damage to parts of the German wire and trenches, while others remained much more guarded. 2nd Division noted that lots of wire had been cleared from the first German trench, but what condition the second line was in was very much anyone's guess.[111] There were also several worrying references to fresh wire that had been thrown out by the defenders.[112] On 9th Division's frontage, the results were again mixed. While the wire and parapets of Madagascar Trench were heavily damaged, contrary to previous information, some wire on the southern face of Mad Point was still intact. While the barbed wire left in front of Little Willie and the west face of the Hohenzollern Redoubt was deemed 'satisfactory', observers were unable to give a definite report on the state of Fosse Trench.

The wire at the north-western end of Big Willie also remained uncut.[113] L Brigade RFA (9th Division), bombarding the cottages in Madagascar, recorded that 400 high-explosive shells were fired at this, with a good 'visible effect'. It was, however, 'impossible to tell what real damage had been done'.[114]

The results of the bombardment further south were equally divided. Brigadier-General Trefusis noted that although the German wire in front of his brigade was 'nearly all cut', there remained 'some about halfway between our line and the Germans' that needed to be cleared away.[115] On the front of both 1st and 15th Divisions, the results of the day seem to have been satisfactory.[116] IV Corps' 'General Progress Report' on the evening of 24 September echoed this.

> Reports from artillery and infantry observers show that practicable passages have been made at intervals all along the Fourth Corps Front. In some places the wire is reported [to be] very thick and though considerably thinned is not yet practicable to troops. In a few places in the front line and in many in the second line the wire is difficult or impossible to observe and the result is doubtful.[117]

By the evening of 24 September, after four trying and frustrating days, I Corps had almost to admit failure. Its war diary simply stated that 'the wire was reported *generally* to be *satisfactorily* cut'.[118] The final job was to cut a path through the British wire that lay in front of their trenches. This was cut diagonally on the evening of 24/25 September.

How effective was the preliminary bombardment? While there had been some success, particularly where the German lines lay under good observation, the cumulative effects of four days of shelling had clearly fallen short of the objectives listed in 'General Principles for the Attack'. The German wire had proven extremely resilient to all but the most accurate shelling and still lay in large quantities along the front. Trench and strongpoint destruction had been equally haphazard and a considerable number of the deadly machine gun posts that dotted the German line were still intact and able to offer considerable resistance to any infantry attack. As befitted their limited resources, both the shelling of the second line and the attempts at counter-battery fire seem to have completely failed in gaining their objectives.

Cutting the barbed wire was perhaps the pressing and persistent problem British artillery faced in this period. But the references to uncut (or insufficiently cleared) wire that greeted the attacking battalions on 25 September are numerous and speak volumes about the failure of the preliminary bombardment. This was particularly noticeable on the front of

2nd Division. All three brigade war diaries, as well as various other sources, mention uncut wire and unsuppressed enemy machine gun posts when they attacked on 25 September.[119] In what was a disturbing comment on the failure of the bombardment in his sector, Lieutenant-Colonel H.C. Potter (CO 1/King's, 6 Brigade) mistakenly thought 'that no wire cutting had been done on the battalion front as reliance was placed entirely on the expected effect of our gas'.[120] 1st Division was equally unsuccessful, testament to a lack of guns and an unfavourable sector of the front. Both attacking battalions of 1 Brigade complained about uncut wire,[121] while 2 Brigade completely failed to clear away the enemy obstacles in its way. Faced with, as one officer put it, 'one of the strongest and widest belts I saw during the war',[122] repeated attacks could not to reach the enemy line, which had been completely undamaged by the bombardment.[123]

Poor staff work did not help. In particular, there does not seem to have been an effective transmission of information between those battalions in the front line and their supporting artillery batteries. For example, numerous patrols had warned Lieutenant-Colonel F.G.M. Rowley (CO 1/Middlesex, 19 Brigade) that the enemy wire in his sector was still intact and in places up to twenty-five yards thick, but nothing was done about it – with deadly consequences when the infantry tried to bypass it on 25 September.[124] Likewise, Lieutenant-Colonel A.C. Northey (CO 9/Scottish Rifles, 28 Brigade) complained that the machine gun posts at Strongpoint and Railway Redoubt had been practically undamaged by the bombardment. Although repeated efforts were made to communicate this to higher command, he did not 'observe any alteration in the treatment of these points'.[125] This may well have reflected either a lack of ammunition or a belief that the gas would deal with these before the infantry went 'over the top', but Northey was not told why this was so.

For the bombardment to be effective, the infantry in the front line had to check the state of the German lines regularly and make sure that any repair work was kept to a minimum. But on some sectors this not carried out. Neither 28 nor 2 Brigade sent out patrols to check the state of the German wire before the attacks went in. This was an omission of crucial importance because of the difficulty of observing the state of the German wire in these sectors. If patrols had been sent out, it would have been obvious that a much heavier bombardment was needed.[126] It seems that in 28 Brigade, 'the desire to save the men from being exposed to our own artillery fire' contributed to the decision not to patrol,[127] but why 2 Brigade failed to do so is unclear. It is even more puzzling when considering that during August 1st Division had been regularly sending patrols to the German wire, although a report had been filed on 3 August that 'Lone Tree cannot be visited by day'.[128] There are perhaps similarities to what John Terraine observed about the preliminary bombardment for the Battle of the Somme the following year. It seems that the British tendency to 'look on the bright side' also occurred at Loos.[129] Captain J.C. Dunn even recorded how 'I did not like to hurt the gunner's feelings by saying how little sign there was of cut wire'.[130] Amazingly, this was not an isolated phenomenon.

Certain sectors of the front clearly had better artillery preparation than others, but results could still be mixed. The Hohenzollern Redoubt is a particular example. Because of its tactical importance it was heavily bombarded not only by 9th Division's field artillery and two extra batteries from 7th Division, but also by much of the heavy artillery within I Corps. But it seems that only one side of the redoubt was properly shelled. The war diary of 26 Brigade, the unit that overran it on 25 September, noted that 'Nearly all the German wire in the greater part of our front was efficiently cut by our artillery'.[131] On the contrary, 28 Brigade, attacking from the northern side, was faced with 'practically intact' enemy wire, which completely stopped its attack.[132] 7th Division experienced a similar 'mixed' effect. While 22 Brigade reported that enemy wire was 'very thick and had not been cut by our guns',[133] the wire-cutting in 20 Brigade seems to have been 'most effective', with good gaps made.[134]

The pre-battle problems with IV Corps' artillery organisation do not seem to have been too debilitating. Indeed, the preliminary bombardment was most successful on the right of the British line. Both 15th and 47th Divisions managed to clear large amounts of enemy wire from the German front line. While both 44 and 46 Brigades reported that the German wire was 'well cut',[135] a report on 4 October confirmed that wire-cutting had been 'excellent' within 47th Division.[136] Patrick MacGill, a stretcher-bearer with 141 Brigade, noted that the wire had been 'cut to little pieces by our bombardment'.[137]

> The German trench [MacGill added] had suffered severely from our fire; parapets were blown in, and at places the trench was full to the level of the ground with sandbags and earth. Wreckage was strewn all over the place...[138]

15th Division had been equally successful. Its divisional history recorded how on 'reaching the enemy trenches, the effect of the accurate and intense artillery fire was apparent. The front line was badly damaged – in fact, in some places was non-existent – and the communication trenches leading to Loos were filled with dead and dying men.'[139] When John Buchan visited the battlefield five days after the fighting had begun, he was amazed at what he found. The Loos Road Redoubt was now, he explained, 'a monument to the power of our artillery. It is all ploughed up and mangled like a sand castle which a child has demolished in a fit of temper.'[140] But these successes remained the exception rather than the rule. As regards the long-range firing at the German second line, this seems to have been ineffective. According to 1st Division, the machine gun posts and dugouts in the second line were 'practically untouched' and when 21 Brigade reached Cité Trench it found its wire obstacles were 'undamaged'.[141] This seems to have not been unusual. When the doomed attack of 24th Division reached the German second line between Hulluch and Cité St Auguste on 26 September, numerous personal accounts and war diaries testify that its covering wire entanglements were completely undamaged and, as one observer put it, 'absolutely intact'.[142]

How effective were the air operations conducted by the RFC? Its artillery spotting seems to have been generally successful, but considering the grave weaknesses inherent in the bombardment plan and within British artillery during this period, its effect was understandably limited. Teething problems with air–artillery co-operation were also in evidence. According to one observer:

> The greatest difficulty was experienced at first in getting the gunners to conform to the best methods of ranging for air observations. They were a strongly individualistic corps and each battery commander had his own theories about working his guns and many at first intensely resented being interfered with.[143]

There were also organisational difficulties. A memorandum issued on 25 October admitted that in future operations it would be necessary to clearly designate zones for each squadron to work in, 'to prevent confusion caused by two machines trying to range on [the] same target'.[144] The effect of the aerial bombing campaign was also limited. Considering the fledgling nature of the air war, the damage that aerial bombing did to German communication networks and infrastructure was necessarily light, but it was considerably greater than had previously been achieved. Bombing flights went up to thirty-six miles behind the German lines and dropped over five and half tons of munitions. The main rail lines were apparently damaged in 16 different places, with 5 or 6 trains 'practically wrecked'.[145] However, an RFC report concluded that although 'considerable interference' had been caused to the German rail network, 'no great damage' had been done.[146]

The counter-battery operation was similarly ineffective. As Peter Chasseaud has explained, counter-battery results 'before and during the battle were disappointing, and showed up the limitations of First Army artillery intelligence work, the artillery command structure and the gunnery itself'.[147] German artillery was undoubtedly quiet during the bombardment (*Sixth Army* only contained 325 field and 150 heavy guns), and this seems to have been a reflection of both poor German and British counter-battery work, as well as an understandable desire to avoid getting into an 'artillery duel'.[148] Brigadier-General A.A. Montgomery believed that it 'does not appear that the injury inflicted on the German artillery and personnel or material was very great'. He did, however, think that British batteries maintained 'an undoubted superiority over the German artillery during the operations'.[149] But this was largely irrelevant. Lieutenant-Colonel W.R. Warren, serving as a brigade artillery commander in Indian Corps, noted the unrealistic optimism that many air observers and battery commanders had regarding artillery shoots.[150] He also voiced a familiar complaint that as German batteries tended to fall silent as soon as any shells neared their position, this was often taken 'as evidence of destruction', when in fact they were unscathed.[151] Warren subsequently added that 'all known batteries' on his front came to life again on 25 September.

What of those 'on the other side of the hill'? It is not known exactly how many German soldiers became casualties during the bombardment, but it was probably not a great number. An estimate by IV Corps reckoned that *117th Division* suffered only 120 casualties prior to 25 September.[152] Because German defenders usually evacuated all but the most essential personnel from the first line when a bombardment was going on, they held their lines with only small numbers of men. The majority of its soldiers would therefore have been sheltering from the shells in deep dugouts or secure in the support lines. The regimental history of *157 Infantry Regiment* confirmed that even after three days of bombardment the losses in the front-line battalion were 'relatively small' and the morale of the troops was 'very good'.[153] So poor was the British bombardment that when Crown Prince Rupprecht (GOC *Sixth Army*) met his corps commanders on 22 September, he was unimpressed with British artillery preparation and refused to believe that an attack was imminent.[154]

It is clear therefore that British artillery fire was simply not *heavy* enough. The Brigade Major of 26 Brigade complained that the bombardment 'struck us all as quite childish and futile… no volume at all'.[155] This was a common concern and was echoed in *Goodbye To All That* (1929).[156] As Lieutenant Colonel Warren noted:

> The whole programme appeared too deliberate, scattered and long drawn out for the amount of ammunition available. In many cases insufficient rounds were allotted to heavy guns for destructive tasks, particularly for counter-battery shoots.[157]

This is confirmed by statistics taken from the papers of AA & QMG First Army. Table 3 shows that around five times more shells were fired during the preliminary bombardment at Loos that at Festubert, four months before.

Table 3. The number of rounds fired during the preliminary bombardments of the Battles of Festubert (13–15 May 1915) and Loos (21–24 September 1915)[158]

	Festubert	Loos
Field guns	33,802	209,745
Field howitzers	5,102	32,554
Counter-battery	1,736	7,221
Heavy howitzers	3,307	16,958
TOTAL	43,947	266,478

But this is misleading. Table 4 puts these figures into sharp perspective. It shows the numbers of rounds fired *per yard of front* during the preliminary bombardments of both battles. Although at Loos there was a slightly higher amount of field gun, field howitzer and heavy howitzer shells fired, the differences between the two bombardments is hardly significant. The preliminary bombardment at Festubert had been a day shorter than at Loos and fired fewer shells, but the greater amount of front to be bombarded at Loos more than cancelled these factors out.

Table 4. The number of rounds expended per yard of front during the preliminary bombardments of the Battles of Festubert (13–15 May 1915) and Loos (21–24 September 1915)[159]

	Festubert	Loos
Field guns	11.2	13.1
Field howitzers	1.7	2
Counter-battery	0.57	.05
Heavy howitzers	1.1	1.8

From these statistics it is reasonable to assume that the results of the following infantry attacks would be similar. Festubert had been a success, with gains made and consolidated, but the attacks had been made at 11.30p.m. and 3.15a.m., at night and at dawn respectively. At Loos the British would be 'jumping the bags' hours later. This was the result of Haig's 'spreading' of his guns. Enemy artillery strength may well have been spread over a wide area, but by doing so, Haig effectively neutralised his own artillery.

5

THE FIRST DAY (I): 25 SEPTEMBER 1915

At 6.30a.m. on 25 September 1915, following a forty-minute discharge of chlorine gas and smoke, the first waves of six British divisions clambered out of their trenches and began making their way across no-man's-land. Simultaneously, British artillery, which had been bombarding the German front line with shrapnel, lifted to engage targets further into the enemy position. This marked the beginning of First Army's main 'all-out' infantry assault south of the La Bassée canal. Fighting was heavy and continuous all morning. Although stubborn German resistance slowed and even stopped the advance in places, some striking success was achieved on the southern sector of the battlefield. 47th (London) Division took all its objectives with relatively light casualties, and in what was the most spectacular advance of the day, 15th (Scottish) Division stormed two German defensive lines, captured the village of Loos and took Hill 70. On the northern sector of the battlefield, however, a different battle was unfolding. 2nd Division's attacks were repulsed, and while 9th (Scottish) Division managed to take the Hohenzollern Redoubt, it could not get much further, becoming bogged down around Fosse 8. In the central section of the British line, 7th and 1st Divisions had managed, after initial setbacks and heavy resistance, to capture their first objectives, but were unable to reach the second German position.

From a close study of the available eyewitness accounts, war diaries and after-action reports it is possible to reconstruct the events of the morning of 25 September and provide a full account of what occurred once the main assault began. It will be seen that even before the infantry had left their trenches, the ambitious plans drafted in the run-up to the battle began to unravel. The gas attack was perhaps the most obvious example, the inflexibility of General Sir Douglas Haig's plan demanding that it be released even in the face of an unfavourable wind. The discharge of smoke undoubtedly helped, but the gas was largely a failure. The subsequent infantry assault also experienced mixed success. The bravery and determination of the British infantry was as noticeable as ever, but against uncut wire, which still existed in many places, and facing heavy German fire, the attacking battalions sustained severe casualties. Owing to the looseness of the 'all-out' tactical plan, combined with relatively poorly trained infantry and heavy officer casualties, many battalions had virtually ceased to exist as coherent formations once the German front line had been crossed. The actions of the German Army on 25 September will only be alluded to, but it should be understood that they were heavily outnumbered. Facing the eighteen British brigades were only five German regiments belonging to *117th* and *14th Divisions* of General Sixt von Armin's *IV Corps*.[1]

Before looking at what happened on the British front south of the La Bassée canal after the infantry went 'over the top', it will be useful to review the discharge of chlorine gas and smoke, which was perhaps the most memorable feature of the fighting on 25 September. How effective had the gas and smoke been in killing or incapacitating the German defenders or weakening their morale? Although this has been obscured by both the general confusion of the battlefield and a number of post-war writings, it seems to have been mixed, being particularly unhelpful on the left of the British line, but becoming more useful over the more favourable terrain on the right.[2] However, some aspects of the gas attack have been misunderstood and require further explanation, particularly the series of protests that were mounted by several officers in the face of unfavourable weather conditions and the confused series of events at the Chateau of Hinges during the early morning as Haig and his staff agonised over whether to go ahead and release the gas.

The most glowing account of the gas operation at Loos was written – as perhaps was to be expected – by Lieutenant-Colonel C.H. Foulkes (CO Special Brigade). With selective quotes culled from various intelligence sources, German newspapers and prisoner reports, Foulkes concluded that 'our gas attack met with marked success, and produced a demoralising effect in some of the opposing units, of which ample evidence was forthcoming in the captured trenches'.[3] Foulkes's account may be deeply biased – he was keen to show how effective gas was – but it is not entirely inaccurate. It is clear that where the ground and weather conditions were not too unfavourable, the gas could assist the infantry advance. This was especially the case on the southern sector of the battlefield occupied by 15th and 47th Divisions. A report by 46 Brigade confirmed that once the gas was released, rifle and machine gun fire immediately erupted from the German trenches, but 'it was distinctly noticeable how the hostile rifle fire gradually decreased in volume as the fumes reached the German line'.[4] Because 47th Division occupied higher ground than the Germans, the gas rolled down the valley and travelled 'fairly well' towards the enemy positions.[5] Again, enemy rifle and machine gun fire was immediately opened, but it was inaccurate and after all the cylinders had been emptied and the discharge completed, there was a noticeable slackening off in enemy fire.[6]

The smoke had also proved successful. Although it can be difficult to assess the effectiveness of the smoke candles (and bombs in some cases) because the discharge was mixed with gas, it is clear that they were of considerable use. Aided by a line of smoke candles and a barrage of phosphorous smoke balls, 7/Seaforth Highlanders stormed the southern face of the Hohenzollern Redoubt without prohibitive casualties.[7] 15th Division also benefited from smoke. According to Captain K.G. Buchanan (2/Royal Scots), 44 Brigade had apparently 'suffered no casualties from the time of leaving their trenches until they had gone forward some forty yards'. Up to this point they had been hidden by the gas and smoke.[8] Two subsequent reports confirmed that the smoke candles had been 'extremely effective' in forming a screen for the attacking infantry.[9] Even on the more unfavourable fronts the positive impact of smoke was widely recognised. 19 Brigade's 'Summary of Operations' recorded that its attacking waves were safe within the smoke screen, but as soon as this lifted 'the assaulting troops came under heavy rifle and machine-gun fire'.[10] Because no smoke candles had turned up in the front trenches of 1 Brigade, the attacking battalions were left with only a number of smoke bombs available to throw out into no-man's-land. Nevertheless, even these crude devices proved 'entirely successful' in screening the attacking waves.[11] Similarly, on the front of 2 Brigade the clouds of smoke 'protected all the men from German fire'.[12] Although the German Official History believed that the effect of the gas 'varied between temporary disability and total loss of the ability to fight', it also admitted that under the 'smoke cloud, the British advanced in large, well-structured groups'.[13]

Nevertheless, however useful smoke proved, it seems to have been completely overshadowed by the problems experienced with the gas. Even on those areas where the gas was believed to have succeeded, reports were often conflicting. While 140 Brigade admitted that the 'enemy had not suffered to any great extent by our gas',[14] 44 Brigade also noted that a burst cylinder had caused problems when it caught the leading waves in its gas.[15] On parts of 46 Brigade's sector, the local effect of the gas was far from beneficial. Indeed, if a lone piper had not marched up and down the parapet oblivious to the dangerous fumes and 'piped' the men out of the trench, 7/KOSB may have been seriously delayed.[16] Two optimistic reports by 7th Division also concluded that although gas and smoke 'were a leading factor in the success… the effect was moral and in no way physical'.[17] In the central section of the British line the gas had poor results. The Medical Officer of 8/Black Watch (26 Brigade) could only find three Germans killed by gas, although he did believe it had a 'considerable morale effect'.[18] 22 Brigade's gas discharge was 'ineffective',[19] if not the 'utter failure' one senior officer believed.[20] On the front of 20 Brigade, the wind 'blew very lightly towards the enemy' so that 'the whole of no-man's-land became hidden in dense fog'.[21] According to Sir James Edmonds:

> The advance was at first completely enveloped in the gas cloud, and here, too, the smoke-helmets brought more curses than blessings from all ranks. After a few minutes the men, almost suffocated, had to remove them to get breath, many being subsequently incapacitated by the gas fumes.[22]

1 Brigade's discharge was equally unsuccessful. Colonel C. Russell Brown (CRE 1st Division, 2 October 1915) remembered how the gas had 'a very stupefying effect on the troops', which 'did much to spoil the impetus of the attack'.[23] The wind conditions were unfavourable and no-man's-land was soon filled with a dense cloud of gas.[24] Some cylinders then began to leak into the front trenches, causing a number of casualties and some confusion.[25]

Things were even worse in 2 Brigade. The wind was not only unfavourable, beginning to change direction as soon as the gas was released, but owing to the slope of the ground, it rolled back towards the British lines.[26] 2 Brigade also suffered from occupying a bulge in the front; the result of the attempt made throughout August and September to close with the distant German defences. This proved to be 'singularly unfortunate' as clouds of gas that had been released by 15th Division further to the south began to roll across its fire trenches.[27] An officer of the Special Brigade, Captain J.N. Pring, remembered how the gas 'formed a dense cloud lying only a few feet above the ground', which blew across the front line when the wind changed direction.[28] In the resulting confusion about 400 men from the assaulting battalions were put out of action. More men were brought up, only for them to be gassed by a further discharge. While the gas may have been of limited success on the south of the battlefield, it was to prove particularly troublesome on the front of 2nd Division in the north. The failure of this discharge has been the subject of sustained criticism. In particular there are numerous references to a series of protests by a number of senior officers, including several members of the Special Brigade, about the feasibility of releasing the gas in such poor conditions. It seems that their concerns were either ignored or refused, at least initially.[29] The gas officers then released the gas, so the accounts tell, only for it to be blown back in the faces of their own men with predictably dire consequences. Although somewhat overstated, these instances highlight not only the difficult weather conditions on the morning of 25 September, but also, more importantly, the confusing and inflexible plan that First Army had adopted for the Battle of Loos.

The best-known protest is perhaps the 'bloody balls-up' episode from Robert Graves's *Goodbye to All That* (1929). According to Graves, a captain belonging to the Special Brigade had contacted divisional headquarters and told them that owing to the poor weather conditions it was impossible to discharge the 'accessory'. He had apparently been told that the 'accessory' was to be 'discharged at all costs'.[30] Another officer within 2/Royal Welsh Fusiliers, Captain J.C. Dunn, recorded a similar story, albeit with the brigade commander, Brigadier-General P.R. Robertson, trying to cancel the discharge, again without success.[31] Similar stories echo back from this sector of the battlefield, but according to Edmonds, the only 'really strong' protest came from Lieutenant A.B. White, attached to Brigadier-General A.C. Daly's 6 Brigade.[32] The wind conditions were especially unfavourable in this sector. White remembered how just before Zero Hour the wind was 'blowing very lightly from the south-south-west and varying considerably in direction'. He therefore 'decided not to carry on and warned the men to do nothing without further orders'.

> At 5.48a.m. [White continued] I got on to the Brigade on the telephone and informed the general that I was unable to carry on. He replied that he had already spoken to the 2nd Division about the wind being unsuitable, and that he had received a direct order to carry on. In these circumstances he ordered me to let the gas off.[33]

With White in the trenches was Lieutenant-Colonel H.C. Potter (CO 1/King's, 6 Brigade) who was told by 2nd Division that he must 'order the officer to discharge the gas, if he refused shoot him!' Somewhat alarmed, White replied that 'he was quite ready to discharge the gas only fearful of the consequences'. Fortunately, Potter was then told that if the wind was still not favourable the gas could immediately be turned off.[34] It was 5.58a.m. before White and his officers – struggling with leaking cylinders and rusting stopcocks – managed to start the discharge. Although the chlorine started encouragingly, drifting 'slowly towards the German lines', ten minutes before the infantry were to attack, the wind changed direction and began blowing back towards the British line. White turned the gas off, but this did not prevent 'large quantities' of it swamping the front trenches and causing considerable confusion.

A similar situation occurred further north. Attached to Brigadier-General C.E. Corkran's 5 Brigade, north of the canal, was Captain C.E.S. Percy-Smith and Second Lieutenant J.W. Sewill, both of whom protested against the discharge.[35] According to Sewill:

> I immediately rang up and spoke to the Brigade Major – a Major in the KRR – and told him I had reported unfavourable [*sic*] on the wind all night, that it was then calm and drizzling and that I would not be responsible for the effect of the gas on our own men. He replied, 'very well I will inform division. Ring me up again.' Only twenty minutes before Zero I got onto him again and he said 'carry on. It is a *Corps* order.'[36]

With a faint wind blowing almost parallel to the British trenches, the gas was released, with predictably lamentable consequences. Sewill recorded how he lost half his section 'gassed in 5 minutes'. A dense volume of chlorine then enveloped the front trenches of 5 Brigade – much of it probably emanating from 6 Brigade on the right – and badly gassed the leading platoons of 9/Highland Light Infantry.[37] Unsure of the situation in front a reconnaissance patrol was sent out, but being met by heavy gunfire the attack was abandoned.[38]

Who was to blame for this fiasco? Sewill thought Foulkes was at fault,[39] while Edmonds criticised both Captain Ernest Gold, First Army's meteorological officer, and 'a hopelessly dull, but rigidly obedient divisional commander' who can only be Major-General H.S. Horne (GOC 2nd Division).[40] Both Liddell Hart and Foulkes agreed with Edmonds that Horne was at fault because he had overruled a number of protests. This remains problematic, however. Although Horne was later to become one of Haig's most reliable army commanders, relatively little is known about him.[41] Were there any other candidates? Foulkes did hint that the decision to go ahead with the gas discharge might have come 'perhaps from still higher authority',[42] and Sewill was apparently informed that it was a corps order.[43] What about GOC I Corps, Lieutenant-General Hubert Gough? He is perhaps a stronger candidate than Horne. His offensive zeal was well known, he had counselled Haig against the cancellation of the gas discharge earlier in the day and had been criticised by subordinates officers in 9th Division for his interference in brigade orders.[44]

But this debate was a little irrelevant and neither Edmonds nor Liddell Hart correctly guessed who was really responsible. They missed the point that the plans for the 'all-out' attack simply did not entertain any possibility that the gas would *not* be released. Therefore, Horne had little choice in the matter. Despite the fact that Foulkes (and Haig) had made it clear that Special Brigade officers would have executive responsibility for the discharge on their fronts, these arrangements collapsed in the frantic moments before the attack. Because the plans were so dependent on the gas, subordinates who acted upon this theoretical independence were bluntly told that they *must* go ahead and release the gas. The roots of this debacle stemmed not from the poor weather conditions that have often been blamed, but from the contradictory and inflexible attack plans that had been drafted at First Army. Indeed, it seems that the one person who has never been blamed for what occurred on 25 September has been the man who was responsible for planning and executing the attack. He devised the plan for Loos and enshrined its contradictions, and he ordered the gas discharge to go ahead even in unsuitable weather conditions. It was Haig's fault.

As has been discussed earlier, the forty-minute discharge of gas and smoke was naturally dependent on the strength and direction of the wind, but because First Army's plan had been placed in the grey area between Sir John French and Sir Douglas Haig, what would happen if the weather was unsuitable – the one factor the British could not control – was left unresolved. While French had been insistent that Haig must press his main attacks on 25 September, the commander of First Army was adamant that major offensive operations could only go ahead when covered by a gas discharge. The contradictions and flaws inherent in First Army's plan, which had not been resolved in the planning stages, were finally played out in the grounds of the Chateau of Hinges on the morning of the attack when a decision whether to go ahead or not *had* to be made. What had happened at Hinges? The weather had been fitful all night, with low clouds, light rain and, more ominously, a faint south-south-westerly breeze. Captain Ernest Gold had calculated that for a successful gas discharge the required wind direction lay between north-west and south-west with a speed of at least four miles per hour.[45] His weather reports had been filtering into Hinges all night with frustratingly inconsistent results.

> At 9p.m. the wind had changed from south-east to south. By 10p.m. it was south-south-west and west, but its speed at five feet about the ground was only two to four miles per hour. At midnight the wind remained in the south-west; but at times the speed fell so low in some places that conditions could only be described as calm.[46]

Haig met Gold at 3a.m. and asked his opinion. Gold replied that although he could not guarantee anything, it was probable that the wind would be stronger and at its most favourable at sunrise, which was at 5.50a.m. Accordingly Haig fixed Zero Hour for this time. The infantry would attack forty minutes later.

It is a commonly held assumption that Haig made his decision whether to go ahead or not with the gas discharge on the basis of smoke that issued from a cigarette belonging to his ADC, Major Alan Fletcher. This episode was recorded in Haig's diary, with the smoke drifting 'in puffs towards the north-east', and has generally been accepted by historians.[47] However, it seems that this was little more than a dramatic tale and the key factor that swayed Haig's decision came not from Fletcher but from Foulkes. Just after 5a.m. Haig asked Foulkes if his Special Brigade officers would turn on the gas if the wind was not favourable on their particular fronts. Foulkes replied that 'they won't turn the gas on if the wind is not favourable'.[48] This seemed to reassure Haig, allowing him to order the attack secure in the knowledge that on the fronts where the conditions were completely unfavourable no gas would be released. No British troops would therefore become gassed.

Haig was still not sure. He put a phone call through to Lieutenant-General Hubert Gough to ask him whether it was too late to stop the main attack and go through with the smaller two-division programme instead. Alarmed at the seemingly fatal paralysis of command at such a crucial time (it was now nearly 5.20a.m.), Gough replied that no such change could take place in time.[49] Although Gough has since been criticised for this, he 'considered it was too late to get the orders to the men in the front trenches. Nor did it appear at the moment that the wind was definitely unfavourable. To postpone the attack would have exposed the men assembled for the attack in the trenches to serious risks and disadvantages.'[50] Whether it would have been possible to alert the attacking divisions in time is a moot point; certainly there were a number of schemes that had been arranged to ensure the swift delivery of orders to the troops in the trenches, but time was running out fast. Haig's mind was therefore made up for him. The main attack would to go ahead as planned. This decision was made not on the basis of a lone cigarette, but on the reassurance that gas would not be released on any unfavourable fronts. And because the wind was not *completely* unsuitable, Haig went ahead with the main attack using this 'fail-safe' system only to see it collapse lower down the chain of command.[51]

The dramatic events at Hinges and the horrid dilemma at the front over whether to release the gas have dominated writing on the first day of the battle. But the historian must be aware of overemphasising the role that gas played in what subsequently occurred when the infantry went 'over the top'. While gas was of immense importance in how the 'all-out' attack was planned and developed, its impact on the battlefield was not as significant and has perhaps been overstated. The release of chlorine gas undoubtedly caused a number of problems for the attacking infantry, by dislocating several brigades and causing casualties (and certainly making going 'over the top' a more trying experience than it otherwise might have been), but it did not always define the success or failure of the British assault. Of far more importance was how the battle had been planned at the operational level, the effectiveness of the preliminary artillery bombardment and the resistance of the Imperial German Army. How then had the British attacks fared?

The left-hand attack was conducted by Hubert Gough's I Corps, which enjoyed a troubled day on 25 September. Difficulties were especially evident with Major-General H.S. Horne's 2nd Division, tasked with forming the northern flank guard. Situated on the extreme left of the British line just north of the La Bassée canal around the village of Givenchy, 5 Brigade had to secure the line Chapelle St Roch–Canteleux, while 6 and 19 Brigades, further to the south, were to advance on Auchy and the Railway Triangle, eventually reaching a German support trench known as Canal Alley, which was to be converted into a strong defensive line. 2nd Division's attacking brigades may have, in places, entered the German line, but nowhere did they hold any enemy ground by the end of the day. Although further attacks were planned for later in the morning, in response to appeals from lower down the chain of command, these were cancelled at 9.45a.m.[52] The failure of 2nd Division stemmed from a number of factors, most notably the poor ground conditions, the lack of thorough artillery preparation and the troubled discharge of the gas, but some progress had been initially made. The unenviable task of creating a diversion half an hour before the main infantry attacks went in was given to 5 Brigade. Despite the unfavourable wind conditions, but aided by surprise, the attack initially went well. The attacking battalions (2/Highland Light Infantry, 1/Queen's and 2/Oxfordshire) were able to capture the opposing German trench, but once through the enemy position, the leading companies ran up against fierce resistance. Owing to a lack of bombs and an inability to light the ones they had, they were forced to evacuate their gains.[53] By 9.40a.m. both battalions were back in the relative safety of their own trenches. A second, smaller attack was to take place by 9/Highland Light Infantry at 6.30a.m., but owing to the disabling effects of the gas discharge and heavy machine gun fire, it was abandoned.

The bad ground conditions were particularly acute on the front of 6 Brigade in the Cuinchy sector. Although only 200 yards wide, no-man's-land was of a most inhospitable nature and huge craters littered the landscape. Because the attacking battalions (1/South Staffordshire and 1/King's) were forced to tread narrow paths between the craters in single file, they were easy targets for enemy riflemen and machine gunners. The attack of 6 Brigade simply withered away under enemy fire. Only scattered groups of men reached the German wire, which was uncut and impossible to get through.[54] The attack of 19 Brigade was little better. As the opposing lines were so close together, its leading battalions (1/Middlesex and 2/Argyll & Sutherland Highlanders) had to vacate the original front line (which was used as the gas trench) and launch their attack from a supporting position about 30–40 yards to the rear. When the infantry finally moved out, advancing into clouds of their own gas, they could make little progress against stubborn resistance.[55] According to Colonel F.G.M. Rowley (CO 1/Middlesex), the attacking waves 'were all shot down within ten minutes'.[56] It was equally bleak on the left, where 2/Argyll & Sutherland Highlanders were attacking Mine Trench. When the leading platoons encountered the German wire, still uncut, the advance stopped. Two platoons of the supporting battalion, 2/Royal Welsh Fusiliers, were hurriedly brought forward to assist the stricken attack, but they 'lost 150 men immediately on getting over the parapet' and could not assist.[57]

Attacking on the right of 2nd Division was Major-General G.H. Thesiger's 9th (Scottish) Division. Deployed along a frontage of 1,500 yards, 28 and 26 Brigades were ordered to carry the German front trenches from the Vermelles–La Bassée railway to the left of 7th Division, including capturing the formidable Hohenzollern Redoubt. Once these objectives had been secured (and supported by 27 Brigade), the division would head eastwards through the mining area of Fosse 8 towards the German second line between Haisnes and Cité St Elie. The operations of 9th Division on 25 September have been remembered largely for 26 Brigade's epic capture of the Hohenzollern Redoubt, an achievement that founded the excellent reputation that 9th Division would subsequently enjoy within the BEF. Even so this attack had initially got off to a bad start. 5/Cameron Highlanders, delayed by the refusal of the gas cloud to move towards the German line, were badly enfiladed by Mad Point, but 7/Seaforth Highlanders managed to drive through a storm of machine gun and shellfire and break into the redoubt.[58] The thorough artillery bombardment had cleared away most of the wire entanglements in this sector.[59] After hastily securing the redoubt, the battalions reformed and pushed on towards Fosse 8. By 7.40a.m. 7/Seaforth Highlanders were east of the mining buildings and moving towards Cité St Elie trench. By 8a.m. both battalions were in touch.[60]

The achievement of 26 Brigade would prove, however, to be the high point for 9th Division during the Battle of Loos and the attack of 28 Brigade on the left was reminiscent of what had happened further north; the wire had not been cut and the infantry were unable to progress. The divisional history gloomily wrote that 'before vicious machine-gun fire from Madagascar Trench, Railway Work and Mad Point, the attack melted away'.[61] While 10/Highland Light Infantry was faced with 'very well aimed and directed rifle and machine-gun fire the moment they got over the parapet',[62] 6/KOSB 'disappeared into a motley fog' and when no news was forthcoming, the second-in-command, Major W.J.S. Hosley, ordered the two remaining companies to move out. Unfortunately, as the regimental history recorded, they walked into 'the jaws of death' and 'were met with terrific gusts of machine-gun fire'.[63] Incredibly, some men managed to get into Madagascar Trench, but they could not hold out for long.

The ordeal of 28 Brigade had, however, only just begun. 9th Division had received a message from 28 Brigade at 9.10a.m. reporting that its attacks had been repulsed.[64] Shortly after an order arrived from I Corps that 28 Brigade must renew the attack against the German defences north of the Hohenzollern Redoubt. 9th Division's subsequent order made it clear who was responsible.

> Corps have ordered a bombardment of Madagascar houses – Mad Point – Madagascar Trench – Railway Work and support trench in rear. Bombardment to begin at 11.30a.m. Finish 12 noon. Last five minutes intensive. 28 Infantry Brigade will assault at 12 noon. Attack at 12 sharp.[65]

The result was a tragic example of how *not* to conduct an attack on fortified trenches manned by an alert, determined defence. The scheduled bombardment crashed down upon the German lines at 11.30a.m. as planned, until it abruptly ceased at noon. Yet 28 Brigade was in no position to take advantage of the shellfire. Its battalions received their orders at different times and had only minutes to prepare. 9/Scottish Rifles were handed their orders at 11.53a.m. while 11/Highland Light Infantry only received a copy ten minutes later. At 12.15p.m., the two battalions scrambled out of the trenches but were 'very quickly held up by machine-gun and rifle fire'.[66] The bombardment had not suppressed the enemy defenders and merely alerted them to the new attack.

Why had 28 Brigade been ordered to renew its attack in such unpromising circumstances? The corps commander, Hubert Gough, made little mention of this episode in his memoirs and perhaps for good reason. Something had clearly gone wrong. *The History of the 9th (Scottish) Division* (1921) was scathing in its criticism of its corps commander, calling the attack a 'forlorn hope', 'an offence against a well-understood military principle', 'futile' and of betraying 'an almost unbelievable optimism'. The history also believed that 'the persistence in a frontal attack showed a serious lack of flexibility in the Higher Command in making use of the division'.[67] Indeed, on reflection it is difficult to avoid being critical of Gough who was beginning to show an over-optimism, aggression and impatience that would become his hallmark when commanding operations on the Western Front.[68] It seems that he made a number of errors on the morning of 25 September, firstly by abandoning his headquarters for crucial periods, and then by showing a marked reluctance to accept that the battle had already turned against him.

After speaking to Haig earlier in the morning over whether or not to release the gas, Gough had spent his time anxiously awaiting news at his headquarters. As a troubled, overcast morning wore on it seemed that 2nd Division had encountered fierce resistance, 26 Brigade had taken their initial objectives, and 7th Division had done well but been held up outside the German second line.[69] The absence of news from 28 Brigade was, however, of some concern. According to his biographer, Gough went forward during the morning:

> along the side road from Vermelles to Auchy, hoping to discover what was happening in 28 Brigade; but the headquarters had been shelled out of its original position and after two wasted hours Gough realised he was completely out of touch with events. He returned to corps headquarters frustrated and worried, with the result that he answered sharply to a young member of his staff who passed him a light remark.[70]

Such an action was not untypical of Gough, who was a very 'hands-on' commander, and is indicative of his inexperience in commanding large formations. He had perhaps not realised that if he was to have any influence on the battle at all, it would be from the end of a telephone line.

News from the battlefield gradually worsened during the day, but this did not make such an impact upon Gough. It seems that he could not get the early – and generally favourable – reports out of his mind. Though 'he realised that he must not rely on these first messages, Gough could not completely suppress a hope that the picture they drew him was in essence correct'.[71] He therefore ignored later, more pessimistic reports and still insisted that a breakthrough was at hand. Frustrated at having wasted two hours riding around behind his lines, Gough seems to have felt under pressure to do something and, therefore, ordered 28 Brigade to renew the attack. And while it is possible that he dismissed the possibility of a flank attack because of concerns over whether it would be possible for his troops to move around to the right through the congested trench network, his decision was still problematic. Surely he had enough experience of trench warfare to understand that if one attack failed, it was usually futile to send more men forward over the same ground? The attitudes of Gough's subordinates should perhaps be considered. There was probably more opposition to renewed attacks in 2nd Division. The sector was generally recognised as being completely unfavourable to a successful advance and the divisional commander was Major-General Henry Horne, an intelligent artillery officer who had commanded the division since the start of the year. On the contrary, Major-General Thesiger had only arrived to command 9th Division on 9 September, just over a fortnight before the offensive began. After arriving he had shown a marked reluctance to become involved in the intricacies of the plan of attack and it is perhaps understandable if Thesiger did not protest strongly about Gough's decision being so new to the job.[72]

The attacks of I Corps were completed by Major-General Sir T. Capper's 7th Division, which was deployed on the right flank of 9th Division. 7th Division held a frontage of 1,400 yards up to the Vermelles–Hulluch road and was tasked with capturing Quarry and Breslau Trenches, including the Pope's Nose Redoubt. The Quarries and an intermediate position called Gun Trench would then be secured, before the leading troops (supported by the reserve brigade) went through the German second line between Hulluch and Cité St Elie. In many ways the experience of 7th Division was similar to that encountered by both 2nd and 9th Divisions, in that heavy German resistance was met all along its front. But in sharp contrast to what had happened further north, both attacking brigades were able to overrun the first series of enemy trenches and in some cases even reach the German second line.

The ground conditions in this central portion of the British front were certainly an improvement on the difficult positions elsewhere on I Corps' front, but they were hardly ideal. Because no-man's-land was a forbidding place – 500 yards wide with long grass that concealed much of the enemy wire – both leading battalions of 22 Brigade (2/Royal Warwickshire and 1/South Staffordshire) suffered from heavy machine gun fire and were unable to break into the German trenches.[73] Lieutenant-Colonel R.M. Ovens (CO 1/South Staffordshire) complained of suffering 'terribly from uncut wire' and how 'becoming a casualty seemed only a matter of time'.[74] But showing considerable fighting spirit a further attack by the supporting battalion (1/Royal Welsh Fusiliers) managed to penetrate the German trenches, which were cleared just after 7.30a.m. Although Slit Redoubt held out for another hour, by 9.30a.m. the brigade was firmly established in the Quarries.[75] Parties of 2/Queen's even pushed on towards Cité Trench and Cité St Elie, but owing to a British bombardment, had to withdraw.[76]

The attack of 20 Brigade on the right also managed to overrun the German front line. As might have been expected, the wind showed no more inclination to blow in the required direction here than it had elsewhere. Lieutenant-Colonel H.H. Tudor (CO XIV Brigade RHA) recorded how 'the whole of no-man's-land became hidden in dense fog'.[77] Enemy resistance was also fearsome, with the Germans manning the parapet of Breslau Trench 'firing away furiously'.[78] But despite these handicaps progress was still made. This probably had much to do with Brigadier-General Hon. J.F.H.S.F. Trefusis's (GOC 20 Brigade) decision to keep the German front line under artillery fire as the leading waves were advancing through no-man's-land. Standard tactics called for artillery fire to cease the moment infantry stepped out of their trenches, but because of the width of no-man's-land and the experience of previous battles, it was decided to 'keep our guns firing on the enemy for three minutes after our infantry had gone over the top in order to keep down the Hun fire from rifles and machine-guns as long as possible'.[79] This seems to have worked. And while 8/Devonshire came up against uncut wire, which slowed up the advance, the battalion on the right (2/Gordon Highlanders) fared better.[80] Because the wire had been cleared and the enemy parapets smashed in by the bombardment, it was able to crash through the German front line. By 9a.m. these battalions had hastily reformed and reached the Lens road in front of the German second line at Hulluch.

While the attacks of I Corps had been partly unsuccessful, with progress only being made on the right half of the corps frontage, Lieutenant-General Sir Henry Rawlinson's IV Corps achieved considerable success over the more suitable terrain in the south. In what was one of the most well-known attacks of the entire war, 15th (Scottish) Division advanced up to two miles into the German defences and 47th (London) Division, attacking on its right, also performed extremely well, taking its objectives with minimal casualties. Nevertheless, IV Corps had not met with complete success and 1st Division, on Rawlinson's left, encountered similar difficulties to those units further north. Attacking in poor weather conditions, facing intact enemy defences and meeting stubborn resistance, only its left-hand brigade was able to bludgeon a path through the German front line with its opening attack. 2 Brigade, on the right, was unable to take the enemy strongpoint at Lone Tree and repeated attacks foundered on uncut wire. It was midday by the time German resistance crumbled in this sector, having been outflanked by British supporting battalions from the rear.

Before looking at the epic advance of 15th Division through Loos and up Hill 70, it is necessary to analyse the attack of Major-General A.E.A.

Holland's 1st Division in more detail. 1st Division was deployed between the Vermelles–Hulluch Road and the left of 15th Division and faced the forbidding German defences on the Lone Tree ridge. After taking the first line Holland's men were to advance down the Loos valley and link up with 7th Division at the southern end of Hulluch and with 15th Division at Puits 14 bis on the Lens–La Bassée road. Owing to the configuration of the ground, both leading brigades would be moving on slightly divergent lines. While 1 Brigade went directly eastwards, 2 Brigade headed off to the south-east. In order to fill in any gap that would be created between them, a separate sub-brigade was formed, known as 'Green's Force'. 3 Brigade, in reserve, was stationed at Le Rutoire.

The attack of 1 Brigade can be briefly summarised. Because the gas was unhelpful (and sorely missing its smoke candles), the leading battalions (10/Gloucestershire and 8/Royal Berkshire) had to contend with heavy machine gun fire from advanced German positions in two small, shell-splattered copses (La Haie and Bois Carré), which had escaped the attentions of the preliminary bombardment. Although these were swiftly dealt with, it was found that much of the wire in front of the German line was uncut, presenting a formidable obstacle. Nevertheless, the battalions managed to get into the enemy trenches, chasing after the garrison, which had retreated to the support line.[81] By 8a.m. the two battalions had established themselves in the southern end of Gun Trench and 1/Cameron Highlanders, the supporting battalion, was moving up in support. The attack of 2 Brigade, however, did not progress according to plan. It had a disastrous day on 25 September, illustrating all the myriad problems with planning, artillery preparation and communication that dogged the British throughout this period.[82] The opening attack, badly dislocated by clouds of gas (probably from 15th Division on its right) delayed the advance by four minutes, and when the leading battalions (1/Loyal North Lancashire and 2/KRRC) began moving out, they were badly enfiladed by two saps, which had not been shelled.[83] Casualties quickly mounted and as the leading lines – mixed up, panicking and confused – reached the German line, it was found that the wire was uncut, and the attack stalled.[84] A second attack at 7.30a.m. by the supporting battalions (2/Royal Sussex and 1/Northamptonshire) again failed to dislodge the enemy defenders.[85] This was, however, not for want for courage. The later award of four Victoria Crosses to members of 2 Brigade bore eloquent testimony to how determined the attacks had been pressed.[86]

The failure to take a strong German position was certainly not unfamiliar to the BEF in 1915, but the events that followed make the action at Lone Tree worth more than a cursory glance. Despite the failure of 2 Brigade's two attacks, the morning also witnessed the employment of

Green's Force in the battle for Lone Tree. Although it had originally been intended to link the divergent advances of 1 and 2 Brigades, the two battalions of Green's Force (1/14th London and 1/9th King's) became involved in the attempts to clear Lone Tree around midday. Unfortunately, when faced with heavy gunfire and rows of uncut barbed wire, its attack – like all previous attempts – came to nothing and was abandoned close to the enemy wire.[87] The decision to continue attacking Lone Tree head-on has been heavily criticised with blame falling on the divisional commander, Major-General Holland. According to Robin Prior and Trevor Wilson, Holland's decision to use Green's Force against Lone Tree was 'a baffling decision', which reinforced failure.[88] Similarly, Robin Neillands has written that Holland's orders showed either 'excessive optimism, or a complete misjudgement of the enemy'.[89] However, from a close study of 1st Division's papers, it is possible to see that the real problem at Lone Tree was not the stupidity of the divisional commander, but a tragic misunderstanding that reveals much about the problems with command and control on the Western Front at this period.

The main criticism of Holland centres on his decision to order Green's Force to make a *frontal* assault on Lone Tree. Because the enemy trenches on either side had been overrun by British forces it is assumed that he should have ordered a more promising flanking manoeuvre in order to bypass the uncut belts of wire and get behind the German defenders.[90] The order that Holland sent to Green's Force is central to this argument. According to both the British Official History and the two regimental histories of the London Scottish, at 9.10a.m. Holland ordered Green's Force to attack, 'with one battalion on either side of Lone Tree'.[91] However, after a lengthy search of 1st Division's papers, such an order has not come to light. According 1st Division's log of messages, an order *was* issued at 9.10a.m., but it read as follows:

> Sussexs [*sic*] are reported to be held up by wire in front of German trenches south of LONE TREE. Support with your two battalions attacking Germans on flank if possible.

Therefore, far from ordering a renewed *frontal* assault, it seems that Holland was very aware of the need to attack on the flank 'if possible'. Similarly, another message was sent to Green's Force at 10a.m.

> It is essential that the 2nd Brigade should get forward without delay. Push in your attack on the German flank at once.

Once again Holland mentioned the possibility of attacking the German *flank* rather than its frontal defences. The message at 10a.m. is perhaps attributable to the influence of IV Corps' commander, Henry Rawlinson, who had phoned Holland and bluntly informed him that 'it would be as well to ignore the Germans still holding them up [2 Brigade], and push on'.[92] Nevertheless, Holland's preference for flanking manoeuvres can also be seen in his conduct of operations during the rest of the day. By 10.55a. m. Holland had arranged for a 'strong bombing party' to begin rolling up the German front line from Northern Sap, and likewise, elements of 3 Brigade had been ordered forward at 11.10a.m. in the wake of 1 Brigade on the left.[93] Although the war diaries differ on the exact time (or times) of surrender, it seems that just before 3p.m. resistance finally ended at Lone Tree. 1st Division's account records that at 2.50p.m. the Germans opposite 2 Brigade surrendered, but a second group held out until 3.30p.m. when 2/Welsh (3 Brigade), which had crossed no-man's-land at Bois Carré and then wheeled right, found itself directly behind Lone Tree.[94]

This reassessment of the attack at Lone Tree may have lifted some of the blame that has fallen on Major-General Holland's shoulders, but there are still unanswered questions that surround the conduct of Green's Force during 25 September. Owing to the death of three runners, Holland's order to attack Lone Tree did not reach Lieutenant-Colonel Edgar Green (CO Green's Force) until 10.55a.m. and it was past midday by the time he was ready to launch the assault.[95] Puzzlingly, it seems that Green did indeed receive an order to attack 'on either side of Lone Tree' because it formed the subject of a heated discussion between Green and Major J.H. Lindsay (CO 1/14th London). According to the London Scottish regimental history, Lindsay was so concerned about these orders that he suggested to Green that if his men were allowed to move to the rear and then swing around to take the enemy in the flank, the 'spirit' of the order would be complied with and better results obtained.[96] Unfortunately, Lindsay was ignored. It seems that Green felt that the specific mention of attacking '*on either side of Lone Tree*' precluded any prospect of conducting a flanking manoeuvre. As Major J. Paterson (1/14th London) later argued, Green believed his orders 'made it necessary to say *no*' to Lindsay.[97] So why, if he had received orders that allowed the possibility of attacking Lone Tree from the flank, did Green insist on another frontal assault? This remains unclear, but if Green had – through whatever means – received orders to attack 'on either side of Lone Tree' he may well have simply misunderstood them. It is possible that while Green thought of 'Lone Tree' as the cherry tree in no-man's-land (and, therefore, directed his attack on either side of this tactical feature), this was not what 1st Division actually meant. Holland probably saw 'Lone Tree' as the 600 yards of front trench still held by the enemy and wanted Green's Force to attack on either side of this, in other words, by conducting a flank attack. In any case, Holland had made it clear before the battle (in an order penned to his brigadiers) that 'any offensive action taken will be his orders and that he will accept full responsibility for the results',[98] and it is not inconceivable that these words were in Green's mind when he was considering his actions at Lone Tree.

Fortunately for First Army, the factors that had caused such difficulties for 2 Brigade did not apply to the remaining divisions of IV Corps. Major-General F.W.N. McCracken's 15th (Scottish) Division was deployed between just north of the Vermelles–Loos road and Fosse 7. Attacking on a front of 1,500 yards, the leading brigades had to capture two large strongpoints, known as the Loos and Lens Road Redoubts, before they could advance eastwards towards Loos. Once the village was secured, 15th Division would head towards Hill 70, and supported by 45 Brigade, push past the German second line at Cité St Auguste. As has been mentioned previously, 15th Division conducted the most spectacular attack on 25 September, with both leading brigades breaking the German line and advancing deeply into the enemy position. Facing the Loos Road Redoubt on the left of the divisional frontage was 46 Brigade. Because the thick belts of wire that protected the German trenches had been 'cut thoroughly', the attacking battalions (7/KOSB and 10/Scottish Rifles supported by two companies of 12/Highland Light Infantry) were able to push through the clouds of gas and clear the German front line.[99] On the right, heavy enemy resistance and the shelling of its crowded front trenches could not prevent 44 Brigade from pressing home its attack against the Lens Road Redoubt with 'great dash'.[100] And while the leading battalions (9/Black Watch and 8/Seaforth Highlanders) suffered heavy casualties from machine gun fire, they pressed on 'in good order and with determination' towards the village of Loos, still shrouded in smoke.

The second phase of the assault, as 46 and 44 Brigades pushed on eastwards through the village of Loos and up to the long slopes of Hill 70, remains one of the enduring and celebrated images of the battle. Sir James Edmonds even compared the British troops that captured the village to 'a bank holiday crowd'.[101] However, there was a darker side to this advance that has rarely been discussed. Very soon after the German front line had been broken the attack of 15th Division began to go wrong. For 46 Brigade the situation was far from secure. The failure of 2 Brigade to capture Lone Tree meant that its left flank was completely open and although elements of its leading battalions had pressed on across the Loos Valley and reached Puits 14 at about 9a.m., these forward troops soon became isolated. A pre-battle order had warned against being 'drawn into an attack on Loos', but after being fired on by snipers, the rest of the brigade changed direction and became mixed up in the streets of Loos.[102] Regarding 44 Brigade, it had breached the Loos Defence Line by 7.10a.m. and soon after began to filter into the village.[103] As the Scottish soldiers bombed and bayoneted their way through Loos, the attack began to lose its initial cohesion. Battalions became mixed up, entangled and disorientated in the ruined village.[104]

It has often not been realised just how debilitating the initial advance had been, even for battalions that had taken their objectives successfully. Casualties were everywhere heavy, and many battalions, having few officers left, became disorientated in the gas and smoke. The direction of 15th Division's advance also began to waver. By 10a.m. most of the attacking battalions were thoroughly mixed up, and as they filtered through the shattered, sniper-infested streets of Loos, their line of advance suddenly began to warp to the right. Captain D. Strang (8/Seaforth Highlanders, 44 Brigade) believed that 'the pylons ['Tower Bridge'] seemed to exercise a fascination on the firing line',[105] and Brigadier-General M.G. Wilkinson (GOC 44 Brigade) also recorded that during the fighting through Loos, 'there was a tendency for the left of the attack to swing round towards the south pivoting on the right flank – this was partly due to the confirmation of the ground but principally I think from a natural tendency to follow prominent features such as the PYLONS at Loos and the [Double] crassier.'[106] This loss of direction and cohesion was undoubtedly connected to the crippling officer casualties, but it was also the result of the decision to attack 'all-out' with little chance to pause and reform before pushing onto further objectives. The very looseness of the attack plans mitigated against any attempt to control the advance.

There also seems to have been a lowering of discipline as units overran German defensive positions, especially in Loos village. Contained in numerous personal accounts, and (more interestingly) in several war diaries, are references to a seemingly widespread abuse of German prisoners. Although every battle surely contains such instances, Loos seems to have gained an unenviable reputation as a battle that was particularly bad for captured German soldiers. It is extremely doubtful whether any divisional or brigade orders specifically requested attacking troops *not* to take prisoners – indeed none has ever been found – but abuse clearly occurred on a greater scale than was usual for British operations. Although the Germans made no serious stand in Loos village – the Scottish advance had simply been too fast – it is clear that the fighting was close, bitter and bloody. Sergeant J.M. Cavers (10/Gordon Highlanders, 44 Brigade) remembered how the 'street fighting was very hot; barricades were climbed, houses bombed and enemy detachments made prisoner'.[107] Private A.G.C. Townsend (20/London, 141 Brigade) also noted how 'a lot of the Germans threw down their rifles and put up their hands for mercy', and were then captured.[108] But it was often not so simple and Townsend also recorded how those German machine gunners hidden in houses 'made a stubborn resistance' and were 'soon made short work of'. Indeed, so close was the fighting that it was often difficult to control those men who were intent on murdering Germans, especially because there were so few officers to rein them in.[109]

Perhaps the most outspoken account of the murder of German prisoners at Loos was recorded by Private H. Panton (7/Cameron Highlanders, 44 Brigade).[110] When in the village Panton took a German officer prisoner, recording the following:

> The German we did not know what to do with so we sent him on in front and as he got a few yards away I shot him. At another part of the village we came across three or our lads who had discovered some Huns in a cellar hiding. Once lad was fair [*sic*] mad and wanted to bayonet each one as they came up the stair. We held him back for a little but the fourth Hun was a huge chap and as we came up his brains were scattered along the wall by a shot from this chap. The others we eventually disposed of. I could tell you hundreds of other such incidents but they are all too gruesome.

Although it is rare to find such a candid account of murder, this was, as Panton suggests, not an isolated incident.[111] A number of other sources also testify to the collapse of discipline after the front line had been crossed. Major J. Stewart (9/Black Watch, 44 Brigade) told his wife that his battalion took very few prisoners at Loos and that 'the main thing' was 'to kill plenty of HUNS with as little loss to oneself as possible.'[112] On 13 February 1916, Captain J.L. Jack (2/Cameronians) recorded a '*highly disgusting incident*', very similar to Panton's account, told to him by an army chaplain who had served at Loos.[113] Other parts of the battlefield also witnessed instances of prisoner killing. When 8/Gordon Highlanders (26 Brigade) overran the Hohenzollern Redoubt on 25 September, between 40–50 Germans were found 'apparently hidden in deep dug-outs'. The war diary records that 'these men were *attended to*'.[114] Why did such episodes occur? It is difficult to make any wider, generalised conclusions about the reason for these murders. It certainly does not indicate a kind of 'barbarisation' of warfare that Omer Bartov has described on the Eastern Front during the Second World War,[115] but it is perhaps indicative of a collapse of morale following the extreme shock of battle on inexperienced troops who had lost most of their officers, were frightened by the gas and smoke, and maddened by sniper fire.

In vivid contrast to the dramatic events around Loos, the attack of Major-General C. St L. Barter's 47th Division, was a much more controlled affair. 47th Division conducted the most successful attack of the entire day, achieving its limited objectives within three hours and spending the rest of the day consolidating its newly won positions. The reason why such success had been achieved seems to have stemmed from a combination of the limited objective, which allowed for thorough preparation, the promising ground conditions and a concentrated artillery bombardment. Overlooking a series of open fields south-west of Loos, 141 and 140 Brigades were ordered to breakthrough the first German line between the right of 15th Division and the Double Crassier, before forming a defensive flank along a German support trench. The opening attack had been aided by a diversionary 'Chinese' attack with specially made dummies and wooden figures that had been organised by 142 Brigade. This seems to have drawn considerable enemy rifle and machine gun fire.[116]

With a favourable wind and good ground, the leading battalion (1/18th London) of 141 Brigade swept over no-man's-land and was soon upon the German front line, where after a swift fight, most of the bewildered defenders broke and ran. Within ten minutes it was through the first line of trenches, and had been 'leapfrogged' by the two supporting battalions (1/19th and 1/20th London), which continued the advance. After reaching the Loos Defence Line the brigade then changed direction and headed south-east, through Garden City towards the Loos Crassier and Chalk Pit Copse.[117] By 9.30a.m. these positions had been taken, although some confusion had been experienced over the exact extent of 1/19th London's objectives. As a result, some men became lost and mixed up with the Scottish troops that were fighting in Loos and moving up the slopes of Hill 70.[118] Although some dislocation and confusion was inevitable in such large-scale operations, 47th Division's attack was remarkable for its crisp execution. The leading battalions of 140 Brigade (1/6th and 1/7th London) were equally successful in capturing the German support trench that ran from the Double Crassier to the Béthune–Lens road. 1/6th and 1/7th London reached the German front line without hindrance; the gas and smoke rolling down into the valley and effectively screening their advance.[119] By 8a.m. the battalions had reached their final objectives and started consolidating their gains.

Reviewing the events of the morning of 25 September 1915, it will be seen that the key to understanding them does not lie, as so many commentators have alleged, with the gas attack before the infantry went 'over the top'. Although the gas was undoubtedly a highly novel feature of the battle that has made an indelible impression on many of the memoirs, novels and secondary accounts that deal with Loos, it was not of supreme importance to the success (or not) of the British attacks. This lay with the four-day preliminary artillery bombardment that had shelled the German lines in the days preceding the attack. Where the British guns had been able to concentrate their fire upon well-observed sections of the German line, considerable damage could be achieved, as occurred on the southern sector of the battlefield occupied by 15th and 47th Divisions. But where the German lines were difficult to observe or where British artillery was weak (particularly in 1st and 2nd Divisions), the results were far from satisfactory. As a result the attacking infantry found it very difficult to make gains without at least heavy, and sometimes devastating, casualties.

Writing about battlefield command and control in 1917, John Lee has argued persuasively that 'After two years of bitter experience the British army was perfectly aware that modern battle was a truly chaotic environment', and had learnt to cope with this chaos in two ways. Firstly, 'the whole attack was subordinated to the artillery plan', which meant the infantry were given precise, achievable objectives, would follow closely a 'creeping' barrage and would also be protected by various standing barrages. Secondly, infantry battalions were organised and trained 'in a totally standardised way'. They were split into four sections, with the Lewis gun and rifle grenade troops providing fire support, while rifle and bombing sections were to close with the enemy as quickly as possible.[120] This standard operating procedure was reproduced in various tactical pamphlets, notably SS143 (*Instructions for the Training of Platoons for Offensive Operations*) and SS135 (*Instructions for the Training of Divisions for Offensive Action*), and was well understood throughout all levels of the BEF. These reforms provided the basis for much British success from 1917 onwards.[121] However, regarding Loos, it will be seen that both these points do not apply. Firstly, the plan of attack had been subordinated to the gas attack, *not* the bombardment, and had been formulated on the assumption that it would prove utterly devastating and allow British troops to clear two German defensive lines without facing heavy resistance. Moreover, as shown in Chapter 3, the tactical plan at Loos was based not on precise, achievable objectives, but on the assumption that units would attack 'all-out', and go as far as they could 'into the blue'. Indeed, when a number of battalion commanders had expressed concerns over the scope of these orders, they were discouraged from halting their advance and told by senior officers that no intermediate objectives could be given.

How important were infantry tactics to the success of failure of the main attacks? Of course, the manner in which British troops moved across no-man's-land cannot be ignored, but it seems not to have been the vital factor and complements recent work on 1 July 1916. According to Robin Prior and Trevor Wilson:

> As long as most German machine-gunners and artillerymen survived the bombardment, the slaughter of the attacking infantry would occur whatever infantry tactics were adopted. To rush German machine-guns might slightly increase the rate of survival over those who walked towards them, but the different was not significant.[122]

A similar situation existed at Loos. Even when battalions involved used simple and slow-moving formations success could be achieved, often because the pre-battle artillery preparation had cut the barbed wire and smashed the German trenches. 9/Black Watch (44 Brigade) captured the Lens Road Redoubt with 'Perfect steadiness... There was no shouting or hurry; the men moved in quick time, packing up their 'dressing' as if on ceremonial parade.'[123] Similarly 7/Seaforth Highlanders (26 Brigade) crossed no-man's-land at a 'steady walk' but were still able to make their way into the Hohenzollern Redoubt.[124]

This is not to say that all battalions attacked in inflexible or slow, linear formations and it seems that a considerable proportion of battalions used 'fire and movement' tactics on 25 September. According to the regimental history the attack on Pekin Trench by two battalions of 27 Brigade (11 and 12/Royal Scots) was 'striking proof of the efficiency of their training and would have done credit to a battalion of regulars. Working by small groups, each supporting the advance of its neighbour by covering fire, they swiftly lessened the distance between them and their goal by a series of short sharp rushes.'[125] Similarly, 5/Cameron Highlanders (26 Brigade) apparently advanced upon the German line by rapid rushes, each of eighty yards, and Rifleman Walter Young (1/18th London, 141 Brigade) recorded how his battalion crossed no-man's-land in 'rushes of about 80 yards at a time, then down for a minute, then another rush and so on'.[126] 1/20th London (141 Brigade) also captured Chalk Pit Copse by using 'fire and movement' tactics.[127]

But even if 'fire and movement' tactics were used success was not guaranteed. This depended upon the state of the German defenders, whether the wire had been cut and the situation on either flank. Green's Force attacked Lone Tree with 'short rushes', but it was unable to bypass thick belts of uncut wire,[128] and 2/Worcestershire (5 Brigade, attached to Carter's Force) failed to recapture the Quarries on 26 September, despite advancing in successive lines 'at a steady double'.[129] Poor tactics, however, undoubtedly meant that greater casualties were sustained than might otherwise have been the case had looser, more flexible attack formations been employed. According to one eyewitness, the men of 1/Middlesex (19 Brigade) 'went over the top as though on parade and were all shot down within ten minutes' during their doomed attack on Railway Redoubt.[130] Similarly, within 8/Devonshire (20 Brigade) 'A' and 'D' Companies started off too early and ran into 'C' Company in no-man's-land. This resulted in great crowds of men at the gaps in the German wire, which only increased the casualty rate.[131]

Why was there so much difference in what tactics were used? Considering the inexperience of a great number of British troops, it is perhaps surprising that there was no real discussion within high command about which tactical formations should be employed at Loos. As Prior and Wilson have noted, even with the complete mix of divisions within IV Corps (regular, territorial and new army), 'there was virtually no heart-searching about the infantry tactics that should be adopted, and no suggestion that non-regular troops might be incapable of conforming to the relatively sophisticated attack formations of the old army'.[132] It seems that as long as the attack was pressed home with speed and momentum – to the 'full extent' of its power in other words – commanding officers were free to devise their own formations. Artillery tactics were equally 'loose'. While 20 Brigade kept its artillery firing on the German front line for at least three minutes after most batteries had ceased (to cover the movement of infantry through no-man's-land), this effective tactic seems not to have been replicated by other brigades.[133]

To conclude then, it is probable that even had the wind conditions been perfect on 25 September, First Army would have achieved a similar level of success. This is not to say that the gas and smoke were unimportant, but they must be seen within their proper context. Certainly the smoke seems to have been useful in screening the movement of many battalions through no-man's-land, but when this cover was broken the German defenders were free to wreak havoc on the exposed British battalions. It also had the unfortunate effect of disguising a number of tactical features on the battlefield and helping to cause some confusion and loss of direction amongst the attacking battalions. Admittedly, the chlorine gas may have been effective on certain local sectors, particularly for 47th Division, but the primary reason why the attacks of 15th and 47th Divisions were successful stemmed from the ground conditions that gave the British good artillery observation over the German lines, as well as the detailed pre-battle preparation that both divisions had undertaken. Again, for other divisions artillery seems to have been the key factor. The failure of 2nd Division emanated from the inability of British guns to destroy the belts of wire that protected the German trenches and the strength of enemy resistance in this sector, and likewise, it is doubtful whether 2 Brigade would have been able to capture Lone Tree even if the gas had reached the enemy trenches because the wire was so thick as to delay any frontal advance for a considerable time. Whatever else the gas and smoke might do, it could *not* cut belts of barbed wire. But would First Army be able to exploit the gains that had been made at such cost during the morning and continue the advance into the afternoon?

6

THE FIRST DAY (II): 25 SEPTEMBER 1915

By mid-morning on 25 September 1915, First Army's main attack south of the La Bassée canal had reached its high-water mark. Although the British had not managed to make a complete breakthrough, considerable success had been achieved. As has been discussed in the previous chapter, 2nd Division and the left-hand brigade of 9th Division had been unable to make any progress, but matters had improved elsewhere with most of the other brigades being within sight of the German second line at this time. And while German resistance at the second line hardened with every passing hour, the British still had considerable fighting power left on the battlefield. Indeed, if First Army's ambitious objectives were to be achieved, the gains of the morning would need prompt exploitation. But the continuation of this partial success would prove largely beyond the capabilities of the BEF and many of the problems that had been experienced at Neuve Chapelle – such as poor communication, lack of artillery support, the movement of reserves and the difficulty of mounting of renewed attacks – would again be encountered. While the BEF could achieve a break-in, it could not yet manage a break-out.

Notwithstanding the mixed success of the opening assault, with five brigades being stopped in their tracks, the excellent artillery preparation in the south had allowed 15th and 47th Divisions to make major gains and provide the battle with perhaps its most famous episode as columns of kilted Scottish soldiers streamed through Loos and ascended Hill 70. According to the British Official Historian, Sir James Edmonds:

> The fighting in Loos had drawn together the mass of the 44th and 46th Brigades, so that soon after 8a.m. on a narrow front of about six hundred yards near the eastern exits of the village there was a great gathering of Scottish units. As they streamed out thoroughly intermingled, and began the ascent of Hill 70 in a somewhat leisurely manner they had had, in the words of a battalion diarist, 'the appearance of a bank holiday crowd'. For the moment there was a lull in the noise of battle, and their advance appeared to be unopposed.[1]

What happened once 15th (Scottish) Division reached the crest of Hill 70 is well known. Instead of going directly *eastwards* towards Cité St Auguste as planned, when the leading elements of 44 Brigade, about 1,500 men in total (which had began to ascend Hill 70 at 8.30a.m.)[2] reached the high ground, they began moving *southwards* towards the northern outskirts of Lens. By this time groups of German survivors had managed to rally and after being reinforced by a battalion of *178 Regiment (123rd (Saxon) Division)* and a battalion of *22 Reserve Regiment* (*117th Division*), they were able to man the second line around Cité St Laurent and Dynamitière and prevent the attackers from reaching their positions.[3] The situation only worsened as the morning wore on and by around 10a.m. German resistance began to increase alarmingly. Seeing the attackers swarming around Hill 70, enemy gunners began shelling it and sweeping it with machine gun fire. The position of 15th Division could have collapsed completely were it not for the equally exhausted state of the enemy and the steady influence of a number of British senior officers, who realised how serious the situation had become.[4] Although it was difficult to stop the crowds of mixed-up Scottish soldiers from continuing past Hill 70, a line was dug on the near side of the crest in an effort to avoid the murderous fire on the hill.

In retrospect, it seems that although much was made of the advance of 15th Division on 25 September, both at the time and ever since, it was not the clean breakthrough that had been envisaged by General Sir Douglas Haig. Admittedly, Loos has been popularly associated with a breakthrough and German sources certainly betray the sense of shock and panic at the deep penetrations that had been made. The German Official History recorded that by mid-morning the situation in Loos was 'extremely serious', with the British seemingly on the verge of a complete breakthrough.[5] A German regimental history concurred, noting that Lens 'was in great danger' and that parts of the town had to be evacuated.[6] Certain British writers have echoed this 'near-victory' thesis. According to Captain Basil Liddell Hart, the attack of 15th Division was 'a near approach to a breakthrough',[7] and Alan Clark believed the attack of 8/Royal Berkshire (1 Brigade) to have been 'the cleanest break on the whole front of the offensive'.[8] More recently, Paddy Griffith has written that the 'infantry actually came close to complete victory'.[9]

How true was this? While the German High Command was certainly initially alarmed by the speed of the British attack in the south (the northern half of the battlefield did not cause such concern), it soon regained its balance as reinforcements were rushed to the threatened sectors. Robin Prior and Trevor Wilson are unimpressed by the notion of a breakthrough at Loos, concluding with regard to 15th Division that even by as early as 10.30a.m. there were between 700 and 800 German soldiers 'in the area from Lens North to Cité St Auguste'. This was, of course, more than enough to pin down the 1,500 mixed-up Scottish soldiers that reached Hill 70.[10] Indeed, on a close reading of the available sources, it seems that the idea of a breakthrough at Loos is largely a chimera, perhaps even a post-battle justification for such an ambitious plan of attack. While a scattered party of 1/Cameron Highlanders (1 Brigade) entered Hulluch briefly, this was exceptional.[11] It is clear that in many cases, once the attacking battalions had crossed the German front line, they were in no state to go much further. According to Brigadier-General Hon. J.F.H.S.F. Trefusis (GOC 20 Brigade), the 'thrust' of his brigade 'had spent itself' by 10a.m.[12] Supporting battalions found it equally difficult to get into the German second position. Captain P.S. Brindley (9/Devonshire, 20 Brigade) remembered how once his battalion had reached Gun Trench, it consisted of a 'mere handful of men' and he regarded any attempt to attack Cité St Elie as being 'useless'.[13] Even full strength battalions fared little better. By as early as 11a.m. Haisnes was 'strongly held' by the enemy, with both 11 and 12/Royal Scots being unable to take it.[14]

To understand why there was no 'decisive' breakthrough at Loos, it is necessary to examine how the British attempted to support the gains that had been made in the opening assault. Despite the great emphasis placed in the operation orders on the importance of battalions attacking 'all-out', it was clear that they could not go unsupported forever and would, sooner or later, require reinforcement. And until large reserve units (XI Corps) were on the battlefield, it was the task of the supporting battalions and reserve brigades of I and IV Corps to continue the attack. But this was not easy. Merely getting to the old British front line – let alone crossing no-man's-land – was fraught with difficulty. Persistent enemy shelling, long-range machine gun fire and the all-pervading 'fog of war', which at Loos literally meant lingering gas and smoke, hampered the attempts of not only the infantry, but also the artillery, to get forward. Indeed, it seems that this secondary phase of the battle, with the British attempting to support their initial gains, was the point when First Army 'lost' the Battle of Loos.

Immediately after the leading waves had left their assault trenches, the movement of support and reserve battalions began. For these units, moving up initially to the vacated front-trenches and then trying to reinforce the leading troops could be a trying experience. As one regimental history recorded, 'all the carefully drawn-up plans for the regulation of traffic in the communication trenches broke down during the stress of battle'.[15] It usually took between three and four hours for the reserve brigades to reach the old British front line. After being ordered forward soon after 6a.m., 21 Brigade reached its assigned position at 9.30a.m.[16] Similarly, 45 Brigade had arrived at the vacated British front line trenches by about this time.[17] But for other units, however, the journey forward was not as straightforward. It took four hours for Brigadier-General C.D. Bruce's 27 Brigade to reach the vacated British front lines, in what was described as a 'dreadful nightmare'.[18] Lieutenant-Colonel H.H. Northey (CO 6/Royal Scots Fusiliers) recalled how the trenches were 'absolutely choked with dead and wounded'.[19] It took 1/8th London (140 Brigade) three hours to move the one and half miles to the old German front line,[20] and 3 Brigade also recorded slow progress through the cluttered communication trenches of 1st Division.[21]

Crossing no-man's-land was an extremely perilous business. Because not all of the German strongpoints had fallen in the initial attack, enfilade fire swept across certain sectors of the front, particularly on the north of the battlefield. When the battalion headquarters of 5/Cameron Highlanders (26 Brigade) went forward at 7.30a.m. the officers present found out that 'the whole line of advance was enfiladed by heavy machine-gun and rifle fire from Mad Point'.[22] By the time one of its supporting battalions (8/Black Watch) had got past this obstacle, it was 'seriously diminished'.[23] So congested were the communication trenches behind 7th Division's front with wounded soldiers that 9/Devonshire (20 Brigade) was forced to move across the open towards Gun Trench. By the time it had got there, enfilade fire had caused heavy losses in officers and men.[24] Also because a number of the wounded, lying out in no-man's-land, occasionally fired their rifles to attract attention to their plight, the battlefield could be a bewildering place for those battalions moving up.[25]

It would take many more hours before the supporting and reserve battalions were in a position to continue the attack. And by the time they could do so, German reinforcements, especially machine gun detachments, had often arrived just in time to man parts of the second line and to hold up the advance. The leading battalions of 27 Brigade (11 and 12/Royal Scots) reached Pekin Trench at about 8.45a.m.[26] After skilfully trying to move forward, fierce fire from the upper stories of buildings in Haisnes and Cité St Elie prevented any further movement.[27] It was a similar situation in 20 Brigade. Its supporting battalions tried to cross the German second line, but the belts of protective wire had not been cut and accurate machine gun fire from *Stützpunkt II* and Hulluch prevented any attempts at this. And 21 Brigade, to the chagrin of some, was split earlier in the morning.[28] Instead of being used as a whole brigade, one half was sent to support the attack on Cité St Elie, while the other was to try and get into Hulluch. The left half of 21 Brigade (2/Yorkshire and 1/4th Cameron Highlanders) reached the Quarries at midday, while the right half of the brigade (2/Bedfordshire and 2/Wiltshire) sustained many casualties from machine guns in Cité St Elie and eventually ended up along Stone Alley and Gun Trench.[29] Although scattered elements of 1 Brigade entered Hulluch through a small gap in its protecting wire, they were held up by two companies of the reserve battalion of *157 Infantry Regiment* (*117th Division*).[30] The remnants of the brigade then reformed on the southern end of Gun Trench and Alley 4, with a senior officer not considering it advisable to attack the village until more support was received. The attack on the second line would have to wait.

If the British were to press the attack on the second line it was essential that the forward troops were supported with accurate artillery fire. But it seems that once the main assault had gone in, British artillery was unable to provide the infantry with the support they required. As had been the case throughout the preliminary bombardment, dust and bad light, as well as gas and smoke, made observation 'practically impossible'.[31] Heavy enemy shelling – a sure sign of the failure of British counter-battery fire – also compounded familiar communication difficulties. XXII Brigade RFA (7th Division) reported that the telephone wires for its FOOs were 'repeatedly cut' during the day.[32] Although XXXVI Brigade RFA (7th Division) only had one of its telephone cables cut, this still interrupted communication between all its units.[33] LI Brigade RFA (9th Division) was equally unsure of the situation in front of it and despite numerous attempts to ascertain how the attack had progressed, little information could be gained during the morning.[34]

The task of finding out what was going on and trying to correct British shelling was down to the liaison officers attached to the infantry. The difficulties these officers faced were legion. For example, L Brigade RFA (9th Division) spent most of 25 September anxiously awaiting orders to move forward. By 8a.m., when no information about the infantry attack had been received, an officer and two telephonists were sent forward to 'pick up' any information. Unfortunately, two of the party were killed as they laid out the line.[35] The diary of a young subaltern, P.H. Pilditch, attached to 1/6th London (140 Brigade, 47th Division), describes such difficulties. Although he was supposed to observe the progress of the shelling and send back information on targets, because he had not been supplied with either telephone equipment or signallers, there was little he could do. He spent the day 'helping to reconstruct the [captured German] parapet'.[36] On the following day when he had received the necessary equipment, his efforts to help British guns destroy a number of German machine gun posts on the Double Crassier were largely in vain. According to Pilditch, the battery 'shot deplorably'. He ascribed this either to worn-out guns or 'else the gun laying [must have been] shockingly poor'.

A vivid example of the failure of British artillery to support the infantry attack is contained in the Middlesex regimental history. Before the opening assault went in all artillery batteries were to shell the German first line, before lifting onto targets deeper into the enemy position. The system worked well enough if initial resistance was not too heavy, but if the attack went awry and the infantry were unable to progress, things rapidly fell apart, as the summary of messages between 19 Brigade and 1/Middlesex testify. At 6.57a.m. 19 Brigade asked for 'any news? How far have you advanced?' This was followed by a spate of messages from Lieutenant-Colonel F.G.M. Rowley (CO 1/Middlesex) detailing his battalion's plight.

6.50a.m.	Much opposition to our front. Please ask guns to shell Les Briques Trench.
7a.m.	Reserve Company has got on, but we are being very heavily fired at.
7.16a.m.	Line held up. Very heavy fire.
7.20a.m.	Ask guns to shell German front-line trench. Railway Trench I mean.
7.26a.m.	Don't think gas is affecting us or Germans. They are holding their front-line trench. Our battalion is all out in area between their front trench and ours. 2/Royal Welsh Fusiliers are now up. It is essential now to shell hostile front trenches.
7.30a.m.	Reported casualties probably 400, but impossible to tell. Have observed an enormous number fall.
7.55a.m.	Must shell German first line. Our men are all out in front. Almost all must be killed or wounded. Please shell first line.[37]

In just over one hour, Rowley had asked his supporting artillery to shell the German front line *five times*. Problems with artillery staff work were obviously being experienced because it proved so difficult for guns to be diverted from their prearranged fire-plans. But this precise scenario had been detailed in I Corps' Operation Order No. 106, which had been issued on 20 September, so it could not have been a totally unexpected proposition.[38]

Even if the attacks went according to plan, good artillery support was far from assured. As the reserve infantry brigades had already found out, it was often a time-consuming and taxing business to move past the series of trenches into open ground. LXXII Brigade RFA (15th Division) had trouble getting past a number of trenches because not all had been properly bridged.[39] The ground itself was also not conducive to good gunnery positions. Lieutenant-Colonel R.M. Ovens (CO 1/South Staffordshire, 22 Brigade) complained that because the ground was so open it was 'well nigh impossible to get the artillery to useful shelling range of Cité St Elie and its defences'.[40] So swept by fire were the open fields north of Loos that LXXIII Brigade RFA (15th Division) lost ten horses during the day.[41] While batteries that remained in the positions they had occupied throughout the preliminary bombardment did not suffer too heavily from enemy shellfire, for those that moved forward, severe casualties could be sustained. The artillery of 1st Division seems to have been hit particularly hard on 25/26 September. Five of the senior officers within XXVI Brigade RFA were all hit, 'and the command of both its batteries devolved on young subalterns'.[42]

But even so, it is clear that some intrepid gunners did manage to provide useful support for the infantry. The war diary of 12th Battery (XXXV Brigade RFA, 7th Division) recorded that after moving closer to the front line, 'Effective fire was opened on Puits Trenches and houses in [Cité] St Elie'.[43] On seeing the enemy front line fall, Lieutenant-Colonel H.H. Tudor (CO XIV Brigade RHA) ordered a section of 'T' Battery to advance eastwards along the Vermelles–Hulluch road. According to Tudor, 'T' Battery went 'down the road at a steady gallop', and although the leading driver and several horses were shot, the guns were positioned in a slight hollow near the German front line. They then opened fire on hostile infantry seen entering Cité St Elie.[44] Considering how lethal and confusing the battlefield was during the day, it is surprising just how many artillery batteries limbered up and made their way forward.[45] But because the battlefield was such a difficult environment, especially following the loss of the Quarries during the night, most of the batteries were withdrawn to their previous positions under the cover of darkness.

Despite the disappointing failure of the British to support and enlarge upon the advances of the morning, it is clear that further gains were not impossible, but would depend upon the arrival of large-scale reinforcements. It was during the afternoon that the bulk of the two leading divisions of XI Corps (21st and 24th Divisions) arrived on the battlefield; tired, bewildered and suffering from an 'appalling ignorance of the situation'.[46] It will be recalled that XI Corps had not had an easy march forward and had been delayed by the combined effects of overcrowding, poor traffic control and a lack of prior planning. Once on the battlefield, however, its problems multiplied rapidly. Not only were the battalions unsure about what lay ahead of them and had difficulty crossing the muddy battlefield in the darkness, which was 'intersected with trenches and barbed wire',[47] but also owing to a complete lack of suitable maps, they found it impossible to locate their exact position and had to march on a compass bearing of 112 degrees.[48] According to Lieutenant-Colonel Cosmo Stewart (GSO1 24th Division) the crossing of the battlefield was fraught with difficulty. He later remarked that 'the animals slipped on the boards of hastily made bridges and several vehicles tumbled into the trenches'.[49] A more unpromising introduction to war can hardly be imagined.

Eventually, however, the reserve divisions reached their allotted deployment areas. Within 24th Division, 71 Brigade had concentrated just south-east of Le Rutoire by 9p.m.[50] and 72 Brigade reached the old trenches of 1st Division at Lone Tree at 11.05p.m.[51] After a long, tiring night marching through the trenches, 73 Brigade, which had been sent to bolster the situation around the Hohenzollern Redoubt, gradually relieved 26 Brigade around 1a.m.[52] It was, however, more difficult for the brigades of 21st Division, which were to march a considerable distance further across the battlefield. 63 Brigade had taken over its positions in Chalk Pit Wood around midnight, relieving the remnants of 2 and 44 Brigades, but the situation remained extremely confusing for the other formations of 21st Division.[53] So bad did things get that two battalions of 62 Brigade (8/East Yorkshire and 10/Yorkshire) became lost, moved south-east and came under heavy enemy machine gun fire from Chalk Pit Copse, suffering a number of casualties before being pulled back.[54] Although this was an unfortunate (and singular) incident, it did not bode well for the following day.

But what were these tired, soaked-through brigades to do now that they were on the battlefield? In view of the heavy casualties sustained on 25 September and the difficulties the British had experienced when trying to reinforce and support the gains made during the morning, it is difficult to understand why Haig wanted to use XI Corps to mount an ambitious attack on the German second line for the following morning. According to Edmonds, the decision to attack with 21st and 24th Divisions was simply the result of indifferent communication and inaccurate reporting. This has been accepted by historians ever since.[55] Edmonds believed that early and generally optimistic messages emanating from the battlefield had convinced Haig that 'First Army was on the crest of the wave of victory; that it had broken through the German second and last line of defence in two central and vital places, Cité St Elie and Hulluch; and that a break-through at Haisnes and Cité St Auguste was imminent.' But he went on to write: 'The reports, as we know, had overestimated the successes, and the great losses suffered were scarcely mentioned.'[56] Admittedly, Edmonds had a point. The morning's reports had indeed reflected the sweeping success achieved on certain sectors of the front, but they had not all been so sanguine, and as the day dragged on, an increasing number of messages began to appear that told of units being 'held up by machine-gun fire' and the like. Indeed, from a close reading of the First Army war diary for this period, it is difficult to agree with Haig's breezy assertion in his diary that 25 September had been 'a very satisfactory' day 'on the whole'.[57]

Much of the writing that deals with the nature of command and control on the Western Front has tended to emphasise those factors that inhibited communication on the battlefield. Because of the unprecedented scale of the fighting, combined with the limitations of existing technology, the First World War was the only war in history fought without effective voice control.[58] In trench warfare, as Martin van Creveld has written, 'effective command often ended where the wire did'.[59] This meant that once troops had left the shelter of their own trenches, commanders in the rear found it very difficult to get an accurate assessment of the progress of the attack. Telephone wires were often cut by shellfire; visual signalling was generally ineffective (especially in bad weather) on smoky, shell-swept battlefields; runners were vulnerable to shell and small arms fire; and wireless sets were not yet available in sufficient numbers (and able to withstand the rigours of the field) to make a major difference to the flow of information. A combination of these factors had a deadening effect on the ability of British units to achieve a higher operational tempo than the enemy on a number of occasions, most notably the Battle of Neuve Chapelle (10–12 March 1915) and several times during the Battle of the Somme (for example on 1 and 14 July 1916).

Was this the case during the Battle of Loos? As soon as the main British assault south of the La Bassée canal began, First Army's command and control arrangements came under pressure from enemy shells and long-range machine gun fire. On certain sectors of the front communication broke down as telephone wires were cut, runners were killed and signalling proved useless in the poor weather conditions. For example, news of 28 Brigade's failed attack against Madagascar Trench filtered up the chain of command only slowly. A German shell hit the headquarters of 10/Highland Light Infantry, which killed most of the signalling staff, and as many officers had become casualties, exact information on what had happened only reached brigade headquarters when Major H.C. Stuart staggered in at noon.[60] Attacking on the other side of the Hohenzollern Redoubt was 5/Cameron Highlanders (26 Brigade). It attack may have been successful but its commanding officer (Lieutenant-Colonel D.W. Cameron of Lochiel) later wrote that 'There was practically no communication of any sort' on 25 September.[60] Indeed, the events of the coming days would show the Hohenzollern Redoubt to be a particularly lethal sector of the battlefield, under direct enemy observation and pounded by shellfire.

As British units, particularly those in the centre of the attack, moved away from their 'jumping off' positions, communication became, in many cases, progressively worse. Once 15th (Scottish) Division had broken through the first line of German trenches, communication between the front troops and divisional headquarters began to falter. Lieutenant-Colonel H.R. Wallace (CO 10/Gordon Highlanders) sent a message to 44 Brigade at 9.06a.m., reporting all the telephone wires had been cut,[62] and Brigadier-General M.G. Wilkinson (GOC 44 Brigade) also confirmed that during the afternoon communication was 'to a great extent lost and only kept up to a limited extent by runners'.[63] Similarly, Major R.H.D. Tompson (acting AA&QMG 7th Division between 12 and 22 September 1915) noted that it was 'Very difficult to get any information, and [the] situation [was] obscure everywhere'.[64] Little assistance could be gained from the RFC. The weather conditions, which were generally unfavourable for aerial observation, were aggravated by the gas discharge, with observers recording large clouds of smoke stretching some three miles from the German lines.[65] Indeed, while the smoke and gas discharge had helped to conceal the movement of troops through no-man's-land, it had also hindered the observation of the infantry.

However, not all areas of the battlefield were hit equally hard and communication functioned much better on other sectors. Having received messages reporting the failure of the attacks of 6 and 19 Brigades south of the La Bassée canal, and the unlikelihood of any further attempts succeeding, by as early at 9.45a.m. Major-General H.S. Horne (GOC 2nd Division) had decided to abandon operations for the day.[66] In part this was due to the fact that 2nd Division had not made any major gains, its operations were not vital to the success of the main assault, and it could also rely on buried cable from its own front line. Similarly, despite being unable to take the German position at Lone Tree, 2 Brigade remained in good communication with 1st Division all day.[67] On the southern sector of the battlefield, communication between 47th (London) Division headquarters and its brigades was 'well maintained' throughout the battle.[68] And even for the hard-pressed 44 Brigade, runners could still reach brigade headquarters in only thirty-four minutes.[69] It will be seen, therefore, that although getting accurate information to and from the front at Loos was never an easy matter, communication held up surprisingly well on 25 September. Those sectors where it had completely broken down (for example 28 Brigade) were largely irrelevant to the future of the British offensive. Admittedly, messages from 15th Division around Loos and Hill 70 may have been forced to rely on runners, but it seems that enough news made its way back from the battlefield for a rough appreciation of the situation to emerge.

How did the progress of the battle appear to General Sir Douglas Haig and his staff, anxiously awaiting news at the Chateau of Hinges? News of the fighting had been filtering in soon after the initial attacks began and they made encouraging reading.[70] At 6a.m. I Corps reported that the 'gas was going splendidly in front of 9th Division', and thirty-five minutes later the attack of 5 Brigade (2nd Division) had apparently advanced 'unopposed'. IV Corps experienced a similar situation and apart from what seemed like a temporary setback on the front of 2 Brigade, all attacks were progressing well. At 6.40a.m. IV Corps wired that the 'gas appeared to be effective' and five minutes later 1st Division was reported to be 'advancing rapidly'. By 7.05a.m. it was known that 47th Division had 'got off well' and forty minutes later it was confirmed that 15th Division too was 'getting on well', having reached the German support trenches. At 9.45a.m. IV Corps informed First Army that Loos and Puits 14 had been taken, and an hour later 7th and 9th Divisions were reportedly in Cité St Elie. By midday elements of 1st Division were apparently in Hulluch. Although the reports of British troops in the villages on the German second line were untrue (with the exception of a party of 1/Cameron Highlanders in Hulluch), most of the information received at Hinges was generally accurate and the great logistical operation that had preceded the battle enabled a considerable flow of information to be maintained even in the face of heavy shelling and long-range machine gun fire.

With the encouraging news of British success, the issue of XI Corps now resurfaced. The first mention of the reserves on 25 September seems to have come from Lieutenant-General Sir Henry Rawlinson (GOC IV Corps) who, in the first flush of success, put a telephone call through to Hinges at 8.30a.m. suggesting that XI Corps be moved up at once.[71] Rawlinson was obviously anxious to exploit the great success of 15th Division. He had apparently been told, rather optimistically, that he 'need keep nothing in reserve as the moment we had been successful another corps would be pushed through us'.[72] General Sir Douglas Haig agreed with his corps commander and immediately sent a staff officer to find the Commander-in-Chief and urge him to make sure XI Corps was ready to advance. But instead of being at GHQ in St Omer, Sir John French had spent the morning at Chateau Philomel, three miles south of Lillers, where, because of poor communications – there was only the normal French telephone system to rely on – he was much less able to direct operations.[73] Although French was eventually found and swiftly agreed to move 21st and 24th Divisions up, by this time it was around 9.30a.m. and precious time had been lost.[74] Sir John eventually arrived at Hinges two hours later. It was agreed that when the first brigade of 24th Division (73 Brigade) arrived on the battlefield it would come under I Corps' orders and make for Vermelles.[75] It was hoped that these troops would allow 9th Division to push on through the German second line. The leading brigade of 21st Division (62 Brigade) was attached to 15th Division and ordered to support the positions around Hill 70. Therefore, by the early afternoon of 25 September two brigades of the reserves divisions had already been parcelled off to I and IV Corps, leaving only four brigades still directly under the control of XI Corps. The Guards Division remained in GHQ reserve.

Events, however, rapidly ran away from Haig and First Army as the tide of battle began finally, and irrevocably, to turn against the British during the afternoon. It is clear that Haig knew (or *should* have known) great setbacks had occurred, especially on the north of the battlefield. Even on the more favourable terrain in the south, where 15th (Scottish) Division had done so well, Haig could not have failed to realise that the enemy was counterattacking in some strength. As early as 7.45a.m. reports had arrived from I Corps warning that the attacks had broken down north of the La Bassée road and ten minutes later a message from IV Corps told of 1st Division's problems with the gas. By 1p.m. I Corps admitted that the situation around Hulluch was unclear, and IV Corps reported that the Scottish battalions on Hill 70 were being heavily counterattacked and 'it was questionable whether 15th Division would be able to hold it'.[76] An hour later Haig was informed that the renewed attack of 28 Brigade had failed. By 3.50p.m. confirmation was received from 1st Division that it had finally cleared the enemy from Lone Tree, but this was the last of the good news. At 5.20p.m. a wire informed First Army that the attack on Cité St Elie had failed, and soon after this 2nd Division admitted that it had been unable to make any progress.

Despite the increasingly unsatisfactory news, the orders to XI Corps do not seem to have changed, indeed if anything, they became more ambitious. At 2.35p.m. 21st and 24th Divisions were ordered to 'push forward at once between Hulluch and Cité St Auguste and occupy [the] high ground between Haisnes and Pont à Vendin'. At 3.30p.m., despite knowing for two and a half hours that German counter-attacks were being made against Hill 70, and making no mention that two brigades had already been detached from its command, XI Corps was informed that:

> The IV Corps have captured Hill 70 east of Loos. The I Corps have entered Hulluch. The XI Corps (less Guards Division) will advance with a view to securing the crossings over the Haute Deule canal at Loison-sour-Lens – Harnes and Pont à Vendin.

News from the battlefield did eventually begin to curtail the scope of XI Corps' attack plans. At 7.50p.m., just as the leading reserve units were finally entering the battlefield, XI Corps received another set of instructions. This time it was a little more cautious. XI Corps was ordered to 'Secure and entrench a line from Hill 70 to the western end of Hulluch and link up with troops on the right and left'; to send out strong patrols towards the Haute Deule canal; and to bring up divisional artillery and be ready to continue the attack at daybreak in conjunction with neighbouring troops.

The orders for all three corps were finalised in the early hours of 26 September.[77] The plan that emerged eventually was a two-step staged offensive that would initially (at 9a.m.) take Hill 70 and Hulluch, thus clearing the flanks, so that the reserve divisions could then break the German centre. IV Corps would take Hill 70 and Hulluch, while I Corps pushed onto Cité St Elie. XI Corps' order called for 21st and 24th Divisions to be pushed through the German second line once the flanks had been secured. What would happen if this failed was not mentioned. But even this relatively straightforward (if somewhat sketchy) plan suffered from confusion and contradiction. It seems that Rawlinson thought he was commanding both 21st and 24th Divisions and the orders for I Corps made no mention of 73 Brigade, despite it being placed under Gough's command on the morning of 25 September.[78] It was surely obvious that the complete lack of clearly understood and definite orders, combined with a command structure that was rapidly collapsing under the strain of battle, did not bode well for the following day.

Why had Haig given the reserve divisions such ambitious orders in the face of the mixed news from the battlefield? There does not seem to have been any systematic, let alone detailed, plans for what the reserve divisions would do once they had reached the front. Haig did, however, have one rough idea. After the enemy had been sufficiently weakened, XI Corps would go forward and complete the victory. This uncertain situation was reflected in the orders issued to the reserve divisions throughout 25 September, and although these were modified several times in response to developments on the battlefield, there was no fundamental re-think about what they should do despite the increasingly grim news that arrived at Hinges. They were simply to attack, break the German second line and reach the Haute Deule canal. As had been a feature of much of the pre-battle preparation, Haig's chronic over-optimism was allowed to cloud his judgement and, if not ignore, then certainly suppress, much of the uncomfortable information he received at Hinges. Seemingly unable to get the early, encouraging reports of success out of his mind, as soon as Haking's corps entered First Army's area of operations, Haig pushed them forward as aggressively as possible, with apparently little thought about what they would do, except march eastwards and push through any lingering resistance in line with his belief in the structured battle.

According to Prior and Wilson, Haig's plan for 26 September was 'possessed of not a single redeeming feature',[79] but there has been little explanation of why such attacks went ahead. Communication between the firing line and the headquarters in the rear was undoubtedly problematic during the battle, but as shown, First Army had a fairly accurate – if delayed – picture of events on the battlefield. Yet from the orders issued to XI Corps, it is clear that this news had less of an impact on Haig than his pre-battle expectations, his belief in the structured battle and what a general reserve should (theoretically) accomplish. He decided, therefore, upon a very big second day, with poor artillery support and limited intelligence, in the knowledge that German reinforcements had arrived and were menacing British forward positions. And even given the mixed success of the first day, the plan for 26 September bordered on the reckless. Such a complex, inter-related and rushed attack was unworkable, and the reserve divisions had little understanding of the situation.

Before moving on to discuss the second day at Loos, when the reserve divisions finally went into action, it is necessary to review the events of 25 September more widely, including the casualties that had been suffered and the performance of the German Army. Nothing illustrates the industrialised slaughter at Loos better than the high level of British casualties. Exact figures for 25 September are difficult to assess, with the Official History recording a round figure of 470 officers and 15,000 other ranks.[80] If anything this estimate errs on the side of caution. Indeed, the average number of soldiers that died per division on 25 September 1915 was actually *higher* than the number sustained on the worst day of British military history, 1 July 1916.[81] According to the CD-ROM, *Soldiers Died in the Great War 1914-1919*, total recorded deaths for the six attacking divisions at Loos were 6,350. Using the accepted ratio of one death for every three soldiers who were wounded or missing, it is clear that casualties for the first day could have been as high as 19,000. Because they were almost continually in action between 25 and 27 September, statistics for those divisions in the central sectors of the battlefield are not specific for the first day, but they were certainly heavy. During the Loos operations 9th Division sustained

5,868 casualties.[82] There were 5,199 casualties in 7th Division.[83] 1st Division suffered 4,316 casualties.[84] Losses in 15th Division were very high, and as the divisional history noted, out of a total fighting strength of over 19,000 men, 6,606 died or were wounded in the battle.[85] The divisions on the flanks suffered far fewer losses, and because of their limited roles, exact figures for 25 September are much easier to come by. Casualties in 47th Division only amounted to sixty officers and 1,352 other ranks,[86] although 2nd Division suffered more heavily with ninety-one officers and 2,234 other ranks being recorded as killed, wounded or missing.[87]

Because Scottish divisions were making the main attacks, they suffered particularly heavily. By the evening of 25 September some battalions had been virtually destroyed. 5/Cameron Highlanders (26 Brigade) could muster only eighty soldiers and no more than forty-six men from 6/KOSB could be assembled.[88] 8/Black Watch (26 Brigade) also lost approximately seventy per cent of its strength during the main attack.[89] When Lieutenant-Colonel G.S. Cartwright (CRE 15th Division) went forward a little later in the day, he noticed how no-man's-land was 'carpeted with their [9/Black Watch] dead, lying so thickly that they almost touched all the way across'.[90] But it was not just Scottish units that suffered and some English battalions were also hit hard. While 10/Gloucestershire (1 Brigade) had barely 130 survivors by nightfall, 8/Devonshire (20 Brigade) lost nineteen officers and 600 men out of a total strength of 750.[91] Similarly, 2/Royal Warwickshire (22 Brigade) could muster only 140 men by nightfall.[92] Lone Tree was a particularly lethal sector of the battlefield, and when it was relieved later in the day, the strength of 2 Brigade only amounted to 1,550 all ranks.[93]

The *nature* of these losses was particularly shocking. Officer casualties were nothing short of disastrous. Even in relatively successful attacks, losses in certain units could be devastating. Despite being part of the most well-conducted divisional attack on 25 September, of the eighteen officers who went into action with 1/7th London (140 Brigade), ten were killed and four were wounded.[94] It was a similar situation within 15th Division and all company commanders in 9/Black Watch (44 Brigade) became casualties.[95] Equally grim statistics emerged from the central and northern sectors of the battlefield. The war diary of 10/Gloucestershire (1 Brigade) recorded that sixteen officers out of twenty-one had been hit,[96] and every officer – save three – were either killed or wounded within 8/Devonshire (20 Brigade).[97] Even 9/Devonshire, the reserve battalion of 20 Brigade, which did not actually take part in the initial attack, sustained grievous losses. According to its war diary:

> The CO, the second-in-command, and four company commanders all fell within a few yards of our front line, no-man's-land being swept by overhead machine-gun fire and shrapnel.[98]

21 Brigade sustained grievous losses trying to reinforce the forward positions. By the time it had reached Gun Trench, 2/Wiltshire had lost seven officers and 200 other ranks, while in 2/Bedford, the CO, Adjutant and all four company commanders, as well as over 200 men had been hit.[99] 9th Division also suffered appallingly. 26 Brigade's war diary recorded that 'a large number of our officers were killed and wounded',[100] and the ill-fated 28 Brigade fared as bad. While 10/Highland Light Infantry lost eighty-five per cent of its officers, twelve of the nineteen officers who went into action with 6/KOSB were killed and seven were wounded.[101]

But it was in the realm of *senior* officer casualties that Loos gained an almost unassailable place in the pantheon of British military disasters. It has not often been realised just how severe officer casualties were at Loos, and the devastating effect this had on the units concerned. Nine lieutenant-colonels (or acting battalion commanders) had been killed and twelve had been wounded.[102] And again, even in units that took part in attacks that were relatively successful, casualties could be very heavy. Owing to a burst of machine gun fire, Lieutenant-Colonel H.D. Collison-Morley (CO 1/19th London, 141 Brigade), his second-in-command and adjutant were all killed.[103] So bad were officer losses in 8/Seaforth Highlanders (44 Brigade) that only the adjutant remained to write up the report on the battalion's attack. He confirmed that:

> The losses were disastrous to the battalion with regard to senior officers. The colonel [Lieutenant-Colonel N.A. Thompson] and second in command, who had gone over the parapet well-forward, were left not far from our own trenches, and the four [company] commanders were in a similar case.[104]

In 10/Highland Light Infantry (28 Brigade), Lieutenant-Colonel J.C. Grahame was carried off the field suffering from the effects of the gas, his adjutant was killed and a German shell hit the battalion headquarters, which killed most of the signalling staff.[105] Perhaps reflecting the aggressive character of the divisional commander, high-ranking officer casualties suffered in Major-General Sir Thompson Capper's 7th Division were the worst of any division for the entire battle.[106] No less than five lieutenant-colonels had been killed and three wounded. Of Brigadier-General Trefusis's five commanding officers in 20 Brigade, two had been killed in action and another two seriously wounded. Afterwards he lamented that Lieutenant-Colonel E.I. de. S. Thorpe (CO 2/Border) was the 'only one left'.[107] Within 22 Brigade, Lieutenant-Colonel B.P. Lefroy (CO 2/Royal Warwickshire) was mortally wounded at the wire, while both 2/Royal Warwickshire and 1/South Staffordshire lost a number of company commanders.[108]

Why were regimental officer casualties so high? Common to all battalions, both Regular and New Army, were widely held notions on what duties officers were supposed to undertake. They were expected not only to be paternalistic towards their men and look after their welfare, but also to embody the ideal of an unselfish Christian gentleman.[109] According to one recent historian, one of 'the most important methods used by the British regimental officer… was to act as a leader in the most literal sense'.[110] And in the field these ideas rapidly turned into a 'model of heroic leadership' whereby officers were expected to lead by example, which in trench warfare, often meant that they were first 'over the top'.[111] On such a murderous battlefield as Loos it is of no surprise that a significant percentage of junior officers were killed or wounded. Indeed, so strong were these ideas of 'heroic leadership' that even senior regimental officers risked their lives by making themselves highly visible to their men. Lieutenant-Colonel F.W. Ramsay (CO 1/9th King's, Green's Force) even walked across no-man's-land carrying his distinctive white wand![112] An even more eccentric episode concerns Lieutenant-Colonel E.B. Macnaughten (CO XXXIX Bde RFA, 1st Division). In order to reassure his batteries, Macnaughten apparently 'had a table set with linen, cloth, napkins, and plates and put up at 'Lone Tree'… fully exposed to shellfire… where he took his lunch just as if in his mess in billets.'[113]

As well as the many examples of heroic leadership, another factor that increased officer casualties was the British uniform. While other ranks were issued with a khaki serge jacket with trousers and puttees, officers wore a jacket that had an open collar with lapels and numerous pockets, they were also expected to wear a dark khaki tie.[114] As might have been expected, German snipers found these differences especially helpful and were able to target British officers relatively easily. Captain L. McNaught-Davis (8/Lincolnshire, 63 Brigade) remembered how enemy snipers were hidden in the upper branches of trees in Bois Hugo and were 'picking off our men'.[115] Although British officers would gradually lose their distinctive uniforms in the trenches, by donning a private's uniform and arming themselves with a rifle and bayonet, it is evident that a majority of officers in this period wore traditional uniforms and suffered accordingly.

How had the Germans fared? Despite operating under considerable numerical inferiority, they had proved formidable adversaries. *IV Corps* had fought exceedingly well, doing just enough to blunt the initial British attack long enough for reinforcements to arrive and solidify the line. But this success had been bought at heavy cost, with the battalions defending the first line being in many cases wiped out. The Germans, however, had suffered far less than their attackers. Between 21 and 29 September, *Sixth Army* recorded casualties of 657 officers and about 29,000 other ranks.[116]

Losses were particularly heavy in *117th Division*, with 5,600 casualties, and *123rd (Saxon) Division*, which lost 2,500 men. *26 Reserve Infantry Brigade* (*117th Division*), heavily involved at Loos, suffered over 2,000 casualties. Perhaps reflecting the relatively high instances of the murder of prisoners, it seems that relatively few German soldiers were captured at Loos. For example, 9th Division captured barely five officers and 168 other ranks[117] although 47th Division did slightly better, recording eight officers and 302 other ranks, with three field guns being taken.[118]

Most German units had suffered heavily by the end of the day, but their defensive tactics had proved effective. It seems that relatively few defenders were left in the trenches when the British attacked, with only enough to crew the machine guns, the majority sheltering in the support trenches. This was particularly noticeable on the front of 2nd Division. According to the divisional history:

> All along the line it had been noticed that the enemy's front-line trenches were but lightly held until the attack began; then after opening a very heavy fire from his support trenches, he rushed men up to the front line in time to meet the assaulting parties and decimate them almost on the wire.[119]

Although artillery would become the major man-killer in later years of the war, the machine gun was still the most deadly weapon on the battlefield in 1915. Heavy machine gun fire could be devastating against lines of unprotected infantry, especially those in clumsy linear formations. According to the historian of 8/Black Watch (26 Brigade), 'probably at no other time during the whole war did the 8th ever come under machine gun fire so intense and deadly as that at Loos'.[120] Most of the German machine guns were firing on prearranged lines, and as was experienced by the British the following year on the Somme, a great number of these were sited low. The war diary of 19 Brigade recorded how many of its wounded were hit in 'the lower part of the legs or ankles'.[121] But even so, resistance was often much stronger at the support line. This was the case with 22 Brigade,[122] and 19 Brigade recorded communication trenches that were 'packed with men. It would seem that [the] enemy fires from his support trenches at the first assault while other troops rush up the front line.'[123] This could be slightly surprising. Once it had crossed no-man's-land, 8/Royal Berkshire (1 Brigade) found the German front line 'practically deserted'.[124]

Sixth Army had launched several counter-attacks across the open during the day. Most of them, apart from the recapture of the Quarries during the night of 25/26 September, were unsuccessful, simply melting away against heavy British rifle fire. They seem to have been characterised by the weight of numbers; perhaps a reflection of rushed preparations or

1 *Above:* The Loos battlefield.

2 *Right:* Earl Kitchener of Khartoum, British Secretary of State for War.

3 *Above:* Field-Marshal Sir John French, Commander-in-Chief BEF.

4 *Left:* Crown Prince Rupprecht of Bavaria, GOC German *Sixth Army*.

5 *Right:* General Ferdinand Foch, Commander French *Groupe d'Armées du Nord*.

6 *Below:* General Joseph Joffre, French Commander-in-Chief (right) and Sir John French (on left talking to liaison officer) at Calais railway station, June 1915.

7 Sir John French leaving Joffre's headquarters at Chantilly.

8 *Opposite:* General Sir Douglas Haig (GOC First Army).

9 Lieutenant-General Hubert Gough (GOC I Corps).

10 Lieutenant-General Sir Henry Rawlinson (GOC IV Corps).

11 *Left:* General Sixt von Armin (GOC German *IV Corps*).

12 *Below:* 'Tower Bridge' and Loos village.

13 *Above:* British troops marching through a French village, summer 1915.

14 *Below:* A Scottish battalion moving up to the front.

15 Irish Guardsmen wearing PH gas helmets.

16 German barbed wire defences.

17 High-explosive shell exploding in no-man's-land.

18 View of 'The Dump' and Miners' houses from the British front line.

19 View of Fosse 8 and Corons de Maroc.

20 Artist's impression of the British infantry assault.

21 Soldiers of the 47th Division advancing towards the enemy lines.

22 View of Loos and Hill 70

23 Ruined street in Loos village.

24 Carnage on the battlefield.

25 German troops in the Quarries.

26 View of the 'Field of Corpses'.

27 British troops in trenches near the Quarries, October 1915.

28 The attack on 13 October 1915.

simple ignorance of British forward positions. A counter-attack against 9/Devonshire (20 Brigade) 'came on in several thick lines'.[125] Colonel L.G. Oliver (CO 13/Middlesex, 73 Brigade) remembered a similar situation. According to him, a German counter-attack marched, 'in columns of platoons and were mowed down like grass'.[126] Similarly, on 26 September, 2/Welsh (3 Brigade) watched German forces readying to counter-attack. At 10.50a.m., 'Masses of Germans came out of Bois Hugo and advanced in one great mass but five heavy shells fell right in the middle of them and the whole lot turned around and bolted.'[127] When counter-attacks were properly supported and well planned, however, they were very difficult to resist. At 10.30a.m. the reserve battalion of *178 Regiment*, billeted in the northern part of Lens, received an order to march for Cité St Laurent to stop British troops from getting through the second line.[128] By the skilful use of enfilade fire from the railway embankment, combined with a rush forward, the crest of Hill 70 was captured in the early afternoon and the mixed-up Scottish battalions were sent reeling back in disorder. But although rushed attacks across the open were usually repulsed, German infantry outmatched and consistently outperformed the British in bombing operations. This was largely due to their superior model of grenade, which was available in far greater numbers than the primitive British varieties. German rifle grenades were also notably effective.[129] For example, on the morning of 25 September, when 6/Cameron Highlanders (45 Brigade) tried to bomb up the German trenches towards Lone Tree, it barely progressed 60 yards before being stopped by a strong barrier, 'manned by hostile bombers with a machine gun'.[130] This was not an untypical experience. The depressingly familiar experiences of British troops in and around Fosse 8 and the Hohenzollern Redoubt in the coming days would prove how inferior the British were in this respect.[131]

When examining the events of 25 September, it will be seen that the real failure of the British was in being unable to achieve a higher operational tempo than the German defenders and move their support and reserve units forward quicker than enemy reinforcements. This meant that by the time First Army had marshalled enough strength to advance upon further objectives, long-range machine gun fire effectively stopped the infantry in their tracks. Why had First Army been unable to bring its supporting battalions forward quick enough? The failure of the preliminary bombardment was an important factor. Because a number of German strongpoints (particularly Mad Point and Lone Tree) were relatively unscathed by British shellfire, they were able to enfilade any movement on either side. The complete failure of British counter-battery fire also left German artillery free to shell the battlefield. Considering the large number of British troops crammed into the lines south of the La Bassée canal,

German shells, more often than not, found a target. Moreover, the failure to support the gains of the first day also stemmed from the way the battle had been planned. Because it was envisaged that the attacking battalions would go a considerable way into the German position, little attempt had been made to institute a careful and methodically organised system of reinforcement and relief. Battalions were told – in somewhat vague terms – to simply attack 'all-out'. Whereas in later years troops would go forward according to a detailed plan of 'leapfrogging', with the movement of units being highly-structured and well-known, the situation at Loos was chaotic. Communication trenches were in many cases small, cramped, too few in number and often under heavy German shellfire. This meant that a number of battalions, frustrated at the lack of progress, simply climbed out of them and advanced across the open, often with devastating results. As has been shown, once the initial attacks had broken down, very few officers and men had any idea about where they were supposed to be, or what they were supposed to be doing. It was a disastrous situation and one that would only get worse as the British continued their attacks in the following days.

7

THE SECOND DAY: 26 SEPTEMBER 1915

26 September 1915 was a day of disaster for the BEF. Primarily remembered for the abortive attack on the German second line by the reserve divisions (21st and 24th Divisions) and their subsequent retreat from the battlefield, it also featured heavy fighting around Hill 70, Hulluch and the Quarries as the British attempted to capitalise upon their gains of the previous morning. And while the character of the fighting could differ greatly on each side of the battlefield, from the close-fought bombing attacks on the northern sector, to the sweeping infantry movements further south, the experiences of I, IV and XI Corps during the day were remarkably similar. Early German counterattacks unbalanced the British and when First Army attempted to get forward, its operations were characterised by poor organisation, weak artillery support and a lack of information. Many of the attacks were also terribly rushed. Little ground was secured, heavy casualties were sustained and for the reserve divisions at least, the day ended in ignoble retreat.

Making sense of the second day of the Battle of Loos can be problematic. Although the fighting on the first day was at times confusing, it is not too difficult to trace the movements of different battalions throughout the day. Units began 25 September in clearly defined positions and with familiar objectives. On the following day, however, things were different.

They began it scattered, considerably below strength (excepting, of course, the reserve divisions) and with little or no idea of where they were supposed to be going and what resistance lay in their path. The fighting that subsequently occurred was so close, fluid and free flowing that it is at times impossible to assess what happened accurately. Nevertheless, without gas and smoke to confuse the issue, it is clear that Haig's ambitious plans for 26 September fell apart rapidly when confronted with the situation at the front. Lacking artillery support and suffering from a catastrophic breakdown in command and control (including poor staff work, few adequate maps and a lack of planning for the secondary stage of the offensive), the renewed attacks were lamentable failures, with the attacking battalions unable to progress in the face of unsuppressed enemy machine gun fire and uncut belts of barbed wire.

Before discussing what has traditionally been regarded as the main drama of the day – 21st and 24th Division's attack on the German second line – it is necessary to examine the operations that were intended to stabilise First Army's position on the northern sector of the battlefield, which had been under increasing pressure since the afternoon of the previous day. At 1a.m. part of *117th Division*, reinforced by *26 Reserve Brigade*, delivered an attack on the British positions around Fosse 8 and the Quarries. This operation was part of a series of local counter-attacks ordered the previous afternoon by the commander of *IV Corps*, General Sixt von Armin, and did much to determine the character of the second day. By nightfall on 25 September, the Quarries were garrisoned by a mixture of British units from 20 and 21 Brigades (7th Division), all under-strength, tired and soaked to the skin. For the next two hours utter chaos reigned in this sector and at 2a.m., after getting word that the Quarries had been abandoned, an intense British bombardment began, forcing the surviving defenders to retire. By 3a.m. most of the British units had retreated back to the old German front line in some confusion.[1]

The loss of the Quarries on the night of 25/26 September highlighted the real difficulties that the British found in trying to react to the enemy and counterattack effectively at this period of the war. It also marked the loss of British initiative on the northern sector of the battlefield, which First Army would spend the rest of the battle trying desperately to regain. It is little wonder that a slightly bewildered corps commander, Lieutenant-General Hubert Gough, could later write how he was 'faced with fresh anxieties'.[2] Instead of planning to get into Cité St Elie and the second German line, he was forced to concentrate on shoring up his own position. But this was not easy. The difficulties of organising reinforcements, moving up troops and getting artillery forward that had been experienced on

25 September were to be repeated in the following days. As the supporting battalions and reserve brigades had already discovered, moving through the maze of trenches and getting into the correct positions took a great deal of time and effort. Brigadier-General W.A. Oswald's 73 Brigade (24th Division) had been ordered to relieve 26 Brigade (9th Division) at 5.21p.m. the previous evening.[3] According to one regimental officer:

> No clear view of the ground, still to be covered, had been possible by daylight, and in the darkness the business of crossing a maze of muddy trenches, shell holes, broken entanglements and the debris of battle caused endless confusion, loss of direction and stragglers.[4]

This was not an unusual experience and those battalions tasked with recapturing the Quarries faced similar difficulties. One of 7th Division's staff officers, Lieutenant-Colonel G.H. Boileau, grimly noted how the men of 9/Norfolk (71 Brigade) were 'dropping with fatigue' from their exhausting approach march by the time they had reached the front line.[5]

First Army made two attempts to recapture the Quarries; two attempts to enter Hulluch; and two attempts to retake Hill 70 on 26 September. All failed, and for similar reasons. They were rushed, piecemeal attacks against a hardening defence, and were conducted with poor artillery support, woefully inadequate preparation and almost non-existent staff work. The battalions involved tended to be already tired and hungry when they went into action – in some cases they had suffered heavy casualties, were mixed up and leaderless – and because the situation was often vague, they were only given a basic objective with the bare minimum of battlefield intelligence. The first attempt to secure the Quarries was made by 9/Norfolk, which had been detached from 71 Brigade the previous evening,[6] and never had a chance of succeeding. Such was the state of the British trenches that the battalion had only reached the old German front line by 5.30a.m., and as a result, had little time to reconnoitre the ground. The attack at 6.45a.m. was a predictable failure.[7]

Subsequent attacks fared little better. 2/Worcestershire experienced a whole catalogue of problems as it endeavoured to move up to the front.[8] The battalion received its orders to move out at 1.15a.m. on the morning of 26 September. It was to 'march today so as to reach the fields west of Annequin and south of the La Bassée road at 9a.m. tomorrow to form part of a detached brigade under Colonel [B.C.M.] Carter'. Because the message had been handed to brigade signallers at 12.55a.m., some confusion was experienced about what day the order was referring to. Battalion staff were, however, eventually informed that the attack was to be delivered on 26 September. Just over an hour later the battalion received a more detailed order concerning the exact line of march it was to take. Unfortunately, the wrong map square was given and further delay was caused in correcting this error. The battalion started marching at 4a.m. and it was over twelve hours later (4.15p.m.) when it reached the British front line from where the assault was to take place! The subsequent attack, horribly rushed, was beaten back by heavy enemy gunfire, with the survivors taking cover in an old half-dug German trench in the middle of no-man's-land.

The attempt to secure Hulluch by 3 Brigade (1st Division) was an even more vivid example of how First Army had in many cases completely lost control of its front-line battalions on 26 September. Orders for 2/Welsh only arrived at 10.20a.m., barely forty minutes before they were supposed to move out. The battalion was to take the village of Hulluch in conjunction with 1/Black Watch and 1/South Wales Borderers (also of 3 Brigade), but it seems that a combination of unexpected enemy movements and heavy shelling, which destroyed the only telephone set at battalion headquarters, resulted in 2/Welsh attacking alone.[9] The assault was swept away by heavy machine gun fire from six German machine gun teams in the upper storeys of the Hulluch. When the remaining two battalions of 3 Brigade finally advanced against Hulluch at midday, the same gunners, who had proved so devastating to the attack of 2/Welsh, also raked the battalions with heavy fire.[10]

The renewed attempt to secure Hill 70 also failed. By the morning of 26 September the situation of 15th (Scottish) Division was highly precarious. Units were mixed up, often leaderless, tired, short of ammunition, food and water, and were occupying only thin trenches below the crest. Half of 45 Brigade was sheltering in Loos, while two battalions (13/Royal Scots and 11/Argyll and Sutherland Highlanders) had relieved several groups of mixed-up Scottish troops and were spread out on the slopes of Hill 70. The unpromising situation did not go unnoticed and Major-General F.W. McCracken (GOC 15th Division) complained about renewing the attack, but was overruled by his corps commander (Lieutenant-General Sir Henry Rawlinson).[11] Disregarding the opinion he had formed following the Battle of Neuve Chapelle (10–12 March 1915) that 'when the enemy has been able to man his second line of defence it is a waste of life to attack him until the heavy guns are able to pulverise these localities', Rawlinson does not seem to have been too perturbed by the difficulty of the operation.[12] In any case, he made no attempt to communicate any private fears higher up the chain of command. He later recorded in his diary that 'All looked well for breaking enemy's last defences'.[13] To be fair to Rawlinson, there was little he could do. The taking of Hill 70 and Hulluch were operations vital to the success of the main attacks to take place later in the morning. If Hill 70 and Hulluch were still in enemy hands by the time the remaining units of 21st and 24th Divisions attacked at 11a.m., German troops would be able to enfilade the advance onto the second line, which would place the whole operation in jeopardy. Whatever his reservations the objectives *had* to be taken.

Major-General McCracken's fears were, however, justified. Orders for the attack had arrived at the headquarters of 15th Division at 5a.m., but as might have been expected, they took much longer to reach the battalions in the front line.[14] While some battalions of 45 Brigade received their orders in good time, others were only handed theirs between 7 and 8a.m., just as the preliminary bombardment was about to begin. Indeed, orders only reached 13/Royal Scots at 9a.m.[15] The attack was to be led by 45 Brigade at 9a.m., supported from the north by 62 Brigade, after an intensive bombardment lasting an hour. It seems that the troops had advanced punctually, but against heavy enemy rifle and machine gun fire, progress was limited. Although elements of the attacking battalions (7/Royal Scots Fusiliers, 11/Argyll & Sutherland Highlanders and 13/Royal Scots) managed to push on through the perimeter trench and drive the enemy garrison from the redoubt, as was typical of such poorly organised attacks, the gains were impossible to preserve.[16] Fierce enfilade and cross fire swept the summit, causing heavy casualties and forcing the battalions to settle back below the crest line where cover was available.

Why had it proved so difficult to take Hill 70? Lack of artillery support was a key factor. Although a number of batteries had managed to get forward during the previous day, most had been moved back during the night, and the majority of 15th Division's guns were still behind the British front line on the morning of 26 September.[17] For those few batteries that had moved forward, heavy enemy shelling was a constant problem. The war diary of LXXIII Brigade RFA recorded that after reaching a position north of Loos, its guns were 'subjected to artillery, rifle and maxim fire', which was fortunately directed too high.[18] Similarly 'B' and 'C' Batteries had three horses killed, and when LXXI Brigade RFA moved forward to a position west of Loos, it was heavily shelled all day.[19] Poor organisation only hampered matters. The history of the Royal Artillery admitted that 'the heavies continued to work on counter-battery tasks and their fire was not really co-ordinated with the rest. Indeed, ammunition soon became so short that rates of two rounds per battery per minute were being imposed!'[20] Ironically, the bombardment was 'extremely accurate',[21] but owing to the lateness that many units received their orders, a number of battalions had been unable to move back in order to avoid the shellfire and suffered accordingly.[22]

The late arrival of orders seems to have been a particular problem for 62 Brigade. Scheduled to support the attack from the north, 13/Northumberland

Fusiliers did not receive notification of the preliminary bombardment and that they would be required to pull their companies back to avoid the shelling. The war diary recorded that 'before the withdrawal could be ordered our shells were dropping amongst our own men'.[23] The battalion was forced to retreat and then had to abandon the attack. The war diary of 45 Brigade bitterly lamented the performance of 62 Brigade because it 'never came on, though had it done so it seems extremely probable that the position would have been carried'.[24] However, this was never likely. 62 Brigade had originally been asked to support the Scots from the north, but owing to difficulties of getting the men into the correct positions, it had been decided that 62 Brigade would simply support 45 Brigade closely in the rear.[25] Two battalions (10/Yorkshire and 12/Northumberland Fusiliers) had taken part in the attack, advancing towards Hill 70 on either side of the Loos–Hill 70 track, about 200 yards behind 45 Brigade. But, as might have been expected, under heavy enemy gunfire the attack wavered and while parties of 12/Northumberland Fusiliers managed to get over the crest and break into the enemy trenches, they ran into 'very severe' machine gun fire and were forced to retreat.[26]

While the flanking operations on 26 September have been largely forgotten, the actions of the reserve divisions have been the subject of much myth and misunderstanding. It is commonly assumed that *both* 21st and 24th Divisions advanced upon the German second line at 11a.m., losing over 8,000 men in 'little over an hour' in the long grass of what became known as the '*Leichenfeld von Loos*' (the 'field of corpses').[27] Although often repeated, this is incorrect. According to official figures, 21st Division suffered 4,051 casualties, and the 24th Division another 4,178.[28] But these, it should be noted, were sustained during the whole day and not in 'little over an hour' as is commonly assumed. Exact German casualties for 26 September are harder to ascertain. They were much less than the British, although certainly not the 'zero' as quoted by Alan Clark.[29] Regarding the actual operations, historians have often confused two separate actions. Only one and a half brigades of 24th Division actually reached the 'corpse field' – half of the division had been sent to bolster the line further north – while two brigades of 21st Division had been heavily counterattacked by *153 Infantry Regiment* around Bois Hugo and Chalk Pit Wood since daylight and never reached the German second line.

Dealing first with the German counterattack through Bois Hugo, which has been consistently neglected in writing about the second day of the Battle of Loos, it will be seen that this was one of the most important events of the day, fatally unbalancing 21st Division and doing immense damage to 72 and 71 Brigades when they advanced later in the day. What had happened? During the hours of darkness 63 Brigade had taken up advanced positions around the Chalk Pit and Bois Hugo and started digging in, but by as early as 9a.m. enemy pressure had begun to increase. 63 Brigade was facing the brunt of a vicious German counter-attack conducted by troops of *153 Infantry Regiment (8th Division)*, part of *106 Regiment* and *178 Regiment (123rd (Saxon) Division)* from the far side of Bois Hugo.[30] Although British resistance, especially rifle fire, seems to have been most effective – 'heavy casualties' were apparently caused in the attacking German waves[31] – by 10.15a.m. parties of 8/Lincolnshire and 12/West Yorkshire were flooding back across the Lens–Hulluch road to the cover provided by the Chalk Pit.[32] Although a second line was quickly formed, barely fifteen minutes later large parties of the brigade were retreating steadily westwards.[33]

Command and control had clearly broken down under the stress of battle. When two companies of 10/York & Lancaster were sent to reinforce 8/Lincolnshire, the order was misunderstood and the whole battalion rushed down through Chalk Pit Wood into an enemy bombardment. Despite being only 1,000 yards apart, a message from 63 Brigade took over an hour to reach 64 Brigade.[34] By 10.30a.m. 14/Durham Light Infantry, which had been sent forward to support the troops in Bois Hugo, collided with the retiring elements of 63 Brigade. According to 64 Brigade's war diary:

> On coming round the northern end, and seeing the 14/Durham Light Infantry against its western edge they [elements of 63 Brigade] apparently [mis]took them for Germans owing to their wearing long greatcoats, and made a change of direction as if to attack the 14/Durham Light Infantry in flank.[35]

The error was soon realised, but not before 14/Durham Light Infantry had passed through the lines of retreating men into heavy machine gun fire from Bois Hugo.[36] Unfortunately, the harrowing fate that befell 14/Durham Light Infantry was not unique to 64 Brigade, and the day witnessed a number of errors, mistakes and 'blue on blue' incidents.

The experience of 64 Brigade on 26 September can be divided into two sections, which although separate, were remarkably similar, and can be briefly summarised. The first concerns the harrowing experience of 14 and 15/Durham Light Infantry. In accordance with the orders to resume a large-scale advance, both battalions had been ordered forward to secure Puits 14 at 11a.m., but instead of moving eastwards, the battalions were drawn to the right and advanced southeast. As they did so they were fired upon by German troops in Bois Hugo and Chalet Wood. However, instead of dealing with these enemy positions, they continued marching towards

Hill 70, where they were finally brought to a halt by heavy machine gun fire from the crest. The war diary of *106 Reserve Regiment*, part of which garrisoned Hill 70, noted that the effect of this fire from two sides 'was very considerable, whole lines being mown down by the machine guns'.[37] The second part of 64 Brigade's operations on 26 September concerns the remaining two battalions (9 and 10/KOYLI), which were again also unwittingly diverted south-east. Brigadier-General G.M. Gloster (GOC 64 Brigade) had originally been 'averse to throwing in the battalions', and thought it best to remain in position and await further developments or reinforcements.[38] Unfortunately, and seemingly without any orders, 9/KOYLI suddenly began moving off eastwards at 1.45p.m. In some alarm and confusion, and having completely lost control of his own battalion, the commanding officer (Lieutenant-Colonel C.W.D. Lynch) ran after it in a vain attempt to stop the advance. In his absence, it was hurriedly decided that 10/KOYLI should follow up in support, but the two battalions were *not* to go further than the Loos–Hulluch road. But it seems that these orders did not reach a number of company commanders and advancing into storms of shellfire, the battalions marched *past* the road and *continued up* the slope of Hill 70, straight into a number of trenches held by survivors of 15th Division. 9 and 10/KOYLI did not last long; they were 'crumpled up by flanking enemy machine gun fire and shrapnel', and then began to retreat, coming back towards the British lines.[39]

At 11a.m. therefore, owing to the failure to secure Hulluch and Hill 70, and the disabling effects of the German counter-attack through Bois Hugo, the 'main' British attack would now only consist of 72 Brigade, supported in the rear by two battalions of 71 Brigade. This was woefully inadequate to take such a strongly defended and wired position. By the morning of 26 September, the German second line between Hulluch and Cité St Elie was manned by six composite battalions of infantry.[40] The second line had not been 'softened' to any great extent by the preliminary bombardment, and in any case, extra wire entanglements had been thrown out during the night. Details of the epic march of the six battalions through shellfire across open ground (which would be later christened the 'corpse field') up the low rise upon which lay the German second line can be found in numerous regimental histories, war diaries and personal accounts. All make for harrowing reading. It is clear that the failure to secure the flanks meant that 72 Brigade not only came under machine gun and rifle fire from German troops manning the second line, Bois Hugo and Hulluch, but was also shelled by the artillery of *117th* and *8th Divisions*.[41] During the advance to the 'corpse field', Colonel E. Vansittart (CO 8/Royal West Kent, 72 Brigade) urgently penned a message reporting 'very heavy frontal, as well as enfilade fire from both flanks, and shelling from our left rear'.[42] It is also possible that 9/East Surrey came under *reverse* fire from Bois Hugo.[43] A more unpromising position can hardly be imagined and, as might have been expected, when the thinned ranks of 72 Brigade reached the German wire, which was uncut, covered in long grass and about twenty yards deep,[44] the advance came to a standstill. The German position remained unbroken. General Haig's gamble had failed.

Reaction to the failure of 21st and 24th Divisions to break the German second line was swift and not entirely praiseworthy from British High Command. When Haig received the news later that afternoon he became angry and threatened to have the man who had sent it court-martialled for spreading alarmist reports.[45] Rawlinson was equally dismayed, believing that the divisions involved had 'behaved badly'.[46] In a letter to Lord Kitchener, written three days later, his opinions had not changed. He felt that the attack on the second line had failed because of 'Bad discipline and want of food and secondly to attacking an entrenched position strongly wired and held without adequate artillery support'.[47] Haig also confided to his diary that the reason for the debacle 'is said to be that the men had not been fed'.[48] Haig, and to a lesser extent Rawlinson, fought on a 'moral battlefield' and it is clear that fears over the 'quality' of the New Army clouded their judgements and, in effect, excused the lamentable failures of the second day. Although exact information about the fate of the reserves would take several days to gather, it was generally accepted by Haig and his staff that the reason for the failure of the attacks was because of the inexperience of the troops (with their late arrival) and *not* because they had been given an impossible task to perform. As Haig's diary recorded, the new divisions 'did not look out for themselves'.[49]

But was this correct? How much of the disaster was down to internal weaknesses (such as poor training, morale and fighting skills) within the divisions, as Haig and Rawlinson stressed, and how much related to other factors? The bulk of the evidence, especially that emanating from the battlefield, does *not* support the view taken by the British High Command. Indeed, on reading the numerous war diaries and personal accounts, it is very difficult to take any other view that the reserves, especially 21st Division, were committed to an extremely dangerous situation, hampered by a catastrophic series of handicaps, including lack of information, the poor condition of the men, heavy enemy attacks and very little artillery support. As regards 24th Division, to paraphrase Rawlinson, the *main and only reason* the attack failed was because of 'attacking an entrenched position strongly wired and held without adequate artillery support' and not simply 'want of food'. Haig and Rawlinson's reaction was consistent with their belief in the importance of morale, discipline and 'offensive spirit' on the battlefield, and reflected both their suspicions of wartime volunteers and the difficulty there were having in coming to terms with the changing nature of warfare with its industrialised levels of slaughter.

Sir James Edmonds was of a similar opinion. The verdict recorded in the British Official History was kinder to the reserve divisions, but did not completely exonerate them. Edmonds spent several pages discussing the 'many legends', which 'have grown up as regards the failure of the 21st and 24th Divisions at Loos'.[50] Although the troops were admittedly brave, Edmonds believed that the attacks were doomed to fail because of the lack of adequate staff work and training, particularly so that officers could 'take advantage of every opportunity and meet every situation'. While he believed that the 'exertions demanded' of them were 'small as compared with those of the original five divisions of professional soldiers of the BEF', he was forced to admit that the divisions were 'asked to do a nearly impossible task'. He squared this circle by blaming Sir John French for his decision to keep the reserve divisions under his own control and neglecting the tactical decisions made by First Army once the reserve divisions were on the battlefield. Edmonds was clearly not telling the whole story.

In a report written by Major-General G.T. Forestier-Walker (GOC 21st Division) on 15 October 1915, he cited seven reasons for the retirement as well as seven other points for consideration.[51] These included the effect of artillery fire on new troops; the exhausted state of the men; the loss of senior officers at critical times (especially in 63 Brigade); the assault on Hill 70 taking place two hours before the main attack; the poor state of British artillery and heavy casualties. Forestier-Walker also mentioned the lack of water, intermingling, loss of officers and the loss of equipment. He was certainly not happy with the way his division had been employed. He later complained that 'even seasoned regular divisions would have had to do extraordinarily well to have coped successfully with not only the enemy in front, but with the bad staff work of higher commanders, the frequent counter-orders and the disgraceful lack of organisational control in the district behind the front line'. To employ the two reserve divisions in such a situation was, according to him, 'nothing short of criminal'.[52] A report by Major-General J.E. Capper (appointed GOC 24th Division, 3 October 1915) concurred with Forestier-Walker's opinion, if a little more tactfully. It noted that 'unofficial reports… cast a most undeserved slur on the conduct of the infantry in this division'.[53] Capper was of the opinion 'that the conditions before the men were engaged were very trying indeed, that when called upon to act, both officers and men advanced gallantly and did their best, and that the best trained troops in the whole of the British or any other army would have found it difficult to succeed where the infantry of the 24th Division failed'.

Whatever Haig and Rawlinson may have thought, the attack on the 'corpse field' showed the excellent cohesion, bravery and determination possessed by many New Army battalions. According to eyewitness accounts, the advance of 72 Brigade towards the enemy position, despite requiring a quarter-circle move in its line, was carried out with perfect precision. And although advancing into a lethal re-entrant in the German line and being under 'very heavy frontal, as well as enfilade fire from both flanks, and shelling',[54] the battalions managed to reach the enemy wire in sufficient numbers to have broken the line had there been a way through. Captain B.A. Fenwick (9/East Surrey, 72 Brigade) believed that the wire 'was reached in sufficient force to take the position but it was absolutely intact'.[55] Colonel Vansittart agreed. He later remarked to Edmonds that 'had the wire entanglement been cut, we should assuredly have carried the position'.[56] As one regimental history recorded, although 'the position was desperate… some gallant but unavailing efforts were made to get through the wire'.[57] But this was impossible. Although numerous fire-suppression and wire-cutting parties were hurriedly arranged and went to work, most of the men were left 'trying to tear away uncut German wire with their hands'.[58]

A point of some criticism was the manner of 21st and 24th Division's retirement from the battlefield and there are a number of conflicting reports on this. Even as to the basic fact of whether it was a retirement, retreat or rout, there is no agreement. The most severe indictment can be found in the 2/Welsh war diary, which recorded that 'To [our] amazement and disgust the whole corps [*sic*] on our right turned around and bolted in wild panic – throwing away equipment. In this rout they all bunched together and made a good mark for German shrapnel and machine guns in Hulluch and consequently lost twice as many as they did advancing.'[59] Rawlinson also believed that the reserve divisions had 'bolted' and been panicked by German gas shells.[60] Apparently several senior officers attempted to rally scattered parties of men, but with seemingly little success. According to a report by 46 Brigade:

> Many attempts were made by General Matheson [GOC 46 Brigade] and other officers to check this tide, but all in vain, with the exception of a few of 15 Division who somehow had got mixed up in it and who at once obeyed the orders given them. No attempt was made by any of these troops to stand. The men seemed incapable of grasping what was said. Ordered to get into the trenches and reform, the men merely stared vacantly into one's face and walked on. They appeared bereft of comprehension and yet not a sign of a German was to be seen.[61]

How true was this? It seems that the retreat from the second line began at about 1.30p.m. At roughly the same time the survivors of 21st Division on the slopes of Hill 70 started to retire. Although a number of British infantry held out in the long grass before the German lines sniping and helping the keep enemy fire down, they were relatively few in number.[62] The remaining survivors drifted back desolately until being rallied at the old British front line (around Lone Tree) by several senior officers.[63] Although it is evident that some equipment was either lost or thrown away, there was no large-scale casting away of arms, and as for the accusation that the men 'bolted in wild panic' this seems unlikely.[64] Certainly the advances of both 72 and the two battalions of 71 Brigade had been conducted with the utmost *sangfroid*, and the retirement seems to have been equally calm.[65] Capper believed that the retirement as carried out 'on the whole in an orderly manner, though from loss of officers and NCOs there was naturally some confusion in places'.[66] The Official History also recorded that the men, 'came back at a walk, but without order or formation'.[67] By 6a.m. the following morning, 21st and 24th Divisions (except 73 Brigade) had been taken out of the line and were sleeping among the wet fields around Noyelles and Sailly La Bourse.[68] It was evident that something had gone disastrously wrong.

On reflection, a mixed picture of the capabilities of 21st and 24th Divisions emerges from the battle. Although those units of 24th Division that reached the 'corpse field' showed incredible cohesion, determination and fighting spirit in the face of grave odds, the operations further south around Bois Hugo and Hill 70 revealed weaknesses in both leadership and training. Good leadership is vital in maintaining fighting ability against the 'friction' of war. But as Gary Sheffield has written, one of the reasons for the poor performance of XI Corps was 'the failure of battlefield leadership'.[69] There was no shortage of officers willing to follow the unspoken code of heroic leadership, but some officers were certainly substandard and found it very difficult to cope in such bewildering circumstances. 64 Brigade's war diary admitted that during the retirement 'regimental officers and NCOs did not give much assistance in trying to rally the men' and even noted that the NCOs were 'useless'.[70] Similarly, the retreat of 12/West Yorkshire (63 Brigade) from its positions around 10.30a.m. seems to have emanated from its CO, Lieutenant-Colonel R.A.C.L. Leggett, rather than from any specific enemy threat.[71] 8/Bedfordshire (71 Brigade) also seem 'to have been badly led'.[72]

Weaknesses were evident from their training. Even such a staunch defender of his men as Forestier-Walker admitted that the soldiers of 12/West Yorkshire and 10/York & Lancaster (both of 63 Brigade) 'did not behave with credit', and that at least 300 men of the division 'abandoned their rifles without excuse'.[73] According to the war diary of 63 Brigade, 10/York & Lancaster showed 'a certain amount of reluctance to remain in the trenches under shellfire',[74] and similarly, men of 12 and 13/Northumberland Fusiliers (62 Brigade) would not take cover in a trench because it contained several dead bodies, owing to a miners' superstition.[75] Although it was attached to I Corps between 25 and 27 September, the experience of 73 Brigade sheds useful light on these weaknesses. According to Brigadier-General R.G Jelf (GOC 73 Brigade from 26 September 1915):

> no communication of any kind had been established with my battalions either by wire or orderly and I attribute this to the fact that all battalions and the brigade staff were quite ignorant of the rudiments of what to do in the trenches, and how communications etc. were established, and the method of drawing rations etc., they have never been in trenches in their life before.[76]

But while these examples do not reflect well on the units concerned, they were not solely the result of poor soldiers being poorly led, and as Jelf had hinted at, they were reflective of a larger failure. The reserve divisions were totally inexperienced, having had only rudimentary training in musketry, marching and digging, with few large-scale manoeuvres and little combined training, let alone any chance at holding front-line trenches.[77] Their training had also overlooked the use of the navigating officers that had been found necessary in pre-war manoeuvres.[78] Equipment was another problem area. 24th Division was particularly short of spare parts for its machine guns, having had to borrow supplies from other units, and the Guards Division was reported as being thirty-eight miles short of telephone wire two days before the battle.[79] And again, in what was a considerable oversight at GHQ, XI Corps was issued with only the standard establishment of wire-cutters.

When the corps commander, Richard Haking, spoke to survivors soon after the retirement, a common reply was apparently 'We did not understand what it was like'.[80] This reflected a common truth. It should be emphasised how inexperienced all ranks were, and how appalling were the conditions they faced on 26 September. According to the British Official History, the thirteen battalions of 21st Division contained only fourteen regular or ex-regular officers.[81] A similar proportion of regulars was contained within 24th Division, and while most of the senior officers within both divisions were regulars, most were retired Indian Army officers, including Major-General Sir J.G. Ramsay (GOC 24th Division). And when considering the harrowing inferno they entered on 25 September, it is little wonder they found it so difficult to adjust to the tempo of battle. Indeed, while he had criticised various aspects of 73 Brigade's performance in the trenches, Brigadier-General Jelf confidently asserted that 'after many months of trench warfare... it would have taxed to the utmost the resources of any Regular brigade with plenty of experience behind them, to have kept themselves supplied under similar conditions'.[82] This seems a fair conclusion.

Reviewing the events of 26 September it will be seen that the failure of the British to secure either Hulluch or Hill 70, or break the German second line in between, stemmed from a number of interrelated factors. Perhaps the most weighty was the information vacuum on the battlefield; something which, according to one war diary, was 'nothing short of disastrous'.[83] All units were afflicted by this lack of information. For example, Lieutenant L.G. Duke (8/Queen's, 72 Brigade) received an order to attack written in indelible pencil. Because of the wet weather it was almost illegible.[84] Similarly, the adjutant of 8/Lincolnshire (63 Brigade), a Captain Topham, apparently complained to one of his fellow officers how 'it's awful. I've got no orders, no nothing, not even a compass bearing'.[85] As Major J. Buckley (9/KOYLI, 64 Brigade) later wrote:

> The historian has no conception of the vagueness of everything at the time... nobody, from the brigade commanders downwards, had any idea of the situation at any stage of the proceedings.[86]

It seems that even divisional headquarters were equally starved in this matter. According to Captain H. Pattison (8/Lincolnshires, 63 Brigade), when he arrived at 21st Division Headquarters on the afternoon of 26 September, trying to obtain entrenching tools, he was personally asked by Forestier-Walker, 'where brigade HQ was and where the battalions were, as neither he nor his staff had the least idea'.[87] Forestier-Walker later echoed this to Edmonds, writing that no information 'of the slightest value' had been given to him.[88]

Considering this information vacuum, it is of no surprise that artillery support was consistently poor on 26 September. As might have been expected, a great deal of difficulty and frustration was experienced as the artillery of the reserve divisions endeavoured to get into the correct positions with the correct orders. A central problem was that there did not seem to be any prior arrangements for artillery support. As many of the artillery batteries of the reserve divisions arrived at Le Rutoire, the congestion rapidly began to cause serious problems. According to one artillery brigade, 'the night was pitch dark; heavy rain was failing, the roads and fields crammed with cavalry, infantry, cooks, carts, pontoons and men'.[89] Orders were few and far between, often contradictory or simply irrelevant. The experience of Major Hon. R.G.A. Hamilton (CO CVIII Brigade RFA, 24th Division), in his vain efforts to locate Brigadier-General B.R. Mitford (GOC 72 Brigade), was a common one. According to him:

> We wandered about in the dark for three hours, being shelled all the time by heavy guns. It was an absolute nightmare: everyone we asked said something different; that the brigade was just in front, that it was two miles to the right, that it was a mile to the left, and so on.[90]

And while Hamilton never did find Mitford, Lieutenant-Colonel D.R. Coates (CO CVII Brigade RFA, 24th Division) also spent most of the night of 25/26 September in a fruitless search for Brigadier-General M.T. Shewen (GOC 71 Brigade). Coates's instructions said that Shewen should have been at Le Rutoire, but 'no trace' could be found, and with neither officers nor orderlies to guide him, 'nor could it be ascertained definitely that he [Shewen] had ever been there'. By 1a.m. on 26 September Coates had still not been able to find Shewen. Because his artillery batteries were required to support the attack of 71 Brigade that morning, he was forced to entrench east of Le Rutoire and await further orders.[91]

This complete lack of organisation resulted in many batteries occupying positions that were either too exposed or too far to the rear. Because there had been little reconnaissance of the ground, and it was in any case difficult to locate anything on such a 'featureless plain', instead of being under the cover of the Lone Tree Ridge, a number of artillery brigades were situated on open ground to the west and south-west of Le Rutoire. As soon as the morning mist lifted and they began firing, flashes from their barrels attracted enemy attention.[92] For example, XCV Brigade RFA (21st Division) was 'heavily shelled with gas' at 2p.m. and had to abandon its headquarters,[93] and the shooting of XXII Brigade RFA (7th Division) was hindered by not only 'active sniping' but also by heavy shelling.[94] Poor staff work only aggravated matters. Despite 'D' Battery of CIX Brigade RFA being 'pushed well forward… owing to a misunderstanding its ammunition supply failed and… [it was] temporarily withdrawn'.[95] There are also numerous complaints about shells falling short, but how widespread this was is difficult so say. As the war diary of 64 Brigade laconically noted, British guns were 'assaulting our own people in the back most of the day'.[96] But some batteries were able to provide effective support. 30th Battery (XXVI Brigade RFA, 1st Division) apparently stopped an enemy counter-attack south of Hulluch during the morning and 117th Battery caused the same force 'heavy casualties'.[97] Similarly, 'C' Battery of XCIV Brigade RFA (21st Division) shelled Hill 70 and 'D' Battery 'turned effectively' on German troops deploying north-west of Bois Hugo.[98] But such examples seem to have been rare. Why was artillery support so poor? While this certainly reflected the hurried construction of XI Corps, it also had much to do with the situation that existed at First Army headquarters. Lieutenant-Colonel C.G. Stewart (GSO1 24th Division) believed that the 'almost total absence of any arrangements for artillery support' stemmed from the fact that it 'appeared to be regarded as unnecessary owing to the defeat of the Germans'.[99] Therefore, from Stewart's testimony it would seem that the over-optimism and ambition that pervaded all aspects of First Army's pre-battle preparation also leaked into artillery planning.

The chronic congestion on the battlefield on the evening of 25/26 September also meant that it was very difficult for first line transport, especially the cookers, to link up with the forward troops. Only 72 Brigade received a hot breakfast on the morning of 26 September; the other brigades having to be content with their iron rations.[100] But while their empty stomachs certainly made the men uncomfortable, the lack of enough water strained their morale even further. One veteran remembered how the men were 'awfully thirsty'.[101] Ironically the constant drizzle and rain did bring some relief. The British Official History generally absolved the staff officers of 21st and 24th Divisions of too much blame, recording their 'tremendous efforts' to bring rations up:

> The Quartermasters had made many attempts during the night to get in touch with their units, but, after wandering aimlessly in the dark through the mud and debris of the battlefield, they had, with few exceptions, abandoned the search.[102]

But others were not so forgiving. Brigadier-General R. Ford (DA&QMG XI Corps) believed that the problem lay in the 'total inefficiency' of two AA&QMGs: Colonel R.H.D. Thring and Colonel H.T. Kenny of 21st and 24th Divisions respectively. Showing a typical disdain for Indian Army officers, Ford recalled that they were both 'elderly, and with Indian experience only, knew nothing of their jobs, and I was instrumental in having both instantly removed'.[103] Ford was being perhaps a little hard on the officers concerned. He seems not to have liked any of the senior officers within 21st and 24th Divisions. His comments do, however, reveal how poor relations were between the two divisions and its parent corps. It is doubtful whether any other officers could have done a great deal better if placed in a similar situation. The crowding and confusion behind the British lines were not the sole fault of these men, but were symptomatic of larger failures within First Army.

As has been shown previously, successive British attacks against the Quarries, Hulluch and Hill 70, as well as the main assault on the German second line, were fatally handicapped by the complete breakdown in command and control. Because there had been little attempt to structure the opening advance, and compounded by heavy officer casualties, many battalions had little idea where they were supposed to be going or what they were supposed to be doing. Indeed, many units operated in a fog of uncertainty. Often without orders, or only receiving them hours late, they were unable to operate effectively on the battlefield. Nevertheless, this should not blind the historian to failures in the British *system* of command. Indeed, it is impossible to understand the events of 26 September without reference to a number of consistent problems experienced at this time.

Command was clearly a problem within XI Corps. It seems that the senior officers did not work well together and relations between them rapidly frayed once in action. Admittedly, this probably had much to do with the very rushed formation of XI Corps, which was only born on 29 August 1915, did not appoint a CE (Brigadier-General L. Jones) until 11 September, and only had a BGRA from 12 September, but one also suspects that personality clashes occurred. The commander of 24th Division, Major-General Ramsay, who was relieved shortly after the battle, did not possess the confidence of his men or his superiors. Ramsay was an experienced 59 year-old Indian Army officer who had been 'dug out' of retirement in 1914 and sent to command 24th Division. He was clearly unsuited to the pace of modern war on the Western Front. According to Brigadier-General Ford, on the morning of 27 September, 'while in bed Ramsay… tendered his resignation which the corps commander readily accepted'. Ford added that Ramsay was 'entirely unfitted to command a division and he knew it'.[104] As Brigadier-General H.M. de F. Montgomery (BGGS XI Corps) later told Edmonds, 'The whole thing was a nightmare of uncongenial companions and impossible situations, and while… I have the feeling that, although I have no reason to complain at having been made a scapegoat after the melancholy fiasco was over, as I undoubtedly made serious mistakes, there were others who might with equal or greater justice have shared the same fate.'[105]

Problems within XI Corps were not confined to poisonous relationships between its senior officers. In a letter to the British Official Historian after the war, Lieutenant-Colonel C.G. Stewart (GSO1 24th Division) complained about a number of problems he had experienced on 25–26 September. It will be recalled that according to Edmonds the reason why elements of XI Corps had been ordered to make the disastrous attack on the German second line on 26 September emanated primarily from poor communication on the battlefield. Edmonds wrote that 'rumours had been stated as facts, and the great losses suffered in the first assault had been scarcely mentioned' and British High Command had, therefore, not realised how bad the situation was in the front line. Stewart, however, objected to this:

> How could it occur that one division after another received and forwarded incorrect reports of what was happening up in front? And, who was responsible for 'rumours' being reported and accepted as 'facts'? It was common knowledge in the Army that F.S.R. [*Field Service Regulations*] laid down that the reliability of information requires consideration and if necessary confirmation; and that a 'rumour' is not good enough. Also, that the superior authority must be kept informed as to the state and condition of the fighting troops. Did this not point to some defect in our training[?][106]

Stewart did indeed believe that this was so. 'I think the cult of optimism in such matters was carried too far. In this case, a "rumour" was accepted without apparently being confirmed, because it was optimistic. But when a message is sent, which endeavoured to give an accurate idea of what was taking place, it is described as "despondent"; and the author… gets himself disliked, to use a mild term.' Stewart spent over four hours at the front with 21st and 24th Divisions and reported the poor situation to Brigadier-General B.R. Mitford (GOC 72 Brigade), who apparently called him 'despondent'. According to Stewart 'I was told at the time, that because my message was written in red pencil, it was a sign that the officer who sent it was unnerved!'

What was going on? Admittedly, Stewart's comments may have suffered from some exaggeration, but his letter highlights a number of serious systematic failings in the British command structure that cannot simply be ignored. Why did situations like this occur? In part it reflected the deteriorating situation at the front, which brought out latent problems within the British command structure, which was 'top-down', rigidly hierarchical, distrustful of giving subordinates too much freedom and weighted towards the offensive in war.[107] But it also stemmed from the great pressure that Haig's 'all-out' attack placed upon subordinates, particularly corps and divisional commanders, who were reluctant to cancel attacks. Many senior officers were undoubtedly aware that if they did not achieve the required results, their positions could be in danger. More work needs to be done on the pattern of promotion and dismissal within the BEF, but from a cursory study of salaries, it is clear that many senior officers who held temporary rank (which were not substantive or permanent) would face a not inconsiderable drop in salary if they were 'degummed' and sent home.[108] Many were perhaps understandably keen to retain their positions and avoid incurring the wrath of senior officers.

How much pressure did Haig place upon his subordinates? Haig was not a particularly 'hands-on' commander and in many ways he was not in the habit of getting involved in specific tactical matters. There are, however, a number of references to pressure that Haig placed upon subordinates. At 2.15p.m. on 27 September Haig visited Gough at his headquarters and was 'visibly worried', 'sharp' and 'cross'; perhaps because he had just been informed of the death of Major-General George Thesiger (GOC 9th Division).[109] It is evident that following this visit Gough became somewhat 'sharp' himself. He later admitted that 'I also must have been very worried, and perhaps those below me thought the same of me'.[110] But in many respects Haig did not have to pressurise his corps commanders, who were all well aware of the scope and ambition of the attack. Haking was unlikely to offer any dissent, being a confident 'thruster' with an inherent faith in the power of the offensive.[111] Haig may have ordered XI Corps forward onto the German second line, but Haking took his men in without any doubts. One observer recalled a speech Haking gave to the men of 2 (Guards) Brigade shortly before the battle. Apparently he 'spoke very confidently, comparing the German line to the crust of a pie, behind which, once broken, he said, there is not much resistance to be expected. He ended up by saying, "I don't tell you this to cheer you up. I tell it you because I really believe it."'[112] It is evident that Haking took too little account of the 'despondent' news emanating from the battlefield.

A constant problem at Loos was getting orders to the right formations at the right times. Too often units were handed their orders with only minutes to spare; sometimes they were hours out of date. This resulted in attacks that were appallingly rushed, often with dire consequences. For example, because orders had not arrived (they would do so at 5.20p.m.), 72 Brigade was *verbally informed* by a staff officer that it was to attack the German second line at 9.45a.m. on 26 September.[113] When battalions were ordered to attack, despite failures of preparation and communication, a number of protests emerged from officers who were unwilling to carry out their orders. So low did Lieutenant-Colonel E.H.D. Stracey (CO 9/Norfolks, 71 Brigade) consider the chances of a successful counterattack against the Quarries that he protested (in vain) about 'the futility of attacking so strong a position with only one battalion'.[114] Major-General McCracken had also protested about renewing the attack on Hill 70 in the morning, but had been overruled by his corps commander. Admittedly, such protests were firmly in a minority, with most officers obeying their orders as directed, but they do nevertheless merit further analysis for the light they shed on the nature of command in the BEF at this period of the war. One of the fundamental principles of *Field Service Regulations* (1909) may have been the faith placed in 'the man on the spot', but it seems that this was not always followed, especially when a seeming lack of sufficient 'offensive spirit' was shown. As Tim Travers has explained, between 1914 and 1916 a not-insignificant proportion of officer removals – or 'degummings' as they were called – were motivated by a desire on the part of British High

Command to promote the correct level of aggression and fighting spirit.[115] For those that did not show such spirit, little mercy could be expected. According to Travers, 'Faced with obviously hopeless attacks, commanders were reluctant to complain, suggest alternatives, or even refuse to attack, for fear of GHQ reprisals, although some brave souls did'.[116]

One notable dismissal occurred on 26 September and although it was not connected to a refusal to carry out orders, it seems to have had something to do with a lack of aggression and 'offensive spirit'. Brigadier-General W.A. Oswald (GOC 73 Brigade, 24th Division) was 'degummed' by Hubert Gough as he moved up to the front with his troops. Why had Gough taken such a drastic step? Although he gained a reputation during the war for being particularly ruthless towards subordinate officers whom he did not consider were good enough, Gough tended not to do it when the unit concerned was heavily engaged.[117] It seems that Gough was deeply concerned about the capacity of 73 Brigade to hold its positions around Fosse 8 in the face of fierce bombing attacks from men of *91 Reserve Regiment*.[118] Almost as soon as 73 Brigade had begun relieving 26 Brigade, the attacks began; 27 Brigade's later withdrawal from Fosse Alley and the loss of Quarries only adding to the beleaguered situation.[119] But in spite of considerable difficulties, 73 Brigade held its ground. Curiously, Gough seems to have believed that 73 Brigade's problems stemmed *not* from the difficult position they were in, having recently taken over unfamiliar positions under attack with little support, but rather from the capability of their commanding officer, Brigadier-General Oswald. So concerned did Gough eventually become that Oswald was relieved of command during the morning.

Brigadier-General H.R. Davies (GOC 3 Brigade) believed that Oswald had apparently 'broken down mentally', but there seems little supporting evidence for this.[120] On the contrary, according to a report by 12/Royal Fusiliers, 'B' company and half of 'A' company were led to their positions 'in person' by Oswald, which hardly suggests someone on the verge of collapse.[121] However, the Brigade Major of 26 Brigade, who was present when 73 Brigade reached the headquarters of 26 Brigade at 9p.m. on the evening of 25 September, had some damning words for 73 Brigade.

> They imagined they came for a normal trench relief. The brigadier's first question to me was 'What are the trenches like which we take over? Is it a quiet sector?' An old and earnest man… he was removed by the corps commander that night.[122]

Although from this it would seem that Oswald was not in total control of the situation, it reflected badly on both First Army's and I Corps' staff work. When considering the complete lack of information or support Oswald's brigade received, he did well in keeping his men together. But if Oswald had not broken down, then why was he relieved at such a crucial time? It seems that Gough's notorious antipathy for Indian Army officers, especially retired 'dugouts' – both of which Oswald was – had a decisive impact on his decision. While it does not seem that, Oswald aside, any senior British officers were relieved during the battle (although several were relieved afterwards), the threat of dismissal was never far from the surface as is illustrated by the curious case of 64 Brigade.

The disastrous series of events that resulted in the dismemberment of 64 Brigade (21st Division) highlight what damage an inflexible and rigid command structure could do. As will be recalled, one of the most puzzling mysteries of the day was the unexpected movement of 9/KOYLI at 1.45p.m. towards Hill 70, seemingly without orders. According to Lieutenant-Colonel K. Henderson (Brigade Major 64 Brigade) this was prompted by the 'misplaced zeal' of a 'very gallant and zealous but over-excited junior divisional staff officer'.[123] The staff officer – who was later identified as GSO3 21st Division – arrived at 63 Brigade Headquarters just before 9/KOYLI had started off. The staff officer apparently 'arrived breathless and excited from their direction and had been trying to stem the flood of retreat… and urged a fresh attack at all risks and with every available man'. He urged Brigadier-General G.M. Gloster (GOC 64 Brigade) to resume the advance at once, adding that he was 'sure the divisional commander would insist on attacking again'.[124] Henderson was nonplussed:

> In spite of my vehement dissent, he overbore Brigadier-General Gloster, and it was then the COs of the two KOYLI battalions were summoned to take their orders; orders which were nipped in the bud by the action of the 9/KOYLI.[125]

Why did Gloster listen to the young and clearly excited staff officer, and ignore his presumably trusted Brigade Major? Gloster's later comment to Henderson, that if he 'did nothing he might be blamed, whereas if we at least tried he would be free from censure', provides a clue.[126]

As darkness fell on 26 September it was obvious that General Haig's grand plan for an advance up to the Haute Deule canal lay in ruins. Repeated attempts to secure the Quarries, Hulluch and Hill 70 had failed, the main attack on the German second line had been bloodily repulsed, and I Corps' position around the Hohenzollern Redoubt and Fosse 8 was weakening in the face of constant enemy pressure. Indeed, it is difficult to avoid the conclusion that 26 September had been anything other than a complete disaster for First Army. Every attack it launched was beaten back. Little ground was gained. The fighting around Hill 70, Bois Hugo and the 'corpse field' was simply a shambles. Units blundered into the enemy, into other British units (particularly 63 and 64 Brigades of 21st Division), retired, advanced and lost in most cases half their strength. Nobody knew what was happening, what to do or where to go.

British operational and tactical performance on 26 September had been weak in every area. The lack of uniform attack formations that had been noticeable the previous day was again evident on 26 September. While 2/ Worcestershire and two companies of 1/KRRC (both of Carter's Force) attacked the Quarries 'by alternate platoons and sections, so as to ensure the 'fire and movement' of pre-war training',[127] other battalions used much simpler formations. Captain L. McNaught-Davis (OC 'D' Company, 8/ Lincolnshire, 63 Brigade) personally led three bayonet charges through Bois Hugo before he was captured during the afternoon.[128] Owing to the confusion on the battlefield certain units of the reserve divisions do not seem to have operated any tactical formation at all. According to Lieutenant-Colonel Henderson, the attack of 9 and 10/KOYLI (64 Brigade) was 'just a crowd surging forward without any notion of what to do or where to go, except that as before Hill 70 acted as a magnet'.[129] And while 2/Worcestershire, a coherent battalion, was able to conduct a properly organised attack, because so many other British units – especially those strung out on Hill 70 – were mixed up, disorganised and had suffered heavy casualties, it was extremely difficult to restore order. According to one subaltern, the fighting on Hill 70 was 'a dog's breakfast… we were all just fighting as infantry, machine-guns [*sic*], everybody all mixed up'.[130]

This tactical inadequacy was often, however, combined with heroic leadership, although how effective this was remains unclear. In order to compensate for the disadvantages British troops were operating under, including lack of artillery support and rushed preparations, it seems that many officers resorted to sometimes desperate acts of gallantry and courage. Heroism among officers was common on the second day, especially among those battalions of 21st and 24th Divisions that were undergoing their 'baptism of fire'. For example, during the attack on Hill 70, Lieutenant-Colonel A. de S. Hadow (CO 10/Yorkshire, 62 Brigade) and Major W.H. Dent (alongside two other senior officers) recklessly exposed themselves to enemy fire by shouting 'Charge!' and rushing forward. All were shot and killed.[131] Similarly, Lieutenant-Colonel H.E. Walter (CO 8/Lincolnshire, 63 Brigade) died whilst fighting in Bois Hugo, and despite being shot in the shoulder early on, the 64 year-old Colonel R.C. Romer (CO 8/Buffs, 72 Brigade) led his battalion into the 'corpse field' until another bullet felled him.[132] But it was not just officers of the reserve divisions that led from the front. Lieutenant-Colonel A.F. Douglas-Hamilton (CO 6/Cameron Highlanders, 45 Brigade) was a prime example, leading his men in repeated attempts to wrest control of Chalet Wood from the enemy, before finally falling in 'a gallant but hopeless gesture… at the head of his men'.[133]

In the absence of reliable communication between the front line and the headquarters in the rear, many senior officers instinctively tried to get nearer to the front. But rather than producing circumstances whereby such commanders could control their units, it brought them into closer touch with the enemy, often with devastating results. Brigadier-General C.D Bruce (GOC 27 Brigade) was captured by a German patrol in the Quarries as he endeavoured to use a telephone set,[134] and although accounts disagree over the exact circumstances of the death of Major-General Sir T. Capper (GOC 7th Division) it is clear that he should have been much further back.[135] Major-General Forestier-Walker was another commander frustrated by this seeming lack of control, so much that he rode up past the German front line in a vain attempt to see for himself, and was nearly killed. According to one onlooker, 'I saw him… approaching from westward, walking along calmly with shells bursting literally all round him.' Eventually his small party was persuaded to take cover, whereby they 'all cowered down in the trench… continuously sprayed with dirt and gravel and once nearly buried by falling earth, all from the shelling'.[136]

British casualties on 26 September had again been considerable, heaviest among those brigades of 21st and 24th Divisions that had been in action. And as had been a feature of the previous day, senior officer casualties were very high, with another twenty being killed, wounded or captured.[137] Regimental officers had also suffered devastating losses. Several examples will suffice. While twenty-two officers were hit in 8/Lincolnshire (63 Brigade),[138] 14/Durham Light Infantry (64 Brigade) lost its commanding officer (Lieutenant-Colonel A.S. Hamilton), four company commanders, the adjutant and another seventeen officers.[139] During the attack on Hill 70, 12/Royal Scots (45 Brigade) suffered appallingly. According to the regimental history:

> As soon as 'C' Company topped the parapet, Major G.D Macpherson, Captain G.S. Robertson, and many of the men were shot down before they had moved a yard.[140]

In its doomed attack against the Quarries, thirteen officers became casualties within 9/Norfolk (71 Brigade),[141] and within 72 Brigade, all the officers of 8/Royal West Kents had fallen, and only three emerged unscathed from 8/Queen's.[142]

Despite the obvious success of the local counter-attacks against the Quarries and Bois Hugo, a picture of German battlefield performance at Loos remains mixed. Many of the same problems that hampered the British, such as the difficulty of moving units into position, especially with sketchy knowledge of enemy deployments, and all whilst in bad weather, applied equally to the Germans. The men of *14th Infantry Division*, who threw the British back from Fosse 8, were 'up to their knees in mud', yet they still came on in waves of bombers.[143] *153 Infantry Regiment (8th Division)*, ordered to sweep the British from Hill 70, experienced a whole series of problems as it marched towards the firing line. Units blundered into each other in the darkness, were confused about where British troops were, and which positions they were supposed to be retaking.[144] Indeed, although the German Army would later gain a reputation for being a master of the offensive art,[145] their counter-attacks at Loos were largely bloody failures, being massed infantry attacks that were repulsed by heavy British rifle and machine gun fire. For example, during the night of 25/26 September, poorly executed counterattacks against the eastern side of the Loos Crassier and from Cité St Laurent were both repulsed.[146] According to a German regimental history, the 'nocturnal' counter-attack of *153rd* and *93rd Regiments (8th Division)* failed owing to a 'lack of preparation'. Apparently the troops remained out in no-man's-land until daybreak when they were 'shot to pieces' by 15th and 47th Divisions.[147] It seems that aided by strong defensive positions, the sketchy German forces were able to do enough damage to the poorly conducted British attacks to safeguard their position south of the La Bassée canal, but when they attempted to manoeuvre in the open, they became vulnerable to many of the same factors that had hampered First Army.

The second day has been almost totally remembered for the tragic failure of the reserve divisions to break the German second line, but as has been shown, this narrow focus has prevented a thorough understanding of the events of 26 September 1915 from emerging. The story of the second day was not simply 72 Brigade's doomed march towards the 'field of corpses', but of the complete breakdown in command and control on the battlefield, the failure of the important flanking attacks and the effective German counter-attack through Bois Hugo at 9a.m. The deteriorating situation on the battlefield also highlighted a number of problems within the British structure and system of command, which could not cope with the information vacuum, the unexpected movement of enemy units and the lack of artillery support. The cumulative effect of these factors meant that by the time the renewed offensive began (at 11a.m.) the enemy had stolen the initiative. The British attacks were thus fatally undermined and left to wither in the face of heavy machine gun and shellfire. But having endured such a disaster, could the BEF continue the battle?

8

RENEWING THE OFFENSIVE: 27 SEPTEMBER - 13 OCTOBER 1915

The Battle of Loos is primarily remembered for the dramatic events of the first two days when almost all the British gains were made and when the vast majority of the casualties were incurred. That the battle continued for a further three weeks has been largely forgotten or ignored.[1] Apart from Sir James Edmonds, historians have made little attempt to see the events at Loos between 27 September and 13 October as a coherent whole. Perhaps this is understandable. The attacks conducted by the British in this period were not decisive; they were generally small in scale and had little result other than increasing the number of casualties and reducing First Army's stocks of ammunition still further. Nevertheless, this later period of the battle is notable for several reasons and merits some reassessment because many of the factors, both operational and tactical, that had hindered British battlefield performance on 25–6 September were again encountered, such as the friction between Sir John French and Sir Douglas Haig, the difficulties of command and control, poor weather and the lack of adequate infantry fire support.

The abject failure of the British attacks on 26 September left the prospect of any further large-scale advances distinctly bleak. The headquarters of the German *Sixth Army* confidently informed OHL that it did not harbour any doubts about to its ability to prevent a British breakthrough.[2]

A steady flow of German reinforcements were already making their way into the lines south of the La Bassée canal. The *Guard Corps*, which had recently been employed on the Eastern Front, was sent to Artois with *2nd Guard Division* joining General Sixt von Armin's *IV Corps*.[3] Nevertheless, pressure from the French Army meant that once the offensive had been started, it could not be terminated easily. At the request of their ally, therefore, the British kept pushing forward, but because of the fundamental disagreement between Sir John French and Sir Douglas Haig over the extent of the attack, the poor communication between the two and their deteriorating relationship, the operations of First Army continued with a momentum of their own and without proper, thorough discussion and detailed planning. This was to have important repercussions for British operations in this period, particularly the final effort to secure Fosse 8 on 13 October 1915.

Fighting continued to rage in Artois and Champagne, but it was becomingly increasingly clear that Joffre's war-winning offensive was bogging down.[4] Although the French in Champagne had managed to break the German first line and take approximately 14,000 prisoners, as had happened to the British, they were unable to get through the second line, which was heavily wired and well supported by artillery. In Artois, the French Tenth Army had suffered so badly on 25 September that by the following morning it had been forced to suspend its operations until the attacking troops could be relieved and further artillery preparation made. Renewed attacks were pressed during the afternoon, with the village of Souchez finally falling to French infantry, but the situation was so confused that the French Commander-in-Chief, General Joseph Joffre, was forced to direct General Foch (Commander *Groupe d'Armées du Nord*) to close down the operations of Tenth Army later that day, albeit taking care 'to avoid giving the British the impression that we are leaving them to attack alone'.[5]

Pressure from Joffre may have meant that British operations had to continue, but French and Haig were still keen to keep pressing the enemy. For Sir Douglas Haig, he was well aware that the failure to break the German second line meant that his troops were now pinned into the breaches they had made on 25 September. Now more than ever, the dominating feature of the battlefield became Hill 70 and if the British and French were to make further gains, it had to be taken. Sir John French was equally concerned, rather melodramatically explaining to Foch that if he had been the Commander-in-Chief of the 'whole western Allied front', he would have 'put every available man in just north of Hill 70 and "rush" a gap in the enemy's line'.[6] Owing to the failures of 21st and 24th Divisions the only troops immediately available belonged to Major-General the Earl of Cavan's Guards Division,[7] which was finally placed under First Army control at 1.45p.m. on 26 September. It spent the rest of the day marching towards the sound of the guns and arrived on the battlefield around midnight.[8] At 11.30p.m. Lieutenant-General Richard Haking (GOC XI Corps) received orders to submit plans for the capture of Hill 70 to be conducted the following afternoon.

Considering the heavy shellfire and the almost total confusion on the battlefield by the evening of 26 September, the preparations for the attack on Hill 70 were inevitably rushed. As one young officer later recalled, 'I do not think that I or any of my fellow subalterns ever received any information as to what was expected of us'.[9] Little could be done during the night and the morning was spent in feverish discussions and frantic communication. To aggravate matters the orders of the attack were changed later in the afternoon to take account of the deteriorating situation around Fosse 8. Haig had originally wanted to call the attack off, but Haking doubted whether it would be possible to do so in time. Haig did, however, insist that the troops go no further than the line Chalk Pit–Puits 14–Hill 70.[10] XI Corps' orders also stated that if 2 (Guards) Brigade failed to secure its objective of Bois Hugo, the attack of 3 (Guards) Brigade against Hill 70 should not take place. Unfortunately, news to this effect only reached 3 (Guards) Brigade *after* its troops had begun moving out.

When the attack finally got underway some progress was achieved but Hill 70 and Bois Hugo remained in enemy hands. A smoke discharge was successful in screening the approach of 2 (Guards) Brigade to the environs of Chalk Pit Wood,[11] but as had occurred on 25 September, while smoke would allow infantry to close with their objective, it would not allow them to take it if the Germans chose to resist.[12] As 1/Scots Guards and elements of 2/Irish Guards attempted to cross the open ground towards Puits 14 bis, they were met with 'terrific fire from the enemy's maxim guns' and the attack stalled.[13] The attack of 3 (Guards) Brigade was also unsuccessful. After an epic march through 'considerable and growing shellfire' across open ground, the brigade began filtering into Loos.[14] Once inside the rubble-strewn village, however, the brigade became disorganised. Because 4/Grenadier Guards had been caught in a bombardment of gas shells as it entered the village from the north-west, 1/Welsh Guards were hurriedly ordered to lead the attack instead. It began at 5.30p.m. and as soon as the lines of infantry crested the summit and became visible to the German defenders, devastating swathes of machine gun fire swept through their ranks and the advance rapidly faltered.[15] Senior officers on the spot decided that further progress was impossible and that a withdrawal to about 100 yards below the crest of Hill 70 should be conducted.[16]

The attack of the Guards Division was fatally undermined by poor artillery support. One gunner officer, Major Hon. R.G.A. Hamilton (CO CVIII Brigade RFA, 24th Division), who had floundered around the battlefield on the night of 25/26 September trying to find Brigadier-General B.R. Mitford (GOC 72 Brigade), spent the following night in depressingly similar circumstances. He was supposed to find Brigadier-General G.P.T. Feilding (GOC 1 (Guards) Brigade) to brief him on the situation but, as might have been expected, this proved virtually impossible.[17] After working his way down the old German front line 'with great difficulty' Hamilton eventually found Feilding at 3p.m. Others were not so fortunate, however. Major J.D. Anderson (CO XCVII Brigade RFA, 24th Division) went into Loos to consult with Brigadier-General F.J. Heyworth (GOC 3 (Guards) Brigade) 'as regards how the guns could best assist' but because the village was under heavy shellfire, which cut all the telephone wires, he could not communicate with his batteries and returned, dejected, at 6.30p.m.[18]

As well as the logistical difficulties of getting artillery batteries into the correct locations, matters were not helped by a disagreement within XI Corps about what type of artillery preparation should precede the attack. Haking eventually decided that between 12.30 and 3p.m. Puits 14 would be bombarded by all the available heavy batteries before the guns of the Guards Division subjected the German lines to intensive shelling between 3.40 and 4p.m. The infantry would then attack.[19] Haking's idea of lifting the heavy artillery from the German front line at 3p.m., when it would then begin shelling more distant targets, seems to have been somewhat controversial. Lieutenant-General Sir Henry Rawlinson (GOC IV Corps), who met Haking at 10a.m., seems to have wanted a different approach. 'I think this was a mistake,' he noted, adding that 'if I had been doing it I should have kept every available gun on the objective for the attack up to the very last moment.'[20] Unfortunately, Rawlinson kept his concerns to himself and Haking's poor handling of artillery gave his troops even less chance of securing their objectives. The repulse of the Guards Division from Hill 70, combined with the alarming loss of Fosse 8, meant that further attempts to breakthrough the German lines would have to wait, at least until First Army could be reorganised and resupplied.[21]

Following the failure of the Guards Division's operations around Hill 70, the focus of British efforts began to drift northwards. Although Fosse 8 had been lost after a fierce German counter-attack on 27 September,[22] 73 Brigade (24th Division) had managed to improvise a front line position on the east face of the Hohenzollern Redoubt.[23] Fighting continued over the next week as First Army desperately pushed reinforcements into the line in a frantic attempt to stem enemy progress and recapture the lost ground. Unfortunately, the confusion over objectives, the lack of proper planning and the poor artillery support that had been characteristic of British operations between 26 and 27 September were again encountered. Between 27 September and 5 October, 28th Division was deployed in this sector and was ordered to recapture Fosse 8. It efforts were unsuccessful. The experience was undoubtedly a difficult one and was also notable for the palpable bad feeling, controversy and bitter argument that the battle engendered between the officers of 28th Division and GOC I Corps, Lieutenant-General Hubert Gough. Curiously the entire episode only occupies a handful of pages in the usually concise British Official History, perhaps a reflection of the confusion that existed on the battlefield as well as the controversy of the action.[24]

Major-General E.S. Bulfin (GOC 28th Division) had bad memories of the battle. He later wrote to Sir James Edmonds that 'I have a very confused memory of Loos – a sort of horrid nightmare. I was under Hugh [*sic*] Gough – and I never want to serve under him again. I remember he ordered me to attack a Fosse – of course the whole thing was hopeless.'[25] On 20 October, shortly before he was to return to England on two months' sick leave, Bulfin met Brigadier-General C.E. Pereira (GOC 85 Brigade). According to Pereira, as well as suffering from poor eyesight, Bulfin 'could not get on with General Gough who accused the Division of being slow and who was always pressing for attacks without what General Bulfin considered sufficient artillery preparation'.[26] Tension and frustration was also evident from Gough's account. He did not have a high opinion of Bulfin. In *The Fifth Army* (1931), Bulfin appears as 'a bluff, red-faced man' who 'at once on entering the room commenced to explain [to Gough] that infantry were not cavalry'.[27] Gough subsequently added that 'it seemed to me that he was more intent on instructing me how to command a corps than he was to deal with the serious problem before his division and to help the troops already in great difficulties round Fosse 8'.

Was there any truth behind these accusations? Bulfin's argument that his division had been placed under unnecessary pressure is difficult to deny. As 85 Brigade moved up to the front on 27 September, Brigadier-General Pereira was continually bombarded with messages from both corps and division not only to relieve 73 Brigade and elements of 9th (Scottish) Division, but also to recapture Fosse 8. At 4.15p.m. Pereira even received a message *direct* from the corps commander 'ordering an immediate counter attack across the open', something which was clearly impossible.[28] What subsequently occurred does not rebound to the credit of I Corps. Pereira was wounded, with command thus devolving on Lieutenant-Colonel A.C. Roberts (CO 3/Royal Fusiliers). Roberts was immediately visited by Lieutenant-Colonel R.H. Hare (GSO1 28th Division) and told that he must now make the attack on Fosse 8. Owing to the abysmal situation on the ground, Roberts reported at 6a.m. the following day that the attack was 'impossible to carry out' because his battalions were still not in position. At 7.15a.m. on 28 September, Lieutenant-Colonel C.A. Worthington (CO 2/Buffs) and Lieutenant-Colonel G.H. Neale (CO 3/Middlesex), had managed to reach the front line and carry out a brief reconnaissance. They reported that it was impossible to carry out the attack and requested permission to conduct it that evening. Rather predictably this did not go down well with either 28th Division or I Corps. Lieutenant-Colonel Hare visited 85 Brigade headquarters again at 8a.m. and told Roberts that he had definite orders for the attack and was 'to assist in having them carried out'.[29] Roberts's orders stated that 'The attack must take place at once with the utmost resolution, there must be no cause for delay until the fosse is taken'.[30] Despite these desperate appeals, the attack of 85 Brigade on the morning of 28 September was a predictable disaster. 2/Buffs only managed to reach their prescribed jumping-off position at 10a.m., long after the preparatory bombardment had ceased, and as soon as the leading company went 'over the top' it was greeted by hails of bullets from the enemy gunners occupying Slag Alley.[31] By 11a.m. 2/Buffs were back in their original trenches and 3/Middlesex, after bombing up Dump Trench and getting involved in a fierce grenade contest with the enemy, had to disengage because of lack of ammunition.

If anyone had expected that this failure would have shaken Gough out of his preoccupation with recapturing Fosse 8, they would have been disappointed. On 29 September 84 Brigade entered the line and over the next few days it conducted a number of poorly supported and generally unsuccessful attacks against the German positions of Little Willie and the Chord. As might have been expected, 84 Brigade's attacks were generally rushed, without adequate preparation or artillery support and tended to be on a small-scale, often with just two or three companies being involved. They were also largely devoid of lasting gain.[32] A similar situation faced 83 Brigade, which relieved 84 Brigade on 3 October. Once again its commanding officer was repeatedly ordered to make premature and ill-prepared attacks against hardening German positions. Labouring under the immense difficulties of relieving mixed-up troops that were under constant enemy bombing attacks while also planning his own counter-stroke, Brigadier-General H.S.L. Ravenshaw eventually organised an attack against Little Willie on the morning of 4 October by two battalions (2/East Yorkshire and 1/KOYLI). This also achieved little; the expected preliminary bombardment never arrived and the attacking companies were 'practically wiped out' by hostile machine gun and rifle fire.[33]

28th Division's failure to regain Fosse 8, or even secure its position around the Hohenzollern Redoubt, did not go down well with British

High Command. As Andy Simpson has noted, 28th Division suffered a 'stinging rebuke' from I Corps on 6 October for the way it had framed orders for its brigades.[34] A brief paper on the problems with staff work and command in 28th Division's papers listed twelve points for consideration including misleading and inaccurate reports; improper distribution of staff work; lack of contact with the divisional engineers; 'want of discipline and soldierly bearing' in 3/Middlesex (85 Brigade); and the 'disgraceful' retreat of 2/Cheshire (84 Brigade) from the Hohenzollern Redoubt. The list also noted the 'great slackness and a complete want of *co-ordination* and *cohesion* in the Division', and 'Too much "laisser faire [*sic*]"'.[35] Brigadier-General T.H.F. Pearse (GOC 84 Brigade) was also accused of lacking 'energy' and 'discipline'. There was also 'insufficient energy in the command'. Amazingly the report also noted that 'it is not the business of the Corps to command Division – that is the business of the Division'.

Was such a damning report justified? On 20 October Brigadier-General Pereira complained that the whole of 28th Division was 'under a cloud',[36] and given Gough's low opinion of Bulfin and his understandable desire to excuse the failure to secure Fosse 8, this was not entirely surprising. 28th Division admittedly suffered numerous problems with its staff work and command, but many of these were generally inherent in the BEF at this period in the war and were not unique to Bulfin's division. Although Haig believed that 28th Division had 'not proved equal to the task',[37] after reviewing the numerous personal accounts, war diaries and after-action reports for this period it will be seen that although inexperienced, 28th Division suffered from no lack of courage or conviction. Indeed the war diaries of the division detail a considerable number of epic actions, heroic attacks and gallant leadership, which resulted in the later award of two Victoria Crosses.[38] But the division was hampered by a number of serious factors: the weather was wet; enemy pressure was constant and unyielding; artillery support was poor; basic supplies of water, food and ammunition often did not arrive on time; and on a number of occasions its battalions were ordered to conduct operations without sufficient preparation and against the opinions of those officers on the ground.

It is worth noting how appalling was the situation that faced 28th Division during this period. According to Brigadier-General Pereira, when he advanced up the Central Boyau on the afternoon of 27 September, he had to contend with 'constant delays', particularly when moving past the troops he was supposed to relieve. With 'infinite difficulty', he managed to 'get the trench clear for the brigade', but 'The trench was very deep and narrow, wounded men were trying to come down it, further on there were dead bodies and equipment blocking the way'.[39] Moving through this muddy labyrinth was incredibly trying. The German Official History recorded that the Bavarian units detailed to retake the Hohenzollern Redoubt on 27 September sank 'up to their calves in thick slime'.[40] When 1/Suffolk (84 Brigade) attempted to march to the British positions opposite Little Willie on the afternoon of 2 October, it took over seven hours and then only one company had reached its intended destination.[41] Maps were another problem. Even if they were available, and in many cases they were not, the heavy shelling, poor weather, constant movement of troops and incessant digging meant that within a few days even the most up-to-date maps were virtually useless.[42] In this morass guides were often little help. 83 Brigade did receive a number of guides from 9th Division but none 'knew the way and were quite useless stating that they had never been there before'.[43] The trenches were also highly dangerous, those at Big Willie for example being shallow and vulnerable to fire from the Dump.[44]

When operations were pressed in this lethal environment it was essential that British troops were able to count upon the support of their own artillery and the firepower of their rifles and grenades. Unfortunately, all seemed to have worked poorly under the difficult conditions. The factors that had hindered British artillery fire between 25 and 27 September were still much in evidence, particularly the difficulty of observing and locating enemy concentrations, and the perennial complaints about worn guns, inexperienced crews, poor ammunition and lack of communication. One of 9th Division's field artillery brigades voiced a common concern on 27 September. It was:

> Extremely hard to know or hear of how things stand, one minute in possession of HOHENZOLLERN REDOUBT and the next not, the same remark applies to the DUMP.[45]

According to a German regimental history, British artillery fire on 28 September was 'almost all far off target',[46] and because the opposing lines were often close together and regularly changed hands, British gunners were sometimes reluctant to shell trenches for fear of hitting their own troops.

British troops also suffered from a lack of organic fire support. Rifles were prone to jamming in the muddy trenches and grenades were little help. Whereas the German Army had long appreciated the value of such weapons, the British had only one type in service by 1914.[47] During the opening months of 1915, however, the British rapidly learnt the value of the grenade. A grenade company was formed in each brigade early in the year by taking thirty men from each battalion and training them in the use of grenades.[48] But the effectiveness of these groups depended largely upon the quality of the bombs they were using and by September 1915 British bombs came in several varieties including the infamous 'hairbrush', 'jam-pot' and 'cricket-ball' designs.[49] These infamous weapons were notoriously unreliable and the personal memoirs and battalion war diaries for Loos are littered with references to these faulty or useless grenades.[50] Indeed, according to Hubert Gough, the bomb 'played an especially great and decisive part' in failure on the battlefield, particularly concerning the actions of 73 Brigade and 28th Division.[51] It would not be until the arrival of large numbers of the Mills grenades, with its standardised time fuse, that British troops would be able to hold their own in bombing fights with the enemy. Over 11,000 Mills bombs had arrived in France by the time Loos was fought, but owing to poor planning most had been given to the Guards Division, which did not see action until 27 September.[52]

After the failure of the renewed British efforts to secure Hill 70 and Fosse 8, life south of the La Bassée canal gradually settled down into a routine of trench reliefs and working-parties. Nevertheless this did not ease the strain on the troops.[53] As the British gradually built up their new trenches, constructed dugouts and brought up supplies – all whilst in bad weather – they had to contend with heavy and continuous shellfire. Because Hill 70 and the Dump remained in enemy hands, German artillery observers were able to keep a constant watch over the British lines and direct shellfire where required. The British could make little reply. The aircraft of the RFC were unable to spot German guns because of the low cloud and mist.[54] So heavy was the shellfire that it was found virtually impossible to bring artillery forward to support the renewed offensive without it being subjected to devastating counter-battery fire.[55] According to one officer, it was 'almost suicide to drive guns into the open by daylight'.[56]

The British front line and battery positions south of the La Bassée canal were 'heavily shelled' on 2 October, 'very hostile shelling' was recorded again on 4 October and likewise on the following day the front and support line trenches were 'shelled continuously'.[57] Such heavy shellfire inevitably took its toll. On 29 September the headquarters of 2 (Guards) Brigade in Loos was 'very badly bombarded all day by 8" shells'.[58] At 11a. m. a shell buried several senior officers including Lieutenant-Colonel A.G.E. Egerton (CO 1/Coldstream Guards), who was killed.[59] A similar episode mortally wounded Lieutenant-Colonel G.H.C. Madden (CO 1/Irish Guards, 1 (Guards) Brigade) on 11 October.[60] On 2 October Major-General F.D.V. Wing (GOC 12th Division) was killed by shellfire at his advanced reporting centre near the front,[61] and the following day, as elements of 5 (Cavalry) Brigade cleared the battlefield around Vermelles, a shrapnel shell killed Brigadier-General F. Wormald, the brigade commander.[62] Even after the main fighting had ended, the Loos battlefield was still an unhealthy place to linger.

On the evening of 27 September Sir John French bluntly informed General Joffre that unless the French Tenth Army 'attacked with energy and quickly', he would be forced to suspend his operations.[63] In response it was arranged that while the British continue their efforts to reach Pont à Vendin, the French IX Corps (17th, 18th and 152nd Divisions) would move up and take over the positions currently held by 47th (London) Division on the extreme right of the British line. It was hoped that the deployments would be completed between 28 and 30 September. However, owing to the bad weather and traffic congestion, it was the morning of 2 October before the French were finally in position.[64] In line with these reliefs, a reorganisation of the British front line began on 28 September and was completed in the following week. 3rd (Cavalry) Division, which had been hurriedly moved up to hold the village of Loos on the night of 26/27 September,[65] was relieved by elements of 1st Division. The front of IV Corps now ran from the Béthune–Lens road to the Loos–Puits 14 track. XI Corps now consisted of 12th (Eastern), 46th (North Midland) and the Guards Division and was in the line parallel to the Lens–La Bassée road to a point west of Hulluch where it joined I Corps.

As 28th Division struggled in the ruins of the Hohenzollern Redoubt, discussions regarding the renewed offensive continued apace. On the evening of 30 September First Army issued orders regarding the resumption of the attack.[66] Now scheduled for 3 October, it was arranged that XI Corps would secure the Lens–La Bassée road and finally capture the woods of Bois Hugo in conjunction with the French IX Corps, which would then be in position on its right. On the northern sector of the battlefield, I Corps would continue its efforts to retake Fosse 8, while preparing for a gas attack south of the La Bassée canal.[67] The commanders of I and XI Corps were invited to 'submit their projects as soon as possible'.[68] This renewed offensive did not take place, however, on 3 October. Much to Sir John French's chagrin, the date of the offensive was continually postponed and only took place on 13 October. On 30 September Foch wanted to delay any attack until 4 October,[69] and by 3 October, the attack had been rearranged to take place on 5 October. But the worrying developments around Fosse 8 and the Hohenzollern Redoubt conspired to thwart these plans. Under the heading of 'Secret & Pressing', Haig wrote to GHQ on 4 October:

> Owing to the heavy fighting that had taken place continuously during the last three days and to the large amount of work which has been necessary in order to secure the positions gained against further attacks by the enemy, it will not be possible to undertake the attack on FOSSE No. 8 and the QUARRIES until the troops are rested. Also, in spite of our attempts to

> keep the enemy fully engaged and to prevent his working on his entrenchments and wire, aerial photographs and observations show that considerable work has been done and that it will be necessary to prepare a regular plan of attack on similar lines to the preparation for previous attacks.[70]

Haig proposed to postpone the offensive until plans had been completed and full arrangements made.

The attitude of GHQ to this request (and the requests for further postponements that came in the coming days) was recorded in the diary of Lieutenant-General Sir Henry Wilson (Chief Liaison Officer to GQG). On 4 October Wilson noted that this was 'the second time Haig has done this. We agreed with the French to attack on the 4th, then Haig changed to the 5th, and now Haig has changed again to the 10th.'[71] While Wilson had a low opinion of Haig – his diary for this period is littered with snide references to the commander of First Army[72] – Sir John French was also unimpressed. His reply to Haig highlighted the growing gulf between the two men.

> Chief approves of postponement but he is surprised and regrets it is necessary as he has not before heard of continuous heavy fighting except at HOHENZOLLERN. It is understood that postponement is only for two or three days and it is necessary that attack should be made as early as possible.[73]

Somewhat chastened by Sir John's 'surprise and regret', Haig sent a collection of reports to GHQ later in the day explaining the reasons for the postponement. 'The attached reports show clearly,' Haig wrote, 'that the fighting on the front of the Quarries, FOSSE No. 8 and the HOHENZOLLERN Redoubt has been continuous and heavy, that the enemy on this front has made incessant counter attacks, and that the shelling, rifle and machine gun fire on the whole of the front south of the canal has been abnormal.'[74] Haig also noted that 1st, 2nd, 7th, 15th and 47th Divisions had been 'much knocked about' and 28th Division had not 'proved… equal to the task'. Haig hoped that arrangements would be 'sufficiently advanced' for the attack on Fosse 8 to be conducted on 10 October. 'If any further explanation is required,' Haig added, with perhaps a touch of exasperation, then 'I shall be glad to come to Headquarters and give it.'

Sir John's position was a difficult one. Even Wilson, hardly his biggest admirer, admitted on 9 October that he felt sorry for him 'because he is in Haig's hands over this business'.[75] Pressure from General Joffre, who had 'represented to the Commander-in-Chief the disadvantage to the allied operations… entailed by the postponement',[76] only added to Sir John's predicament. Perhaps he was still unaware of the magnitude of the 'all-out' attack that I, IV and XI Corps had conducted on 25 and 26 September and could not understand how Haig had managed to 'knock about' five full-strength British divisions in a matter of days. And once again the two differing conceptions of the battle held by the two officers produced friction. For Haig, the man who had been the author of the ambitious 'all-out' attack, he was aware very early on that, in his opinion at least, a great victory had been lost. As he confided to his diary on 27 September, further progress had not been achieved largely because of 'the initial mistake of the C-in-C in refusing to move up the Reserve Divisions close to the rear of the attacking troops before the commencement of operations'.[77] In his diary entry for the following day, Haig lamented the renewed construction of enemy defences at Pont à Vendin and recorded that when the Commander-in-Chief 'remains blind to the lessons of the war in this important matter (handling of reserves) we hardly deserve to win'.[78]

Conversely, the Commander-in-Chief found it difficult to understand why Haig could not continue to support the French with steady continuous attacks as he had been ordered to. Again there seems to have been a curious lack of communication between GHQ and First Army because while Sir John continually stressed to Haig that the 'general international situation... imperatively demand[ed] an early resumption of the offensive',[79] Haig had to tell him that without adequate reinforcements and proper planning, an 'early resumption' to the offensive was impracticable.

This dichotomy was never resolved and the tensions between French and Haig only widened as the days went by, with Sir John recording on 5 October that Haig seemed 'unable to grasp the situation as a whole',[80] and Haig noting (of French) that it 'seems impossible to discuss military problems with an unreasoning brain of this kind'.[81] It is also evident that Sir John no longer felt able to interfere too greatly in Haig's operations. In late September General D'Urbal (GOC French Tenth Army) had complained to Wilson about the 'rude and discourteous' manner of Haig and his Chief of Staff, Richard Butler. Sir John had apparently promised to speak to Haig about this matter, but it seems nothing came of it. French was, Wilson recalled, 'infatuated with Haig so he wouldn't say much'.[82]

Sir John's emotional and physical state deteriorated further during this period. While he was encouraged by the great number of telegrams he received on 28 September congratulating him on his sixty-third birthday, these could not dispel the gathering gloom in his headquarters,[83] and he was clearly depressed by the results of the Allied offensive, occasionally even slipping into defeatism. After a visit to French's headquarters on 28 September, Haig recorded that Sir John 'seemed tired of the war, and said that in his opinion we ought to take the first opportunity of concluding peace otherwise England would be ruined'.[84] Yet, typically, he also suffered a number of mood swings. On 8 October Sir John met Haig at St Omer. According to Haig's account, Sir John was 'in a chastened mood!' and was 'evidently anxious to make amends for the fiery letters which had been sent to me by his orders'.[85]

As well as the need to conduct the necessary reconnaissance, rest the infantry and bring up the gas cylinders and smoke candles, the renewed offensive was delayed by a heavy German counter-attack on 8 October. Although this attack did not result in any major loss of ground, it interfered with the programme for bringing the gas cylinders into the trenches during the night of 8/9 October.[86] Because Haig planned to use gas and smoke for the renewed offensive, the same delicate process of negotiation, over what would happen if the weather conditions were unsuitable, which had consumed the days before the main assault, were again encountered. They were almost identical to the arguments and discussions in the weeks before the main attacks on 25 September and again revealed the fractured communication that existed between GHQ and First Army. Between 5 and 12 October a flurry of letters passed between the two headquarters about the date for the renewed attack, with Haig continually asking for flexibility when to strike and GHQ always pressing that the attacks should go in on the date arranged with the French. At no stage does there seem to have been a thorough and open discussion about what the requirements of gas entailed and how this would naturally dictate the date of the attack. Instead French and Haig muddled on, arguing from completely different standpoints and, unsurprisingly, being unable to move from them. A brief insight into this lack of communication can be gained from a private letter to Haig from Sir William Robertson (CGS GHQ) on 6 October.[87] Because Sir John felt that he was 'liable to be misunderstood', Robertson confirmed (on Sir John's behalf) that 10 October was 'definitely to be the day of the attack'. But clearly having little idea about what Haig was actually intending to do, Robertson also asked whether First Army was making a feint north of the La Bassée canal, when the preliminary bombardment was scheduled to begin, and would Haig 'kindly let me have a brief outline of your proposals'.

GHQ had officially informed Haig earlier that day that the Commander-in-Chief approved 10 October as the date of the attack.[88] But because the weather might be unfavourable and the Germans better prepared, Sir John requested that Haig assure him that 'the success of your plan is not dependent on the use of gas'. This was a rather odd statement because the primary reason why Haig had requested a postponement to 10 October was to allow time for the gas cylinders to be detrained and moved up to the front trenches. Haig had even sent GHQ a programme of events on

5 October detailing his proposed plans for the following days. The units around Fosse 8 would be relieved on the night of 5/6 October, and during the following two nights, the trenches would be prepared for the arrival of the gas and smoke equipment. Final reliefs would be made on the night of 8/9 October before conducting a thorough reconnaissance of the ground on 9 October. The attack would then take place the following day.[89]

These plans seem to have either been misunderstood or ignored by Sir John French, probably because of his reluctance to incur the wrath of Joffre and Foch. GHQ's letter of 6 October also went on to state that 'your large superiority in guns and the good supply of ammunition available… should be capable of producing such an effect upon the enemy and his defences as to justify us in anticipating success, without undue loss, even if gas cannot be used.'[90] Haig replied on 8 October. He fully agreed with Sir John's opinions. The 'prospects of success', Haig wrote, 'will be much enhanced by waiting until the preparations are complete'.[91] Haig now wanted the attack to take place on 13 October or the nearest date after with favourable weather conditions. Although this postponement was approved, Haig was warned that 'every possible effort' should be made to carry it on 12 October.[92] GHQ also informed Haig that he should be prepared to make his attack without the use of gas, so that 'it may in any case be carried out no later' than 13 October.

As these frantic, sometimes confused, discussions between GHQ and First Army continued, the rationale behind the whole operation began to weaken. Sir John may have fretted over Haig's continual delays and postponements, and feared the wrath of Joffre and Foch, but ironically, on the eve of the renewed offensive, he began to have severe doubts over whether to conduct an operation at all. GHQ contacted Haig on 12 October and informed him that because the French X Corps had failed to progress and that General D'Urbal was 'at present at a standstill',[93] the British offensive would, therefore, be fought for local tactical reasons. After securing Fosse 8, Haig was directed to capture those positions that would allow him to maintain his troops 'without difficulty in the salient which you have created in the enemy's lines'.[94] As had occurred before 25 September, the issues over the timing of the assault were never satisfactorily resolved and Haig was again left anxiously waiting for the wind. His final letter before the attack, written on 12 October, confirmed that all the arrangements had been made, and the operation could go ahead on 13 October. He did, however, point out that he was 'strongly of opinion' that if the weather was unfavourable it should be delayed until the first suitable opportunity.[95] Fortunately for Haig he was spared the horrific dilemma that he had faced on the morning of 25 September, with wind conditions that bordered on the unsuitable, because on the afternoon of 13 October there was an ideal south-westerly wind blowing across the battlefield with a strength of about five miles per hour.[96] Accordingly, the attack went ahead. But how was it planned and conducted?

The attacks on 13 October marked the final stage of the Battle of Loos. Although spasmodic bombing sorties continued in and around the Hohenzollern Redoubt throughout October and into the following month, this was the last large-scale attempt to recapture the Quarries and Fosse 8 by the British during 1915. Its repulse effectively brought the battle to an end. On 15 October Sir John French informed Haig that owing to the failures of the French operations in Champagne and Artois, and in view of recent setbacks, First Army should now confine itself only to those operations necessary to secure its left flank around Auchy and Haisnes.[97] The grand plans for an advance up to the Haute Deule canal had now to be given up. Haig met his corps commanders on 16 October and told them that the offensive was now over and that they should 'settle down for the winter'.[98]

The final stages of the Battle of Loos may have been overshadowed by the events of 25 and 26 September, but they were the subject of much acrimony and bitter debate in the years after. Despite being present on 1 July 1916, 46th Division (the formation that had been tasked with retaking Fosse 8) underwent its worst day of the entire war on 13 October, suffering over 3,500 casualties. Even Edmonds was moved to write that the attack 'had not improved the general situation in any way and had brought nothing but useless slaughter of infantry'.[99] In many ways the attack on 13 October typified much that was wrong with the BEF in this period. It will be recalled that a number of important elements of the plan were never satisfactorily settled, a consequence of the poor communication between GHQ and First Army. First Army's operational plans were also faulty, containing that familiar dose of over-optimism, muddled thinking and an inability to learn seemingly obvious lessons from previous failures that had so contributed to the disappointments of the preceding three weeks.

The object of the attack was to 'secure a strong line of defence including FOSSE No. 8 and the QUARRIES, which is capable of resisting immediate and subsequent counter-strokes'.[100] 12th Division would attack on a 2,000 yard front from the Vermelles–Hulluch road to a German trench known as The Window, while 46th Division (again attacking a front of about 2,000 yards) would be deployed on the left of 12th Division up to the Vermelles–Auchy road, aiming to capture the Hohenzollern Redoubt and Fosse 8. The operation was planned from the outset to be strictly limited, which meant that British artillery would not waste its shells on far-away targets. Haig admitted on 6 October that while the 'ultimate objective' remained Pont à Vendin, before this could be achieved it would be necessary to secure the left flank. Haig also went on to state that:

> The proposed operations were different to those just finished in so far as in the last operation there were reserve close behind ready to push through, whereas the operations proposed for the near future were more with the definite object of taking FOSSE No. 8 and the QUARRIES and securing sufficient ground to the N.E. to secure our left flank in the next offensive.[101]

In line with these directions the corps commander, Haking, made it clear that he 'did not propose to go a yard further in the direction of AUCHY LEZ LA BASSÉE than the line specified'.[102] While XI Corps captured Fosse 8 and the Quarries (with the support of 'every available gun'), IV Corps would be involved, with 1st Division pushing forward to the Lens–La Bassée road. The attack would also be assisted by the use of smoke as a 'barrier' on its flanks to cover the infantry and confuse the enemy.[103]

In some respects the plans for 13 October were a considerable improvement on what had gone before. At certain stages of the planning process it is clear that efforts were made to ascertain what had occurred earlier in the battle and what lessons could be learnt from them. In stark contrast to the orders before 25 September, Haking's attack plans noted that the attacking brigades 'must be given very clear and definite objectives, as regards the direction of their advance, the exact place they are to get to and the work to be done directly they get there'.[104] There was also an emphasis upon the transport of hand grenades to the firing line, the importance of keeping communication trenches clear, and the need for machine guns to be taken forward in the attack. In an echo of the tactics that had been used earlier in the year at Festubert, divisional commanders were instructed to place 18-pounders in the front trenches to help suppress enemy fire, while mountain guns were also to be made available to accompany the attacking troops.[105] At a First Army conference on 6 October it was agreed that 'Every available gun would be at the disposal of XI Corps', and smoke would also be dispersed over a wide front 'so as to induce the enemy to distribute his fire'.[106]

Efforts were also being made lower down the chain of command. On 7 October, Lieutenant-Colonel Hon. J.F. Gathorne-Hardy (GSO1 7th Division) visited the headquarters of 46th Division and shared with them his experiences of the recent operations.[107] Gathorne-Hardy highlighted nine points to consider for the forthcoming operation. Most were practical lessons revealed by the recent fighting, including the need to fill in trenches 'so as to force the Germans to attack over the top'; having an adequate supply of bombs; the need to train British troops in the use of

German grenades; the importance of depth in an attacking battalion; the value of smoke candles for consolidation; and the need to detail specific units to methodically clear captured enemy positions. 46th Division also interviewed an unnamed officer who had taken part in the capture of Fosse 8 on 25 September and discussed with him a number of important matters, such as the nature of the ground, the layout of German trenches and the location of barbed wire.[108] 12th Division laid out a full-size plan of the ground around the Quarries with sandbags and likewise 46th Division built its own dummy trench system.[109] The brigades of 46th Division were also involved in extensive bomb training, including the use of the new Mills bombs, which were available in considerable numbers for the attack.

While these activities were certainly encouraging and reflected a growing professionalism within the BEF, the old problems with command lingered. As usual, as the attack drew ever closer, over-optimism and a growing ambition began to make their presence felt. Although the attack was to be a limited operation, it still involved three divisions over a wide stretch of front and, as might have been expected, Rawlinson was worried. At Hinges on 6 October he 'suggested that the attack on CITÉ ST ELIE and HULLUCH should be made a subsequent operation',[110] but these words seem to have fallen on deaf ears. Contrary to Rawlinson's concerns, Haking believed that there were good grounds for optimism.

> In spite of the short time available there is little doubt that with the assistance of smoke and of such gas cylinders as we can get into the trenches in the time, and with the very powerful artillery support placed at our disposal by 1st Army, we have a better chance of gaining our limited objective ever [*sic*] than the troops who made the original attack on 25th Septr [*sic*], partly because the enemy is now more shaken and disorganised and partly because we are in a position to produce a tremendous artillery bombardment against a very small portion of the enemy's front. The enemy's failure, with heavy losses, in his attack on 6th will also be a great advantage to us.[111]

While there was little evidence that the enemy were – in Haking's words – 'shaken and disorganised', which was little more than wishful thinking, the real problem was artillery support. Because the attack on Fosse 8 would be preceded by a 'tremendous' bombardment with 'every available gun' against a relatively short stretch of front, it seems to have been assumed by First Army and XI Corps that it would completely suppress all resistance and allow the attacking troops to capture their objectives without heavy loss.

What artillery support was available for the attack? The attack of 12th Division was to be supported by thirty batteries of field artillery (mostly 18-pounders and 4.5" howitzers) firing at the German positions between

Hulluch and just north of the Quarries.[112] 46th Division's attack would be preceded by the fire of twenty-six batteries of field artillery directly against Fosse 8. Three groups of heavy artillery, No. 5 Group HAR (Brigadier-General T.A. Tancred), No. 1 Group HAR (Brigadier-General G. McK. Franks) and the Siege Group (Brigadier-General W.J. Napier), directly under Haking at XI Corps headquarters, would also support the attack by demolishing enemy trenches, targeting machine gun positions, stopping hostile counter-attacks and conducting counter-battery work. As usual counter-battery work was given a low priority and a considerable proportion of these heavy guns, which arguably should have been used to try and suppress enemy batteries, were concentrated against Fosse 8 during the intensive bombardment 'when counter-battery work is not so important'.[113]

Artillery preparation was to be split into several clear sections.[114] During 10 and 12 October divisional artillery would commence wire-cutting while the heavy guns searched out enemy trenches and strongpoints. This would continue into the morning of 13 October, when at 12 noon an intensive heavy bombardment would begin, lasting for one hour. At 1p.m. the gas and smoke would be released as the fire of the heavy artillery lifted upon Corons de Pekin, Corons de Maroc, Pentagon Redoubt and the Dump. Divisional artillery would remain sweeping the front trenches with shrapnel and at 2p.m. the infantry would go 'over the top'. This tactic seems to have originated from Haking and echoed the earlier artillery preparation for the Guards Division on 27 September when concern had been expressed about lifting the heavy artillery from the German front line before Zero Hour. Haig had even telephoned Haking on 28 September, telling him that 'He thinks it was a mistake not keeping the heavy howitzers on longer, and that was the reason of the failure.'[115] But in spite of these misgivings Haig (characteristically) did little to influence XI Corps' artillery plan for 13 October. Why did Haking order the heavy artillery to lift from the enemy trenches before Zero Hour? While there was an understandable concern that heavy shells would disperse the gas and smoke, which shrapnel would not do,[116] Haking also 'wanted to give the enemy *a chance of running away* and for this reason he thought it would be a good plan for his guns to start bombarding the front of the hostile defences and then gradually lift'.[117]

This may have sounded well to the staff of First Army and XI Corps but Major-General Hon. E.J. Montagu-Stuart-Wortley (GOC 46th Division) was distinctly unimpressed.[118] He would later complain that his division had been 'hurried into the trenches' with barely enough time 'to become acquainted with the actual position',[119] something that the officers of 28th Division would have been very familiar with. After seeing the ground for himself, Stuart-Wortley was of the opinion that only a step-by-step advance using the power of artillery could succeed in wresting Fosse 8 from the Germans. Unfortunately, his concerns were overruled and in another example of the gross over-optimism that infected First Army headquarters, he was apparently told that because his attack was to be preceded by 'the fire of 400 guns', his men would probably 'reach Fosse 8 *without firing a shot*'.[120] Haking seems to have been mesmerized by the power of the bombardment and honestly believed that under this fire German resistance would crumble. He gave a number of speeches to the attacking brigades in the days before the attack, which were strikingly reminiscent of those he had given to 21st and 24th Divisions before their 'baptism of fire'.[121] To say that Haking was being over-optimistic is an understatement; either he was guilty of seriously misleading the troops under his command, or he was simply ignorant of the severe limitations operating on British artillery in this period. The bombardment was not only littered with technical problems, but also did little damage to the German defences.[122]

As well as artillery preparation, another element of the attack was the employment of gas and smoke.[123] Interestingly, gas does not seem to have been the central and dominating component of the attack plans that it had been on the first day; perhaps reflecting a growing disillusionment with cylinder discharge. Whereas on 25 September the British had staked everything on the devastating effect of gas, artillery was regarded as being the key weapon on 13 October, with gas being a useful accessory. In the days preceding the attack 3,170 gas cylinders were brought up from the rear and dug into sandbagged entrenchments in the British front line.[124] There seems to be some confusion about the effectiveness of the chlorine gas discharge on 13 October as there had been about 25 September. Edmonds believed that it 'did not provide even the limited assistance which it had given on the 25th September; in fact it chiefly served to give the enemy warning that an infantry assault was imminent'.[125] As might have been expected, Lieutenant-Colonel Charles Foulkes (CO Special Brigade) disagreed. Noting the 'perfect' weather, with a south-westerly breeze of five miles per hour, Foulkes wrote that the 'enemy's rifle and machine-gun fire stopped almost at once when the gas reached them, and the infantry of the 46th Division reached the redoubt at 2p.m. with very little loss'.[126] Although the attacks on 13 October were a disappointment, Foulkes attributed this to the 'superiority of the German hand-grenade', and a delay in the assault against Hulluch, which allowed time for the Germans to recover. Foulkes also noted the 'new form of apparatus', which prevented much leakage and spillage in the British trenches. This positive interpretation was subsequently echoed by Donald Richter, who wrote that the gas attack on 13 October was 'a far greater technical success than those of September'.[127]

Technical improvements may have smoothed out a number of the difficulties that had been encountered on 25 September, but the discharge was still a lamentable failure. According to Brigadier-General G.C. Kemp (GOC 138 Brigade):

> The gas attack was more disconcerting to the attack than to the defence, for some of it blew back onto our trenches and a good deal settled down into the shell holes and remains of trenches in the open between the Hohenzollern and the Dump and Corons, while mighty little reached the objective where most of the enemy were. It gave the enemy warning of just when the attack was to be expected and drew down an artillery bombardment before our men could leave the trenches.[128]

Further to the south the gas seems to have drifted encouragingly towards the German lines but did little harm to the defenders. The smoke also filled no-man's-land, but by the time the British attacked, it had begun to disperse, leaving the attackers exposed to German fire. According to 35 Brigade's war diary, 'The smoke cloud was commenced, the wind was rather strong from the SW and the cloud was not entirely satisfactory, it varied very much in intensity.'[129] Similarly, on the front of 37 Brigade the smoke 'did not last long enough to cover the attack',[130] with the war diary of 6/Buffs recording that by 2p.m. 'all the smoke had cleared'.[131] Perhaps the most unfortunate aspect of the gas attack was that it attracted enemy artillery fire. On the front of 1/5th Leicestershire (138 Brigade), shellfire burst cylinders in three places, which filled the trenches with gas.[132] With the infantry on the northern sector of the attack 'packed like sardines' into the trenches, the result was horribly predictable; with one survivor recalling that many men were 'unable to reach the protective cloths in their pockets'.[133] There are also worrying references to the state of drunkenness among some battalions before they went 'over the top'. According to one survivor, 'we were given as much rum as we liked, [and] everybody was nearly drunk after that'.[134] As might have been expected, when the infantry finally clambered out of their trenches and advanced towards the German trenches, little success was achieved.

The main attack was conducted by 46th Division. 138 Brigade attacked on the left, achieving some initial success, but at heavy cost. The opening attack, conducted by 1/4th Leicestershire and 1/5th Lincolnshire, managed to break into the Hohenzollern Redoubt 'with comparatively little loss', but as the infantry attempted to push on further, they came under accurate German machine gun fire from Mad Point and the mining buildings around Fosse 8.[135] The advance came to a standstill about 100 yards short of Fosse Trench, with bombing parties meeting heavy German resistance.

If Fosse 8 was still to be secured it was essential that 138 Brigade receive support on its right from Brigadier-General E. Feetham's 137 Brigade. Unfortunately, in what was perhaps the most miserable episode of the entire day, Feetham's attack rapidly collapsed under a devastating weight of fire. The left-hand battalion (1/5th North Staffordshire) went 'over the top' into a 'hail of bullets' and against 'very deadly machine gun and rifle fire' could not progress.[136] The attack on the right fared similarly. Before the leading companies of 1/5th South Staffordshire could reach the front line 'all the officers and most of the men had fallen'.[137] The attack launched from Big Willie by the rest of the battalion was also completely unsuccessful.[138]

To the right of 46th Division lay Major-General A.B. Scott's 12th (Eastern) Division, deployed on a front of two brigades between the Quarries and the Vermelles–Hulluch road. It is evident that the artillery bombardment and the gas and smoke discharge were no more successful on this sector than they had been on the front of 46th Division. The attack on the Quarries was conducted by 35 Brigade. On the left, two companies of 7/Suffolk managed to break into the north-western face of the Quarries, and after heavy fighting were able to link up with elements of 7/Norfolk, which had attacked on the right.[139] Further to the right lay Brigadier-General C.A. Fowler's 37 Brigade, which was assigned the task of capturing Gun Trench. The attack was led by 7/East Surrey. Although suffering badly from heavy enfilade fire from the left, the battalion was able to secure Gun Trench. Reinforcements were gradually sent up during the afternoon, with elements of 6/Queen's helping to prevent a hostile counter-attack. The rest of the brigade was less successful with the infantry of 6/Buffs being mown down by German machine guns.[140]

The disappointing results of the British offensive were to be repeated on the rest of the attacking frontage. The task of securing the Lens–La Bassée road between the Chalk Pit and Hulluch was entrusted to Brigadier-General A.J. Reddie's 1 Brigade (1st Division, IV Corps). Reddie was given the unenviable 'short straw' of conducting what was essentially a holding operation, which was undertaken with little hope of success.[141] It was also unusual in that there was to be very little depth in the attack. Reddie's entire brigade was to operate on a front of 1,400 yards: 1/Cameron Highlanders were deployed on the left, directly opposite Hulluch; with 10/Gloucestershire on their left; followed by 1/Black Watch; 8/Royal Berkshire and 1/14th London (Scottish). The experience of 1/Cameron Highlanders was typical of what happened that afternoon. According to the war diary, 'The Company attacking over the open suffered severe losses from machine gun and rifle fire from the northerly and north-easterly flanks and was unable to gain the German position'.[142]

10/Gloucestershire made little headway against heavy shell and rifle fire; the attack of 1/Black Watch was devastated by two German machine guns firing from the flanks, which 'did much execution'; 8/Royal Berkshire was halted within 75 yards of its own line; and the two attacking companies of 1/14th London (Scottish) went to ground in no-man's-land.[143] Robin Prior and Trevor Wilson have aptly summarised the attack of 1 Brigade as a 'complete failure' and it is difficult to disagree with them.[144]

The later stages of the Battle of Loos may not have seen fighting on the same scale and intensity as the first two days, but combat was still severe, with nine Victoria Crosses being won in actions south of the La Bassée canal during this period.[145] The operations were also far from cheap. British casualties had been continuous and heavy with 46th Division being hit particularly hard. Suffering casualties of 180 officers and 3,583 other ranks, as Edmonds later wrote, 'it was long before the division recovered from the effects' of 13 October.[146] Although they were not sustained in a single engagement, the casualties of 12th Division were almost as high, totalling 117 officers and 3,237 other ranks between 30 September and 21 October.[147] The Guards Division recorded a total of 2,041 casualties at Loos.[148] And again senior officer casualties continued to mount. Between 27 September and 15 October, at least twenty-five senior officers were killed, wounded, gassed or invalided home.[149]

One of the most notable aspects of the later stages of the Battle of Loos was the deteriorating level of staff work and planning. The attack on 13 October was particularly bad in this respect, being riddled with errors, omissions and lack of detail. As 21st and 24th Divisions had already found to their cost, the lack of adequate maps of the battlefield proved disastrous. According to Captain G.J. Worthington (1/5th North Staffordshire, 137 Brigade), adequate reconnaissance of the ground was 'a difficult matter' because the maps supplied to him were 'in many respects incomplete[,] inaccurate and the trenches themselves had been considerably damaged in the recent fighting'.[150] Guides could offer little help. When the senior officers of 1/5th Lincolnshire visited the trenches opposite the Hohenzollern Redoubt on 8 October, 'No guides appeared to be available and the occupants of the trenches, including officers, seemed to know very little about them. Most of them had no idea of the number of the trench they were occupying. Very little information was gleaned from this visit, except what could be seen through periscopes.'[151] It is doubtful whether these problems could have been overcome in the short space of time available to plan for the renewed offensive, but certain aspects of the operation were simply careless. For example, according to the war diary of 7/Norfolk (35 Brigade), the smoke cloud that had been produced for its attack on

13 October had cleared from no-man's-land by 2p.m. and the enemy could be seen manning the parapet, apparently because the smoke discharge had ended at 1.40p.m., instead of continuing (as arranged) for another twenty minutes.[152] Grenades were another source of anxiety. As British troops desperately tried to hold their fragile gains in the Hohenzollern Redoubt and the Quarries, it was found with horror that 'many of the bags and boxes of bombs sent up during the afternoon were found to contain bombs without detonators'.[153] Similarly, during 35 Brigade's attack on the Quarries, when the supplies of Mills grenades ran out, recourse had to be made to the infamous 'cricket-ball' varieties, but because the men had not been issued with the correct striking equipment even these could not be used.[154]

Problems were not confined to poor staff work lower down the chain of command and many of those senior officers in charge of the renewed offensive did not perform terribly well. Indeed the high casualties and lack of success on 13 October prompted one of the fiercest attacks on British High Command during the entire war, when Lieutenant-Colonel J.C. Wedgwood, a Staffordshire MP and notorious radical, compiled a report on the attack of 137 Brigade (against Big Willie) and sent it to the Prime Minister, Herbert Asquith.[155] Although nothing was done with Wedgwood's report, his criticisms about the poor planning and over-optimism of the attack were valid and there were a number of problems with British High Command during these operations. At the highest level Sir John French was largely irrelevant. He had virtually abdicated responsibility to Haig before the battle and at no time did he show any real determination to get to grips with the situation, find out what Haig was planning and make sure his wishes were acceded to. Haig, on the other hand, continued to direct operations in a calm and confident manner, albeit realising that the chances of a real breakthrough had slipped through his fingers on the afternoon of 25 September. But once again Haig's performance was marred by his persistent over-optimism and his seeming inability to keep his subordinate commanders in check. The command decisions of Richard Haking were again poor and he was guilty of making the same mistake twice. His insistence on ordering the heavy artillery to lift from the German front trenches before Zero Hour during the attacks on 27 September and again on 13 October, despite warnings from Rawlinson and Haig that this would cause more problems than it solved, does not reflect well on his capabilities.

Reviewing the events at Loos between 27 September and 13 October it will be seen that the performance of the BEF was mixed. While there were certain improvements in tactical ability, such as the growing supply of Mills bombs and the impressive repulse of the German counterattack on 8 October, the later stages of Loos revealed a number of persistent problems.

Effective command and control on such a difficult battlefield, especially with German observers on Fosse 8 and Hill 70, was found to be virtually impossible. All British operations in this period were affected, in varying degrees, by the failure of orders to arrive, the lack of adequate supplies, and the difficulty of finding direction among the mass of trenches, particularly around the Hohenzollern Redoubt. Enemy shelling was persistent, often demoralising and devastating. British artillery support was weak and the RFC could do little in the poor weather. British attacks were undoubtedly pressed with courage and determination, but because there had been little time to make clearly understood and well-thought-out plans, and combined with poor artillery support, the gallantry of the infantry was to be in vain.

CONCLUSION: LOOS, THE BEF AND THE 'LEARNING CURVE'

Military operations at Loos did not officially cease until 4 November 1915, but the failure of the attack on 13 October effectively brought the battle to an end. The fighting between 27 September and 13 October had made little gain at considerable cost and merely postponed the inevitable reckoning after the battle. Intrigues against Sir John French began almost as soon as the attack on the German second line on 26 September had failed.[1] Within days Haig was complaining to Kitchener about French's apparent mistakes over the reserves,[2] and Sir John's despatch, published in *The Times* on 2 November,[3] brought the disagreements between GHQ and First Army to boiling point. Containing misstatements over the movement and timing of the reserve divisions, the despatch presented Haig with a heaven-sent opportunity. He quickly outmanoeuvred the embattled Commander-in-Chief and demanded the full story be published. Sir John's tepid efforts to kill the subject failed abysmally and by 6 December he had been forced out, setting sail for England a few days before Christmas.

This study has explained both how the BEF came to be involved in a major offensive in the autumn of 1915 and how it planned and executed such an operation. It is now necessary to review what conclusions can be drawn before looking at the influence of Loos on future British battlefield performance. As regards the political and military situation in the summer of 1915, as demonstrated in Chapter 1, the enormous influence of the Eastern Front needs to be understood if a clear picture of British strategic thought in this period is to emerge. Although the autumn witnessed the waning of Lord Kitchener's power and authority over his cabinet colleagues, he was still able to exert a considerable influence over the direction of the British war effort between May and August. The increasing number of depressing – some bordering on alarmist – reports emanating from the east have been largely neglected by historians, but it is evident that Russia was of singular significance for the Secretary of State. While rumours of French war-weariness undoubtedly caused concern, it is clear that the 'Russian news' unsettled Kitchener and proved to be the main factor in his decision to sanction British participation in Joffre's offensive.

The portrait of Field-Marshal Sir John French that emerges from these pages is consistent with the findings of his modern biographers, Richard Holmes and George Cassar. But two points need to be stressed. French's oft-repeated mercurial temperament may have been evident throughout the early stages of the planning process, but his determination, once his mind had been made up against attacking north of Lens, should not be underestimated. Considering how insecure he felt during this period, his stubborn refusal to be bullied into committing his troops to an offensive in a murderous landscape of slagheaps was laudable. Sir John's failing state of health should also be noted. This seems not to have been noticed, or to have often been brushed over with little comment by historians, but it is clear that French's poor health between late August and early September badly affected his handling of allies and subordinates alike. And even if Sir John had been absolved of blame for XI Corps' disastrous debut at Loos, it is likely that he would have been unable to cope with the strain of another campaigning year.

What about the First Army commander? Understanding Haig's role in both the planning and execution of Loos is crucial and has been extensively discussed in Chapter 2. He was, in many ways, the key figure. Although Haig emerged from the battle with his reputation enhanced – by December he was Commander-in-Chief – his performance at Loos was clearly flawed. Indeed, the planning of the battle at both operational and tactical levels was problematic. Haig's report of 23 June had been a realistic and sober appreciation of the difficulties of the proposed ground, but in the following months this attitude disappeared. Ordered to attack to the 'full extent' of his power, Haig was allowed considerable operational leeway in how he did this. But he seems to have misunderstood these orders and instead of planning for a subsidiary (albeit powerful) supporting attack, he committed First Army to a major breakthrough effort that it simply could not achieve.

Why did Haig do this? In order to understand why this was so it is necessary to understand both Haig's character and education. The lessons that Haig had learnt at the Staff College in the late 1890s meant that he saw warfare in a very traditional and structured way. According to Haig's teachers, victory went to the side with the highest discipline and morale. This would be achieved by a series of 'all-out' offensives that would wear out the enemy's main forces before the 'decisive' blow was struck by one's own reserves. This was the framework in which Haig planned the Battle of Loos, which was designed to be an 'all-out' and 'decisive' attack, not the limited, supporting operation that has sometimes been assumed. Haig's character – in particular his consistent optimism – should also be considered. This is an important, and perhaps insufficiently appreciated, factor in how the battle was fought. This manifested itself in three ways. Firstly, despite being well aware of the deficiencies of his artillery, both in guns and ammunition, he persisted in spreading his fire across too large an area, believing (despite much evidence to the contrary) that it would deal effectively with the enemy defences. Haig's attitude to gas has been poorly understood, but it can be seen that far from being unimpressed by the new technology, Haig believed that, given the correct winds, it would prove utterly devastating and allow his men to bypass two lines of German defences without much resistance. Sadly, Haig proved impervious to the nagging doubts from some of his subordinates about the likely effectiveness of gas. It seems that on 22 August, after attending a demonstration of cylinder-released chlorine, Haig's mind was made up. Gas would give him the decisive victory. But if doubt remains over the extent of Haig's chronic optimism in the run-up to the battle, his conduct once the fighting began is revealing. Despite disturbing evidence about the strength of German resistance emanating from the battlefield, Haig rushed XI Corps into action as aggressively as possible, with disastrous results.

A mixed picture also emerges of those lower down the chain of command. From the evidence presented, the performances of First Army's corps commanders, Gough, Rawlinson and Haking, will cause little drastic revision to their reputations. Gough performed reasonably well, although the decision to renew the attack of 28 Brigade and the dismissal of Brigadier-General W.A. Oswald (GOC 73 Brigade) were indicative of his natural aggression and frustration when the battle did not develop as planned. The starvation of reserve units from I Corps on 26 September effectively meant that Gough's attacks were allowed to die out without any large-scale attempt to push through the second line in his sector, although it did not prevent him from urging 28th Division to conduct a number of rushed and wasteful operations in increasingly difficult circumstances. Regarding IV Corps, Rawlinson's capabilities as a commander, including his role in the Battle of Loos, have been examined in some detail in *Command on the*

Western Front (1992).[4] His preference for limited 'bite and hold' attacks, and his reluctance to upset Haig's desire for more ambitious operations, was a recurring feature of Rawlinson's war. His experiences at Loos were little different. While being one of the most tactically astute commanders in the BEF, he proved sadly deficient in using his insights about artillery and the 'bite and hold' to conduct operations effectively.[5] When looking at the third key corps commander, Richard Haking, it will be seen that although he undoubtedly faced a difficult job in welding together XI Corps into an efficient fighting force for Loos, he proved unequal to the task. The poor relations between the senior staff under his command do not reflect well on his managerial skills. Haking's performance on the battlefield was even more lacklustre. He had relatively little to do on 25–26 September. He seems to have 'lost' his corps and had little involvement in the tactical plans for the attack on the second day. In any case, he offered no dissent to Haig's plans. His performance during the later stages of the battle was also poor and, like Haig, his over-optimism, traditional understanding of artillery and underestimation of the enemy were constant problems.

What about the rest of the BEF? As shown in Chapter 3, the logistical arrangements prior to the battle were impressive in scale, but weak in detail. The installation of over 5,000 gas cylinders in the front trenches had been a miracle of improvisation, hard labour and determination, but suffered from clumsy organisation. Loos was simply too big and too ambitious a battle for the BEF at this time. Although an unprecedented amount of manpower, supplies and firepower was assembled for the main operations south of the La Bassée canal, and a massive digging operation was conducted, lack of trained staff – from medical personnel to traffic control officers – hampered the efforts that were made. These factors were again in evidence during the preliminary bombardment. Whilst on paper the numbers of guns and ammunition available were impressive, there were too many targets and too many yards of enemy trench to bombard. Mechanical breakdown was common, many shells were of poor quality, intermittent bad weather did not help and not enough was done by the infantry manning the front line trenches to make sure that the enemy garrisons did not repair their defences. The failure of the preliminary bombardment along at least half of the British front line meant that much would depend, as Haig had always believed, on the effect of the discharge of chlorine gas and smoke. Unfortunately the misunderstandings that had bedevilled the planning of the attack were never resolved and First Army attacked on 25 September into indifferent wind conditions. With this in mind, and when considering the German anti-gas measures (as well as the dilution of the chlorine across such a wide front), it will be seen that the gas attack was never likely to achieve its ambitious goals. While reports can be conflicting, the gas discharge seems to have helped on the southern sector of the British front (which probably owed much to the good ground conditions), but was highly damaging further north.

When the leading British battalions finally went 'over the top' on the morning of 25 September, their attack was undoubtedly pressed with courage and determination (as shown by their high casualty rates), but the secondary attempts to reinforce and capitalise upon these gains highlighted the inherent difficulties of conducting a successful 'all-out' attack. As at Neuve Chapelle, adequate command and control broke down almost as soon as the leading waves began crossing no-man's-land. Because they had lost so many officers, many attacking battalions were virtually 'decapitated' by the time the German front line had been taken. Thus it proved extremely difficult for these units, exhausted and having suffered heavily, to continue onto the German second line against intermittent machine gun fire. Reserve units, often equally as tired, fared little better. Although still outnumbering the enemy, British infantry simply did not have the fighting power to subdue those localities that needed capturing. Artillery support was generally poor on both days. Hampered by bad weather, heavy enemy shelling and its technological limitations, British artillery was unable to open a way to the second line.

What of XI Corps and the debacle of the second day? Logistical confusion and poor staff work loom large in any discussion of the fate of the reserve divisions. It will be seen that the debacle of the reserves on 26 September stemmed from a number of interrelated causes, both internal and external. At the broadest level it was the result of the differing conceptions between French and Haig over how the reserves were to be used and who had control of them, but it perfectly highlighted a number of other weaknesses in the BEF. 21st and 24th Divisions were very 'green', with only a handful of experienced regulars, few maps, little information, poor artillery support and shortages of water. It can be no surprise that they failed in capturing the German second line. Nevertheless, the dire situation on the front of First Army on the morning of 26 September meant that even had both reserve divisions been hardened veterans with good support, the results would not have been much different to what actually occurred. Haig's decision to use 21st and 24th Divisions to make renewed attacks on the second day was clearly a gross mistake.

Another factor in the British failure to exploit the initial gains was the performance of the German *Sixth Army*, particularly General Sixt von Armin's *IV Corps*, which bore the brunt of First Army's main assault. Although heavily outnumbered and out-gunned, the defensive tenacity of the German defenders south of the La Bassée canal was remarkable. Admittedly the strength of the German defences took the sting out of much of the British attack, but the fighting skill of the machine gun teams, who were able to move into position relatively quickly (particularly into the villages on the second line) and inflict enough damage onto the clumsy British attempts to move forward, was enough to prevent any major exploitation. German counter-attacks in the open were not as effective, however, particularly the abortive operation on 8 October, but in the close-fought trench warfare around the Hohenzollern Redoubt and the Quarries, superior German equipment in bombs and trench mortars, combined with poor British command and control (with battalions rushed into ill-advised and poorly prepared attacks), meant that First Army was never able to recapture these localities after being counterattacked in the days after 25 September.

A neglected feature of the battles of 1915 was their lethality. Officer casualties were a particularly grisly feature of Loos. A close analysis of casualty statistics contained on the CD-ROM *Soldiers Died in the Great War, 1914-1919*, reveals that the first day of the Battle of Loos was very similar to the day usually cited as the worst in the history of the BEF: 1 July 1916.[6] On average, for 25 September 1915, 1,058 soldiers died per division. The figures for 1 July 1916 reveal that 1,017 soldiers died per division. Although 1 July was the bloodier day because it had three times as many divisions involved, the figures for Loos show that for those engaged, it was certainly as devastating, and perhaps even slightly worse.[7] Officer casualties were particularly disastrous. Within two days of battle over *forty* senior officers, including a divisional commander and several brigadier-generals, had become casualties, twenty of them fatalities. Such wastage could not be sustained. It was clear that the BEF – already critically short of experienced officers – simply could not afford to lose such valuable men. For Sir William Robertson (CGS GHQ) this was a huge problem. Reeling from the loss of another divisional commander (Major-General F.D.V. Wing, GOC 12th (Eastern) Division, was killed on 2 October), Robertson wrote:

> Three divisional commanders have been killed in action during the past week. These are losses the army can ill afford and the Field-Marshal Commander-in-Chief desires to call attention to the necessity of guarding against a tendency on the part of senior officers such as divisional and corps commanders to take up positions too far forward when fighting is in progress. ...[8]

The BEF, as Robertson fully realised, was now paying the price for fighting a major action against a formidable foe, with an army that was ill-equipped, half-trained and too few in number to gain the victory wanted so badly.[9]

Following the disappointing results of the renewed offensive at Loos, fighting died down on the British sector of the Western Front. The winter would see a continuous stream of New Army divisions arriving in France and Belgium and the extension of the British front line further southwards through the rolling chalk hills of Picardy. This would be the location for the next offensive undertaken by the BEF. Following the joint Allied conference at Chantilly between 6 and 8 December 1915, it was agreed that the coming year would see four simultaneous Allied offensives, with the Italians, Russians, French and British all making concentric assaults designed to put the Central Powers under crushing pressure without the chance to use their interior lines to shuffle reserves to and from the threatened sectors. The British part in this Allied offensive was the Battle of the Somme, which began on 1 July 1916 in conjunction with the French Tenth Army. The results of the first day on the Somme have often been discussed and it remains the worst single day in British military history, with nearly 60,000 casualties being sustained in a desperate day of unrelenting enemy machine gun and shellfire.

Reviewing the experience of the BEF during this period, it would seem at first glance that very little was learnt from Loos because of the poor results and heavy casualties of 1 July. This, however, would be a gross oversimplification. Notwithstanding the disappointing results of the opening of the Somme offensive, Loos undoubtedly had a considerable effect on British operational methods and marked an important milestone in the BEF's 'learning curve'. The BEF that existed in July 1916 was very different to the force that had gone into battle at Loos. The decision to concentrate Britain's fighting strength on the Western Front meant that the BEF gradually increased in size and complexity throughout the winter of 1915–16. On 1 January 1916 the BEF contained 38 infantry divisions (including two Canadian divisions) and five cavalry divisions split into three armies and which totalled just under one million men.[10] By 1 July it had absorbed another nineteen divisions, including a New Zealand division, four Australian divisions and five territorial divisions.[11] It also began taking over more trench frontage from the French and by the opening of the Somme offensive, the British front line ran from the Ypres Salient in the north to Maricourt just north of the river Somme.

The increase in the size of the BEF was mirrored in a vast increase in the scale and complexity of its logistical base. In particular, more resources were being put aside to deal with the inevitable toll of casualties. For the offensive on the Somme, the number of regimental stretcher bearers per battalion was doubled to thirty-two, special relay posts were established every 1,000 yards, a number of extra communication trenches were constructed solely for the removal of wounded from the trenches, and regimental aid posts and advanced dressing stations were improved by increasing protection, accommodation and comfort.[12] Unfortunately, even these rigorous arrangements proved inadequate for the scale of the casualties suffered on 1 July 1916. The Battle of Loos also sparked a major reappraisal of traffic control within the BEF. The inglorious and exhausting approach march of XI Corps has already been discussed, but it illustrated the limited resources, lack of preparation, and poor staff work that existed in the areas behind the front line of First Army. According to Gary Sheffield, the problems that had been experienced with traffic control at Loos 'brought about the birth of modern traffic control in the British Army. The high level of success in campaigns since Loos can be attributed in large part to the Corps of Military Police learning from their mistakes on 25 September 1915.'[13] For future operations it was made clear that the quartermaster staff needed to work closely with the APM to make sure that traffic was properly co-ordinated and controlled. Policing and traffic control in the rear areas of the British front became ever more sophisticated following the debacle at Loos. For example, in July 1916, 18th Division's sector included 'diversionary tracks, roadside bays and a breakdown lorry for the clearance of wrecked vehicles'.[14] This should be contrasted with the confusing road traffic arrangements prior to Loos when a staff officer complained that 'it was most difficult to effect a traffic circuit at all, without encroaching on the areas of other divisions'.[15]

As well as undergoing organisational and administrative changes, the weapons systems available to the BEF began to mature. Chief amongst these developments was the continued growth and evolution of the Royal Artillery. By 1 July 1916 British artillery was more accurate than it had been the previous year, although it still suffered from 'dud' shells and worn guns.[16] The numbers of guns and shells available increased dramatically during 1916, although whether there was still *enough* for the coming offensive was a source of some discussion in the British War Cabinet. By June 1916 Britain was producing between 140–150 heavy guns and 120,000 shells per week.[17] For the attack on 1 July Fourth Army had at its disposal 1,000 field guns, 233 howitzers and 180 counter-battery guns.[18] 'Cap-badge' resistance from certain sections of the Royal Artillery was beginning to weaken and more use was being made of meteorological, atmospheric and technical readings to improve the accuracy of shelling. Of particular importance was the systematic development of counter-battery fire.[19] Field survey companies were formed on 10 February 1916 and given executive authority to employ the new methods of flash-spotting and sound-ranging to locate enemy batteries.[20] The accuracy of British artillery was also helped by the continual expansion of the RFC. When the Somme offensive began it had grown from twelve squadrons to twenty-seven squadrons – of eighteen machines as opposed to twelve in 1915 – and contained improved types of aircraft such as the F.E.2b, the D.H.2 and the French Nieuport Scout.[21]

How the BEF handled its guns was also improving. On 23 October 1915 the position of GOCRA, which replaced the old BGRA at corps headquarters, marked a further step forward in the command of artillery. While BGRAs had been merely advisors with no power to actually command batteries, the GOCRA possessed executive power to command batteries within each corps. This arrangement did, however, take until the end of 1916 to become definite.[22] The bombardments that British artillery fired also became ever more complex after the Battle of Loos. It is possible that a rudimentary 'creeping' barrage – a moving wall of shells that would 'lift' or 'jump' onto further targets with the infantry following in its wake – was fired by 15th (Scottish) Division at Loos,[23] but it was still a very novel technique when the Somme offensive began. Although several corps utilised 'a creeping element' in their barrages on 1 July 1916 (to make sure that differences in terrain were adequately covered by shellfire), most corps used a 'lifting' barrage.[24] The fighting that occurred during the summer and early autumn on the Somme proved a vital testing ground for new artillery techniques. The 'creeping' barrage, which had not been fully understood and was only executed 'shakily' in July 1916, had been – as the history of the Royal Artillery comments – 'perfected and with confidence' by October and November.[25] By the end of the battle there was also a noticeable decrease in the amount of faulty or 'dud' ammunition that was being fired.

Concurrent with these developments in artillery were changes in the structure of the British division. Many senior regular officers instinctively regarded the New Armies with great suspicion and the inglorious circumstances surrounding 21st and 24th Divisions on 26 September 1915 did nothing to allay these concerns.[26] But how was the BEF to turn these 'green' divisions into hardened formations, able to survive the test of battle? Several solutions were drawn up in the months following Loos, including the 'stiffening' of New Army divisions with the substitution of a regular brigade for one of its original brigades,[27] and the development of the raid – known somewhat caustically as 'winter sports' – to inculcate battlefield craft into inexperienced units.[28] The amount of firepower that divisions could wield also increased. By September 1916, an average British division contained an extra field artillery brigade, three medium trench mortar batteries and a heavy trench mortar battery. Instead of having four Vickers machine guns, each infantry battalion was now equipped with twelve Lewis guns, three brigades of light trench mortar batteries and an extra sixteen Vickers machine guns brigaded into machine gun companies.[29] The urgent need for a reliable and effective grenade had been recognised early in 1915, but it was not until the arrival of large numbers of Mills bombs in 1916, with their safe time-fuse mechanisms, that British troops were able to hold their own during bombing fights with the enemy. These bombs could either be thrown or fired from the muzzle of a rifle with a blank cartridge. By 1 July 1916 all British units had also been issued with steel anti-shrapnel helmets.

In response to the sobering experience at Loos British infantry tactics began to evolve. Because a large number of Royal Engineer field companies had gone forward with the assaulting battalions on 25 September, they had sustained heavy casualties. It was decided that in future such companies should remain further to the rear and only go forward when the situation was suitable.[30] The influence of Loos was also evident in Fourth Army's 'Tactical Notes' of May 1916. For example, on 'The General Form of Attack', it was stressed that '*each body of troops must be given a definite objective to attack and consolidate*'.[31] If successive waves of men were passed through onto its final objective, this would obviate the 'confusion and lack of control that is bound to occur when one body of troops is given too distant an objective, and reached it in an exhausted and somewhat disordered condition, and is in consequence unable to resist a counter-attack successfully'. This was precisely the situation that 15th Division had found itself in once it had reached Hill 70 on 25 September 1915. As regards the employment of reserves, the influence of Loos was clear. 'Tactical Notes' stressed that reserves 'must be placed so that they can follow up directly' and that they must 'know exactly what is expected of them'. It was noticed at Loos that because a number of battalions had lost direction once the German front line had been crossed, future attack schemes 'should be simple and involve as few changes of direction as possible'.

There were a number of technological developments in the BEF between the Battle of Loos and the beginning of the Somme offensive that should also be considered. Perhaps the most revolutionary weapon that emerged from the battles of 1915 was the British 'tank'. Although not employed on 1 July, tanks made their debut on the Western Front on 15 September 1916. They were not a decisive, war-winning weapon – the Mark I tank was 26 feet in length, weighing 28 tons with a top speed of only 3 mph[32] – but their appearance undoubtedly marked a major accession of strength for the BEF and they would gradually improve throughout the war. Gas was another weapon that was continually improved and refined. The widespread disappointment with gas that followed the Battle of Loos did not hinder the development of British chemical warfare. Although gas would never again be the central component of a British offensive, it would prove an important auxiliary weapon, particularly when it was fired from shells in counter-battery shoots. By February 1916, Lieutenant-Colonel Charles Foulkes's Special Brigade had grown to a strength of 5,000 officers and men, split into twenty-one companies. Foulkes was also beginning to experiment with different types of agent (including phosgene and white phosphorous) and with various methods of delivery (such as mortars, flamethrowers and the infamous Livens projector).[33] Cylinder discharge was not used on a large scale on 1 July 1916 but the Special Brigade had conducted thirty gas attacks during the previous week (using both red and white star gas), which contributed to the general weakening of German defenders and their morale before the battle.[34]

Notwithstanding these improvements the period between September 1915 and July 1916 was not notable for any fundamental change in the way British High Command planned and devised operations. It seems that following the sobering experience at Loos a number of key lessons remained unlearnt by a number of senior British commanders and was to prove disastrous for the much bigger operation that was attempted on the Somme. Much of the blame lies with the commander who had been primarily responsible for the ambitious 'all-out' attack at Loos, General Sir Douglas Haig. He remained suspicious of any attempt at battle that did not aim at a total 'decisive' breakthrough and again attempted to do this on 1 July 1916. When this was combined with his difficult relationship with Henry Rawlinson (GOC Fourth Army), who was in charge of the attack on the Somme, a hopelessly muddled plan was developed that ended in disaster.

At the beginning of 1916 Haig reaffirmed his faith in the 'decisive' battle. In a paper entitled 'General Factors to be Weighed in Considering the Allied Plan of Campaign During the Next Few Months', dated 16 January 1916, Haig discussed the need for a simultaneous Allied offensive to be conducted in the coming year in order to 'deprive the enemy of the advantages of his interior lines'.[35] After discussing the relative merits of a series of smaller operations designed to wear down the enemy – something akin to Rawlinson's 'bite and hold' idea – Haig finally opted for his preferred method of a *decisive* offensive. He believed (rather spuriously) that such an attack would be quicker to mount and consume less ammunition than smaller, less ambitious attacks. Why did Haig continue to believe that a 'decisive' offensive was not only possible but also within his grasp in 1916? The events of Loos clearly had some resonance with Haig and influenced his approach to the campaign of 1916. Almost as soon as news from the fighting began to filter into the various headquarters on the morning of 25 September 1915, British commanders began assessing the results of the assault and trying to glean important lessons for future operations. But, as will be seen, Loos defied obvious explanation and the lessons of the battle were (seemingly) not straightforward with many senior British officers taking totally different things away from the battle. It seems that the debacle over the reserves and the dismissal of Sir John French clouded many of the real reasons for the failure of Loos, particularly the scope of the ambitious attack that had been planned and developed within First Army headquarters. It allowed many senior officers to write the battle off as a near miss that could have been so much more had the General Reserve been in place, and look no further for the causes of defeat. It was generally accepted that as long as sufficient reserves were in place for future operations the breakthrough would look after itself.

For Sir Douglas Haig the results of the Battle of Loos seemed to underline all that he held true for operations on the Western Front. Indeed, far from causing him to modify his ambitious faith in an 'all-out' decisive battle, the disasters of the second day only confirmed what he saw as the fundamental validity of his methods. Haig remained true to his long-cherished principles and simply interpreted the battle *through* these beliefs. His attitude to what had happened on the first day and the confused deployment of the reserves all fitted into this mental paradigm. This was revealed in his somewhat urgent letter to Kitchener on 29 September 1915.

> You will doubtless recollect how earnestly I pressed you to ensure an adequate Reserve being close in rear of attacking divisions and under my orders! It may interest you to know what happened. No reserve was placed under me. My attack, as has been reported, was a complete success. The Enemy had no troops in his second line, which some of my plucky fellows reached and entered without opposition. Prisoners state the Enemy was so hard put to it for troops to stem our advance that the officers' servants, fatigue-men, etc., in Lens were pushed forward to hold their end line to the east of Loos and Hill 70.[36]

Haig subsequently complained that the reserve divisions only arrived on the battlefield at 6p.m., when they should have gone into action '12 hours previously'. 'This, you will remember,' Haig continued, 'I requested should be arranged by GHQ and [Sir William] Robertson [CGS GHQ] duly concurred in my views and wished to put the reserve divisions under me, but was not allowed.' As a result the enemy had been given precious time to bring up reinforcements and defeat the later British attempts to move forward. Needless to say, that this was a partial and not entirely accurate account of the battle did not occur to Haig. Loos had simply been a defeat snatched from the jaws of victory owing to the incompetence of Sir John French.

Why did Haig remain aloof from the real problems experienced at Loos? In many ways, it was not in Haig's character to be self-critical. He was a robust, stubborn and deeply confident man. He had been given command of the BEF following the departure of Sir John and perhaps could be forgiven for thinking that this promotion vindicated the methods he had used at Loos. He could also have been unaware of the true depth of the problems experienced during the battle, possibly because he did not bother to order a thorough investigation. Because he (partly) blamed the failure of the 21st and 24th Divisions (and also 46th Division) on their lack of discipline, morale and 'offensive spirit', it was relatively easy not to look for the causes of defeat closer to home. Haig also remained robustly optimistic. He wrote to Lady Haig on 18 October of how he believed that 'the situation for the Allies is more favourable now than at any previous time in the war'.[37] Given the imminent ruin of the Balkans, the near collapse of the Russian war effort, the recent failure of the large Allied offensives on the Western Front, and the continued stalemate in the Dardanelles, it is difficult to see where Haig's faith came from. It is perhaps noticeable that from this time, as John Terraine has written, 'an element in him – certainly not new, but hitherto less evident – begins to be marked: a religious faith, planted in him by his mother in his earliest years'.[38]

Even the more perceptive Sir Henry Rawlinson initially seems to have concurred with Haig's views. As he explained to Lord Kitchener (and reiterated in letters to other correspondents), if the reserve divisions had been on the battlefield at midday on 25 September, 'I am quite certain that they would have been successful and that we should have broken through the enemy's second system of defences and been able to send on the cavalry to Pont à Vendin and Carvin.'[39] Robin Prior and Trevor Wilson have suggested, probably correctly, that Rawlinson's *post mortem* of the Battle of Loos suffered from 'an inability on his part to reach a dispassionate judgement on military events in which he had been intimately involved' as well as his desire to seek the dismissal of Sir John French. Nevertheless, Rawlinson's natural inclination towards limited-objective 'bite and hold' attacks remained and would again surface during the lengthy discussion process prior to the Battle of the Somme. Ominously, by as early as March 1916 Rawlinson was anticipating a 'tussle' with Haig over the choice of a limited or unlimited attack on the Somme.[40]

The views of Haig and Rawlinson – that Loos would have been a complete success but for the late arrival of XI Corps – would later become enshrined in the British Official History. However, not all officers who had been involved in the battle were convinced of this rosy appreciation and some had nagging doubts about the ambition of the attack, the effectiveness of gas and the issue of the reserves. Brigadier-General C.E.D. Budworth (BGRA IV Corps, MGRA Fourth Army 1916) believed (correctly) that the lack of artillery support had been the crucial factor in the failure at Loos. According to Budworth, in future the British should either fire short 'hurricane' bombardments or wait until they had enough guns and shells to totally destroy the German position.[41] In a lecture about Loos and its implications for future operations, Rawlinson's Chief of Staff at IV Corps, Brigadier-General A.A. Montgomery, believed that there were ten main lessons to be drawn from the battle.[42] These included the importance of a defensive flank; the need for reserves to be held in readiness close behind the assaulting troops; careful preparation; and the dangers of positioning divisional or brigade headquarters too close to the front where they could be shelled. Of more interest was Montgomery's discussion of the scope of future operations. He commended the attack of 47th (London) Division, but noted that its mission was 'far easier' than the tasks given to the other divisions deployed further north, which had to make 'all-out' attacks. Nevertheless, because the limited objective attack was 'easier' Montgomery noted that 'it does not follow that it is always the correct one', adding that the failure of the 'all-out' attack did 'not prove it was a mistake'. According to Montgomery, the 'all-out' attack failed because of a 'faulty method of execution' and not the 'the selection of the wrong form of objective'.

Although Montgomery's lecture certainly pointed in the right direction, the dissemination of lessons from recent operational experience was hampered in the BEF by what Tim Travers has called a 'proper *system* for learning' and 'a proper *system* for rational decision making'.[43] This meant that apart from the efforts of a few dedicated officers, it was very difficult for an empirical appreciation of Loos to emerge. It seems that in 1915–16 the BEF was really undergoing two separate, and often divergent, 'learning curves'. For while there was continual growth and development lower down the chain of command as divisions, brigades, the RFC and Royal Artillery got to grips with new technology and tactics and tried to understand how to use them effectively, the British High Command did not undergo a similar empirical advance in wisdom. Some lessons were learnt, but the consistent desire for 'decisive' breakthrough operations, which was in line with pre-war thought, meant that most major British attacks would be plagued by over-optimism well into 1917.

This conflict was noticeable in the approach to the Somme offensive of 1916. The planning of the Somme has been discussed at length, most recently by Robin Prior and Trevor Wilson.[44] At the highest level, it was, in many ways, not much of an improvement on that before Loos. The crucial relationship between Haig and Rawlinson remained difficult throughout 1916 and resulted in the hopelessly muddled plan for the Somme.[45] Haig favoured a deep breakthrough operation following a 'hurricane' bombardment, but Rawlinson preferred a more deliberate operation. Whereas at Loos, Haig, spurred on by the thought of using gas, had dismissed Rawlinson's concerns and opted for an 'all-out' attempt to break through the German lines, he was not as firm before the Somme. The two officers exchanged numerous letters, reports and many hours of conversation, but – in a situation that was reminiscent of Loos – do not seem to have ironed out their basic differences of opinion. An uneasy compromise was eventually reached, with the far-reaching objectives remaining, but the short bombardment being sacrificed in order for a longer, more methodical shoot to take place. And again, the preliminary bombardment was spread over too wide an area of front, with both Haig and Rawlinson being mesmerised by the unprecedented numbers of guns and shells available and ignoring worrying concerns from lower down the chain of command. Over 1.5 million shells were fired at the German defences, but their effect on the hardened dugouts and deep belts of wire was not enough to allow the waves of attacking British infantry to crash through the German front line. Only on the right of the British line (XIII Corps) was any progress made.

The attack on 1 July revealed that serious mistakes had been made by British High Command. Indeed, it is difficult to deny that although definite improvements occurred in the months after Loos, a number of important lessons from the fighting of 1915 were ignored or forgotten. These lessons then had to be painfully *re-learnt* during the brutal five-month campaign on the Somme. British infantry tactics, codified in Fourth Army's 'Tactical Notes', remained primarily based upon the linear module of 'waves' based upon weight of numbers and the bayonet. There was also an emphasis consistent with pre-war thought on the continuing relevance of discipline, morale and human factors. Because British High Command remained sceptical of the ability of New Army units to conduct the relatively sophisticated 'fire and movement' tactics possessed by the regular army, 'Tactical Notes' laid down an exhaustive list of practices, including specific infantry formations and the correct use of machine guns, mortars and artillery support. Curiously, General Rawlinson made no attempt to enforce these ideas and as at Loos, corps and divisions were left to devise their own formations. Although this was helpful when commanders used modern tactics – for example, Brigadier-General J.B. Jardine (GOC 97 Brigade) ordered his men out into no-man's-land before the attack – such good practice was not enforced until much later. For example, Haig and Rawlinson were both aware of the partial success of smoke in shielding the attacking infantry at Loos on both 25 and 27 September, but did not use it on 1 July 1916. Had it been used, it is probable that casualties amongst the attacking battalions would have been reduced considerably.

Counter-battery fire operated on a similar basis. One of the key lessons of the battles of 1915 had been the difficulty of reinforcing forward troops through a curtain of shellfire, and if the British were to rediscover manoeuvres on the battlefield, it was essential that enemy shellfire be reduced to a minimum. But counter-battery fire was given a low priority during the preliminary bombardment for the Somme. As Prior and Wilson have noted, Rawlinson may well have been convinced after Loos that the key to battlefield success was reducing German artillery fire, but for various reasons he seems to have paid little attention to it. As a result counter-battery fire was 'allowed to degenerate under Fourth Army neglect into a matter wholly at the whim of the individual corps commanders'.[46] Why was counter-battery fire given such a low priority given its fundamental importance to the success of the infantry assault? Possibly the unprecedented artillery resources available to Fourth Army blinded Haig and Rawlinson into thinking that it would be enough to devastate all the German defences over a wide area, but one is still left with the lingering suspicion that not enough had been done to analyse previous operations and improve on them for future attacks.

The plans and preparations for the Somme offensive may have been faulty at the highest level, but for those troops on the ground, the run-up to the battle was ironically a much more encouraging experience than it had been before Loos. Whereas the attacking divisions (apart from 47th Division) on 25 September had been issued with very little information, few maps and told to attack 'all-out' and go off 'into the blue', the Somme offensive was a much more thoroughly organised affair. As one veteran of both battles later commented, the 'secrecy and fog regarding the tactical situation and the topography' of Loos 'contrasted with the minutely detailed preparation and complete information imparted to all ranks before the Somme attack on 1 July 1916'.[47] The attacking divisions were issued with hundreds of maps and aerial photographs of their sectors, and were able to rehearse over practice grounds in the rear of the line. However, an unfortunate similarity between the two offensives was the amount of labour entrusted to the British infantry who were plagued by working-parties and fatigues. Many divisions only had one week to train their men before the assault on 1 July.[48]

Despite its infamous opening, by the end of the Somme campaign the BEF had been blooded and was a much leaner, fitter fighting machine. Vital experience had been gained at all levels and 1917 would see the fruits of this bitter campaign, with a succession of promising set-piece attacks at Arras, Messines, Third Ypres and Cambrai. As the BEF grew more experienced during 1916–17, more and more command was devolved to subordinates. As Andy Simpson's work has shown, far from being the 'postbox' of 1914, British corps began to assume increasing levels of responsibility during 1915–16, particularly in the artillery fireplans for attacks.[49]

The formal recognition of the corps artillery commander (GOCRA) in December 1916 reflected the increasing centrality of artillery in the BEF's operations. The infantry were also evolving. In December 1916 GHQ issued SS 135, a pamphlet entitled *Instructions for the Training of Divisions for Offensive Operations*, and this was followed in February 1917 by *Instructions for the Training of Platoons for Offensive Actions* (SS 143). These pamphlets placed a great emphasis on the platoon becoming a self-contained firebase and recognised the need to adopt looser, more flexible infantry formations without losing cohesion.[50]

There can be little doubt that Haig improved as a commander during the war. In particular, he learnt to appreciate logistics during 1916. While logistics had not featured too heavily in his plans for Loos, the partial breakdown in supply on the Somme during August 1916 meant that it could no longer be ignored. Haig's enthusiastic support for the former Deputy General Manager of the North-Eastern Railway, Sir Eric Geddes (appointed Director General of Transportation at GHQ on 6 December), who conducted a far-reaching reform of British logistical and transport infrastructure, from the base ports to the front, was indicative of a new concern for the problems of sustaining a mass army.[51] According to Prior and Wilson, both Haig's and Rawlinson's performances improved when they had, in effect, less to do. While at Loos they were deeply involved in planning the battle and devising how to use the available technology, including artillery and gas, they gradually assumed less and less responsibility for these matters as the war progressed. During the later stages of the war, particularly by 1918, Haig and his army commanders could concentrate on setting operational objectives and count on their subordinates, who were by now fully versed in their respective roles and using technology that was familiar and had been well developed over the previous four years to carry them out.[52] This was simply not possible in 1915.

It is hoped that this study will contribute to a growing appreciation of a poorly understood period of the BEF, but much work remains to be done on 1915. Neuve Chapelle has been discussed in some detail, but First Army's battles of May and June remain neglected, especially the important operations around Festubert that followed the debacle at Aubers Ridge. And while the Second Battle of Ypres has recently attracted some welcome attention, a truly satisfactory operational history is still required.[53] The mechanics of command during this period also merit attention, especially the movement and promotion of what became the middle ranks of the BEF in 1916–18 from a tiny base in 1914–15. A comparative study between First and Second Armies during 1915 would also yield important results on whether the methods of both armies were different and why this was so.

The subsequent controversy about the reserves, and why they had arrived on the battlefield so late, effectively ended Sir John French's tenure as Commander-in-Chief. But this scandal helped to mask some of the more fundamental problems with the Loos attack, so riven was it with contradiction. Although he had once been a protégé of Haig's, Hubert Gough provided one of the most intelligent critiques of Haig's performance during the battle. Commenting on the drafts of the Official History in 1926, Gough asked whether, even if an attack had to be staged to help the French and to pin German reserves, it should have been planned 'on the very ambitious scale that Sir Douglas Haig adopted'.

> Should not the attack have been strictly limited in its objectives? Such an attack, if successful, would have drawn as many reserves as it actually did. It would not have caused such heavy casualties and such disappointment. If the French had met with some marked success in our vicinity it would then not have been difficult to organise and launch fresh attacks on our front. If they failed, as turned out to be the case, heavy casualties in attempting to get forward would have been avoided.[54]

'Haig's optimism in these operations, as in many others,' added Gough, 'obscured his judgement and led to heavy casualties in attempts to advance and decisively defeat the German army, with very insufficient means.' And although these comments were made in the safety of post-war anonymity, it is difficult to disagree with them. Nevertheless, despite suffering from poor health, Sir John cannot escape censure. He should have made it clear, early on, exactly where he wanted the reserves, which would have straightened out Haig's misunderstandings about what type of attack he was expected to make. But French seemingly lost all interest in the battle after Kitchener had forced his hand, and his moral courage, so noticeable in his discussions with Joffre, deserted him when facing Haig.

NOTES

INTRODUCTION

1 Sir J.E. Edmonds (comp.), *History of the Great War: Military Operations France & Belgium, 1915*, vol. 2, *Battles of Aubers Ridge, Festubert and Loos* (London/Nashville: Imperial War Museum/Battery Press, 1995; first published 1928).

2 The standard popular work has, for many years, been P. Warner, *The Battle of Loos* (Ware, Hertfordshire: Wordsworth, 2000; first published 1976). It is, however, deeply flawed and should be treated with caution. It is not a history of the fighting, but a rather uneven collection of personal letters and memoirs from veterans. See also I. Hay, *The First Hundred Thousand. Being The Unofficial Chronicle of a Unit of "K(I)"* (London: Blackwood, 1916); A. Clark, *The Donkeys* (London: Pimlico, 1997; first published 1961), Chapters 10–12; R. Prior & T. Wilson, *Command on the Western Front. The Military Career of Sir Henry Rawlinson 1914–18* (Oxford: Blackwell, 1992), pp. 100–34; D. Richter, *Chemical Soldiers. British Gas Warfare in World War One* (London: Leo Cooper, 1994), pp. 36–93; A. Rawson, *Battleground Europe, Loos – Hill 70* (Barnsley: Leo Cooper, 2002) and *Battleground Europe, Loos – Hohenzollern Redoubt* (Barnsley: Leo Cooper, 2003). For the origins of the battle see R. Williams, 'Lord Kitchener and the Battle of Loos: French Politics and British Strategy in the Summer of 1915', in L. Freedman, P. Hayes & R. O'Neill (eds.), *War, Strategy and International Politics. Essays in Honour of Sir Michael Howard* (Oxford: Clarendon Press, 1992), pp. 117–32.

3 P. MacGill, *The Great Push* (London: Herbert Jenkins, 1916); J.C. Dunn (ed.), *The War the Infantry Knew 1914–1919* (London: Abacus, 2004; first published 1938), Chapter 6; F. Richards, *Old Soldiers Never Die* (London: Anthony Mott, 1983) Chapter 9; R. Graves, *Goodbye To All That* (London: Penguin, 1960; first published 1929), Chapter 15; A. Stuart Dolden, *Cannon Fodder* (Poole: Blandford Press, 1980), Chapter 5; R.B. Talbot-Kelly, *A Subaltern's Odyssey* (London: William Kimber, 1980), Chapter 2; P. Maze, *A Frenchman in Khaki* (Kingswood: William Heinemann, 1934). Loos also appears in several novels, including F.S Brereton, *Under French's Command. A Story of the Western Front from Neuve Chapelle to Loos* (London: Blackie & Son, 1915); H. Willamson, *A Fox Under My Cloak* (Stroud: Sutton, 1996; first published 1955); J. Masters, *Now, God be Thanked* (London: Sphere Books, 1979).

4 Graves, *Goodbye To All That*, p. 156; Stuart Dolden, *Cannon Fodder*, p. 30.

5 D. Lloyd George, *War Memoirs* (2 vols., London: Nicholson & Watson, 1933), I, p. 487.

6 B.H. Liddell Hart, *History of the First World War* (London: Pan, 1975; first published 1930), p. 193; Clark, *The Donkeys*, passim.

7 Edmonds (comp.), *Military Operations France & Belgium, 1915*, vol. 2, p. ix, 399.

8 TNA: PRO CAB 45/120, Brigadier-General J. Charteris to Brigadier-General Sir J.E. Edmonds, 24 February 1927.

9 LHCMA: Burnett-Stuart Papers, 'Memoirs', 6/1–12, Chapter 7, p. 76.

10 J. Terraine, *Douglas Haig. The Educated Soldier* (London: Cassell, 2000; first published 1963), p. 154.

11 G. Corrigan, *The Unwanted Battle* (Stroud: Spellmount, 2006); N. Cherry, *Most Unfavourable Ground. The Battle of Loos 1915* (Solihull: Helion & Company, 2005). Unfortunately, Corrigan's book was not available before this account went to press. Major G. Corrigan to author, 14 February 2006.

12 Perhaps the most extreme books in this school are J. Laffin, *British Butchers and Bunglers of World War One* (Stroud: Sutton, 1992) and D. Winter, *Haig's Command* (London: Penguin, 1992). Laffin's text contains a number of errors. For example he confuses that German gas attack at Ypres in April 1915 with the British gas attack at Loos in September. Although initially well received Winter's *Haig's Command* has been found to contain major problems with its use of evidence and archive material. See J. Grey, 'Denis Winter's "Haig's Command: A Reassessment"', *Journal of the Society for Army Historical Research*, vol. 71, no. 285 (Spring 1994), pp. 60–3.

13 T. Travers, *The Killing Ground: The British Army, the Western Front and the Emergence of Modern Warfare 1900–1918* (Barnsley: Pen & Sword, 2003; first published 1987); T. Travers, 'Technology, Tactics, and Morale: Jean de Bloch, the Boer War, and British Military Theory, 1900–1914', *Journal of Modern History*, vol. 51, no. 2 (June 1979), pp. 264–86; 'The Hidden Army: Structural Problems in the British Officer Corps, 1900–1918', *Journal of Contemporary History*, vol. 17, no. 3 (July 1982), pp. 523–44; 'Learning and Decision-Making on the Western Front, 1915–1916: The British Example', *Journal of Canadian History*, vol. 18, no. 1 (April 1983), pp. 87–97; 'A Particular Style of Command: Haig and GHQ, 1916–1918', *Journal of Strategic Studies*, vol. 10, no. 3 (1987), pp. 363–76; *How the War Was Won* (London: Routledge, 1992); *Gallipoli 1915* (Stroud: Tempus, 2004; first published 2001).

14 The only chapters to deal with 1917 and 1918 in Travers, *The Killing Ground* are mainly concerned with the writing of the Official History, especially the controversial Passchendaele volume and the German Spring Offensive of March 1918. A staunch defence of Edmonds and the Official Histories can be found in A. Green, *Writing the Great War. Sir James Edmonds and the Official Histories, 1915–1948* (London: Frank Cass, 2003). Criticism of *How The War Was Won* can be found in P. Simkins, 'Somme Reprise: Reflections on the Fighting for Albert and Bapaume, August 1918' in B. Bond (ed.), *'Look to your Front' Studies in the First World War by The British Commission for Military History* (Staplehurst: Spellmount, 1999), pp. 147–162; A. Simpson, 'The Operational Role of British Corps Command on the Western Front, 1914–18', D.Phil., University College, London, 2003.

15 For a concise introduction to recent revisionist work on the British Army during the First World War see G.D. Sheffield, *Forgotten Victory. The First World War: Myths and Realities* (London: Headline, 2001). For important other works see J. Bailey, 'The First World War and the Birth of the Modern Style of Warfare', *The Strategic & Combat Studies Institute*, The Occasional, 22 (1996); S. Bidwell & D. Graham, *Firepower: British Army Weapons and Theories of War, 1904–1945* (Boston: Allen Unwin, 1982); R. Prior & T. Wilson, *Command on the Western Front. The Military Career of Sir Henry Rawlinson 1914–18* (Oxford: Blackwell, 1992); P. Griffith, *Battle Tactics of the Western Front: The British Army's Art of Attack 1916–1918* (New Haven & London: Yale University Press, 1994).

CHAPTER 1: THE ORIGINS OF THE BATTLE OF LOOS: MAY–AUGUST 1915

1 The Schlieffen Plan has attracted a considerable body of literature. A brief selection will suffice. See G. Ritter, *The Schlieffen Plan* (London: Oswald Woolf, 1958); F. Fischer, *Germany's Aims in the First World War* (New York: W.W. Norton, 1967); G.E. Rothenberg, 'Moltke, Schlieffen, and the

Doctrine of Strategic Envelopment', in P. Paret (ed.), *Makers of Modern Strategy from Machiavelli to the Nuclear Age* (Oxford: Clarendon Press, 1986), pp. 296–325; T. Zuber, *Inventing the Schlieffen Plan. German War Planning 1871–1914* (Oxford: Oxford University Press, 2002) has called into question traditional interpretations of the Schlieffen Plan. See A. Schliffen, *Schlieffen's Military Writings*, ed. & trans. R.T. Foley (London: Frank Cass, 2002) and R.T. Foley, 'Origins of the Schlieffen Plan', *War in History*, vol. 10, no. 2 (2003), pp. 222–32. For a comprehensive modern account of the historiography see H. Strachan, *The First World War. Volume I, To Arms* (Oxford: Oxford University Press, 2001), pp. 163–80.

2 See R.T. Foley, 'East or West? General Erich von Falkenhayn and German Strategy, 1914–15', in M. Hughes & M. Seligmann (eds.), *Leadership in Conflict, 1914–1918* (Barnsley: Leo Cooper, 2000), pp. 117–137; and H.H. Herwig, *The First World War. Germany and Austria-Hungary 1914–1918* (London: Arnold, 1997), pp. 130–5.

3 For an excellent recent discussion of Falkenhayn's strategic ideas see R.T. Foley, *German Strategy and the Path to Verdun. Erich von Falkenhayn and the Development of Attrition, 1870–1916* (Cambridge: Cambridge University Press, 2005).

4 R. Chickering, *Imperial Germany and the Great War, 1914–1918* (Cambridge: Cambridge University Press, 1998), pp. 52–3.

5 E. Falkenhayn, *General Headquarters 1914–16 and its Critical Decisions* (London: Hutchinson, 1919), p. 56.

6 J. Terraine, *The Great War* (Hertfordshire: Wordsworth, 1997; first published 1965), p. 89.

7 Much of the following is taken from P. Bernard & H. Dubieff, *The Decline of the Third Republic, 1914–1938* (Cambridge: Cambridge University Press, 1985), pp. 29–32.

8 See M.M. Farrar, *Principled Pragmatist. The Political Career of Alexandre Millerand* (Oxford: Berg, 1991); 'Politics versus Patriotism: Alexandre Millerand as French Minister of War', *French Historical Studies*, vol. 11, no. 4 (Autumn 1980), pp. 577–609.

9 J.F.V. Kreiger, *Raymond Poincaré* (Cambridge: Cambridge University Press, 1997), p. 217.

10 L.V. Smith, S. Audoin-Rouzeau & A. Becker, *France and the Great War, 1914–1918* (Cambridge: Cambridge University Press, 2003), p. 80.

11 S.R. Williamson, 'Joffre Reshapes French Strategy, 1911–1913', in P.M. Kennedy (ed.), *The War Plans of the Great Powers, 1880–1914* (London: George Allen & Unwin, 1979), pp. 133–54.

12 C. Barnett, 'The Western Front Experience as Interpreted Through Literature', *R.U.S.I. Journal*, vol. 148, no. 6 (December 2003), p. 56.

13 J.C. Joffre, *The Memoirs of Marshal Joffre*, trans. T. Bentley Mott (2 vols. London: Geoffrey Bles, 1932), II, p. 327.

14 IWM: French Papers, PP/MCR/C32, French Diary, 'Minutes of Meeting at Chantilly', 24 June 1915.

15 Joffre, *The Memoirs of Marshal Joffre*, II, p. 394.

16 D. Stevenson, 'French Strategy on the Western Front, 1914–1918', in R. Chickering & R.S. Forster (eds.), *Great War, Total War. Combat and Mobilization on the Western Front, 1914–1918* (Cambridge: Cambridge University Press, 2000), p. 306.

17 LHCMA: Robertson Papers, 3/1/13, 'Notes from Conversations 4 June'.

18 Basil Liddell Hart declaimed 'What a majestic conception was this plan of Joffre's, and how utterly unrelated to the material conditions of modern warfare!' B.H. Liddell Hart, *History of the First World War* (London: Pan, 1975; first published 1930), p. 195. For other criticisms of Joffre's strategy see D. Porch, 'The French Army in the First World War', in A.R. Millett & W. Murray (eds.), *Military Effectiveness Volume I: The First World War* (London: Unwin Hyman, 1998), p. 215; G.H. Cassar, *Kitchener. Architect of Victory* (London: William Kimber, 1977), p. 379; Terraine, *The Great War*, p. 61.

19 For example, in September 1914, 12,000 75mm shells were being manufactured daily. By October 1915 the total had risen to over 150,000 per day. Joffre, *The Memoirs of Marshal Joffre*, II, p. 391.

20 For the 'cult of the offensive' see A.J. Echevarria II, 'The 'Cult of the Offensive' Revisited: Confronting Technological Change Before the Great War', *Journal of Strategic Studies*, vol. 25, no. 1 (March 2002), pp. 128–57. See also D. Porch, *The March to the Marne. The French Army 1871–1914* (Cambridge: Cambridge University Press, 1981), Chapter 11 and 'The French Army and the Spirit of the Offensive 1900–1914' in B. Bond & I. Roy (eds.), *War and Society. A Yearbook of Military History* (London: Croom Helm, 1975), pp. 117–43; M. Howard, 'Men Against Fire: The Doctrine of the Offensive in 1914', in Paret (ed.), *Makers of Modern Strategy from Machiavelli to the Nuclear Age*, pp. 510–26.

21 TNA: PRO WO 158/13, 'Note for the General Officers Commanding Army Groups', 14 September 1915.

22 A. Clayton, *Paths of Glory, The French Army 1914–1918* (London: Cassell, 2003), p. 22.

23 Ibid., p. 30.

24 Porch, 'The French Army in the First World War', p. 202.

25 Porch, *The March to the Marne*, p. 213.

26 See P. Guinn, *British Strategy and Politics, 1914 to 1918* (Oxford: Clarendon, 1965); J. Gooch, *The Plans of War. The General Staff and British Military Strategy c. 1900–1916* (London: Routledge & Kegan Paul, 1974); D. French, *British Strategy and War Aims 1914–1916* (London: Allen & Unwin, 1986) and *British Economic and Strategic Planning 1905–1915* (London: George Allen & Unwin, 1992); W.J. Philpott, *Anglo-French Relations and Strategy on the Western Front, 1914–18* (London: Macmillan, 1996)

27 A.J.P. Taylor, *English History, 1914–1945* (Oxford: Oxford University Press, 1965), p. 34.

28 G.H. Cassar, *Asquith as War Leader* (London: Hambledon, 1994), p. 109.

29 M. Hankey, *The Supreme Command 1914–1918* (2 vols., London: George Allen & Unwin, 1961), I, p. 334.

30 For Kitchener see G. Arthur, *Life of Lord Kitchener* (3 vols., London: Macmillan, 1920); Viscount Esher, *The Tragedy of Lord Kitchener* (London: John Murray, 1921); P. Magnus, *Kitchener. Portrait of an Imperialist* (London: John Murray, 1958); Cassar, *Kitchener. Architect of Victory*; T. Royle, *The Kitchener Enigma* (London: Michael Joseph, 1985); P. Warner, *Kitchener. The Man Behind the Legend* (London: Hamish Hamilton, 1985); J. Pollock *Kitchener, Comprising the Road to Omdurman and Saviour of the Nation* (London: Constable, 2001).

31 D. French, 'The Meaning of Attrition, 1914–1916', *English Historical Review*, vol. 13, no. 407 (April 1988), p. 389.

32 French, *British Economic and Strategic Planning 1905–1915*, p. 155.

33 TNA: PRO 30/57/50, Kitchener Papers, Lord Kitchener to Field-Marshal Sir J. French, 2 January 1915.

34 TNA: PRO WO 159/4/6, 'An Appreciation of the Military Situation in the Future', 26 June 1915.

35 Philpott, *Anglo-French Relations and Strategy on the Western Front, 1914–18*, p. 77; French, *British Strategy and War Aims 1914–1916*, p. 103.

36 TNA: PRO CAB 22/2, Minutes of Dardanelles Committee Meeting, 7 June 1915.

37 LHCMA: Clive Papers, 2/1, Clive Diary, 6 June 1915.

38 H.H. Asquith, *Memories and Reflections, 1852–1927* (2 vols., London: Cassell, 1928), II, pp. 106–7.

39 TNA: PRO CAB 37/131/4, Memorandum by A.J. Balfour, 2 July 1915; Cassar, *Kitchener*, p. 382; Philpott, *Anglo-French Relations and Strategy on the Western Front, 1914–18*, p. 79; French, *British Strategy and War Aims 1914–1916*, p. 107.

40 'Joffre's view's about the need for a new offensive were accepted by both Governments with the proviso that we must exercise *prudence* and *caution*.' IWM: French Papers, PP/MCR/C32, French Diary, 6 July 1915. Original emphasis. See also Viscount Esher, *The Tragedy of Lord Kitchener*, p. 141.

41 Asquith, *Memories and Reflections, 1852–1927*, II, p. 107.

42 Viscount Esher, *Journals and Letters of Reginald Viscount Esher, Vol. 3, 1910–1915* (London: Ivor Nicholson & Watson, 1938), p. 252.

43 Hankey, *The Supreme Command 1914 – 1918*, I, p. 349.

44 Joffre, *The Memoirs of Marshal Joffre*, II, pp. 380–1.

45 IWM: French Papers, PP/MCR/C32, French Diary, 'Minutes of Meeting at Chantilly', 24 June 1915.

46 TNA: PRO WO 159/11, Kitchener Papers, Brigadier-General Hon. H. Yarde-Buller (British Mission with GQG *des Armées Françaises*) to Kitchener, 11 July 1915, p. 7. Yarde-Buller seems to have confused his dates. He erroneously recorded that Chantilly followed the conference at Calais on 5 *July*.

47 LHCMA: Clive Papers, 2/2, Clive Diary, 6 July 1915; Hankey, *The Supreme Command 1914–1918*, I, p. 348.

48 Magnus, *Kitchener*, p. 348.

49 Cassar, *Kitchener*, p. 380.

50 Ibid., p. 381.

51 Philpott, *Anglo-French Relations and Strategy on the Western Front, 1914–18*, p. 79; French, *British Strategy and War Aims 1914–1916*, p. 107

52 Cassar, *Kitchener*, p. 381; K. Neilson, 'Kitchener: A Reputation Refurbished?', *Canadian Journal of History*, vol. 15, no. 2 (1980), pp. 220–1; French, *British Strategy and War Aims 1914–1916*, p. 108.

53 Neilson, 'Kitchener: A Reputation Refurbished?', p. 221.

54 Hankey, *The Supreme Command 1914–1918*, I, p. 351.

55 LHCMA: Robertson Papers, 7/5, Lieutenant-General Sir W. Robertson to C. Wigram, 13 July 1915.

56 TNA: PRO WO 159/11, Kitchener Papers, Yarde-Buller to Kitchener, 11 July 1915, p. 11.

57 I.M. Brown, *British Logistics on the Western Front, 1914–1919* (Westport, CT: Praeger, 1998), p. 103.

58 Between 22 April and 31 May 1915 General Sir Horace Smith-Dorrien's Second Army was involved in fighting around Hill 60 and the battle of Second Ypres. Although British attacks were made, they were (strictly speaking) part of a wider defensive operation.

59 Sir John French has attracted relatively little biographical attention: See G. French, *The Life of Field-Marshal Sir John French. First Earl of Ypres* (London: Cassell, 1931); R. Holmes, *The Little Field Marshal. Sir John French* (London: Jonathan Cape, 1981); G.H. Cassar, *The Tragedy of Sir John French* (London: Associated University Presses, 1985). See also Sir John's controversial memoirs, *1914* (London: Constable, 1919).

60 Supported by his officers, Brigadier-General Hubert Gough (GOC 3 Cavalry Brigade) threatened to resign if he was ordered to take part in any move to coerce Ulster into accepting Irish Home Rule. See A.P. Ryan, *Mutiny at the Curragh* (London: Macmillan, 1956); Sir J. Fergusson, *The Curragh Incident* (London: Faber, 1964); I.F.W Beckett (ed.), *The Army and the Curragh Incident* (London: Army Records Society, 1986).

61 R. Holmes, 'Sir John French and Lord Kitchener', in B. Bond (ed.), *The First World War and British Military History* (Oxford: Clarendon Press, 1991), p. 128.

62 See Sir W. Robertson, *From Private to Field-Marshal* (London: Constable, 1921) and *Soldiers and Statesmen 1914–1918* (2 vols., London: Cassell, 1926); V. Bonham-Carter, *Soldier True. The Life and Times of Field-Marshal Sir William Robertson* (London: Frederick Muller, 1963); D.R. Woodward, *Field-Marshal Sir William Robertson. Chief of the Imperial General Staff in the Great War* (Westport, CT: Praeger, 1998). For discussions of Robertson's performance in 1914 see E. Spears, *Liaison 1914. A Narrative of the Great Retreat* (London: Cassell, 1999; first published 1930), p. 217; Brown, *British Logistics on the Western Front, 1914–1919*, pp. 56–7.

63 Sir William Robertson, 'Conduct of the War', 8 November 1915, cited in Woodward, *Field-Marshal Sir William Robertson*, p. 19.

64 N. Gardner, *Trial by Fire. Command and the British Expeditionary Force in 1914* (Westport, CT: Praeger, 2003), p. 2.

65 See Sir C.E. Callwell, *Field Marshal Sir Henry Wilson: His Life and Diaries* (2 vols., London: Cassell, 1927); B. Collier, *Brasshat. A Biography of Field-Marshal Sir Henry Wilson* (London: Seecker & Warburg, 1961).

66 LHCMA: Robertson Papers, 4/3/24, Robertson to Lieutenant-Colonel A. Fitzgerald (Kitchener's Private Secretary), 19 October 1915.

67 Sir J.E. Edmonds (comp.), *History of the Great War: Military Operations France & Belgium, 1914*, vol. 1, *Mons, the Retreat to the Seine, the Marne and the Aisne. August–October 1914* (London/Nashville: Imperial War Museum/Battery Press, 1996; first published 1933), Appendix 8, pp. 499–500.

68 Philpott, *Anglo-French Relations and Strategy on the Western Front, 1914–18*, pp. 53–66.

69 TNA: PRO 30/57/50, Kitchener Papers, French to Kitchener, 3 January 1915.

70 Holmes, 'Sir John French and Lord Kitchener', p. 124.

71 LHCMA: Clive Papers, 2/1, Clive Diary, 3 and 4 June 1915; Robertson Papers, 3/1/13, 'Notes from Conversations 4 June'.

72 TNA: PRO 30/57/50, Kitchener Papers, French to Kitchener, 11 June 1915.

73 IWM: French Papers, PP/MCR/C32, French Diary, 19 June 1915.

74 IWM: French Papers, 7/2 (1), Haig to GHQ, 23 June 1915.

75 Sir D. Haig, *The Haig Papers from the National Library of Scotland*, part 1, *Haig's Autograph Great War Diary* (Brighton: Harvester Press Microfilm, 1987), 20 June 1915.

76 Ibid., 22 June 1915.

77 Haig split the battlefield into four sectors. The first lay south of the Béthune–Lens road. An attack here was not recommended. Not only were the British trenches too far away from the enemy lines, but they were also badly enfiladed by a feature known as the Spoil Bank. Any attack would be stopped by the heavily wired second line. The ground between the Béthune–Lens road

and the Vermelles–Loos road formed a more promising second sector. Observed artillery fire could be brought to bear on part of the German second line (known in this sector as the Loos Defence Line), the trenches were reasonably close together and forming up areas could be dug without too much difficulty. Haig did not recommend an attack on the third sector, running from the Vermelles–Loos road north to the Vermelles–La Bassée railway. The difficulties of the ground, distant trenches, hard soil and enemy observation, were similar to those further south. And again, if an advance proved successful, moving men and supplies up would be far from easy. The fourth sector lay between Cuinchy and La Bassée, an area that Haig believed would offer 'serious resistance'. An attack was practicable, however, because forming up places could be constructed and artillery fire directed onto much of the German position. IWM: French Papers, 7/2 (1), Haig to GHQ, 23 June 1915.

78 Sir J.E. Edmonds (comp.), *History of the Great War: Military Operations France & Belgium, 1915*, vol. 2, *Battles of Aubers Ridge, Festubert and Loos* (London/Nashville: Imperial War Museum/Battery Press, 1995; first published 1928), p. 117.

79 IWM: French Papers, PP/MCR/C32, French Diary, 23 June 1915.

80 When asked by French if his plans had changed, Joffre said that they had not. Although the French Commander-in-Chief did admit that there were 'slight differences' between his position and Foch's (who wanted a major effort in Artois), a second attack would be made, at a place, 'not yet determined'.

81 LHCMA: Clive Papers, 2/2, Clive Diary, 17 July 1915; IWM: Wilson Papers, DS/MISC/80, HHW 25, Wilson Diary, 28 July 1915.

82 IWM: French Papers, 7/5, 'Meeting at St Omer, 11 July 1915 10 a.m.'.

83 IWM: French Papers, PP/MCR/C32, French Diary, 27 July 1915; C. Falls, *Marshal Foch* (London: Blackie & Son, 1939), p. 95; F. Foch, *The Memoirs of Marshal Foch*, trans. T. Bentley Mott (London: William Heinemann, 1931), pp. 237–8.

84 IWM: French Papers, PP/MCR/C32, French Diary, 12 July 1915.

85 IWM: Wilson Papers, HHW 2/80/41, 'Note for Lieutenant-General Sir Henry Wilson', 15 July 1915.

86 IWM: French Papers, PP/MCR/C32, French Diary, 20 July 1915.

87 Ibid., 22 July 1915.

88 LHCMA: Clive Papers, 2/2, Clive Diary, 25 July 1915.

89 IWM: French Papers, 7/2 (1), GHQ to Haig, 22 July 1915.

90 IWM: French Papers, 7/2 (1), Haig to GHQ, 23 July 1915.

91 IWM: French Papers, PP/MCR/C32, French Diary, 24 July 1915.

92 IWM: Wilson Papers, DS/MISC/80, HHW 25, Wilson Diary, 24 July 1915.

93 LHCMA: Clive Papers, 2/2, Clive Diary, 4 August 1915.

94 IWM: Wilson Papers, HHW 2/80/44, 'Report of a Meeting Between Field-Marshal Sir John French and General Foch, Frevent, 27 July 1915'.

95 TNA: PRO WO 158/13, French to Joffre, 29 July 1915.

96 IWM: Wilson Papers, HHW 2/79/33, Joffre to French, 5 August 1915.

97 Apparently Robertson had tried to get Sir John to omit this sentence, which would place the British unreservedly in the hands of the French. Cassar, *The Tragedy of Sir John French*, p. 257.

98 IWM: Wilson Papers, HHW 2/79/35, French to Joffre, 10 August 1915.

99 See R. Prior & T. Wilson, *Command on the Western Front. The Military Career of Sir Henry Rawlinson 1914–18* (Oxford: Blackwell, 1992), Chapter 4.

100 Haig, who was informed of the 'artillery plan' on 7 August, confirmed that it was 'to be made chiefly with artillery and I am not to launch a large force of infantry to the attack on objectives *which are so strongly held as liable to result only in the sacrifice of many lives*'. Haig, *The Haig Papers*, 7 August 1915. Emphasis added. The 'artillery plan' seems to have originated soon after the Frevent conference. Sir John drafted a letter to Foch on 29 July asking him whether Joffre would be satisfied with the neutralisation of enemy batteries south of the La Bassée canal by British artillery fire. It seems that Sir John made this decision without the poisonous influence of Wilson who was away on other matters. He may also have been encouraged by a meeting between Clive and Joffre on the following day. Clive was apparently told that the attack on Vimy Ridge, to be made by the French Tenth Army, was 'going to be an artillery, not an infantry battle.' TNA: PRO WO 158/26, 'Note for General Foch Commanding the Group of Armies of the North', 29 July 1915, not sent; LHCMA: Clive Papers, 2/2, Clive Diary, 30 July 1915; TNA: PRO WO 158/13, Handwritten Note by Major G.S. Clive, 31 July 1915.

101 IWM: Wilson Papers, HHW 2/79/36, Joffre to French, 12 August 1915; Wilson Papers, DS/MISC/80, HHW 25, Wilson Diary, 12 August 1915.

102 Joffre to Millerand, 30 July 1915, cited in Philpott, *Anglo-French Relations and Strategy on the Western Front, 1914–18*, pp. 98–99.

103 BLO: Asquith Papers, MS. ENG. LETT. C. 542/2, Asquith to Mrs S. Henley, 15 August 1915.

104 W.S. Churchill, *The World Crisis, 1915* (London: Thornton Butterworth, 1923), p. 432.

105 IWM: French Papers, 7/4 (2), Kitchener to French, 20 August 1915.

106 R. Williams, 'Lord Kitchener and the Battle of Loos: French Politics and British Strategy in the Summer of 1915', in L. Freedman, P. Hayes & R. O'Neill (eds.), *War, Strategy and International Politics. Essays in Honour of Sir Michael Howard* (Oxford: Clarendon Press, 1992), p. 119.

107 Ibid., p. 120.

108 P.J. Flood, *France 1914–18. Public Opinion and the War Effort* (London: Macmillan, 1990), pp. 107–17, 147–78.

109 K. Neilson, *Strategy and Supply. The Anglo-Russian Alliance, 1914–17* (London: George Allen & Unwin, 1984), p. viii.

110 Neilson, 'Kitchener: A Reputation Refurbished?', pp. 207–27.

111 Haig, *The Haig Papers*, 19 August 1915.

112 Magnus, *Kitchener*, p. 348.

113 Cassar, *Kitchener*, p. 386.

114 Warner, *Kitchener*, p. 187.

115 TNA: PRO CAB 22/2, Minutes of Dardanelles Committee Meeting, 20 August 1915.

116 Royle, *The Kitchener Enigma*, p. 328.

117 See the account in Churchill, *The World Crisis, 1915*, pp. 410–1.

118 IWM: French Papers, 75/46/3, Kitchener to French, undated but from the summer of 1915. According to Sir John this telegram was sent on 18 December 1914. See French, *1914*, p. 355.

119 See M. Hughes, "Revolution Was in the Air': British Officials in Russia During the First World War', *Journal of Contemporary History*, vol. 31, no. 1 (January 1996), pp. 75–97. Knox's experiences are recounted in his *With the Russian Army* (New York: Arno Press, 1971; first published 1921).

120 Neilson, *Strategy and Supply*, p. 30.

121 TNA: PRO WO 106/1058, Knox's Despatch U, 26 May 1915.

122 TNA: PRO WO 106/1062, Knox's Despatch Y, 8 June 1915 and WO 106/1060, Knox's Despatch W, 12 June 1915.

123 TNA: PRO WO 106/1063, Knox's Despatch Z, 18 June 1915.

124 Ibid. One of Knox's colleagues told him that unarmed soldiers were being sent into the trenches 'to wait till someone with a rifle gets killed or wounded'.

125 In a telegram to Kitchener (dated 29 June), Knox reported that the Russian Third Army had suffered 75 percent casualties. TNA: PRO WO 159/13, Knox to Kitchener, 29 June 1915. The following month Knox also reminded Kitchener of the 'colossal' losses Russia had suffered since the outbreak of war, something amounting to 3,800,000. WO 106/1064, Knox's Despatch A1, 4 July 1915.

126 TNA: PRO WO 106/1060, Knox's Despatch W, 12 June 1915. Despatch E2 of 29 August 1915 (WO 106/1068) also commented upon the 'bitter' feelings towards the French.

127 TNA: PRO 30/57/67, Kitchener Papers, Hanbury-Williams to Kitchener, 13 June 1915.

128 TNA: PRO WO 106/997, Despatch LXXIII, 4 August 1915.

129 Viscount E. Grey, *Twenty Five Years, 1892–1916* (2 vols., London: Hodder & Stoughton, 1925), II, p. 211.

130 BLO: Asquith Papers, 117, Memorandum by Sir George Buchanan, 7 August 1915.

131 TNA: PRO 30/57/67, Kitchener Papers, Hanbury-Williams to Kitchener, 11 August 1915.

132 TNA: PRO 30/57/67, Kitchener Papers, Grand Duke Nicholas Nicholaevich to Kitchener, 19 July 1915.

133 TNA: PRO WO 159/11, Kitchener Papers, Yarde-Buller to Kitchener, 24 July 1915.

134 R.H. Bruce Lockhart, *Memoirs of a British Agent* (London: Pan Macmillan, 2002; first published 1932), p. 126. In a vivid illustration of the interconnectedness of the Western and Eastern Fronts, Lockhart's brother, Norman, was killed at Loos. Lockhart's reports – that, arguably, added some pressure on the British to do something in the west – yielded a tragic personal result.

135 BLO: Asquith Papers, 117, Buchanan to Kitchener, 18 August 1915.

136 Bruce Lockhart, *Memoirs of a British Agent*, p. 126.

137 TNA: PRO WO 106/997, Despatch LXXIII, 4 August 1915.

138 TNA: PRO WO 106/998, Despatch LXXIV, 7 August 1915.

139 TNA: PRO WO 106/1067, Knox's Despatch D2, 14 August 1915.

140 TNA: PRO WO 106/998, Despatch LXXV, 15 August 1915.

141 TNA: PRO WO 106/998, Despatch LXXIV, 7 August 1915.

142 TNA: PRO WO 159/4, 'General Staff Note on the General Military Situation', 3 August 1915.

143 TNA: PRO CAB 22/2, Minutes of Dardanelles Committee Meeting, 3 September 1915.

144 TNA: PRO 30/57/57, Kitchener Papers, Kitchener to Millerand, 20 August 1915. Millerand replied on 26 August 1915, telling Kitchener how he was 'deeply touched by your kind letter'. 'Please believe that', he wrote 'I myself have very happy memories of the three days I had the pleasure of spending with you.'

145 TNA: PRO CAB 22/2, Minutes of Dardanelles Committee Meeting, 20 August 1915.

146 Williams, 'Lord Kitchener and the Battle of Loos: French Politics and British Strategy in the Summer of 1915', p. 129.

147 TNA: PRO CAB 22/2, Minutes of Dardanelles Committee Meeting, 20 August 1915. Original emphasis.

148 The meeting did contain, however, one more surprise. After discussing Sir John French's requirements, Kitchener stated that there was 'another *new factor* in the situation'. What this new factor was is unknown, being apparently too secret to include in the minutes. The author has been unable to shed any light on this mystery.

149 French, *British Economic and Strategic Planning 1905–1915*, p. 126; R. Jenkins, *Asquith* (London: Collins, 1978), pp. 342–3.

150 Kitchener to Hamilton, 20 August 1915, cited in W.S. Churchill, *Winston S. Churchill. Volume III Companion, Part 2, Documents, May 1915–December 1916*, ed. M. Gilbert (London: Heinemann, 1972), pp. 1149–50; Foreign Office to Buchanan, 20 August 1915, cited in Neilson, *Strategy and Supply*, p. 96; IWM: French Papers, 7/4 (2), Kitchener to French, 20 August 1915.

151 E. Greenhalgh, 'Why the British Were on the Somme in 1916', *War in History*, vol. 6, no. 2 (1999), pp. 143–73; W. Philpott, 'Why the British Were Really on the Somme: A Reply to Elizabeth Greenhalgh', *War in History*, vol. 9, no. 4 (2002), pp. 446–71; E. Greenhalgh, 'Flames Over the Somme: A Retort to William Philpott', *War in History*, vol. 10, no. 3 (2003), pp. 335–42.

152 Liddell Hart, *History of the First World War*, p. 193.

153 K. Grieves, *The Politics of Manpower, 1914–18* (Manchester: Manchester University Press, 1988), Chapters 1 & 2; Gooch, *The Plans of War. The General Staff and British Military Strategy c. 1900–1916*, p. 317.

154 See N. Stone, *The Eastern Front 1914–1917* (London: Hodder & Stoughton, 1975), pp. 180–91.

155 'The Russian Army has been so weakened by the blows it has suffered that Russia need not be seriously considered a danger in the foreseeable future.' General Erich von Falkenhayn to Chancellor von Bethmann Hollweg, 31 August 1915, cited in Herwig, *The First World War*, p. 179.

CHAPTER 2: OPERATIONAL PLANNING: AUGUST–SEPTEMBER 1915

1 TNA: PRO WO 95/158, 'Précis of First Army Conference of Monday, 6 September 1915'.

2 J. Terraine, *Douglas Haig. The Educated Soldier* (London: Cassell, 2000; first published 1963), p. 156.

3 For a discussion of Haig's command of First Army see N. Lloyd, '"With Faith and Without Fear": Haig's Command of First Army During 1915', forthcoming *Journal of Military History*, 2006.

4 Haig does not lack biographical study. For a comprehensive historiography see K. Simpson, 'The Reputation of Sir Douglas Haig', in B. Bond (ed.), *The First World War and British Military History* (Oxford: Clarendon Press, 1991), pp. 141–62. Also see B. Bond & N. Cave (eds.), *Haig. A Reappraisal 70 Years On* (Barnsley: Leo Cooper, 1999) for the results of modern research. Terraine, *Douglas Haig*, remains the standard defence of Haig's leadership, but for a more critical appraisal see G.J. De Groot, *Douglas Haig, 1861–1928* (London: Unwin Hyman, 1988); T. Travers, *The Killing Ground: The British Army, the Western Front and the Emergence of Modern Warfare 1900–1918* (Barnsley:

Pen & Sword, 2003; first published 1987), Part II; and Travers, 'A Particular Style of Command: Haig and GHQ, 1916–1918', *Journal of Strategic Studies*, vol. 10, no. 3 (1987), pp. 363–76. The recent publication of D. Haig, *War Diaries & Letters 1914–1918*, eds. G. Sheffield & J. Bourne (London: Weidenfeld & Nicolson, 2005) marks a new stage in studies of Haig.

5 Although the two divisions (Lahore and Meerut) of Indian Corps were both smaller than a comparable British division. The corps only totalled around 20,000 men. See G. Corrigan, *Sepoys in the Trenches* (Staplehurst: Spellmount, 1999).

6 Lieutenant-General Sir C.A. Anderson replaced Lieutenant-General Sir James Willcox as GOC Indian Corps on 7 September 1915.

7 Sir D. Haig, *The Haig Papers from the National Library of Scotland*, part 1, *Haig's Autograph Great War Diary* (Brighton: Harvester Press Microfilm, 1987), 13 August 1915.

8 The only biography is A. Farrar-Hockley, *Goughie: The Life of General Sir Hubert Gough* (London: Hart-Davis, MacGibbon, 1975). See also H. Gough, *The Fifth Army* (London: Hodder & Stoughton, 1931), his autobiography *Soldiering On* (London: Arthur Baker, 1954) and G. Sheffield, 'An Army Commander on the Somme: Hubert Gough', in G. Sheffield & D. Todman (eds.), *Command and Control on the Western Front. The British Army's Experience 1914–1918* (Staplehurst: Spellmount, 2004), pp. 71–95.

9 Gough, *The Fifth Army*, p. 94.

10 See I.F.W. Beckett, 'Hubert Gough, Neill Malcolm and Command on the Western Front', in B. Bond (ed.), *'Look to your Front' Studies in the First World War by the British Commission for Military History* (Staplehurst: Spellmount, 1999), pp. 1–12.

11 P. Simkins, 'Haig and the Army Commanders', in Bond & Cave (eds.), *Haig. A Reappraisal 70 Years On*, p. 88.

12 R. Prior & T. Wilson, *Command on the Western Front. The Military Career of Sir Henry Rawlinson 1914–18* (Oxford: Blackwell, 1992). See also F.B. Maurice, *The Life of Lord Rawlinson of Trent* (London: Cassell, 1928).

13 Prior & Wilson, *Command on the Western Front*, pp. 70–3.

14 TNA: PRO WO 95/158, 'I Corps Scheme for the Operations', 22 August 1915.

15 9th (Scottish) Division was the senior division of the First New Army. It had been in France since mid-May.

16 NAM: Rawlinson Papers, 5301-33-25, Rawlinson Diary, 13 August 1915.

17 Ibid., 20 August 1915.

18 Prior & Wilson, *Command on the Western Front*, p. 104.

19 TNA: PRO WO 95/158, 'IV Corps Proposals for an Attack on Loos and Hill 70', 22 August 1915.

20 15th (Scottish) Division was the senior division of the Second New Army. It had been in France since 13 July and had joined IV Corps on 17 July.

21 Rawlinson showed a similar reluctance to plan beyond the capture of the initial locality at Neuve Chapelle in March. See Prior & Wilson, *Command on the Western Front*, pp. 25–35.

22 Haig, *The Haig Papers*, 1 September 1915.

23 IWM: French Papers, PP/MCR/C32, French Diary, 28 July 1915.

24 TNA: PRO WO 95/157, GHQ to Haig, 23 August 1915.

25 Ibid.

26 This was apparently not unusual. See T. Travers, 'The Offensive and the Problem of Innovation in British Military Thought, 1870–1915', *Journal of Contemporary History*, vol. 13, no. 3 (July 1978), pp. 531–53.

27 IWM: Wilkinson Papers, 44 Brigade, 'Preliminary Operation Order', 13 September 1915. Emphasis added.

28 NAM: Rawlinson Papers, 5301-33-25, Rawlinson Diary, 4 September 1915.

29 Haig, *The Haig Papers*, 30 August 1915.

30 Ibid., 17 August 1915.

31 During September Major-General J.P. DuCane (MGRA GHQ) complained that GHQ was 'unapproachable expect by mail'. Cited in Travers, *The Killing Ground*, p. 120, n. 23.

32 IWM: Wilson Papers, DS/MISC/80, HHW 25, Wilson Diary, 13 September 1915.

33 IWM: Fitzgerald Papers, PP/MCR/118, Fitzgerald Diary, 29–31 August 1915.

34 LHCMA: Clive Papers, 2/2, Clive Diary, 19 September 1915.

35 Haig, *The Haig Papers*, Haig to Lady Haig, 16 September 1915.

36 TNA: PRO WO 95/158, 'Précis of First Army Conference of Monday, 6 September 1915'.

37 Prior & Wilson, *Command on the Western Front*, p. 106.

38 Travers, *The Killing Ground*, p. 95.

39 TNA: PRO WO 95/158, 'Précis of First Army Conference of Monday, 6 September 1915'.

40 Much of the following is taken from J. Luvaas, *The Education of an Army* (London: Cassell, 1965), pp. 216–47.

41 G.F.R. Henderson, *Campaign of Fredericksburg* (London: Gale & Polden, 1886); *The Battle of Spiceren, August 6th, 1870, and the Events that Preceded it: A Study in Practical Tactics and War Training* (London: Gale & Polden, 1891).

42 G.F.R. Henderson, *The Science of War. A Collection of Essays and Lectures 1892–1905*, ed. N. Malcolm (London: Longmans, Green & Co, 1905), p. 40.

43 TNA: PRO WO 95/158, 'Précis of First Army Conference of Monday, 6 September 1915'.

44 Rather curiously, in *The Science of War*, Henderson had criticised military history that did not make mention of 'the spirit of war, to moral influences, to the effect of *rapidity, surprise* and secrecy'. Cited in Luvaas, *The Education of an Army*, p. 225. Emphasis added.

45 This point is made in Travers, 'The Offensive and the Problem of Innovation in British Military Thought 1870–1915', pp. 540–1.

46 D. Haig, *Cavalry Studies. Strategic & Tactical* (London: Hugh Rees, 1907), p. 142.

47 *Field Service Regulations, Part I, Operations* (London: HMSO, 1909; amended 1912). See Travers, 'Technology, Tactics and Morale: Jean de Bloch, the Boer War, and British Military Theory, 1900–1914', *Journal of Modern History*, vol. 17, no. 3 (June 1979), p. 273.

48 See A. Simpson, 'The Operational Role of British Corps Command on the Western Front, 1914–18', D.Phil., University College, London, 2003, passim.

49 *Field Service Regulations, Part I, Operations*, p. 126.

50 Ibid., p. 192.

51 Ibid., p. 126.

52 See Travers, *The Killing Ground*, pp. 85–100. To be fair to Haig many senior German officers also shared this adherence to 'decisive' battles. See R.T. Foley, *German Strategy and the Path to Verdun. Erich von Falkenhayn and the Development of Attrition, 1870–1916* (Cambridge: Cambridge University Press, 2005), passim.

53 BLO: Asquith Papers, 13–14, Haig to Hon. H.H. Asquith, 25 June 1915.

54 Haig, *The Haig Papers*, 30 July 1915; Travers, *The Killing Ground*, p. 127.

55 Haig, *The Haig Papers*, Haig to Lady Haig, 15 August 1915.

56 Ibid., Haig to Lady Haig, 24 August 1915. Emphasis added.

57 Ibid., Haig to Lady Haig, 22 September 1915.

58 For the classic account see R. Graves, *Goodbye To All That* (London: Penguin, 1960; first published 1929), pp. 155–66. See also H. Willamson, *A Fox Under My Cloak* (Stroud: Sutton, 1996; first published 1955). Williamson was not, as some commentators have alleged, at Loos. *A Fox Under My Cloak* is a fictional account of Loos. Personal Communication, *Henry Williamson Society* to the Author.

59 C.H. Foulkes, *"GAS!" The Story of the Special Brigade* (London: Blackwood, 1934), Chapter 4; L.F. Haber, *The Poisonous Cloud. Chemical Warfare in the First World War* (Oxford: Clarendon Press, 1986), pp. 52–58; G. Hartcup, *The War of Invention. Scientific Developments, 1914–18* (London: Brassey's, 1988), pp. 96–102; D. Richter, *Chemical Soldiers. British Gas Warfare in World War One* (London: Leo Cooper, 1994), Chapters 2–4, and 'The Experience of the British Special Brigade in Gas Warfare', in H. Cecil & P.H. Liddle (eds.), *Facing Armageddon. The First World War Experienced* (London: Leo Cooper, 1996), pp. 353–64; A. Palazzo, *Seeking Victory on the Western Front. The British Army and Chemical Warfare in World War I* (Lincoln and London: University of Nebraska Press, 2000), Chapter 2. Palazzo correctly shows how gas became the 'central, controlling feature of British planning', but misses the fundamental disagreement between French and Haig over the scope of the attack.

60 Although accepting volunteers, it was believed essential that the Special Brigade be composed of men who knew something of chemistry. Transfer requests were therefore sent out for members of the armed forces with any relevant knowledge or skills. Because it was believed that the Special Brigade would only control the discharge of the gas – this was to be proved false – usual standards of height, fitness and age were waived. In order to help differentiate members of the Special Brigade, who would be working in crowded fire-trenches, successful applicants were promoted to corporal and issued with revolvers.

61 Travelling on average a hundred miles per day, Foulkes gave numerous demonstrations and lectures, and visited virtually every division and corps in First Army to arrange the detailed plans for the use of gas. Foulkes, *"GAS!"*, pp. 61–2.

62 Richter, *Chemical Soldiers*, p. 23.

63 The rubber pipes, however, proved very difficult to manufacture in sufficient numbers and rigid iron ones were substituted instead. Unfortunately, the large number of joints they contained proved leaky.

64 Lieutenant-Colonel C.H. Foulkes to Lieutenant-General Sir W. Robertson, 31 May 1915, cited in Foulkes, *"GAS!"*, p. 40.

65 Haig, *The Haig Papers*, 22 August 1915.

66 Gough, *The Fifth Army*, p. 101.

67 This point was made in B.H. Liddell Hart, *History of the First World War* (London: Pan, 1975; first published 1930), p. 198; Richter, *Chemical Soldiers*, p. 36. Foulkes later denied that the demonstration on 22 August had been 'too successful', because 'only a few cylinders were used to show how gas was emitted'. TNA: PRO CAB 45/120, Lieutenant-Colonel C.H. Foulkes to Brigadier-General Sir J.E. Edmonds, undated.

68 'The arrangement for dropping bombs has been perfected, also a bomb containing chloroform and prussic acid has been produced which is of usually deadly nature. One whiff of the gas is said to be sufficient to kill.' Haig, *The Haig Papers*, 15 August 1915.

69 LHCMA: Montgomery-Massingberd Papers, 7/1, 'Lecture on Battle of Loos Given on 14 December 1915'; TNA: PRO CAB 45/121, Lieutenant-General Sir R.D. Whigham to Edmonds, 9 July 1926.

70 TNA: PRO WO 95/158, 'IV Corps Proposals for an Attack on Loos and Hill 70', 22 August 1915.

71 TNA: PRO WO 95/158, 'Précis of First Army Conference of Monday, 6 September 1915'.

72 See M. Crawshaw, 'The Impact of Technology on the BEF and its Commanders', in Bond & Cave (eds.), *Haig. A Reappraisal 70 Years On*, pp. 155–75.

73 Lord Kitchener had apparently wanted a smaller gas frontage. See Foulkes, *"GAS!"*, p. 60.

74 NAM: Rawlinson Papers, 5201-33-18, 'Letter Book Volume II, May 1915–Aug 1916', Lieutenant-General Sir H. Rawlinson to Lieutenant-Colonel A. Fitzgerald (Kitchener's Private Secretary), 29 August 1915.

75 TNA: PRO WO 95/158, 'Notes on the Conference Held at Hinges at 10.30 a.m. on the 6th September by the GOC First Army'.

76 'At the conference,' wrote Charteris, 'the Indian Corps made difficulties, and were very roughly dealt with by D.H.' J. Charteris, *At G.H.Q.* (London: Cassell, 1931), p. 107.

77 Sir J.E. Edmonds (comp.), *History of the Great War: Military Operations France & Belgium, 1915*, vol. 2, *Battles of Aubers Ridge, Festubert and Loos* (London/Nashville: Imperial War Museum/Battery Press, 1995; first published 1928), p. 396.

78 Travers, *The Killing Ground*, p. xx.

79 Foulkes, *"GAS!"*, pp. 44–45.

80 'Moreover up to the present on my front all prisoners taken have had most inefficient respirators. This looks as if the enemy did not anticipate a gas attack here. His machine gunners are said to have oxygen inhalers which can last for half an hour.' Haig, *The Haig Papers*, 26 August 1915.

81 Charteris, *At G.H.Q.*, p. 107.

82 Haig, *The Haig Papers*, 21 August 1915.

83 Foulkes records that the first batches of metal cylinders, manufactured in Runcorn, when filled, took five minutes to empty. Owing to a breakdown in cylinder supply, different sizes of cylinders were employed and emptied much quicker. Foulkes, *"GAS!"*, p. 45.

84 Haig, *The Haig Papers*, 21 August 1915.

85 Ibid., 26 August 1915.

86 TNA: PRO WO 95/157, Haig to GHQ, 26 August 1915.

87 TNA: PRO CAB 45/120, Foulkes to Edmonds, undated.

88 LHCMA: Foulkes Papers, 2/16, Foulkes Diary, 4 September 1915.

89 Foulkes, *"GAS!"*, p. 56.

90 TNA: PRO WO 95/157, Robertson to Haig, 28 August 1915.

91 Edmonds (comp.), *Military Operations France & Belgium, 1915*, vol. 2, pp. 158–9.

92 For a full forty-minute gas attack on a frontage of 6,300 yards, 5,040 cylinders would be required in 252 bays.

93 Foulkes, *"GAS!"*, p. 60.
94 TNA: PRO WO 95/158, First Army Memorandum, 17 September 1915.
95 Prior & Wilson, *Command on the Western Front*, p. 115.
96 TNA: PRO CAB 45/121, Whigham to Edmonds, 9 July 1926.
97 See for example Edmonds (comp.), *Military Operations France & Belgium, 1915*, vol. 2, p. 397; Liddell Hart, *History of the First World War*, pp. 200–2; Terraine, *Douglas Haig*, pp. 156–70; J.H. Johnson, *Stalemate! Great Trench Warfare Battles* (London: Cassell, 1999; first published 1995), p. 49; R. Neillands, *The Great War Generals on the Western Front 1914–18* (London: Robinson, 1999), p. 218.
98 TNA: PRO WO 95/157, Haig to GHQ, 28 August 1915.
99 XI Corps was formed on 29 August 1915 consisting of 23rd, 24th and the Guards Division. On 4 September it was decided that 23rd Division would be replaced by 21st Division once the latter had arrived in France. TNA: PRO WO 95/880, XI Corps War Diary, 4 September 1915.
100 The decision to use 21st and 24th Divisions at Loos is a controversial one. The Official History records that they were chosen to form a reserve corps because 'not another seasoned division could be withdrawn without endangering the British front'. Edmonds (comp.), *Military Operations France & Belgium, 1915*, vol. 2, p. 139. This is, however, debatable. According to Haig, Sir John believed that 'not having been in the trenches, but fresh from training in open warfare,' 21st and 24th Divisions 'would be better for the attack and pursuit resulting from a successful assault and then our more seasoned units which had become sticky and disinclined to leave their trenches because of the "trench habits" which they had learnt'. TNA: PRO CAB 44/28, Haig's comments on the draft chapters of the Official History, 7 January 1928.
101 Haig, *The Haig Papers*, 1 September 1915.
102 'Loyalty to and consideration for his troops did not appear to have been characteristics of Haking,' P. Warner, *The Battle of Loos* (Ware, Hertfordshire: Wordsworth, 2000; first published 1976), p. 23. See also Graves, *Goodbye To All That*, p. 114; R. Kipling, *The Irish Guards in the Great War* (2 vols., London: Macmillan, 1923), II, pp. 6–7; Travers, *The Killing Ground*, p. 48.
103 Edmonds (comp.), *Military Operations France & Belgium, 1915*, vol. 2, p. 23.
104 IWM: Fitzgerald Papers, PP/MCR/118, Fitzgerald Diary, 12 September 1915.
105 Haig, *The Haig Papers*, 18 September 1915.
106 TNA: PRO CAB 44/27, Haig's comments on the draft chapters of the Official History, 20 February 1927.
107 Sir J. French, 'Loos', 15 October 1915, in *Complete Despatches of Lord French, 1914–1916* (Uckfield: Naval & Military Press, 2001; first published 1916), p. 396.
108 See Travers, *The Killing Ground*, pp. 16–9.
109 IWM: Wilson Papers, DS/MISC/80, HHW 25, Wilson Diary, 24 September 1915.
110 LHCMA: Edmonds Papers, 3/10, 'Memoirs', Chapter XXVI, p. 8.
111 R. Holmes, *The Little Field Marshal. Sir John French* (London: Jonathan Cape, 1981), p. 302.
112 TNA: PRO CAB 45/121, Whigham to Edmonds, 9 July 1926. Whigham was not impressed by this, believing it was 'a bit of special pleading' by Sir John.
113 TNA: PRO CAB 45/121, Field-Marshal Sir W. Robertson to Edmonds, 10 August 1926.
114 For this in 1914 see N. Gardner, *Trial by Fire. Command and the British Expeditionary Force in 1914* (Westport, CT: Praeger, 2003), passim.
115 Apparently, Sir John told Robertson on 2 October that the *second* day of the battle was the correct day for the reserves to go into action. Haig, *The Haig Papers*, 2 October 1915.
116 LHCMA: Liddell Hart Papers, 1/520, General A. Montgomery-Massingberd to Captain B.H. Liddell Hart, 29 September 1927.
117 T. Travers, 'The Hidden Army: Structural Problems in the British Officer Corps, 1900–1918', *Journal of Contemporary History*, vol. 17, no. 3 (July 1982), p. 532.
118 TNA: PRO CAB 44/28, Haig's comments on the draft chapters of the Official History, 1 January 1928.
119 Haig, *The Haig Papers*, 19 September 1915.
120 TNA: PRO WO 95/158, Haig to Robertson, 19 September 1915. Emphasis added.
121 TNA: PRO WO 95/158, Robertson to Haig, 19 September 1915.
122 LHCMA: Howell Papers, 6/2/126–6/2/158, Haig to Howell, 22 September 1915. Thanks to Professor Gary Sheffield for this reference.

123 Sir William Robertson was apparently undecided about who should have control of the reserves. TNA: PRO CAB 45/121, Whigham to Edmonds, 9 July 1926.
124 IWM: French Papers, PP/MCR/C33, French to Mrs W. Bennett, 24 September 1915.
125 TNA: PRO CAB 45/120, Major-General G.T. Forestier-Walker (GOC 21st Division) to Edmonds, 24 January 1927.
126 Foulkes, *"GAS!"*, p. 58.
127 Haig, *The Haig Papers*, 15 September 1915.
128 TNA: PRO WO 95/158, Haig to Robertson, 16 September 1915. Original emphasis.
129 TNA: PRO WO 95/158, First Army to I and IV Corps, 16 September 1915.
130 TNA: PRO WO 95/158, 'I Corps Scheme for the Operations', 17 September 1915.
131 TNA: PRO WO 95/711, 'IV Corps Proposals for an attack on Loos and Hill 70', 17 September 1915.
132 TNA: PRO WO 95/158, Haig to GHQ, 18 September 1915.
133 TNA: PRO WO 95/158, GHQ to Haig, 13 September 1915.
134 TNA: PRO WO 95/158, GHQ to Haig, 18 September 1915.
135 Emphasis added.
136 TNA: PRO CAB 45/121, Whigham to Edmonds, 9 July 1926.
137 TNA: PRO WO 95/158, First Army Operation Order No. 95, 19 September 1915.

CHAPTER 3: PRE-BATTLE PREPARATION: SEPTEMBER 1915

1 E. Wyrall, *The History of the 2nd Division, 1914–1918* (Uckfield, East Sussex: Naval & Military Press, 2000; first published 1921), p. 218.
2 IWM: 87/33/1, War Diary of Major E.S.B. Hamilton (45th Field Ambulance, 15th Division), 7 September 1915.
3 TNA: PRO WO 95/158, 'Précis of First Army Conference of Monday, 6 September 1915'.
4 TNA: PRO WO 95/1229, Memorandum by Major-General A.E.A. Holland, 10 September 1915.
5 J. Buchan & J. Stewart, *The Fifteenth (Scottish) Division, 1914–1919* (Edinburgh & London: William Blackwood, 1926), pp. 28–9.
6 See K. Simpson, 'Capper and the Offensive Spirit', *R.U.S.I. Journal*, vol. 118, no. 2 (June 1973), pp. 51–6.
7 TNA: PRO WO 95/1629, Capper's Note to Troops, 18 September 1915.
8 IWM: French Papers, PP/MCR/C32, French Diary, 28 May 1915; Sir D. Haig, *The Haig Papers from the National Library of Scotland*, part 1, *Haig's Autograph Great War Diary* (Brighton: Harvester Press Microfilm, 1987), 20 June 1915.
9 P. Gibbs, *Realities of War* (London: William Heinemann, 1920), p. 133.
10 P. Maze, *A Frenchman in Khaki* (London: William Heinemann, 1934), p. 119.
11 Sir J.E. Edmonds (comp.), *History of the Great War: Military Operations France & Belgium, 1915*, vol. 2, *Battles of Aubers Ridge, Festubert and Loos* (London/Nashville: Imperial War Museum/Battery Press, 1995; first published 1928), p. 147.
12 G.C. Wynne, *If Germany Attacks. The Battle in Depth in the West* (Westport, CT: Greenwood, 1975; first published 1940), p. 66.
13 TNA: PRO CAB 45/120, Colonel W.G.S. Dobbie (GSO1 1st Division) to Brigadier-General Sir J.E. Edmonds, 7 October 1926.
14 'Between Loos and Fosse 8 the country is flat and open, therefore, there will be problems of sending up supplies and reinforcements when the German front line of trenches has been captured (much difficulty is likely to be experienced in supporting an attack on the German trenches). Villages in the rear of German line are strongly defended, and the ground between them is flat and open, so that a further advance eastward would be extremely difficult.' IWM: French Papers, 7/2 (1), Haig to GHQ, 23 June 1915.
15 These were Vermelles–Hulluch–Vendin Le Vieil, Hulluch–Wingles–Meurchin and Haisnes–Douvrin–Berclau. The Béthune–Lens road led directly south-east.
16 IWM: MISC 134 (2072), 'Administration Arrangements During the Battle of Loos', by Lieutenant-Colonel Hon. M.A. Wingfield, 4 January 1916.
17 The *Sixth Army* held the front from just north of the River Lys near Messines to south of Arras.

18 A good description can be found in A. Clark, *The Donkeys* (London: Pimlico, 1997; first published 1961), p. 168.

19 LHCMA: Robertson Papers, 4/1, Captured German Pamphlet (issued in November 1915), 'Experiences gained in the winter battle of Champagne from the point of view of the organisation of the enemy's lines of defence and the means of combating an attempt to pierce our line', 13 May 1915.

20 For the evolution of German defensive doctrine see M. Samuels, *Command or Control? Command, Training and Tactics in the British and German Armies, 1888–1918* (London: Frank Cass, 1995), Chapter 7; R.T. Foley, *German Strategy and the Path to Verdun. Erich von Falkenhayn and the Development of Attrition, 1870–1916* (Cambridge: Cambridge University Press, 2005), Chapter 7.

21 See for example I. Passingham, *Pillars of Fire: The Battle of Messines Ridge June 1917* (Stroud: Sutton, 1998), pp. 35–8.

22 TNA: PRO CAB 45/120, Lieutenant-Colonel J. Rainsford-Hannay to Edmonds, 8 March 1926.

23 TNA: PRO CAB 45/121, Lieutenant-Colonel J.H. Purvis to Edmonds, 27 February 1926.

24 TNA: PRO CAB 45/121, Brigadier-General M.G. Wilkinson to Edmonds, 8 June 1926.

25 BLL: GS 0309, Account of General Sir Philip Christison.

26 TNA: PRO CAB 45/121, Brigadier-General W.C. Walton to Edmonds, 28 April 1926.

27 IWM: MISC 134 (2072), 'Administration Arrangements During the Battle of Loos', by Lieutenant-Colonel Hon. M.A. Wingfield, 4 January 1916.

28 TNA: PRO CAB 45/120, Colonel G.H. Boileau to Edmonds, 28 February 1926.

29 TNA: PRO CAB 45/120, Colonel D.W. Cameron of Lochiel to Edmonds, 17 September 1926. See also Edmonds (comp.), *Military Operations France & Belgium, 1915*, vol. 2, p. 236.

30 IWM: 88/52/1, 'Narrative of the Operations of the First Battalion of the Post Office Rifles in France 1915–1918', by Captain G.N. Clark, p. 17.

31 TNA: PRO WO 95/2698, '47th Division at Loos'.

32 I.M. Brown, *British Logistics on the Western Front, 1914–1919* (Westport, CT: Praeger, 1998).

33 LHCMA: Montgomery-Massingberd Papers, 6/4, 'Report of 25 September 1915 by OC 187 Company RE'.

34 TNA: PRO WO 95/1275, 3 Brigade War Diary, 19 September 1915.

35 Although written later on in the battle, one account will suffice to illustrate how trying these logistical preparations could be: 'Struggling through a communication trench, carrying not only one's own kit of some 60lbs – but also sundry dead weights like gas cylinders; two 1 gallon petrol tins filled with water, boxes of bombs, chunks of duck-boards, with constant wire overhead; wire underfoot; shells bursting around, wounded men enviedly [*sic*] going back, bodies lying waiting to be put over the top at dark – was a seething nightmare...' IWM: 88/52/1, 'My Life with the Post Office Rifles', Account of Rifleman (later Wing Commander) W.J. Shewry.

36 Buchan & Stewart, *The Fifteenth (Scottish) Division, 1914–1919*, pp. 23–4, n. 1.

37 Haig, *The Haig Papers*, 4 September 1915.

38 IWM: 87/33/1, War Diary of Major E.S.B. Hamilton, 5 September 1915.

39 This distinction between 'gas', 'accessory' and 'roger' seems to have been largely dismissed. 'Take those new gas-companies – sorry, excuse me this once, I mean accessory-companies – their very look makes me tremble.' R. Graves, *Goodbye To All That* (London: Penguin, 1960; first published 1929), p. 151. See also J.C. Dunn (ed.), *The War the Infantry Knew 1914–1919* (London: Abacus, 2004; first published 1938), p. 146.

40 Dunn (ed.), *The War the Infantry Knew 1914–1919*, pp. 146–7.

41 IWM: MISC 26/ITEM 469, German Account of Christmas Truce 1914 and Loos, September 1915; D. Richter, *Chemical Soldiers. British Gas Warfare in World War One* (London: Leo Cooper, 1994), p. 89.

42 See for example F. Richards, *Old Soldiers Never Die* (London: Anthony Mott, 1983), pp. 114–5. When the gas was released in this sector the German defenders placed bundles of straw, which had been doused in petrol and set alight, onto their parapet in order to form a barrier to the gas. Graves, *Goodbye To All That*, pp. 157–8.

43 TNA: PRO WO 95/1911, 15th Division War Diary, August-September 1915; Buchan & Stewart, *The Fifteenth (Scottish) Division, 1914–1919*, pp. 23–4.

44 TNA: PRO WO 95/1733, 'Lecture Given on the Part Played by 9th Division in Battle of Loos', by Lieutenant-Colonel S.E. Holland (GSO1 9th Division).

45 C.T. Atkinson, *The Seventh Division, 1914–1918* (London: John Murray, 1927), p. 199.
46 TNA: PRO WO 95/1629, 7th Division War Diary, September 1915.
47 IWM: 82/30/1, Brigadier-General Hon. J.F.H.S.F. Trefusis Diary, 4 September 1915.
48 TNA: PRO WO 95/2698, 47th Division War Diary, August–September 1915.
49 IWM: MISC 134 (2072), 'Administration Arrangements During the Battle of Loos', by Lieutenant-Colonel Hon. M.A. Wingfield, 4 January 1916.
50 TNA: PRO WO 95/1229, 1st Division War Diary, August and September 1915.
51 TNA: PRO WO 95/1229, Brigadier-General A.J. Reddie to Major-General A.E.A. Holland, 7 September 1915.
52 TNA: PRO WO 95/1229, Major-General A.E.A. Holland to Brigadier-General A.J. Reddie, 8 September 1915.
53 TNA: PRO WO 95/1275, 3 Brigade War Diary, 1 August 1915.
54 'Hostile shelling – support trenches blown in. It appears difficult to keep them in good repair and fit for use.' TNA: PRO WO 95/1275, 3 Brigade War Diary, 16 September 1915.
55 TNA: PRO WO 95/1287, 2nd Division War Diary, September 1915.
56 Dunn (ed.), *The War the Infantry Knew 1914–1919*, p. 144.
57 See Chapter 5.
58 TNA: PRO WO 95/1733, 'General Staff Special War Diary Dealing with Battle of Loos'; A.H. Maude, *The History of the 47th (London) Division, 1914–1919* (Uckfield, East Sussex: Naval & Military Press, 2000; first published 1922), pp. 26–7.
59 Sir W.G. Macpherson, *History of the Great War. Medical Services General History*, vol. 2, *The Medical Services on the Western Front, and During the Operations in France and Belgium in 1914 and 1915* (London: HMSO, 1923), p. 453.
60 Ibid., p. 467.
61 IWM: 91/23/1, Diary of Major R.C. Ozanne (Medical Officer 15th Division), 25 September 1915.
62 IWM: 87/33/1, War Diary of Major E.S.B. Hamilton, 30 September 1915.
63 Macpherson, *Medical Services General History*, vol. 2, p. 467.
64 See the account in J. Ewing, *The History of the 9th (Scottish) Division* (London: John Murray, 1921), p. 59.
65 At Chocques and Merville.
66 Macpherson, *Medical Services General History*, vol. 2, p. 457.
67 Brown, *British Logistics on the Western Front, 1914–1919*, p. 102.
68 TNA: PRO WO 95/181, AA&QMG First Army War Diary, 29 August 1915.
69 See entries to Haig, *The Haig Papers*, 25 June and 14 September 1915.
70 'Much careful forethought is necessary in order to have the requisite stores of all kinds available and on the spot when required.' TNA: PRO WO 95/158, 'Précis of First Army Conference of Monday, 6 September 1915'.
71 For 'umpiring' see Samuels, *Command or Control?*, pp. 49–53.
72 Sir J.E. Edmonds & G.C. Wynne (comp.), *Military Operations France & Belgium, 1915*, vol. 1, *Winter 1914–15: Battle of Neuve Chapelle: Battles of Ypres* (London: Macmillan, 1927), p. 125–6.
73 R.E. Priestley, *The Signal Service in the European War of 1914 to 1918 (France)* (Chatham: W & J Mackay, 1921), p. 64.
74 LHCMA: Montgomery-Massingberd Papers, 7/1, 'The IV Corps Artillery at the Battle of Loos', p. 24.
75 Priestley, *The Signal Service in the European War of 1914 to 1918 (France)*, p. 74.
76 TNA: PRO WO 95/158, 'Communication Between Cavalry and Artillery of Army Corps and Divisions in the Event of an Advance', 24 September 1915.
77 For Loos I Corps had fifteen lofts, each containing eight birds. It is not known whether any were available for IV Corps. The pigeons were to fly to a loft in Béthune with messages. Yet pigeons were obviously not invulnerable and fourteen were killed during the subsequent fighting. Edmonds (comp.), *Military Operations France & Belgium, 1915*, vol. 2, p. 99, n. 1; Priestley, *The Signal Service in the European War of 1914 to 1918 (France)*, p. 92.
78 For the battle of Loos 'a wireless section consisting of two lorry sets, two pack sets, and six short range sets was attached to First Army under a specially-qualified senior officer. Previous to the battle, one pack set was installed in a dug-out on the Béthune–Lens Road near Vermelles, and the short range sets… were arranged to provide emergency communication between each of

four divisions and one of their brigades in the line.' Priestley, *The Signal Service in the European War of 1914 to 1918 (France)*, pp. 88–9.

79 See D. Jordan, 'The Battle For the Skies: Sir Hugh Trenchard as Commander of the Royal Flying Corps', in M. Hughes & M. Seligmann (eds.), *Leadership in Conflict 1914–1918* (Barnsley: Leo Cooper, 2000), pp. 73–4.

80 TNA: PRO AIR 1/529/16/12/70, General Sir Douglas Haig to the War Office, 13 September 1915.

81 H.A. Jones, *History of the Great War: The War in the Air* (6 vols., Oxford: Clarendon Press, 1928), II, pp. 78–9.

82 Each Wing contained four squadrons each of twelve aircraft.

83 The resulting 'Fokker Scourge' arrived, however, too late to be of real importance during the fighting around Loos. When the offensive opened, *Leutnant* Oswald Boelcke, one of Germany's leading pilots, had only four victories to his credit. P. Kilduff, *Richthofen, Beyond the Legend of the Red Baron* (London: Arms & Armour Press, 1994), p. 39.

84 There were no bomb racks and bombing remained very much a case of the pilot or observer throwing explosives out of the plane onto the intended target. In order to improve accuracy some form of sight was needed. This did arrive in time for Loos; a primitive sight developed by two RFC officers, Second Lieutenants R.B. Bourdillon and G.M.D. Dobson, but bombing would remain wildly inaccurate into the Second World War.

85 Jones, *The War in the Air*, II, p. 117. A much-quoted statistic, but one that gives some idea of the fledgling nature of the air war.

86 Heavier sets had been used since the beginning of the war, but because they were heavy (weighing 75lbs) and extremely bulky, they had to be installed in the passenger seats of B.E.2c's, thus leaving no room for an observer. The pilot, therefore, had to do everything himself: fly, spot targets and send messages back, and understandably, even experienced flyers found this very testing.

87 The clock code was developed in January 1915 and was a method for simplifying wireless code. It required a celluloid disc with lettered concentric circles upon it and the figures of the clock written around the outside. These circles represented 10, 25, 100, 200, 300 and 400 yards, and by placing the target at the centre of the disc, fire could be brought to bear onto the target. The letter of the circle would be called for the distance of the shell from the target and the number on the clock for the direction. Zone calls allowed targets of opportunity to be engaged quickly. The battlefield was divided into numbered squares each covering about 3,000 yards. See Jones, *The War in the Air*, II, pp. 86–7, 175–6.

88 R. Prior & T. Wilson, *Command on the Western Front. The Military Career of Sir Henry Rawlinson 1914–18* (Oxford: Blackwell, 1992), pp. 40–1.

89 TNA: PRO CAB 45/120, Account of E.R. Ludlow-Hewitt, 22 September 1926.

90 Each section contained one balloon and its crew.

91 On 4 May 1915 First Army finally got hold of an observation balloon, kindly lent by the French. TNA: PRO AIR 1/529/16/12/70, Haig to GHQ, 25 June 1915.

92 TNA: PRO WO 95/592, I Corps Memorandum, 20 September 1915.

93 Jones, *The War in the Air*, II, p. 130. This is perhaps not surprising when considering the lamentable standard of training possessed by aerial observers during this period and also the reluctance of infantry to signal their position. See D. Jordan, 'The Army Co-Operation Missions of the Royal Flying Corps/Royal Air Force 1914–1918', Ph.D., Birmingham, 1997, pp. 45–54, 92–5.

94 See G. Sheffield, *The Redcaps. A History of the Royal Military Police and its Antecedents from the Middle Ages to the Gulf War* (London: Brassey's, 1994), pp. 58–62.

95 TNA: PRO WO 95/158, First Army to GHQ, 21 October 1915.

96 TNA: PRO WO 95/158, XI Corps to First Army, 3 November 1915.

97 The letter of 10 October does not seem to be in the relevant army files.

98 LHCMA: Montgomery-Massingberd Papers, 6/4–6, 'Telephone Conversations of Lieutenant-General Rawlinson', 25 September 1915.

99 T. Travers, *The Killing Ground: The British Army, the Western Front and the Emergence of Modern Warfare 1900–1918* (Barnsley: Pen & Sword, 2003; first published 1987), p. 17.

100 TNA: PRO WO 95/158, First Army to GHQ, 4 November 1915.

101 TNA: PRO CAB 45/120, Major-General G.T. Forestier-Walker to Edmonds, 24 January 1927.

102 TNA: PRO CAB 45/120, Major R.B. Johnson to Edmonds, undated.
103 TNA: PRO CAB 45/121, Major J. Vaughan to Edmonds, 16 June 1926.
104 TNA: PRO CAB 45/121, Major-General B.R. Mitford to Edmonds, 23 January 1926. Although this military policeman has generally been blamed for incompetence, the question remains as to *why* Mitford had not been given the correct pass.
105 TNA: PRO CAB 45/121, Lieutenant-Colonel H.J.C. Piers to Edmonds, 17 June 1926.
106 TNA: PRO CAB 45/121, Major T.G.F. Paget to Edmonds, 14 June 1926.
107 24th Division only left England at the end of August. TNA: PRO WO 95/2189, 24th Division War Diary, 28 August 1915.
108 The entry to 63 Brigade's War Diary of 21 September reads: 'The Brigade marched very well and there were very few stragglers.' TNA: PRO WO 95/2151.
109 TNA: PRO WO 95/2151, Lieutenant-Colonel C.G. Stewart to Major A.F. Becke, 3 August 1925.
110 IWM: PP/MCR/185, Lieutenant-Colonel A. de. S. Hadow to his wife, 21 September 1915.
111 TNA: PRO WO 95/2189, Lieutenant-Colonel C.G. Stewart to Major A.F. Becke, 3 August 1925.
112 TNA: PRO WO 95/2128, 21st Division War Diary, 24 September 1915.
113 TNA: PRO WO 95/2189, 24th Division War Diary, 24 September 1915.
114 TNA: PRO WO 95/2128, 21st Division War Diary, 24 September 1915.
115 TNA: PRO WO 95/880, Robertson to Haig, 23 September 1915.
116 T. Travers, 'The Hidden Army: Structural Problems in the British Officer Corps, 1900–1918', *Journal of Contemporary History*, vol. 17, no. 3 (July 1982), p. 532.
117 Sheffield, *The Redcaps*, p. 60.
118 IWM: 88/52/1, 'Narrative of the Operations of the First Battalion of the Post Office Rifles in France 1915–1918', by Captain G.N. Clark, p. 17.
119 TNA: PRO WO 95/2268, 'General Pereira's Statement as to 85 Brigade Taking over on 27 September'. 28th Division was moved up to support operations around the Hohenzollern Redoubt on 27 September 1915.
120 TNA: PRO CAB 45/120, Major-General C. Coffin to Edmonds, 19 February 1927.
121 TNA: PRO CAB 45/120, Major J. Buckley (9/KOYLI, 64 Brigade) to Edmonds, 1 January 1927.
122 TNA: PRO CAB 45/120, Major-General C. Coffin to Edmonds, 19 February 1927.
123 IWM: 96/29/1, Account of Second Lieutenant J.H. Alcock (8/Lincolnshire, 63 Brigade).
124 TNA: PRO CAB 45/120, Captain E.H. Smythe to Becke, 8 April 1927.
125 TNA: PRO WO 95/885, AA&QMG XI Corps War Diary, 14 September 1915.
126 IWM: MISC 134 (2072), 'Administration Arrangements During the Battle of Loos', by Lieutenant-Colonel Hon. M.A. Wingfield, 4 January 1916.
127 TNA: PRO CAB 45/120, H.M. de F. Montgomery to Edmonds, 12 January 1926.
128 TNA: PRO CAB 45/120, Major-General Sir F. Maurice to Edmonds, 10 January 1926.

CHAPTER 4: THE PRELIMINARY BOMBARDMENT: 21–24 SEPTEMBER 1915

1 Sir J.E. Edmonds (comp.), *History of the Great War: Military Operations France & Belgium, 1915*, vol. 2, *Battles of Aubers Ridge, Festubert and Loos* (London/Nashville: Imperial War Museum/Battery Press, 1995; first published 1928), Chapter 9; R. Prior & T. Wilson, *Command on the Western Front. The Military Career of Sir Henry Rawlinson 1914–18* (Oxford: Blackwell, 1992), pp. 117–8. See also Sir M. Farndale, *History of the Royal Regiment of Artillery. Western Front 1914–18* (Woolwich: Royal Artillery Institution, 1986), p. 116–27.
2 See I.M. Brown, *British Logistics on the Western Front, 1914–1919* (Westport, CT: Praeger, 1998), Chapter 3; R.Q.J. Adams, *Arms and the Wizard. Lloyd George and the Ministry of Munitions* (London: Cassell, 1978), passim.
3 TNA: PRO WO 95/158, 'General Principles for the Attack', contained in First Army War Diary, 6 September 1915.
4 Prior & Wilson, *Command on the Western Front*, Part II.
5 Edmonds (comp.), *Military Operations France & Belgium, 1915*, vol. 2, p. 40; A. Bristow, *A Serious Disappointment, the Battle of Aubers Ridge, 1915 and the Subsequent Munitions Scandal* (London: Leo Cooper, 1995), passim.

6 Prior & Wilson, *Command on the Western Front*, p. 85.

7 M. Samuels, *Command or Control? Command, Training and Tactics in the British and German Armies, 1888–1918* (London: Frank Cass, 1995), p. 107.

8 Sir D. Haig, *The Haig Papers from the National Library of Scotland*, part 1, *Haig's Autograph Great War Diary* (Brighton: Harvester Press Microfilm, 1987), 11 May 1915; Prior & Wilson, *Command on the Western Front*, p. 94.

9 TNA: PRO WO 95/157, 'Notes of Conferences held at Advanced First Army HQ, Hinges, at 2 p.m. 24 August 1915'.

10 LHCMA: Montgomery-Massingberd Papers, 7/1, 'The IV Corps Artillery at the Battle of Loos', p. 7.

11 There are similarities here with the discussions regarding what the preliminary bombardment would be like before the Somme offensive of the following year. Haig had wanted a short bombardment but this was rejected by Rawlinson (GOC Fourth Army), because he did not have enough guns. This, however, does not seem to have been made clear to Haig.

12 'Artillery conquers, infantry occupies.' J.M. Bourne, *Britain and the Great War 1914–1918* (London: Edward Arnold, 1989), p. 39. Original emphasis.

13 The definitive discussion can be found in S. Bidwell & D. Graham, *Firepower: British Army Weapons and Theories of War, 1904–1945* (Boston: Allen Unwin, 1982), Chapter 5.

14 J. Bailey, 'British Artillery in the Great War', in P. Griffith (ed.), *British Fighting Methods in the Great War* (London: Frank Cass, 1996), p. 29. Bailey also mistakenly writes that the attack at Loos began on 15 September 1915.

15 TNA: PRO WO 95/728, 'Organization of Artillery for Forthcoming Operations', 31 August 1915.

16 Figures taken from TNA: PRO WO 95/181, AA&QMG First Army War Diary, December 1914–December 1915.

17 Figures taken from Edmonds (comp.), *Military Operations France & Belgium, 1915*, vol. 2, p. 174.

18 TNA: PRO WO 158/12, 'Notes on British Offensive', 1 September 1915.

19 TNA: PRO WO 95/1752, LI Brigade RFA War Diary, 23–24 September 1915.

20 TNA: PRO WO 95/2712, VI (London) Brigade RFA War Diary, 23 September 1915.

21 TNA: PRO WO 95/2718, VIII (London) Brigade RFA War Diary, 24 September 1915.

22 Bidwell & Graham, *Firepower*, p. 79. For the Somme see M. Middlebrook, *The First Day on the Somme* (London: Penguin, 1984; first published 1971), p. 88.

23 R. Graves, *Goodbye To All That* (London: Penguin, 1960; first published 1929), pp. 148–9. See also J.C. Dunn (ed.), *The War the Infantry Knew 1914–1919* (London: Abacus, 2004; first published 1938), p. 151.

24 TNA: PRO CAB 45/121, Lieutenant-Colonel A.G. Prothero to Brigadier-General Sir J.E. Edmonds, 1 March 1926

25 TNA: PRO WO 95/728, IV Corps to First Army, 18 September 1915.

26 TNA: PRO WO 95/728, First Army to IV Corps, 20 September 1915.

27 IWM: MISC 175 (2658), Major-General Sir H.H. Tudor Diary, 15 September 1915.

28 Ibid., 15 September 1915.

29 J. Bailey, 'The First World War and the Birth of the Modern Style of Warfare', *The Strategic & Combat Studies Institute*, The Occasional, 22 (1996).

30 T. Travers, 'Technology, Tactics, and Morale: Jean de Bloch, the Boer War, and British Military Theory, 1900–1914', *Journal of Modern History*, vol. 51, no. 2 (June 1979), pp. 264–86.

31 Bidwell & Graham, *Firepower*, p. 68.

32 Prior & Wilson, *Command on the Western Front*, p. 41.

33 Getting accurate and up-to-date maps were a constant problem. As has been shown, a 'cartographic and survey chaos' existed in First Army during this period that did little to help accurate artillery fire. For example, one of the HAR groups was issued with a map that was three months old, and many of the batteries were using the 1:10,000 trench maps; the points on which were about 260 yards too far north! P. Chasseaud, *Artillery's Astrologers. A History of British Survey and Mapping on the Western Front 1914–1918* (Lewes: Mapbooks, 1999), pp. 104–9.

34 I Corps was equipped with 144 18-pounders and IV Corps received 100.

35 S. Marble, 'Artillery, Intelligence and Optimism. Wire-Cutting During the Somme Bombardment', *Stand To! The Journal of the Western Front Association*, no. 61 (April 2001), pp. 36–9. Experimental firing took place during the build-up to Loos. On 14 September 7th Division experimented with 60-pounder guns, firing both shrapnel and lyddite (high explosive) at barbed

wire. The War Diary recorded how 'more damage was done by the lyddite, but that a clear and more well-defined lane was cut by shrapnel'. TNA: PRO WO 95/1629, 7th Division War Diary, 14 September 1915.

36 By August 1915 only 4.4 percent of 18-pounder ammunition in France was high-explosive. Brown, *British Logistics on the Western Front, 1914–1919*, p. 96.

37 Bidwell & Graham, *Firepower*, p. 97.

38 TNA: PRO WO 95/728, 'Organization of Artillery for Forthcoming Operations', 31 August 1915.

39 T. Travers, *The Killing Ground: The British Army, the Western Front and the Emergence of Modern Warfare 1900–1918* (Barnsley: Pen & Sword, 2003; first published 1987), p. 93. Haig hoped that the artillery would 'add to the moral effect produced by the gas'. Haig, *The Haig Papers*, 24 August 1915.

40 *Field Artillery Training 1914* (London: HMSO, 1914), p. 230.

41 Birch to Edmonds, 8 July 1930, cited in Travers, *The Killing Ground*, p. 138.

42 Farndale, *History of the Royal Regiment of Artillery*, p. 121.

43 LHCMA: Montgomery-Massingberd Papers, 7/1, 'The IV Corps Artillery at the Battle of Loos', p. 1.

44 Edmonds (comp.), *Military Operations France & Belgium, 1915*, vol. 2, p. 174.

45 S. Marble, "*The Infantry Cannot do with a Gun Less": The Place of the Artillery in the British Expeditionary Force, 1914–1918* <www.gutenberg-e.org>, Chapter 9, p. 5. On 13 August Haig saw Major-General H.S. Horne (GOC 2nd Division). 'We discussed the 'pros' and 'cons' of forming Corps Artillery,' wrote Haig. 'He is to think over the function and send me his views in writing.' Haig, *The Haig Papers*, 13 August 1915.

46 A.P. Palazzo, 'The British Army's Counter-Battery Staff Office and Control of the Enemy in World War I', *Journal of Military History*, vol. 63, no. 1 (January 1999), pp. 55–74.

47 Details of artillery organisation taken from Farndale, *History of the Royal Regiment of Artillery*, p. 120.

48 Marble, *"The Infantry Cannot do with a Gun Less"*, Chapter 9, p. 6.

49 See Chapter 2.

50 See Chasseaud, *Artillery's Astrologers*, p. 115.

51 Edmonds (comp.), *Military Operations France & Belgium, 1915*, vol. 2, p. 175; TNA: PRO WO 95/157, 'Notes of Conferences held at Advanced First Army HQ, Hinges, at 2 p.m. 24 August 1915'.

52 IWM: Wilson Papers, HHW 2/80/47, 'Proceedings of a Meeting held at Beauquesne, 4pm 26/08/15'.

53 TNA: PRO WO 95/728, 'Organization of Artillery for Forthcoming Operations', 31 August 1915.

54 See TNA: PRO WO 95/711, 'Order Regarding Demonstrations', contained in IV Corps War Diary, 21 September 1915.

55 See N. Lloyd, 'Note on Decoys and Dummies', *Journal of the Society for Army Historical Research*, vol. 81, no. 237 (Autumn 2003), pp. 290–1.

56 TNA: PRO CAB 45/120, Colonel H.E. Braine (Brigade Major 19 Brigade) to Edmonds, undated.

57 TNA: PRO WO 95/1315, CRA 2nd Division, 'Progress Report', 21 September 1915.

58 TNA: PRO WO 95/1746, CRA 9th Division, 'Operation Report', 21 September 1915.

59 R.B. Talbot-Kelly, *A Subaltern's Odyssey* (London: William Kimber, 1980), p. 51.

60 J. Ewing, *The History of the 9th (Scottish) Division* (London: John Murray, 1921), p. 34.

61 C.T. Atkinson, *The Seventh Division, 1914–1918* (London: John Murray, 1927), p. 204.

62 TNA: PRO WO 95/1638, CRA 7th Division War Diary, 21 September 1915.

63 TNA: PRO WO 95/1643, XXXV Brigade RFA War Diary, 21 September 1915.

64 LHCMA: Montgomery-Massingberd Papers, 7/1, 'The IV Corps Artillery at the Battle of Loos', p. 5.

65 J. Buchan & J. Stewart, *The Fifteenth (Scottish) Division, 1914–1919* (Edinburgh & London: William Blackwood, 1926), p. 31.

66 TNA: PRO WO 95/1919, CRA 15th Division War Diary, 21 September 1915.

67 LHCMA: Montgomery-Massingberd Papers, 7/1, 'The IV Corps Artillery at the Battle of Loos', p. 1.

68 R.G.A. Hamilton, *The War Diary of the Master of Belhaven 1914–1918* (Barnsley: Wharncliffe, 1990; first published 1924), p. 69. Although 24th Division was one of the reserve divisions (XI Corps)

and did not take part in the opening attacks, its artillery had been sent up to the front. By 19 September CVI Brigade RFA was deployed in Vermelles in support of 7th Division, CVII Brigade RFA was in divisional reserve, while CVIII Brigade RFA was deployed in Grenay and CIX Brigade RFA had recently taken over gun-pits at Philosophe.

69 TNA: PRO WO 95/1924, LXXII Brigade RFA War Diary, 21 September 1915.

70 TNA: PRO WO 95/2708, Macnaughten Group, 'Progress Report No 1 6pm 21 September 1915'.

71 See Ibid. and TNA: PRO WO 95/1638, CRA 7th Division War Diary, 21 September 1915.

72 TNA: PRO WO 95/1638, CRA 7th Division War Diary, 21 September 1915; PRO WO 95/1315, CRA 2nd Division, 'Progress Report', 21 September 1915.

73 TNA: PRO WO 95/619, CRA I Corps War Diary, 21 September 1915.

74 TNA: PRO WO 95/728, First Army to IV Corps, 21 September 1915.

75 TNA: PRO WO 95/1746, CRA 9th Division, 'Operation Report', 22 September 1915; PRO WO 95/2708, CRA 47th Division War Diary, 22 September 1915; PRO WO 95/1315, CRA 2nd Division War Diary, 22 September 1915.

76 IWM: 91/23/1, Diary of Major R.C. Ozanne, 22 September 1915.

77 TNA: PRO WO 95/1315, 'Report on Result of Day's Firing', 22 September 1915; PRO WO 95/1326, XLI Brigade RFA War Diary, 22 September 1915.

78 TNA: PRO WO 95/1324, XXXIV Brigade RFA War Diary, 22 September 1915.

79 TNA: PRO WO 95/1746, CRA 9th Division, 'Operation Report', 22 September 1915.

80 TNA: PRO WO 95/1638, CRA 7th Division War Diary, 22 September 1915; PRO WO 95/1643, XXII Brigade RFA War Diary, 22 September 1915.

81 TNA: PRO WO 95/728. 'General Report by IV Corps Artillery', 22 September 1915.

82 TNA: PRO WO 95/728, 47th Division to IV Corps, 23 September 1915, 'Report by Divisional Artillery'.

83 IWM: MISC 175 (2658), Major-General Sir H.H. Tudor Diary, 22 September 1915.

84 IWM: 82/30/1, Brigadier-General Hon. J.F.H.S.F. Trefusis Diary, 22 September 1915.

85 TNA: PRO WO 95/1638, CRA 7th Division War Diary, 22 September 1915.

86 TNA: PRO WO 95/728, 'General Report by IV Corps Artillery', 22 September 1915.

87 Ibid.

88 TNA: PRO AIR 1/752/204/6/61, 'Instructions by Lieutenant-Colonel E.B. Ashmore, Commanding First Wing, RFC', 20 September 1915.

89 TNA: PRO AIR 1/2166/209/11/11, First Wing War Diary, 20–22 September 1915.

90 H.A. Jones, *The War in the Air* (6 vols., Oxford: Clarendon Press, 1928), II, pp. 126–7.

91 TNA: PRO AIR 1/2166/209/11/11, First Wing War Diary, 21 September 1915.

92 Communiqué No. 11, cited in C. Cole (ed.), *Royal Flying Corps Communiqués 1915–1916* (London: Tom Donovan, 1990; first published 1968), pp. 48–9.

93 TNA: PRO WO 95/1746, CRA 9th Division War Diary, 23 September 1915; 'Very cloudy, this combined with smoke and dust raised by our fire made observation extremely difficult.' PRO WO 95/2197, CVIII Brigade RFA War Diary, 23 September 1915.

94 Hamilton, *The War Diary of the Master of Belhaven 1914–1918*, p. 71; Dunn (ed.), *The War the Infantry Knew 1914–1919*, p. 151.

95 Haig, *The Haig Papers*, 23 September 1915.

96 TNA: PRO WO 95/1643, XXII Brigade RFA War Diary, 23 September 1915.

97 TNA: PRO WO 95/1315, CRA 2nd Division, 'Daily Report', 23 September 1915.

98 Graves, *Goodbye To All That*, p. 152.

99 TNA: PRO WO 95/1324, XXXIV Brigade RFA War Diary, 23 September 1915.

100 TNA: PRO WO 95/1325, XXXVI Brigade RFA War Diary, 23 September 1915.

101 TNA: PRO WO 95/1746, CRA 9th Division, 'Operation Report', 23 September 1915.

102 TNA: PRO WO 95/1752, LII Brigade RFA War Diary, 23 September 1915.

103 TNA: PRO WO 95/728, 'Progress Report IV Corps Artillery', 23 September 1915; PRO WO 95/1250, XXVI Brigade RFA War Diary, 23 September 1915.

104 V. Tiede, *Das 4. Infanterie-Regiment Nr. 157* (Oldenburg: Stalling, 1922), p. 24.

105 TNA: PRO WO 95/1924, LXXII Brigade RFA War Diary, 23 September 1915; PRO WO 95/728, 'Progress Report IV Corps Artillery', 23 September 1915.

106 TNA: PRO WO 95/2708, CRA 47th Division, 'Artillery Summary', 23 September 1915.

107 TNA: PRO WO 95/2708, 47th Division to IV Corps, 24 September 1915.

108 TNA: PRO AIR 1/1182/204/5/2595, RFC War Diary, 23 September 1915.

109 Reichsarchiv, *Der Weltkrieg 1914 bis 1918. Die Operationen Des Jahres 1915* (Berlin: E.S. Mittler & Sohn, 1933), p. 45.
110 TNA: PRO AIR 1/1182/204/5/2595, RFC War Diary, 24 September 1915.
111 TNA: PRO WO 95/1315, CRA 2nd Division, 'Daily Diary Z2 Group', 24 September 1915.
112 TNA: PRO WO 95/1324, XXXIV Brigade War Diary, 24 September 1915; PRO WO 95/1325, XXXVI Brigade RFA War Diary, 24 September 1915.
113 TNA: PRO WO 95/1746, CRA 9th Division, 'Operation Report', 24 September 1915.
114 TNA: PRO WO 95/1751, L Brigade RFA War Diary, 24 September 1915.
115 IWM: 82/30/1, Brigadier-General Hon. J.F.H.S.F. Trefusis Diary, 24 September 1915.
116 TNA: PRO WO 95/1250, XXVI Brigade War Diary, 24 September 1915; PRO WO 95/1923, L and LI Brigade RFA War Diaries, 24 September 1915.
117 TNA: PRO WO 95/728, CRA IV Corps, 'General Progress Report', 24 September 1915. The 'second line' referred to is almost certainly the Loos Defence Line and not the actual German second line.
118 TNA: PRO WO 95/619, CRA I Corps War Diary, 24 September 1915. Emphasis added.
119 See TNA: PRO WO 95/1352, 6 Brigade War Diary, 25 September 1915; PRO WO 95/1362, 19 Brigade War Diary, 25 September 1915; PRO WO 95/1343, 5 Brigade War Diary, 25 September 1915; PRO CAB 45/121, Major-General P.R. Robertson (GOC 19 Brigade) to Edmonds, 19 February 1926.
120 TNA: PRO CAB 45/121, Colonel H.C. Potter to Edmonds, 27 September 1927.
121 TNA: PRO WO 95/1265, 8/Berkshire and 10/Gloucestershire War Diaries, 25 September 1915.
122 TNA: PRO CAB 45/120, Major P.J.R. Currie (2/KRRC, 2 Brigade) to Edmonds, 16 July 1926. Currie's letter also states that 'even after the surrender of the trench garrison gaps had to be cut to allow the passage of troops moving forward'.
123 'It was quickly seen that the barbed wire, an unusually formidable obstacle, some ten yards in breadth and staked low on the ground, was practically undamaged in front of the brigade.' Edmonds (comp.), *Military Operations France & Belgium, 1915*, vol. 2, p. 211; TNA: PRO WO 95/1267, 2 Brigade War Diary, 25 September 1915.
124 E. Wyrall, *The Die-Hards in the Great War* (London: Harrison & Sons, 1926), I, p. 145.
125 TNA: PRO CAB 45/121, Lieutenant-Colonel A.C. Northey to Edmonds, 27 September 1926.
126 TNA: PRO CAB 45/120, Lieutenant-Colonel E.A. Beck (Brigade Major 45 Brigade) to Edmonds, 3 February 1926.
127 Ewing, *The History of the 9th (Scottish) Division*, p. 34.
128 TNA: PRO WO 95/1229, 1st Division War Diary, 3 August 1915.
129 J. Terraine, *Douglas Haig. The Educated Soldier* (London: Cassell, 2000; first published 1963), p. 204.
130 Dunn (ed.), *The War the Infantry Knew 1914–1919*, p. 150.
131 TNA: PRO WO 95/1262, 26 Brigade War Diary, 25 September 1915.
132 TNA: PRO WO 95/1774, 28 Brigade War Diary, 25 September 1915.
133 TNA: PRO WO 95/1660, 22 Brigade War Diary, 25 September 1915.
134 TNA: PRO WO 95/1652, 7th Division, 'Narrative of Events on Recent Operations'.
135 TNA: PRO WO 95/1934, 'Report by D.W.P. Strang (Captain & Adjutant) 8/Seaforths'; PRO WO 95/1948, 46 Brigade War Diary, 25 September 1915.
136 TNA: PRO WO 95/712, 47th Division to IV Corps, 'Effect of Our Artillery on German Trenches', 4 October 1915.
137 P. MacGill, *The Great Push* (London: Herbert Jenkins, 1916), p. 80.
138 Ibid., p. 85.
139 Buchan & Stewart, *The Fifteenth (Scottish) Division, 1914–1919*, p. 34.
140 J. Buchan, 'The Battlefield of Loos' in *The Times*, 6 October 1915. Thanks to Andrew Rawson for this reference.
141 TNA: PRO WO 95/712, IV Corps War Diary, October-December 1915, 'Report from 1st Division to IV Corps on Damage Done to Enemy's Trenches by Our Fire During Bombardment', 4 October 1915; PRO WO 95/1658, 21 Brigade War Diary, 25 September 1915.
142 TNA: PRO CAB 45/120, Captain B.A. Fenwick (9/East Surrey, 72 Brigade) to Edmonds, 20 December 1918; PRO WO 95/2210, 72 Brigade War Diary, 26 September 1915.
143 TNA: PRO CAB 45/120, Account of E.R. Ludlow-Hewitt, 22 September 1926.
144 TNA: PRO AIR 1/753/204/4/69, 'Memorandum on the Work of the 1st Wing, RFC in the Operations of the 1st Army Between September 21 and October 11 1915', 25 October 1915.

145 Communiqué No. 12, cited in Cole (ed.), *Royal Flying Corps Communiqués 1915–1916*, p. 52.

146 TNA: PRO AIR 1/753/204/4/69, 'Operations of the Royal Flying Corps 22–26 September', 29 September 1915.

147 Chasseaud, *Artillery's Astrologers*, p. 114.

148 Reichsarchiv, *Der Weltkrieg 1914 bis 1918*, p. 54; C.J.C. Street, *With The Guns* (Uckfield, East Sussex: Naval & Military Press, 2003; first published 1916), p. 74.

149 LHCMA: Montgomery-Massingberd Papers, 7/1, 'IV Corps Artillery at the Battle of Loos', p. 11.

150 TNA: PRO CAB 45/121, Lieutenant-Colonel W.R. Warren (CO Brigade Artillery, Lahore Division) to Edmonds, 21 May 1929.

151 Edmonds (comp.), *Military Operations France & Belgium, 1915*, vol. 2, p. 167.

152 LHCMA: Montgomery-Massingberd Papers, 7/1, 'Lecture on Battle of Loos Given on 14 December 1915. Notes on the Line Held by 117th Infantry Division about 25/09/15'.

153 Tiede, *Infanterie-Regiment Nr. 157*, p. 24.

154 Reichsarchiv, *Der Weltkrieg 1914 bis 1918*, p. 45.

155 TNA: PRO CAB 45/121, Lieutenant-Colonel H.W. B. Thorpe to Edmonds, 18 January 1926.

156 Graves, *Goodbye To All That*, p. 155.

157 TNA: PRO CAB 45/121, Lieutenant-Colonel Warren to Edmonds, 21 May 1926.

158 Figures taken from TNA: PRO WO 95/181, AA&QMG First Army War Diary, December 1914–December 1915.

159 Figures taken from Ibid.

CHAPTER 5: THE FIRST DAY (I): 25 SEPTEMBER 1915

1 All German units will be indicated in italics. Each German division consisted of 3 regiments, each one being roughly the equivalent of a British brigade, and deployed in the same standard manner. With an average strength of 780 men, a battalion was stationed in the front line, with one in support (usually in and around the second line) and one in reserve (usually resting in villages or towns east of the second line). *117th Division*'s frontage ran from Fosse 8 to Puits 16, just south of the Double Crassier, and totalled a monumental 8,700 yards. *117th Division* was deployed as follows: *11 Reserve Infantry Regiment* was in the line from the Railway Redoubt to Bois Carré. *157 Infantry Regiment*'s sector ran from opposite Bois Carré to just north of the Loos Road. On the left of *157 Regiment* was *22 Reserve Infantry Regiment*, deployed along the Loos Road to Puits 16 bis. Northwards from Fosse 8, *14th Division* was in the line. North of the La Bassée canal *56 Infantry Regiment* was deployed. It linked up to *16 Infantry Regiment*, which held the line south of the canal to the Railway Redoubt.

2 A. Palazzo, *Seeking Victory on the Western Front. The British Army and Chemical Warfare in World War I* (Lincoln & London: University of Nebraska Press, 2000), p. 68.

3 C.H. Foulkes, *"GAS!" The Story of the Special Brigade* (London: Blackwood, 1934), p. 84.

4 TNA: PRO WO 95/1948, 'Report of 46 Infantry Brigade on Operations Between 21st and 30th September 1915'.

5 A.H. Maude, *The History of the 47th (London) Division, 1914–1919* (Uckfield, East Sussex: Naval & Military Press, 2000; first published 1922), p. 29.

6 TNA: PRO WO 95/2733, 141 Brigade War Diary, 25 September 1915. See also See G.C. Wynne, 'The Other Side of the Hill. The Fight for Hill 70: 25th–26th September 1915', *Army Quarterly*, vol. 8 (April 1924 and June 1924), pp. 261–73.

7 TNA: PRO WO 95/1765, 26 Brigade War Diary, 25 September 1915; 7/Seaforth Highlanders 'Report of Action Sept 25–27'.

8 TNA: PRO CAB 45/120, Captain K.G. Buchanan to Brigadier-General Sir J.E. Edmonds, 15 January 1927.

9 TNA: PRO WO 95/1934, 'Report by D.W.P. Strang (Captain & Adjutant) 8/Seaforths'; PRO CAB 45/120, Report by IV Corps, 2 October 1915.

10 TNA: PRO WO 95/1364, 19 Brigade, 'Summary of Operations, 25 Sept 1915'.

11 TNA: PRO WO 95/1265, 8/Royal Berkshire War Diary, 25 September 1915.

12 IWM: 01/46/1, Diary of Captain J.N. Pring, 25 September 1915.

13 Reichsarchiv, *Der Weltkrieg 1914 bis 1918. Die Operationen Des Jahres 1915* (Berlin: E.S. Mittler & Sohn, 1933), p. 55.

14 TNA: PRO WO 95/2727, 140 Brigade War Diary, 25 September 1915.

15 TNA: PRO WO 95/1934, 'Report by D.W.P. Strang (Captain & Adjutant) 8/Seaforths'.

16 This was Piper D. Laidlaw who 'with a complete *sang froid*, strutted about the parapet playing the "Blue Bonnets"'. He was subsequently awarded the Victoria Cross. S. Gillon, *The K.O.S.B. in the Great War* (London: Thomas Nelson, 1930), p. 390.

17 TNA: PRO WO 95/1652, 'Notes on Recent Operations by Major-General Commanding 7th Division', 4 October 1915; 'Report on Recent Operations, 5 October 1915'.

18 A.G. Wauchope (ed.), *A History of the Black Watch (Royal Highlanders) in the Great War, 1914–1919* (3 vols., London: The Medici Society, 1925–6), III, p. 12.

19 TNA: PRO WO 95/1660, 22 Brigade, 'Narrative of Operations Sept 25–29'.

20 TNA: PRO CAB 45/120: Colonel G.H. Boileau (CRE 7th Division) to Edmonds, 25 January 1926.

21 IWM: MISC 175 (2658), Major-General Sir H.H. Tudor Diary, 25 September 1915.

22 Sir J.E. Edmonds (comp.), *History of the Great War: Military Operations France & Belgium, 1915*, vol. 2, *Battles of Aubers Ridge, Festubert and Loos* (London/Nashville: Imperial War Museum/Battery Press, 1995; first published 1928), p. 227.

23 TNA: PRO CAB 45/120, Colonel C. Russell Brown to Edmonds, 31 October 1929.

24 Foulkes, *"GAS!"*, pp. 73–4.

25 TNA: PRO WO 95/1265, 8/Royal Berkshire War Diary, 25 September 1915.

26 TNA: PRO WO 95/1270, 1/Loyal North Lancashire War Diary, 25 September 1915.

27 All along the front the gas seems to have drifted north, meaning that often assaulting battalions benefited from the gas released by the battalion on their right. This is commented upon in Foulkes, *"GAS!"*, p. 73. Paul Maze's account also confirms this. He wrote that 'the gas which we had released was drifting heavily down across the left of our front, obviously in the wrong direction'. See *A Frenchman in Khaki* (Kingswood, Surrey: William Heinemann, 1934), p. 120.

28 IWM: 01/46/1, Diary of Captain J.N. Pring, 25 September 1915.

29 See for example A. Clark, *The Donkeys* (London: Pimlico, 1997; first published 1961), pp. 147–8; B.H. Liddell Hart, *History of the First World War* (London: Pan, 1975; first published 1930), p. 199.

30 R. Graves, *Goodbye To All That* (London: Penguin, 1960; first published 1929), pp. 157–8. See also TNA: PRO CAB 45/120, Colonel H.E. Braine (Brigade Major 19 Brigade) to Edmonds, undated.

31 J.C. Dunn (ed.), *The War the Infantry Knew 1914–1919* (London: Abacus, 2004; first published 1938), p. 153.

32 LHCMA: Liddell Hart Papers, LH 1/259/35, Edmonds to Captain B.H. Liddell Hart, 5 December 1930.

33 'Attack of the 2nd Division 25/09/15', Lieutenant A.B. White's Account, contained in Sir F. Maurice (ed.), *The History of the London Rifle Brigade, 1859–1919* (London: Constable, 1921), p. 357.

34 TNA: PRO CAB 45/121, Colonel H.C. Potter to Edmonds, 27 September 1927.

35 Captain C.E.S. Percy-Smith, cited in D. Richter, *Chemical Soldiers. British Gas Warfare in World War One* (London: Leo Cooper, 1994), p. 67.

36 LHCMA: Liddell Hart Papers, LH 1/259/35, Second Lieutenant J.W. Sewill to Liddell Hart, 4 July 1930. Original emphasis.

37 TNA: PRO WO 95/1347, 9/Highland Light Infantry War Diary, 25 September 1915.

38 TNA: PRO WO 95/1343, 5 Brigade War Diary, 25 September 1915.

39 LHCMA: Liddell Hart Papers, LH 1/259/35, Second Lieutenant J.W. Sewill to Liddell Hart, 4 July 1930.

40 LHCMA: Edmonds Papers, 3/10, 'Memoirs', Chapter XXVI, p. 8; Liddell Hart Papers, LH 1/259/35, Edmonds to Liddell Hart, 5 December 1930.

41 Liddell Hart, *History of the First World War*, p. 199. For Horne see P. Simkins, 'Haig and his Army Commanders', in B. Bond & N. Cave (eds.), *Haig. A Reappraisal 70 Years On* (Barnsley: Leo Cooper, 1999), pp. 91–2. Horne's letters to his wife, held in the Imperial War Museum, do not exist for September or October 1915.

42 Foulkes, *"GAS!"*, p. 71.

43 LHCMA: Liddell Hart Papers, LH 1/259/35, Second Lieutenant J.W. Sewill to Liddell Hart, 4 July 1930.

44 TNA: PRO CAB 45/120, Colonel D.W. Cameron of Lochiel (CO 5/Cameron Highlanders, 26 Brigade) to Edmonds, 17 September 1926.

45 Foulkes, *"GAS!"*, p. 58.

46 Edmonds (comp.), *Military Operations France & Belgium, 1915*, vol. 2, p. 170.

47 Sir D. Haig, *The Haig Papers from the National Library of Scotland*, part 1, *Haig's Autograph Great War Diary* (Brighton: Harvester Press Microfilm, 1987), 25 September 1915; For the importance of this cigarette see for example J. Charteris, *At G.H.Q.* (London: Cassell, 1931), p. 114; B.H. Liddell Hart, *History of the First World War* (London: Pan, 1975; first published 1930), p. 199; R. Holmes, *Tommy. The British Soldier on the Western Front 1914–1918* (London: Harper Perennial, 2005; first published 2004), p. 420; K. Coleman, *A History of Chemical Warfare* (Basingstoke: Palgrave Macmillan, 2005), pp. 22–3.

48 TNA: PRO CAB 45/120, Captain E. Gold to Edmonds, 13 December 1925.

49 The (incorrect) recollection of Lieutenant-Colonel John Charteris (First Army Intelligence Officer) was that Gough replied 'gas was already turned on'. TNA: PRO CAB 45/120, Brigadier-General J. Charteris to Edmonds, 24 February 1927.

50 H. Gough, *The Fifth Army* (London: Hodder & Stoughton, 1931), p. 106.

51 Richter, *Chemical Soldiers*, p. 87.

52 Edmonds (comp.), *Military Operations France & Belgium, 1915*, vol. 2, pp. 255–6.

53 TNA: PRO WO 95/1347, 2/Highland Light Infantry War Diary, 25 September 1915.

54 TNA: PRO WO 95/1352, 6 Brigade War Diary, 25 September 1915. Captain A.F.G. Kilby (2/South Staffordshire) was awarded a posthumous Victoria Cross for leading his men along the canal towpath towards Embankment Redoubt against heavy enemy fire.

55 TNA: PRO WO 95/1365, 2/Argyll & Sutherland Highlanders War Diary, 25 September 1915.

56 TNA: PRO CAB 45/121, Colonel F.G.M. Rowley to Edmonds, 17 July 1926.

57 TNA: PRO WO 95/1364, 2/Royal Welsh Fusiliers, 'Summary of Operations, 25 Sept 1915'.

58 TNA: PRO WO 95/1762, 7/Seaforth Highlanders, 'Report of Action Sept 25–27'.

59 TNA: PRO WO 95/1762, 'Report of the Action of the 26th Infantry Brigade on 25, 26, 27 Sept 1915 in Vermelles District'.

60 TNA: PRO WO 95/1767, 5/Cameron Highlanders War Diary, 25 September 1915.

61 J. Ewing, *The History of the 9th (Scottish) Division* (London: John Murray, 1921), pp. 36–7.

62 TNA: PRO WO 95/1774, 28 Brigade, 'Narrative of Events on 25/09/15', 3 October 1915.

63 Gillon, *The K.O.S.B. in the Great War*, p. 326.

64 Ewing, *The History of the 9th (Scottish) Division*, p. 37.

65 TNA: PRO WO 95/1775, 9/Scottish Rifles War Diary, 25 September 1915.

66 Ibid.

67 Ewing, *The History of the 9th (Scottish) Division*, pp. 38–9.

68 See G. Sheffield, 'An Army Commander on the Somme: Hubert Gough', in G. Sheffield & D. Todman (eds.), *Command and Control on the Western Front. The British Army's Experience 1914–1918* (Staplehurst: Spellmount, 2004), pp. 71–95.

69 At 8.34a.m. 2nd Division wired the following message: 'Germans still hold Embankment Redoubt… 19 Brigade returned to our front trench… 6 Brigade lying out in front of Brickstacks.' 9th Division wired between 8.40 and 9.30a.m. that 7/Seaforth Highlanders had taken the Slag Heap and 8/Gordon Highlanders were 'going well'. At 9.42a.m. 7th Division was reported to be 'held up west of Cité St Elie' and at 10.03 a.m. the remaining Germans in the front trench opposite 22 Brigade had surrendered. All reports taken from TNA: PRO WO 95/592, I Corps War Diary, 25 September 1915.

70 A. Farrar-Hockley, *Goughie: The Life of General Sir Hubert Gough* (London: Hart-Davis, MacGibbon, 1975), p. 169.

71 Ibid., p. 169.

72 Unfortunately, we do not have Thesiger's account of the battle; he was killed in action two days later. See F. Davis & G. Maddocks, *Bloody Red Tabs* (Barnsley: Leo Cooper, 1995), pp. 106–7.

73 It was described as 'a fire zone of about 500 yards exposed to by heavy-gun, machine-gun and rifle fire, and the battalion had to storm a powerful line of trenches protected by broad strong lines of thick barbed wire'. TNA: PRO WO 95/1664, 1/South Staffordshire War Diary, 25 September 1915. Private A. Vickers (2/Royal Warwickshire) won a Victoria Cross in this attack for cutting two gaps in the wire.

74 TNA: PRO CAB 45/121, Brigadier-General R.M. Ovens to Edmonds, 20 January 1926.

75 TNA: PRO WO 95/1660, 22 Brigade, 'Narrative on Operations of September 25–29'.

76 TNA: PRO WO 95/1664, 'The 2 Battalion "The Queens" Regiment at the Battle of Loos, 25 Sept 1915'.

77 IWM: MISC 175 (2658), Major-General Sir H.H. Tudor Diary, 25 September 1915.

78 C.T. Atkinson, *The Devonshire Regiment, 1914–1918* (London: Simpkin, Marshall, Hamilton, Kent & Co, 1926), p. 95.

79 IWM: MISC 175 (2658), Major-General Sir H.H. Tudor Diary, 23 September 1915.

80 TNA: PRO WO 95/1655, 8/Devonshire War Diary, 25 September 1915.

81 TNA: PRO WO 95/1265, 8/Royal Berkshire War Diary, 25 September 1915.

82 For a full analysis of the events at Lone Tree see N. Lloyd, 'Command and Control in 1915: The Attack on Lone Tree, 25 September 1915', *Stand To! The Journal of the Western Front Association*, no. 74 (September 2005), pp. 5–10.

83 Northern Sap, on the right of the attack, enfiladed the whole line of advance.

84 According to one officer, the barbed wire that protected the German defences at Lone Tree was 'one of the strongest and widest belts I saw during the war', being about ten feet in width and staked low in the ground. TNA: PRO CAB 45/120, Major P.J.R. Currie (2/KRRC) to Edmonds, 16 July 1926. See also PRO WO 95/1272, 2/KRRC War Diary, 25 September 1915.

85 TNA: PRO WO 95/1269, 'Narrative of the Part Taken by the 2nd Royal Sussex in the Action of September 25th 1915'.

86 These were Private G.S. Peachment (2/KRRC), Private H.E. Kenny (1/Loyal North Lancashire), Captain A.M Read (1/Northamptonshire) and Sergeant H. Wells (2/Royal Sussex).

87 See J.H. Lindsay, *The London Scottish in the Great War* (London: Regimental HQ, 1925), p. 77.

88 R. Prior & T. Wilson, *Command on the Western Front. The Military Career of Sir Henry Rawlinson 1914–18* (Oxford: Blackwell, 1992), p. 122.

89 R. Neillands, *The Great War Generals on the Western Front* (London: Robinson, 1999), p. 208. Similar criticism can be found in Clark, *The Donkeys*, pp. 158–9.

90 Edmonds (comp.), *Military Operations France & Belgium, 1915*, vol. 2, p. 216.

91 Ibid., p. 217; Lindsay, *The London Scottish in the Great War*, p. 76; M. Lloyd, *The London Scottish in the Great War* (Barnsley: Leo Cooper, 2001), p. 61.

92 LHCMA: Montgomery-Massingberd Papers, 6/4–6, 'Telephone Conversations of Lieutenant-General Sir Henry Rawlinson', 25 September 1915; Prior & Wilson, *Command on the Western Front*, p. 122.

93 TNA: PRO WO 95/1229, 'Narrative of the Operations of the 1st Division 25th, 26th and 27th September 1915'.

94 TNA: PRO WO 95/1281, 2/Welsh War Diary, 25 September 1915.

95 Edmonds (comp.), *Military Operations France & Belgium, 1915*, vol. 2, p. 217.

96 Lindsay, *The London Scottish in the Great War*, pp. 76–7.

97 TNA: PRO CAB 45/121, Major J. Paterson to Edmonds, 21 January 1926. Original emphasis.

98 TNA: PRO WO 95/1229, Memorandum by Major-General A.E.A. Holland, 10 September 1915.

99 TNA: PRO WO 95/1948, 'Report of 46 Infantry Brigade on Operations Between 21 and 30 September'.

100 TNA: PRO WO 95/1934, 44 Brigade, 'Report on Attack on 25 September', 2 October 1915.

101 Edmonds (comp.), *Military Operations France & Belgium, 1915*, vol. 2, pp. 197–8.

102 TNA: PRO WO 95/1948, 46 Infantry Brigade Order No. 11, 15 September 1915.

103 Fortunately, the Loos Defence Line was unmanned. Its thick wire defences did, however, slow down the advance. Edmonds (comp.), *Military Operations France & Belgium, 1915*, vol. 2, p. 195.

104 J. Buchan & J. Stewart, *The Fifteenth (Scottish) Division, 1914–1919* (Edinburgh & London: William Blackwood, 1926), p. 37–8.

105 TNA: PRO WO 95/1934, 'Report by D.W.P. Strang (Captain & Adjutant) 8/Seaforths'.

106 IWM: Wilkinson Papers, 'Report on Attack on 25th Sept 1915'.

107 TNA: PRO CAB 45/120, Account of Sergeant J.M. Cavers, 20 November 1918.

108 IWM: 86/65/1: Private A.G.C. Townsend, Letter of 1 October 1915.

109 It is worth noting that the famous heroine of Loos, a 17-year-old local girl called Emillenne Moreau, allegedly killed two German snipers in the village. When placed within this context her actions do not seem particularly remarkable, but they do perhaps add weight to the idea that the normal laws of war had broken down in Loos.

110 IWM: P262, H. Panton, Letter of 29 September 1915. Much of Panton's account is recorded in T. Wilson, *The Myriad Faces of War: Britain and the Great War, 1914–1918* (Cambridge: Polity Press, 1988), pp. 260–3.

111 Writing in 1920, the war reporter, Philip Gibbs, compared small groups of Scottish soldiers to 'packs of wolves', prowling around the streets looking for cellars or basements, which were 'crammed with Germans, trapped and terrified, but still defending themselves'. P. Gibbs, *Realities of War* (London: William Heinemann, 1920), p. 144.

112 Major J. Stewart cited in E. Spiers, 'The Scottish Soldier at War', in H. Cecil & P.H. Liddle (eds.), *Facing Armageddon. The First World War Experienced* (London: Leo Cooper, 1996), p. 326. See also N. Ferguson, *The Pity of War* (London: Allen Lane, 1998), p. 384.

113 J.L. Jack, *General Jack's Diary 1914–18. The Trench Diary of Brigadier-General J.L. Jack*, ed. J. Terraine (London: Cassell, 2000; first published 1964), pp. 126–7. Original emphasis.

114 TNA: PRO WO 95/1767, 8/Gordon Highlanders War Diary, 25 September 1915. Original emphasis.

115 See O. Bartov, *The Eastern Front, 1941–45, German Troops and the Barbarisation of Warfare* (Basingstoke: Palgrave Macmillan, 2001; first published 1985), passim.

116 N. Lloyd, 'Note on Decoys and Dummies', *Journal of the Society for Army Historical Research*, vol. 81, no. 237 (Autumn 2003), pp. 290–1.

117 TNA: PRO WO 95/2733, 141 Brigade War Diary, 25 September 1915.

118 Edmonds (comp.), *Military Operations France & Belgium, 1915*, vol. 2, p. 189.

119 TNA: PRO WO 95/2727, 140 Brigade War Diary, 25 September 1915.

120 J. Lee, 'Command and Control in Battle: British Divisions on the Menin Road Ridge, 20 September 1917', in Sheffield & Todman (eds.), *Command and Control on the Western Front*, pp. 119–20.

121 See J. Lee, 'Some Lessons of the Somme: The British Infantry in 1917', in B. Bond (ed.), *'Look to your Front' Studies in the First World War by the British Commission for Military History* (Staplehurst: Spellmount, 1999), pp. 79–87; C. McCarthy, 'Queen of the Battlefield: The Development of Command, Organisation and Tactics in the British Infantry Battalion During the Great War', in Sheffield & Todman (eds.), *Command and Control on the Western Front*, pp. 173–93.

122 R. Prior & T. Wilson, *The Somme* (London: Yale University Press, 2005), p. 115.

123 Wauchope (ed.), *A History of the Black Watch (Royal Highlanders) in the Great War, 1914–1919*, III, p. 124.

124 TNA: PRO WO 95/1762, 7/Seaforth Highlanders, 'Report of Action Sept 25–27'.

125 J. Ewing, *The Royal Scots, 1914–1919* (London: Oliver & Boyd, 1929), p. 189.

126 TNA: PRO WO 95/1762, 'Report on Operations by 5/Cameron Highlanders on 25/26/27 Sept'; IWM: 88/57/1, 'My Life with the Post Office Rifles', Account of Rifleman (later Wing Commander) W.J. Shewry.

127 See the extract from the war diary of *26 Infantry Regiment* in Edmonds (comp.), *Military Operations France & Belgium, 1915*, vol. 2, p. 189, n. 1.

128 Lindsay, *The London Scottish in the Great War*, p. 76.

129 TNA: PRO WO 95/1351. 2/Worcestershire War Diary, 26 September 1915.

130 TNA: PRO CAB 45/121, Colonel F.G.M. Rowley (CO 1/Middlesex) to Edmonds, 17 July 1926.

131 TNA: PRO WO 95/1655, 8/Devonshire War Diary, 25 September 1915.

132 Prior & Wilson, *Command on the Western Front*, p. 108.

133 IWM: MISC 175 (2658), Major-General Sir H.H. Tudor Diary, 23 September 1915.

CHAPTER 6: THE FIRST DAY (II): 25 SEPTEMBER 1915

1 Sir J.E. Edmonds (comp.), *History of the Great War: Military Operations France & Belgium, 1915*, vol. 2, *Battles of Aubers Ridge, Festubert and Loos* (London/Nashville: Imperial War Museum/Battery Press, 1995; first published 1928), pp. 197–8.

2 TNA: PRO WO 95/1934, 44 Brigade, 'Report on Attack on 25 September', 2 October 1915.

3 See G.C. Wynne, 'The Other Side of the Hill. The Fight for Hill 70: 25th–26th September 1915', *Army Quarterly*, vol. 8 (April 1924 and June 1924), pp. 261–73.

4 The presence of several officers was vital in steadying the advance. These officers included Colonel J.W. Sandilands (CO 7/Cameron Highlanders); Lieutenant-Colonel H.R. Wallace (CO 10/Gordon Highlanders); Captain D.W.P. Strang (8/Seaforth Highlanders); a Major Crichton

(10/Gordon Highlanders), and Second Lieutenant F.H. Johnson (73 Field Company, 44 Brigade) who was subsequently awarded the Victoria Cross.

5 Reichsarchiv, *Der Weltkrieg 1914 bis 1918. Die Operationen Des Jahres 1915* (Berlin: E.S. Mittler & Sohn, 1933), p. 55.

6 Reichsarchiv, *Das Koniglich Sachsische 13. Infanterie-Regiment Nr. 178* (Dresden: Wilhelm und Bertha V. Baensch Stifung, 1935), p. 59.

7 B.H. Liddell Hart, *History of the First World War* (London: Pan, 1975; first published 1930), p. 200.

8 A. Clark, *The Donkeys* (London: Pimlico, 1997; first published 1961), p. 156.

9 P. Griffith, *Battle Tactics of the Western Front* (New Haven & London: Yale University Press, 1994), p. 53.

10 R. Prior & T. Wilson, *Command on the Western Front. The Military Career of Sir Henry Rawlinson 1914–18* (Oxford: Blackwell, 1992), p. 126.

11 Edmonds (comp.), *Military Operations France & Belgium, 1915*, vol. 2, p. 213, n. 1; TNA: PRO WO 95/1264, 1/Cameron Highlanders, 'Full Accounts [*sic*] of Operations by 1st Battalion on 25 September 1915'.

12 IWM: 82/30/1, Brigadier-General Hon. J.F.H.S.F. Trefusis Diary, 25 September 1915.

13 TNA: PRO CAB 45/120, Captain P.S. Brindley to Brigadier-General Sir J.E. Edmonds, 26 October 1926.

14 J. Ewing, *The History of the 9th (Scottish) Division* (London: John Murray, 1921), p. 45.

15 J. Ewing, *The Royal Scots, 1914–1919* (London: Oliver & Boyd, 1929), p. 188.

16 TNA: PRO WO 95/1658, 21 Brigade War Diary, 25 September 1915.

17 TNA: PRO WO 95/1942, 45 Brigade, 'Report on Operations From 21 September to 30 September 1915'.

18 Ewing, *The Royal Scots, 1914–1919*, p. 188.

19 TNA: PRO WO 95/1772, Extract from Private Diary of Lieutenant-Colonel H.H. Northey, 'The 6/R.S.F. at the Battle of Loos'.

20 IWM: 88/57/1, 'With the Post Office Rifles in France and Flanders 1915–18', by Rifleman W. Young.

21 TNA: PRO WO 95/1275, 3 Brigade War Diary, 25 September 1915.

22 TNA: PRO WO 95/1767, 5/Cameron Highlanders War Diary, 25 September 1915.

23 TNA: PRO WO 95/1762, 'Report on Operations on 25th to 27th September as far as concerns 8/Black Watch'.

24 C.T. Atkinson, *The Devonshire Regiment, 1914–1918* (London: Simpkin, Marshall, Hamilton, Kent & Co, 1926), p. 97.

25 TNA: PRO CAB 45/120, Colonel G.H. Boileau (CRE 7th Division) to Edmonds, 28 February 1926.

26 TNA: PRO WO 95/1769, 'Report by the 12/Royal Scots on the Operations from 24–29 September 1915'.

27 Ewing, *The Royal Scots, 1914–1919*, p. 189.

28 21 Brigade was 'literally frittered away and was never employed as a brigade at all. It was order, counter order, disorder. Before Zero Hour our plans were cut and dried. Before any information came in they began altering them.' TNA: PRO CAB 45/120, Colonel G. Crossman (Brigade Major 21 Brigade) to Edmonds, 18 February 1926.

29 TNA: PRO WO 95/1658, 21 Brigade War Diary, 25 September 1915.

30 Edmonds (comp.), *Military Operations France & Belgium, 1915*, vol. 2, pp. 212–3.

31 TNA: PRO WO 95/1924, LXXV Brigade RFA War Diary, 25 September 1915.

32 TNA: PRO WO 95/1643, XXII Brigade RFA War Diary, 25 September 1915.

33 TNA: PRO WO 95/1325, XXXVI Brigade RFA War Diary, 25 September 1915.

34 TNA: PRO WO 95/1752, LII Brigade RFA War Diary, 25 September 1915.

35 TNA: PRO WO 95/1751, L Brigade RFA War Diary, 25 September 1915.

36 IWM: Con Shelf, 'The War Diary of an Artillery Officer 1914–1918', by Major P.H. Pilditch, pp. 160–1.

37 E. Wyrall, *The Die-Hards in the Great War* (London: Harrison & Sons, 1926), I, pp. 147–8.

38 'Should the infantry attack be checked at any period prior to 1.20, a special bombardment may be demanded of, and ordered by, the corps. The hour at which this special bombardment will commence will be notified. It will last for thirty minutes from first to last gun, the last five minutes of this period being marked by a rapid rate of fire.' Edmonds (comp.), *Military Operations France & Belgium, 1915*, vol. 2, Appendix 21, p. 467.

39 TNA: PRO WO 95/1924, LXXII Brigade RFA War Diary, 25 September 1915.

40 TNA: PRO CAB 45/121, Brigadier-General R.M. Ovens to Edmonds, 20 January 1926.

41 TNA: PRO WO 95/1924, LXXIII Brigade RFA War Diary, 25 September 1915.

42 LHCMA: Montgomery-Massingberd Papers, 7/1, 'The IV Corps Artillery at the Battle of Loos', p. 26.

43 TNA: PRO WO 95/1643, XXXV Brigade RFA War Diary, 25 September 1915.

44 IWM: MISC 175 (2658), Major-General Sir H.H. Tudor Diary, 25 September 1915.

45 Within 9th Division, by 1p.m. a battery of L Brigade RFA had occupied positions behind the British front line south-west of the Hohenzollern Redoubt. It was joined later by LII Brigade RFA and a battery of LIII Brigade RFA. Further south, Brigadier-General J.G. Rotton (BGRA 7th Division) ordered XXII Brigade RFA forward just after 8a.m., and in the following hour, also ordered XXXV and XXXVII Brigades RFA to move up. By the end of the day two batteries of 1st Division's artillery were at Bois Carré, another two were stationed at Le Rutoire (XXVI Brigade RFA), and one brigade was north of Loos. The artillery of 15th Division had been delayed because 2 Brigade was unable to take the German positions at Lone Tree until late afternoon. Once this had been cleared, however, two batteries of LXXII Brigade RFA moved into position north of Loos, another two dug in around Fort Glatz (north-west of Loos), while the remainder stayed in its gun-pits around Fosse 7. See Edmonds (comp.), *Military Operations France & Belgium, 1915*, vol. 2, p. 230; TNA: PRO WO 95/1923, LXX Brigade RFA War Diary, 25 September 1915; LHCMA: Montgomery-Massingberd Papers, 7/1, 'The IV Corps Artillery at the Battle of Loos', pp. 17–9.

46 TNA: PRO CAB 45/120, Major J. Buckley to Edmonds, 1 January 1927.

47 IWM: 96/29/1, Account of Lieutenant J.H. Alcock.

48 That the reserve divisions had to fall back on approximate compass bearings perfectly highlights the absolute lack of any planning for their deployment. Lieutenant-Colonel K. Henderson (Brigade Major 64 Brigade) recorded that it was 'still pouring and pitch dark, and it was obvious that in these circumstances and in our complete ignorance of the ground and without a guide or any idea where the 63 Brigade whom we were to follow, was, that our move could only be by compass bearing across the two trench systems'. IWM: DS/MISC/2, Account of Lieutenant-Colonel K. Henderson.

49 TNA: PRO WO 95/2189, Lieutenant-Colonel C.G. Stewart to Major A.F. Becke, 3 August 1925.

50 TNA: PRO WO 95/1619, 71 Brigade War Diary, 25 September 1915.

51 TNA: PRO WO 95/2210, 72 Brigade War Diary, 25–6 September 1915.

52 Ewing, *The History of the 9th (Scottish) Division*, p. 51.

53 TNA: PRO WO 95/2157, 63 Brigade, 'Report of Operations 25th, 26th and 27th September 1915'.

54 TNA: PRO WO 95/2151, 62 Brigade War Diary, 25 September 1915.

55 See for example Liddell Hart, *History of the First World War*, p. 202; G.C. Wynne, *If Germany Attacks. The Battle in Depth in the West* (Westport, CT: Greenwood, 1976; first published 1940), pp. 72–3; L. Macdonald, *1915. The Death of Innocence* (London: Penguin, 1997; first published 1993), pp. 514–5.

56 Edmonds (comp.), *Military Operations France & Belgium, 1915*, vol. 2, p. 282.

57 Sir D. Haig, *The Haig Papers from the National Library of Scotland*, part 1, *Haig's Autograph Great War Diary* (Brighton: Harvester Press Microfilm, 1987), 25 September 1915.

58 See for example J. Terraine, *White Heat. The New Warfare 1914–1918* (London: Sidgwick & Jackson, 1980); M. Middlebrook, *The First Day on the Somme* (London: Penguin, 1984; first published 1971), pp. 148–50; G. Sheffield & D. Todman, 'Command and Control in the British Army on the Western Front', in G. Sheffield & D. Todman (eds.), *Command and Control on the Western Front. The British Army's Experience 1914–1918* (Staplehurst: Spellmount, 2004), pp. 1–11.

59 M. van Creveld, *Command in War* (London & Cambridge, Massachusetts: Harvard University Press, 1985), p. 158.

60 TNA: PRO WO 95/1774, 28 Brigade, 'Narrative of Events on 25/09/15', 3 October 1915; WO 95/1775, 10/Highland Light Infantry War Diary, 25 September 1915.

61 TNA: PRO CAB 45/120, Lieutenant-Colonel D.W. Cameron of Lochiel to Edmonds, 3 August 1926. Lochiel also stated that the first message he received 'was to remind me that my weekly strength return due the previous day had not been received and requesting me to expedite; and the second late in the afternoon telling me to hold on to the Fosse 8 at all costs if possible.'

62 TNA: PRO WO 95/1934, 10/Gordon Highlanders to 44 Brigade.

63 IWM: M.G. Wilkinson Papers, 'Report on Attack on 25 September 1915'.
64 BLL: GS 1612, Account of Major-General R.H.D. Tompson.
65 TNA: PRO AIR 1/1182/204/5/2595, Royal Flying Corps War Diary, 25 September 1915.
66 Edmonds (comp.), *Military Operations France & Belgium, 1915*, vol. 2, pp. 255–6.
67 TNA: PRO WO 95/1229, 'Narrative of the Operations of the 1st Division 25th, 26th and 27th September 1915'. For example, 2 Brigade's message to 1st Division, despatched at 7.01a.m. only took eight minutes to arrive at divisional headquarters and similarly, a second message timed at 7.37a.m. arrived at 7.42a.m. Even after 2 Brigade had passed Lone Tree and was heading for the Lens–La Bassée road, messages only took between twenty and twenty-five minutes to reach divisional headquarters.
68 A.H. Maude, *The History of the 47th (London) Division, 1914–1919* (Uckfield, East Sussex: Naval & Military Press, 2000; first published 1922), p. 35.
69 TNA: PRO WO 95/1934, 10/Gordon Highlanders to 44 Brigade.
70 Unless stated otherwise, the following messages are taken from TNA: PRO WO 95/158, First Army War Diary, 25 September 1915.
71 LHCMA: Montgomery-Massingberd Papers, 6/4–6, 'Telephone Conversations of Lieutenant-General Rawlinson, 25/09/15'.
72 LHCMA: Liddell Hart Papers, HL1/520, Montgomery-Massingberd to Captain B.H. Liddell Hart, 29 September 1927.
73 See R. Holmes, *The Little Field-Marshal. Sir John French* (London: Jonathan Cape, 1981), p. 303; TNA: PRO CAB 44/27, Haig's comments on the draft chapters of the Official History, 20 February 1927. This rather startling decision of Sir John's to absent himself from his headquarters at such an important time probably reflected both his natural desire to be closer to the fighting, and his belief that Haig's battle would develop more slowly and methodically than it actually did.
74 TNA: PRO WO 95/880, XI Corps War Diary, 25 September 1915. See also T. Travers, *The Killing Ground: The British Army, the Western Front and the Emergence of Modern Warfare 1900–1918* (Barnsley: Pen & Sword, 2003; first published 1987), pp. 17–8.
75 TNA: PRO WO 95/880, XI Corps War Diary, 25–6 September 1915.
76 At 1.05 p.m. Sir Henry Rawlinson telephoned First Army 'to say the news from the 15th Division is not so good. They might be turned off Hill 70. Being pretty heavily attacked.' TNA: PRO 95/WO 95/712, 'Telephone Conversations of Lieut-General Sir Henry Rawlinson, Bt., K.C.B., C.V.O., from the Commencement of the Attack', 25 September 1915.
77 TNA: PRO WO 95/158, First Army War Diary, 25–6 September 1915.
78 These discrepancies remain a mystery. Although 21st Division had been briefly placed under IV Corps' control at 1.13p.m., this was cancelled at 2.30p.m.
79 Prior & Wilson, *Command on the Western Front*, p. 127.
80 Edmonds (comp.), *Military Operations France & Belgium, 1915*, vol. 2, p. 267.
81 See Appendix II: Total Recorded British Deaths, 25 September 1915 and 1 July 1916.
82 Edmonds (comp.), *Military Operations France & Belgium, 1915*, vol. 2, p. 392.
83 C.T. Atkinson, *The Seventh Division, 1914–1918* (London: John Murray, 1927), p. 231.
84 Edmonds (comp.), *Military Operations France & Belgium, 1915*, vol. 2, pp. 220–3, n. 1, 3.
85 J. Buchan & J. Stewart, *The Fifteenth (Scottish) Division, 1914–1919* (Edinburgh and London: William Blackwood, 1926), p. 49.
86 Edmonds (comp.), *Military Operations France & Belgium, 1915*, vol. 2, p. 191.
87 E. Wyrall, *The History of the 2nd Division, 1914–1918* (Uckfield, East Sussex: Naval & Military Press, 2000; first published 1921), p. 230.
88 TNA: PRO WO 95/1767, 5/Cameron Highlanders War Diary, 25 September 1915; Edmonds (comp.), *Military Operations France & Belgium, 1915*, vol. 2, p. 241, n. 3.
89 Edmonds (comp.), *Military Operations France & Belgium, 1915*, vol. 2, p. 238, n. 1.
90 TNA: PRO CAB 45/120, Brigadier-General G.S. Cartwright to Edmonds, 7 February 1926.
91 TNA: PRO WO 95/1265, 10/Gloucestershire War Diary, 26 September 1915; Edmonds (comp.), *Military Operations France & Belgium, 1915*, vol. 2, p. 229, n. 2.
92 TNA: PRO WO 95/1664, 2/Royal Warwickshire War Diary, 25 September 1915.
93 TNA: PRO WO 95/1267, 2 Brigade, 'Operations 25–30 September 1915'.
94 Maude, *The History of the 47th (London) Division, 1914–1919*, p. 30.
95 TNA: PRO WO 95/1934, 'Report by T.O. Lloyd (OC 9/Black Watch) on Operations of 25/9/15'.
96 TNA: PRO WO 95/1265, 10/Gloucester War Diary, 25 September 1915.

97 TNA: PRO WO 95/1655, 8/Devonshire War Diary, 25 September 1915.
98 TNA: PRO CAB 45/120, Captain P.S. Brindley (9/Devonshire, 20 Brigade) to Edmonds, 26 October 1926.
99 TNA: PRO WO 95/1658, 21 Brigade War Diary, 25 September 1915.
100 TNA: PRO WO 95/1762, 'Report of the Action of the 26th Infantry Brigade on 25, 26, 27 September 1915 in Vermelles District'.
101 TNA: PRO WO 95/1775, 10/Highland Light Infantry War Diary, 25 September 1915; S. Gillon, *The K.O.S.B. in the Great War* (London: Thomas Nelson, 1930), p. 326.
102 See Appendix III: Senior British Officer Casualties.
103 Maude, *The History of the 47th (London) Division, 1914–1919*, p. 31.
104 TNA: PRO WO 95/1934, 'Report by D.W.P. Strang (Captain & Adjutant) 8/Seaforths'.
105 TNA: PRO WO 95/1775, 10/Highland Light Infantry War Diary, 25 September 1915.
106 Capper was well known for his belief in the 'offensive spirit'. As he had written in 1908, 'success in war on a large scale can only be achieved if the troops are possessed of this unconquerable and determined offensive spirit'. K. Simpson, 'Capper and the Offensive Spirit', *R.U.S.I. Journal*, vol. 118, no. 2 (June 1973), p. 53.
107 IWM: 82/30/1, Brigadier-General Hon. J.F.H.S.F. Trefusis Diary, 25 September 1915.
108 Atkinson, *The Seventh Division*, pp. 207–8.
109 E.M. Spiers, *The Late Victorian Army 1868–1902* (Manchester: Manchester University Press, 1992), p. 113.
110 G.D. Sheffield, *Leadership in the Trenches* (London: Macmillan, 2000), p. 146.
111 M.A. Ramsey, *Command and Cohesion: The Citizen Soldier and Minor Tactics in the British Army, 1870–1918* (Westport, CT: Praeger, 2002), p. 188.
112 E. Wyrall, *The History of the King's Regiment (Liverpool) 1914–1919* (3 vols. London: Edward Arnold, 1928), I, p. 187.
113 IWM: Con Shelf, 'The War Diary of an Artillery Officer 1914–1918', by Major P.H. Pilditch, p. 155.
114 S. Bull, *Brassey's History of Uniforms World War One British Army* (London: Brassey's, 1998), pp. 25–7.
115 BLL: POW 043, Account of Captain L. McNaught-Davis.
116 Reichsarchiv, *Der Weltkrieg 1914 bis 1918*, p. 77. 22 guns were also lost (p. 55). It should be understood that whereas the British Army recorded casualties every day, the German Army recorded them much less frequently, sometimes only a few times a month. The German system was less accurate than the British and would not record lightly wounded soldiers who returned to their units within a few days of being hurt.
117 Ewing, *The History of the 9th (Scottish) Division*, p. 57, n. 1.
118 Maude, *The History of the 47th (London) Division, 1914–1919*, p. 31.
119 Wyrall, *The History of the 2nd Division, 1914–1918*, p. 228.
120 Wauchope (ed.), *A History of the Black Watch (Royal Highlanders) in the Great War, 1914–1919*, III, p. 10.
121 TNA: PRO WO 95/1364 19 Brigade, 'Summary of Operations', 25 September 1915.
122 Atkinson, *The Seventh Division, 1914–1918*, p. 208.
123 TNA: PRO WO 95/1364, 19 Brigade, 'Summary of Operations', 25 September 1915.
124 TNA: PRO WO 95/1265, 8/Royal Berkshire War Diary, 25 September 1915.
125 Atkinson, *The Devonshire Regiment, 1914–1918*, p. 99.
126 TNA: PRO CAB 45/121, Colonel L.G. Oliver to Edmonds, 20 February 1926.
127 TNA: PRO WO 95/1281, 2/Welsh War Diary, 26 September 1915.
128 Wynne, 'The Other Side of the Hill. The Fight for Hill 70: 25th–26th September 1915', pp. 261–73.
129 Reichsarchiv, *Das Koniglich Sachsische 13. Infanterie-Regiment Nr. 178* (Dresden: Wilhelm und Bertha V. Baensch Stifung, 1935), p. 61.
130 TNA: PRO WO 95/1942: 45 Brigade, 'Report on Operations 21 Sept to the 30 Sept'.
131 See Chapter 8.

CHAPTER 7: THE SECOND DAY: 26 SEPTEMBER 1915

1 Getting an accurate picture of events in the Quarries is, as one divisional history noted, 'quite beyond attainment'. For details see C.T. Atkinson, *The Seventh Division, 1914–1918* (London: John Murray, 1927), p. 217; TNA: PRO WO 95/1659, 2/Yorkshire War Diary, 26 September 1915; PRO WO 95/1660, 22 Brigade, 'Narrative on Operations September 25–29'.

2 H. Gough, *The Fifth Army* (London: Hodder & Stoughton, 1931), p. 114.

3 TNA: PRO WO 95/2216, 73 Brigade War Diary, 25 September 1915.

4 TNA: PRO CAB 45/120, Lieutenant-Colonel R.R. Gibson (12/Royal Fusiliers) to Brigadier-General Sir J.E. Edmonds, 23 August 1926.

5 TNA: PRO CAB 45/120, Colonel G.H. Boileau (CRE 7th Division) to Edmonds, 28 February 1926.

6 9/Norfolks had been detached from 71 Brigade at 1a.m. on 26 September. A further battalion, 8/Bedfordshire, followed at 3a.m., but was unable to make contact and returned to 71 Brigade the following morning.

7 TNA: PRO WO 95/1623, 9/Norfolk War Diary, 25 September 1915.

8 TNA: PRO WO 95/1351, 2/Worcestershire War Diary, 26 September 1915. 2/Worcestershire was part of a composite battalion formed from three battalions of 2nd Division (2/Worcestershire, 1/KRRC and 1/Royal Berkshire) commanded by Lieutenant-Colonel B.C.M. Carter (1/King's, 6 Brigade).

9 After noticing large numbers of Germans massing in front of *Stützpunkt IV* and then advancing towards Bois Hugo, Lieutenant-Colonel A.G. Prothero (CO 2/Welsh) put a telephone call through to 3 Brigade reporting these movements. Because it was so difficult to change the orders at such late notice, he was told to continue with the attack, whatever the circumstances. At 11 a.m. 1/Black Watch reported to 3 Brigade that masses of Germans had been seen moving to the south-east and also (erroneously) that the Welsh were not advancing. Brigadier-General H.R Davies (GOC 3 Brigade), alarmed at the situation, but having no means to contact 2/Welsh, ordered the two battalions to stand fast and await events. TNA: PRO WO 95/1281, 2/Welsh War Diary, 26 September 1915.

10 TNA: PRO WO 95/1275, 3 Brigade War Diary, 26 September 1915.

11 J. Buchan & J. Stewart, *The Fifteenth (Scottish) Division, 1914–1919* (Edinburgh & London: William Blackwood, 1926), p. 42. McCracken's phone call to Rawlinson, where he expressed his 'doubts as to the fitness of his division to resume the offensive', does not seem to have been recorded in the log of telephone conversations at IV Corps HQ held in LHCMA: Montgomery-Massingberd Papers, 6/4–6, 'Telephone Conversations of Lieutenant-General Rawlinson, 26/09/15'.

12 Rawlinson to Kitchener, 21 April 1915, cited in R. Prior & T. Wilson, *Command on the Western Front. The Military Career of Sir Henry Rawlinson 1914–18* (Oxford: Blackwell, 1992), p. 78.

13 NAM: Rawlinson Papers, 5301-33-25, Rawlinson Diary, 26 September 1915.

14 Sir J.E. Edmonds (comp.), *History of the Great War: Military Operations France & Belgium, 1915*, vol. 2, *Battles of Aubers Ridge, Festubert and Loos* (London/Nashville: Imperial War Museum/Battery Press, 1995; first published 1928), p. 310.

15 J. Ewing, *The Royal Scots, 1914–1919* (London: Oliver & Boyd, 1929), p. 201.

16 Here Private R. Dunshire (13/Royal Scots) won the Victoria Cross for bringing in wounded men.

17 Edmonds (comp.), *Military Operations France & Belgium, 1915*, vol. 2, pp. 311–2.

18 TNA: PRO WO 95/1924, LXXIII Brigade RFA War Diary, 26 September 1915.

19 TNA: PRO WO 95/1923, LXXI Brigade RFA War Diary, 26 September 1915.

20 M. Farndale, *History of the Royal Regiment of Artillery. Western Front 1914–18* (Dorset: Henry Ling, 1986), p. 124.

21 TNA: PRO WO 95/1942, 45 Brigade, 'Report on Operations from 21 September to the 30 September'.

22 Buchan & Stewart, *The Fifteenth (Scottish) Division, 1914–1919*, p. 43.

23 TNA: PRO WO 95/2155, 13/Northumberland Fusiliers War Diary, 26 September 1915.

24 TNA: PRO WO 95/1942, 45 Brigade, 'Report on Operations from 21 September to the 30 September'.

25 TNA: PRO WO 95/2151, 62 Brigade War Diary, 26 September 1915.

26 TNA: PRO WO 95/2155, 12/Northumberland Fusiliers War Diary, 26 September 1915.

27 A. Clark, *The Donkeys* (London: Pimlico, 1997; first published 1961), pp. 163–74; T. Travers, 'The Army and the Challenge of War 1914–1918', in D. Chandler & I.F.W. Beckett (eds.), *The Oxford History of the British Army* (Oxford: Oxford University Press, 2003; first published 1994), p. 221. J. Keegan, *The First World War* (London: Pimlico, 1999; first published 1998), p. 218. See also Prior & Wilson, *Command on the Western Front*, p. 129. The map on p. 128 (map 11) confuses the deployment of 21st and 24th Divisions.

28 Edmonds (comp.), *Military Operations France & Belgium, 1915*, vol. 2, p. 342, n. 1.

29 Clark, *The Donkeys*, p. 173.

30 E.S. Osswald, *Das Altenburger Regiment (Thuringisches Infanterie-Regiment Nr. 153) im Weltkrieg* (Oldenburg: Stalling, 1922), pp. 181–4.

31 Ibid., p. 184.

32 C.R. Simpson (ed.), *The History of the Lincolnshire Regiment, 1914–1918* (London: The Medici Society, 1931), p. 114.

33 TNA: PRO WO 95/2158, 8/Somerset Light Infantry, 'Report on Operations 25th, 26th and 27th September 1915'. It was around this time that Brigadier-General N.T. Nickalls (GOC 63 Brigade) was killed whilst trying to rally his men around Chalk Pit House.

34 At 9.45 a.m. 64 Brigade received a note from 63 Brigade, timed 8.53a.m., which requested a battalion to move up in support because its right flank was being pressed by a German attack on Bois Hugo. 14/Durham Light Infantry was immediately sent forward. TNA: PRO WO 95/2159, 64 Brigade War Diary, 26 September 1915.

35 TNA: PRO WO 95/2159, 64 Brigade War Diary, 26 September 1915.

36 Edmonds (comp.), *Military Operations France & Belgium, 1915*, vol. 2, p. 321.

37 Quoted in Ibid., p. 329.

38 Ibid., p. 328.

39 TNA: PRO WO 95/2159, 64 Brigade War Diary, 26 September 1915.

40 One battalion of *157 Infantry Regiment* was stationed in Hulluch, one battalion of *26 Regiment* lay between Hulluch and *Stützpunkt IV* and three battalions *153 Infantry Regiment* were situated to the south around Bois Hugo. One battalion of *22 Reserve Regiment* was deployed in Cité St Auguste. Edmonds (comp.), *Military Operations France & Belgium, 1915*, vol. 2, p. 316, n. 2.

41 See for example TNA: PRO WO 95/2210, 72 Brigade, 'Diary of Events 5 p.m. 25th September to 4.30 a.m. 27th September 1915'; Anonymous, *The History of the Eighth Battalion the Queen's Own Royal West Kent Regiment 1914–1919* (London: Hazell, Watson & Viney, 1921), p. 19; C.T. Atkinson, *The Queen's Royal West Kent Regiment, 1914–1919* (London: Simpson, Marshall, Hamilton, Kent & Co, 1924), p. 128; R.S.H. Moody, *Historical Records of the Buffs East Kent Regiment (3rd Foot)* (London: The Medici Society, 1922), p. 97; IWM: 76/210/1, Account of F.W. Billman. For German operations see Reichsarchiv, *Der Weltkrieg 1914 bis 1918*, p. 69.

42 TNA: PRO CAB 45/121, Colonel E. Vansittart to Edmonds, 25 January 1926.

43 TNA: PRO WO 95/2210, 72 Brigade, 'Diary of Events 5 p.m. 25th September to 4.30 a.m. 27th September 1915'.

44 TNA: PRO CAB 45/120, Lieutenant L.G. Duke (8/Queens, 72 Brigade) to Edmonds, 20 November 1918.

45 Sir D. Haig, *The Haig Papers from the National Library of Scotland*, part 1, *Haig's Autograph Great War Diary* (Brighton: Harvester Press Microfilm, 1987), 26 September 1915.

46 NAM: Rawlinson Papers, 5301-33-25, Rawlinson Diary, 26 September 1915.

47 NAM: Rawlinson Papers, 5201-33-18, 'Letter Book Volume II, May 1915–Aug 1916', Lieutenant-General Sir H. Rawlinson to Lord Kitchener, 29 September 1915.

48 Haig, *The Haig Papers*, 27 September 1915.

49 Ibid., 27 September 1915.

50 Edmonds (comp.), *Military Operations France & Belgium, 1915*, vol. 2, p. 342–5. Edmonds also included two paragraphs on 'Young and Old Soldiers' taken from Sir J. Kincaid, *Adventures in the Rifle Brigade: Random Shots From A Rifleman*, pp. 348–9, n. 3.

51 TNA: PRO WO 95/2158, Major-General G.T. Forestier-Walker to II Corps, 15 October 1915.

52 TNA: PRO CAB 45/120, Major-General G.T. Forestier-Walker to Edmonds, 24 January 1927. Forestier-Walker was relieved of command on 18 November 1915.

53 TNA: PRO WO 158/32, 'Report from 24th Division', 25 October 1915.

54 TNA: PRO CAB 45/121, Colonel E. Vansittart to Edmonds, 25 January 1926.

55 TNA: PRO CAB 45/120, Captain B.A. Fenwick to Edmonds, 20 December 1918.

56 TNA: PRO CAB 45/121, Colonel E. Vansittart to Edmonds, 25 January 1926.

57 Atkinson, *The Queen's Royal West Kent Regiment, 1914–1919*, p. 129.

58 TNA: PRO CAB 45/121, Brigadier-General C.G. Stewart (GSO1 24th Division) to Major A.F. Becke, 3 August 1926.

59 TNA: PRO WO 95/1281, 2/Welsh War Diary, 26 September 1915.

60 NAM: Rawlinson Papers, 5301-33-25, Rawlinson Diary, 26 September 1915.

61 TNA: PRO WO 95/711, 'General Account of the Operations by Brigadier-General T.G. Matheson Commanding 46 Infantry Brigade'.

62 Among this party of around 500 men was Sergeant A.F. Saunders (9/Suffolk) who was awarded the Victoria Cross.

63 These included Brigadier-General T.G. Matheson (GOC 46 Brigade), Major-General G.T. Forestier-Walker (GOC 21st Division) and Brigadier-General G.G.S. Carey (BGRA XI Corps).

64 TNA: PRO WO 158/32, 'Report from 24th Division', 25 October 1915.

65 The spectacle of thousands of British troops calmly moving eastwards, its lines marshalled by officers on horseback, was watched by men of *153 Infantry Regiment*. The regimental history compared the sight to a 'peacetime exercise', so impressed was the writer by the discipline of the British, moving forward under fierce shrapnel fire. Osswald, *Das Altenburger Regiment*, p. 186. See also TNA: PRO WO 95/1616, 11/Essex War Diary, 26 September 1915; PRO WO 95/2214, 8/Queens War Diary, 26 September 1915; PRO WO 95/2158, 8/Somerset Light Infantry War Diary, 26 September 1915; PRO WO 95/2210, 72 Brigade War Diary, 26 September 1915.

66 TNA: PRO WO 158/32, 'Report from 24th Division', 25 October 1915.

67 Edmonds (comp.), *Military Operations France & Belgium, 1915*, vol. 2, p. 333. The German Official History records that the 'young troops' of 21st and 24th Divisions 'fled back, at first individually and then in larger groups to their initial position and sometimes even past this point'. Reichsarchiv, *Der Weltkrieg 1914 bis 1918*, p. 69.

68 TNA: PRO WO 95/2159, 64 Brigade War Diary, 26 September 1915.

69 G.D. Sheffield, *Leadership in the Trenches* (London: Macmillan, 2000), p. 179.

70 TNA: PRO WO 95/2159, 64 Brigade War Diary, 26 September 1915.

71 TNA: PRO WO 95/2157, 63 Brigade War Diary, 26 September 1915.

72 TNA: PRO WO 158/32, 'Report from 24th Division', 25 October 1915.

73 TNA: PRO WO 95/2158, Major-General G.T. Forestier-Walker to II Corps, 15 October 1915.

74 TNA: PRO WO 95/2157, 63 Brigade War Diary, 26 September 1915.

75 TNA: PRO CAB 45/121, Colonel J.R. Wethered (Brigade Major 62 Brigade) to Edmonds, 19 January 1926.

76 TNA: PRO WO 95/2216, Brigadier-General R.G. Jelf, 'Report on Operations of 73rd Brigade from 26–27 September 1915'.

77 Edmonds (comp.), *Military Operations France & Belgium, 1915*, vol. 2, pp. 293–4.

78 LHCMA: Edmonds Papers, 3/10, 'Memoirs', Chapter XXVI, p. 8.

79 TNA: PRO WO 95/885, AA&QMG XI Corps War Diary, 23 and 24 September 1915.

80 Edmonds (comp.), *Military Operations France & Belgium, 1915*, vol. 2, p. 335. This quote forms the elegiac ending of Alan Clark's account of Loos in *The Donkeys*, p. 174.

81 Edmonds (comp.), *Military Operations France & Belgium, 1915*, vol. 2, pp. 293–4.

82 TNA: PRO WO 95/2216, Brigadier-General R.G. Jelf, 'Report on Operations of 73rd Brigade from 26–27 September 1915'.

83 TNA: PRO WO 95/2159, 64 Brigade War Diary, 26 September 1915.

84 TNA: PRO CAB 45/120, Lieutenant L.G. Duke to Edmonds, 20 November 1918.

85 IWM: 96/29/1, Account of Lieutenant J.H. Alcock.

86 TNA: PRO CAB 45/121, Major J. Buckley to Edmonds, 1 January 1927.

87 TNA: PRO CAB 45/121, Captain H. Pattison to Edmonds, 2 February 1927.

88 TNA: PRO CAB 45/120, Major-General G.T. Forestier-Walker to Edmonds, 24 January 1927.

89 TNA: PRO WO 95/2197, CVII Brigade RFA War Diary, 26 September 1915.

90 R.G.A. Hamilton, *The War Diary of the Master of Belhaven 1914–1918* (Barnsley: Wharncliffe, 1990; first published 1924), pp. 75–6.

91 TNA: PRO WO 95/2197, CVII Brigade RFA War Diary, 25–6 September 1915. According to 71 Brigade War Diary (PRO WO 95/1619), the brigade had concentrated on a crossroads about 500 yards south-east of Le Rutoire by 9 p.m. on the evening of 25 September.

92 Edmonds (comp.), *Military Operations France & Belgium, 1915*, vol. 2, pp. 316–7.

93 TNA: PRO WO 95/2142, XCV Brigade RFA War Diary, 26 September 1915.

94 TNA: PRO WO 95/1643, XXII Brigade RFA War Diary, 26 September 1915.

95 TNA: PRO WO 95/2198, CIX Brigade RFA War Diary, 26 September 1915.

96 TNA: PRO WO 95/2159, 64 Brigade War Diary, 26 September 1915.

97 TNA: PRO WO 95/1250, XXVI Brigade RFA War Diary, 26 September 1915.

98 TNA: PRO WO 95/2141, XCIV Brigade RFA War Diary, 26 September 1915.

99 TNA: PRO CAB 45/121, Brigadier-General C.G. Stewart to Major A.F. Becke, 3 August 1926.

100 Ibid.

101 IWM: 76/210/1, Account of F.W. Billman.

102 Edmonds (comp.), *Military Operations France & Belgium, 1915*, vol. 2, pp. 317–8.

103 TNA: PRO CAB 45/120, Major-General Sir R. Ford to Edmonds, 5 February 1926.

104 TNA: PRO CAB 45/120, Major-General Sir R. Ford to Edmonds, 5 February 1926.

105 TNA: PRO CAB 45/120, Major-General H.M. de F. Montgomery to Edmonds, 12 January 1926.

106 TNA: PRO CAB 45/121, Lieutenant-Colonel C.G. Stewart to Edmonds, 19 January 1926.

107 For command problems in the pre-war British Army and their damaging influence between 1914–18 see for example M. Samuels, *Command or Control? Command, Training and Tactics in the British and German Armies, 1888–1918* (London: Frank Cass, 1995), passim; N. Gardner, *Trial by Fire. Command and the British Expeditionary Force in 1914* (Westport, CT: Praeger, 2003), passim; T. Travers, 'Command and Leadership Styles in the British Army: The 1915 Gallipoli Model', *Journal of Contemporary History*, vol. 29, no. 3 (July 1994), p. 434.

108 Finding exact salaries for the senior officer ranks of the BEF during the First World War is difficult, but the *Army List* for 1897 lists the following salaries: Commander-in-Chief (Headquarters), £4,500; Commander-in-Chief (otherwise), £3,923; General, £2,920; Lieutenant-General, £2,007; Major-General, £1,095; Brigadier-General, £912; Colonel, £730; Lieutenant-Colonel (depending on the services), between £475 (infantry) and £639 (RAMC and RE). Therefore, if a temporary Major-General had been 'degummed', he could possibly return to his permanent rank, which is likely to have been that of Colonel. He would, therefore, lose £365 per year. See also TNA: PRO WO 113/16, 'Memorandum on the Subject of Loans, Attachments, and Interchanges of and between Officers of the Regular Army and Officers of the Forces of the Overseas Dominions', 31 August 1910.

109 Gough, *The Fifth Army*, p. 116; TNA: PRO WO 95/158, First Army War Diary, 27 September 1915.

110 Gough, *The Fifth Army*, p. 116.

111 See T. Travers, *The Killing Ground: The British Army, the Western Front and the Emergence of Modern Warfare 1900–1918* (Barnsley: Pen & Sword, 2003; first published 1987), p. 48. In *Company Training* (1913) Haking wrote that the offensive would succeed, even if opposed by a greater number of defenders, 'as sure as there is a sun in the heavens'.

112 R. Feilding, *War Letters to a Wife*, ed. J. Walker (Staplehurst: Spellmount, 2001; first published 1929), p. 19. Haking's confidence was also commented upon by R. Kipling, *The Irish Guards in the Great War* (2 vols., London: Macmillan, 1923), I, pp. 6–7. Haking believed that the coming offensive was 'the greatest battle in the history of the world' and instructed all platoon leaders to push on whenever possible, even at the risk of uncovering their flanks.

113 TNA: PRO WO 95/2210, 73 Brigade War Diary, 26 September 1915.

114 TNA: PRO WO 158/32, 'Report from 24th Division', 25 October 1915. Stracey was apparently told that only fifty German soldiers were occupying the Quarries, but considering the lamentable level of confusion then reigning on the battlefield, it is difficult to know how this total was arrived at.

115 Travers, *The Killing Ground*, pp. 20–3 and 'The Hidden Army: Structural Problems in the British Officer Corps, 1900–1918', *Journal of Contemporary History*, vol. 17, no. 3 (July 1982), pp. 523–44; M. Brown, *The Imperial War Museum Book of the Western Front* (London: Pan, 2001; first published 1993), Chapter 15; Gardner, *Trial by Fire*, pp. 95–8; S. Robbins, *British Generalship on the Western Front 1914–18. Defeat into Victory* (London: Frank Cass, 2005), pp. 22–4, 61–2.

116 Travers, *The Killing Ground*, p. 20.

117 See I.F.W. Beckett, 'Hubert Gough, Neill Malcolm and Command on the Western Front', in B. Bond (ed.), *'Look to your Front' Studies in the First World War by the British Commission for Military History* (Staplehurst: Spellmount, 1999), pp. 3–4.

118 *91 Reserve Regiment* was also supported by three battalions of *9, 17* and *18 Bavarian Regiments* from *II Bavarian Corps*, which had arrived at Haisnes during the night.

119 Edmonds (comp.), *Military Operations France & Belgium, 1915*, vol. 2, pp. 303–4.

120 TNA: PRO CAB 45/120, Major-General H.R. Davies to Edmonds, 29 April 1926.

121 TNA: PRO CAB 45/120, 'Operations of the 12/Royal Fusiliers, 73 Brigade, 24th Division, Sept 25–28'.

122 TNA: PRO CAB 45/121, Lieutenant-Colonel H.W.B. Thorp to Edmonds, 18 January 1926.

123 TNA: PRO CAB 45/120, Lieutenant-Colonel K. Henderson to Edmonds, 5 February 1926.
124 IWM: DS/MISC/2, Account of Lieutenant-Colonel K. Henderson. This was also witnessed by Major J. Buckley (9/KOYLI, 64 Brigade). TNA: PRO CAB 45/121, Major J. Buckley to Edmonds, 1 January 1927.
125 TNA: PRO CAB 45/120, Lieutenant-Colonel K. Henderson to Edmonds, 5 February 1926.
126 IWM: DS/MISC/2, Account of Lieutenant-Colonel K. Henderson.
127 Edmonds (comp.), *Military Operations France & Belgium, 1915*, vol. 2, p. 346.
128 BLL: POW 043, Account of Captain L. McNaught-Davis.
129 IWM: DS/MISC/2, Account of Lieutenant-Colonel K. Henderson.
130 BLL: GS 0309, Account of General Sir Philip Christison.
131 TNA: PRO CAB 45/121, Colonel J.R. Wethered (Brigade Major 62 Brigade) to Edmonds, 19 January 1926. See also Edmonds (comp.), *Military Operations France & Belgium, 1915*, vol. 2, p. 314, n. 1.
132 Moody, *Historical Records of the Buffs East Kent Regiment (3rd Foot)*, p. 97.
133 He won a posthumous Victoria Cross. See P. Batchelor & C. Matson, *VC' of the First World War. The Western Front 1915* (Stroud: Sutton, 1997), p. 161.
134 For an account of Bruce's capture see F. Davies & G. Maddocks, *Bloody Red Tabs* (Barnsley: Leo Cooper, 1995), pp. 119–20.
135 See Davies & Maddocks, *Bloody Red Tabs*, pp. 53–4.
136 IWM: DS/MISC/2, Account of Lieutenant-Colonel K. Henderson.
137 See Appendix III: Senior British Officer Casualties.
138 Edmonds (comp.), *Military Operations France & Belgium, 1915*, vol. 2, p. 342.
139 TNA: PRO WO 95/2159, 64 Brigade War Diary, 26 September 1915.
140 Ewing, *The Royal Scots, 1914–1919*, p. 201.
141 Edmonds (comp.), *Military Operations France & Belgium, 1915*, vol. 2, p. 303.
142 TNA: PRO WO 95/2210, 72 Brigade, 'Diary of Events 5 p.m. 25th September to 4.30 a.m. 27th September 1915'.
143 Reichsarchiv, *Der Weltkrieg 1914 bis 1918. Der Operationen Des Jahres 1915* (Berlin: E.S. Mittler & Sohn, 1933), p. 75.
144 Osswald, *Das Altenburger Regiment*, pp. 181–4.
145 See M. Samuels, *Command or Control? Command, Training and Tactics in the British and German Armies, 1888–1918* (London: Frank Cass, 1995), passim.
146 Edmonds (comp.), *Military Operations France & Belgium, 1915*, vol. 2, p. 299.
147 Reichsarchiv, *Das Koniglich Sachsische 13. Infanterie-Regiment Nr. 178* (Dresden: Wilhelm und Bertha V. Baensch Stifung, 1935), p. 69.

CHAPTER 8: RENEWING THE OFFENSIVE: 27 SEPTEMBER–13 OCTOBER 1915

1 The most detailed operational account – despite being only 38 pages long – remains Sir J.E. Edmonds (comp.), *History of the Great War: Military Operations France & Belgium, 1915*, vol. 2, *Battles of Aubers Ridge, Festubert and Loos* (London/Nashville: Imperial War Museum/Battery Press, 1995; first published 1928), pp. 350–88.
2 Reichsarchiv, *Der Weltkrieg 1914 bis 1918. Der Operationen Des Jahres 1915* (Berlin: E.S. Mittler & Sohn, 1933), p. 74.
3 Supported by *26 Reserve Brigade, 14th Division* continued to hold the front from just north of the Quarries to the La Bassée canal, while *117th Division* occupied the trenches between the Quarries and *Stützpunkt IV*. *8th Division* held the ground on the left of *117th Division* up to the Lens–Béthune road. A battalion of *3 Guard Grenadier Regiment* moved up to Hulluch on 27 September and on 30 September further reinforcements in the form of *XI Corps*, again from the east, arrived behind the front of *Sixth Army*. On 2 October three battalions of *II Bavarian Corps* were relieved by a battalion of *6th Bavarian Reserve Division*. On 3 October *8th* and *117th Divisions* were strengthened by the arrival of *216* and *233 Reserve Regiments* respectively. Artillery resources were also bolstered by the arrival of *4 Guard Field Artillery Regiment* and three light field howitzer batteries of *2 Guard Field Artillery Regiment*. See Edmonds (comp.), *Military Operations France & Belgium, 1915*, vol. 2, pp. 375–7.

4 Ibid., pp. 267–71, 346–8, n. 1.

5 General Joffre to General Foch, 26 September 1915, cited in Ibid., pp. 347.

6 Sir J. French, *1914* (London: Constable, 1919), p. 371. This comment again revealed how much Sir John had deteriorated as a commander. There was no 'gap' to 'rush'.

7 The Guards Division contained a cross-section of the crème of Edwardian British society, which included numerous members of the aristocracy. The Staff Captain of 1 (Guards) Brigade was Lord Gort, who later rose to prominence and commanded the BEF on its return to France in 1940. The Guards Division also contained a future Prime Minister, Harold Macmillan, and from October 1915 the son of the current Prime Minister, Raymond Asquith. There was also a strong showing from the aristocracy, which included the twenty-one-year-old HRH Edward, Prince of Wales, Lieutenant-Colonel Hon. G. Baring (fourth son of Lord Ashburton), Captain C.H.F. Noel (second son of the third Earl of Gainsborough) and Lieutenant Hon. H.D. Browne (second son of the Earl of Kenmore). Captain L.H. Tennyson (the grandson of the Poet Laureate) and Lieutenant J. Kipling (the only son of Rudyard Kipling) were also in the division.

8 Edmonds (comp.), *Military Operations France & Belgium, 1915*, vol. 2, pp. 340–1; TNA: PRO WO 95/158, First Army War Diary, 26 September 1915.

9 H. Macmillan, *Winds of Change, 1914–1939* (London: Macmillan, 1966), p. 74.

10 TNA: PRO WO 95/158, First Army War Diary, 27 September 1915; C. Headlam, *History of the Guards Division in the Great War, 1915–1918* (2 vols., London: John Murray, 1924), I, pp. 52–3, n. 2.

11 TNA: PRO WO 95/1212, 1 (Guards) Brigade War Diary, 27 September 1915; PRO WO 95/880, Lieutenant-Colonel J.A. Longridge (GSO1 1st Division) to IV Corps, 28 September 1915.

12 According to Brigadier-General G.P.T. Feilding (GOC 1 (Guards) Brigade), 'the whole country was absolutely lost to sight… gunfire balls were at once fired in the air from the German trenches south of Hulluch and the enemy turned the whole of their artillery onto the smoke and fired with rifles as well'. TNA: PRO WO 95/1190, Feilding to the Guards Division, 29 September 1915.

13 TNA: PRO WO 95/1217, 'Operations of 2nd Guards Brigade, During 27, 28, 29 September 1915', p. 3. Lieutenant John Kipling (2/Irish Guards) was posted missing during this attack. See T. Holt & V. Holt, *My Boy Jack? The Search for Kipling's Only Son* (Barnsley: Leo Cooper, 1998), passim. See also W. Ewart & C. Lowther, *The Scots Guards in the Great War, 1914–1918* (London: John Murray, 1925), pp. 115–6.

14 TNA: PRO WO 95/1223, 4/Grenadier Guards War Diary, 27 September 1915. The march of 3 (Guards) Brigade to Loos has become something of a legend. Numerous accounts speak of the bravery and discipline of the men as they spread out into artillery formation and endured heavy shrapnel fire. By portraying the undoubted courage and discipline of the men, these reports arguably deflected attention from the Guards Division's disappointing battlefield debut. See C.H. Dudley Ward, *History of the Welsh Guards* (London: John Murray, 1920), p. 29; it was a display of 'magnificent coolness and discipline' according to Headlam, *History of the Guards Division in the Great War, 1915–1918*, I, p. 59; the most dramatic account can be found in 'The Guards at Loos' in *The Times*, 8 November 1915.

15 Edmonds (comp.), *Military Operations France & Belgium, 1915*, vol. 2, p. 359; Dudley Ward, *History of the Welsh Guards*, pp. 31–5. See also the rather curiously titled 'Account of the Capture of Hill 70 by 3 Guards Brigade, September 27 1915'; and Lieutenant Colonel W. Murray-Threipland to Colonel G.R.C. Lord Harlech, 28 September 1915 (TNA: PRO WO 95/1190).

16 TNA: PRO WO 95/1223, 2/Scots Guards War Diary, 27 September 1915.

17 R.G.A. Hamilton, *The War Diary of the Master of Belhaven 1914–1918* (Barnsley: Wharncliffe, 1990; first published 1924), pp. 77–8.

18 TNA: PRO WO 95/2143, XCVII Brigade RFA War Diary, 27 September 1915.

19 Edmonds (comp.), *Military Operations France & Belgium, 1915*, vol. 2, p. 355, n. 1. See also Headlam, *History of the Guards Division in the Great War, 1915–1918*, I, p. 54.

20 NAM: Rawlinson Papers, 5201-33-18, 'Letter Book Volume II, May 1915–Aug 1916', Lieutenant-General Sir H. Rawlinson to Lord Kitchener (Secretary of State for War), 28 September 1915.

21 Another attempt to capture Puits 14 took place on the afternoon of the following day, 28 September, but was a lamentable failure. This attack seems to have originated directly from Haig, who proved characteristically stubborn in accepting that the Guards Division could not take their objectives without greatly increased support. Haking, Cavan and the commander

of 2 (Guards) Brigade, John Ponsonby, were of the opinion that their men should consolidate their positions and attempt no attack. Headlam, *History of the Guards Division in the Great War, 1915–1918*, I, pp. 65–6. See also TNA: PRO WO 95/1190, 'Operations of 2nd Guards Brigade, During 27, 28, 29 September 1915', p. 4; PRO WO 95/1219, 1/Coldstream Guards War Diary, 28 September 1915; Edmonds (comp.), *Military Operations France & Belgium, 1915*, vol. 2, pp. 365–6.

22 The German attack was made by a *Composite Bavarian Regiment* and *91 Reserve Regiment*.

23 TNA: PRO WO 95/2216, Brigadier-General R.G. Jelf, 'Report on Operations of 73rd Brigade from 26–27 September 1915'. Jelf's role in the defence of the Hohenzollern Redoubt seems to have been somewhat more heroic than his modest report allows. According to one senior officer, Jelf 'personally led a charge to cut out 'C' Company' at midday on 27 September. PRO CAB 45/121, Major T.G.F. Paget (7/Northamptonshire) to Brigadier-General Sir J.E. Edmonds, 14 June 1926.

24 See Edmonds (comp.), *Military Operations France & Belgium, 1915*, vol. 2, p. 352, 364, 369.

25 TNA: PRO CAB 45/120, General Sir E.S. Bulfin to Edmonds, 11 December 1927. Bulfin also added, recalling his time in Palestine in 1917–18, that 'I wish I had been under Allenby at Loos.'

26 TNA: PRO WO 95/2278, Private Diary of Brigadier-General C.E. Pereira, 20 October 1915.

27 H. Gough, *The Fifth Army* (London: Hodder & Stoughton, 1931), p. 117. This was a complaint typical of those who worked under Gough. See TNA: PRO CAB 45/120, Colonel D.W. Cameron of Lochiel to Edmonds, 17 September 1926; and Edmonds (comp.), *Military Operations France & Belgium, 1915*, vol. 2, p. 236.

28 According to Pereira's account, 'I had only the one map with which to explain orders to the COs which made it very difficult and the 9th Division only sent two officers as guides; about a dozen maps showing the German trenches, but not giving all the names arrived just before we went into the trenches so that our taking over could not have been begun in more difficult circumstances. In addition I was given three different situations; first that some of the captured trenches were lost, secondly all the captured trenches were lost, finally that the Hohenzollern Redoubt was still held; this meant three lots of orders.' TNA: PRO WO 95/2278, Private Diary of Brigadier-General C.E. Pereira, 27 September 1915.

29 TNA: PRO WO 95/2268, 'Narrative of the Operations of 26 September to 5 October 1915 in which the 28th Division took part', p. 2.

30 TNA: PRO WO 95/2278, 85 Brigade War Diary, 28 September 1915.

31 TNA: PRO WO 95/2279, 2/Buffs War Diary, 28 September 1915. Eleven machine guns were apparently counted later in Slag Alley.

32 TNA: PRO WO 95/2276, 84 Brigade War Diary, 29 September 1915. 2/Cheshire attacked the Chord on 1 October and was partially successful; 1/Welsh managed to take sections of Little Willie on 1 October, but because their flanks had been uncovered, German bombing attacks were able to recover the lost ground; and 1/Suffolk attacked Little Willie in the early hours of 3 October but failed to hold any gains. See TNA: PRO WO 95/2276, 2/Cheshire War Diary, 1 October 1915; PRO WO 95/2277, 'Account written by Major Hoggan on the 1st October', contained in 1/Welsh War Diary, 1/2 October 1915 and 1/Suffolk War Diary, 3 October 1915.

33 TNA: PRO WO 95/2274, 1/KOYLI War Diary, 4 October 1915; PRO WO 95/2273, 83 Brigade War Diary, 4 October 1915.

34 A. Simpson, 'British Corps Command on the Western Front, 1914–1918', in G. Sheffield & D. Todman (eds.), *Command and Control on the Western Front. The British Army's Experience 1914–1918* (Staplehurst: Spellmount, 2004), p. 101.

35 TNA: PRO WO 95/2268, 'Notes on Staff Work and Command in 28th Division', undated. Original emphasis.

36 TNA: PRO WO 95/2278, Private Diary of Brigadier-General C.E. Pereira, 27 September 1915.

37 TNA: PRO WO 95/159, Haig to GHQ, 4 October 1915.

38 See for example the stirring account of the attack of 1/Welsh (84 Brigade) against Little Willie on 1 October. TNA: PRO WO 95/2277, 'Account written by Major Hoggan on the 1st October', contained in 1/Welsh War Diary, 1/2 October 1915. Second-Lieutenant A.J.T. Fleming-Sandes (2/East Surrey, 85 Brigade) and Private S. Harvey (1/York & Lancaster, 83 Brigade) both won Victoria Crosses on 29 September.

39 TNA: PRO WO 95/2278, Private Diary of Brigadier-General C.E. Pereira, 27 September 1915.

40 Reichsarchiv, *Der Weltkrieg 1914 bis 1918*, pp. 74–5.

41 TNA: PRO WO 95/2277, 1/Suffolk War Diary, 2 October 1915. 'A' Company did, however, lose its commanding officer, Lieutenant Gale, who 'could not be found in the dark'.

42 TNA: PRO WO 95/2268, 'Narrative of the Operations of 26 September to 5 October 1915 in which the 28th Division took part', p. 4.

43 TNA: PRO WO 95/2273, 83 Brigade War Diary, 29 September 1915.

44 PRO WO 95/2273, 83 Brigade War Diary, 30 September 1915.

45 TNA: PRO WO 95/1752, LI Brigade RFA War Diary, 27 September 1915. According to the war diary of XXXV Brigade RFA (7th Division) on 27 September: 'Great difficulty was experienced in recognising the men in this area Fosse 8, and the enemy must have been let off a heavy artillery punishment a great number of times on account of this.'

46 Reichsarchiv, *Das Koniglich Sachsische 13. Infanterie-Regiment Nr. 178* (Dresden: Wilhelm und Bertha V. Baensch Stifung, 1935), p. 61.

47 M. Samuels, *Command or Control? Command, Training and Tactics in the British and German Armies, 1888–1918* (London: Frank Cass, 1995), p. 114.

48 Sir J.E. Edmonds (comp.), *Military Operations France & Belgium, 1915*, vol. 1, *Winter 1914–15: Battle of Neuve Chapelle: Battles of Ypres* (London: HMSO, 2000; first published 1927), p. 95.

49 For details on British grenades see P. Stigger, Note 1668, 'Numerous Matters Relating to Grenades', *Journal of the Society for Army Historical Research*, vol. 81 (2003), pp. 168–77.

50 See A. Stuart Dolden, *Cannon Fodder. An Infantryman's Life on the Western Front, 1914–18* (Poole, Dorset: Blandford Press, 1980), p. 28; TNA: PRO WO 95/2279, 2/Buffs War Diary, 28 September 1915. For a discussion of British close-quarter weaponry see P. Griffith, *Battle Tactics of the Western Front: The British Army's Art of Attack 1916–1918* (New Haven & London: Yale University Press, 1994), pp. 112–119.

51 Gough, *The Fifth Army*, p. 121.

52 Edmonds (comp.), *Military Operations France & Belgium, 1915*, vol. 2, p. 194.

53 Captain Rowland Feilding (1/Coldstream Guards) described this period well. 'The strain upon the men was heavy, but they bore it splendidly and cheerfully. To make matters harder, there was a penetrating rain which soaked us all, and the cold was bitter, so that we were not only practically sleepless, but wet and shivering all the time. We never lay down: there was nowhere to lie but the watery trench. Of course we had no hot food or drink, but mercifully a rum ration was got up which was a Godsend to all.' R. Feilding, *War Letters to a Wife*, ed. J. Walker (Staplehurst: Spellmount, 2001; first published 1929), p. 26.

54 See TNA: PRO WO 95/158 and WO 95/159, First Army War Diary, 27 September–13 October 1915.

55 Edmonds (comp.), *Military Operations France & Belgium, 1915*, vol. 2, p. 368. See also Rawlinson's complaint about the difficulty of bringing field artillery forward close enough to shell the German wire of the second line. NAM: Rawlinson Papers, 5201-33-18, 'Letter Book Volume II, May 1915–Aug 1916', Lieutenant-General Sir H. Rawlinson to Lieutenant-Colonel A. Fitzgerald (Kitchener's Private Secretary), 14 October 1915.

56 Hamilton, *The War Diary of the Master of Belhaven 1914–1918*, p. 81. See also pp. 80–7 for a graphic account of the horrors of being under German counter-battery fire.

57 TNA: PRO WO 95/159, First Army War Diary, 2, 4, 5 October 1915.

58 TNA: PRO 95/1219, 1/Coldstream Guards War Diary, 29 September 1915.

59 See also Feilding, *War Letters to a Wife*, ed. J. Walker, p. 27.

60 R. Kipling, *The Irish Guards in the Great War* (2 vols., London: Macmillan, 1923), I, p. 121.

61 F. Davies & G. Maddocks, *Bloody Red Tabs* (Barnsley: Leo Cooper, 1995), pp. 107–8. It seems that a rather unwise decision to surround the reporting centre with artillery batteries attracted enemy counter-battery fire.

62 Ibid., p. 108.

63 Edmonds (comp.), *Military Operations France & Belgium, 1915*, vol. 2, p. 363.

64 TNA: PRO WO 95/158, First Army War Diary, 28 September 1915.

65 On 28 September 8 (Cavalry) Brigade conducted a thorough search of the village and found 29 German troops still alive hidden in cellars and rubble. TNA: PRO WO 95/1156, 8 (Cavalry) Brigade War Diary, 28 September 1915.

66 TNA: PRO WO 95/158, First Army to I, IV and XI Corps, 30 September 1915.

67 TNA: PRO WO 95/158, First Army War Diary, 30 September 1915.

68 TNA: PRO WO 95/158, First Army to I, IV and XI Corps, 30 September 1915.
69 IWM: French Papers, PP/MCR/C32, French Diary, 30 September 1915.
70 TNA: PRO WO 95/159, Haig to GHQ, 4 October 1915.
71 IWM: Wilson Papers, DS/MISC/80, HHW 25, Wilson Diary, 4 October 1915.
72 See Ibid., 5 October 1915, when Wilson thought Haig had 'botched the whole thing' and was 'absolutely incapable'.
73 TNA: PRO WO 95/159, 'Copy of Telephone Message, Sir John French to GOC 1st Army', 4 October 1915.
74 TNA: PRO WO 95/159, Haig to GHQ, 4 October 1915.
75 IWM: Wilson Papers, DS/MISC/80, HHW 25, Wilson Diary, 9 October 1915.
76 TNA: PRO WO 95/159, GHQ to Haig, 5 October 1915.
77 Sir D. Haig, *The Haig Papers from the National Library of Scotland*, part 1, *Haig's Autograph Great War Diary* (Brighton: Harvester Press Microfilm, 1987), 27 September 1915.
78 Ibid., 28 September 1915.
79 TNA: PRO WO 95/159, GHQ to Haig, 5 October 1915.
80 IWM: French Papers, PP/MCR/C32, French Diary, 5 October 1915.
81 Haig, *The Haig Papers*, 2 October 1915.
82 IWM: Wilson Papers, DS/MISC/80, HHW 25, Wilson Diary, 30 September 1915.
83 According to Sir John's Private Secretary it was the 'General's birthday dinner: So we had to cheer up. I had a very long talk with him afterwards. He is very gratified at all the telegrams but depressed at the failure of the French on our right.' IWM: Fitzgerald Papers, PP/MCR/118, Fitzgerald Diary, 28 September 1915.
84 Haig, *The Haig Papers*, 28 September 1915. See also J. Charteris, *At G.H.Q.* (London: Cassell, 1931), p. 116. Needless to say Haig disagreed with these sentiments.
85 Haig, *The Haig Papers*, 8 October 1915.
86 The attack on 8 October seems to have been a massed infantry assault, which was repulsed all along the line. German shelling had been heavy all morning, but increased in intensity around 3p.m. An hour later, twelve battalions of *7th* and *8th Divisions* moved against the French IX Corps around the Double Crassier and against the British positions near the Chalk Pit. Two German regiments (*153rd* and *216th*) attacked 1st Division, but were repulsed with heavy casualties, chiefly because of the intense rifle and machine gun fire of 1/Gloucestershire and 9/King's. Further north, the Germans advanced in 'massed formation' against 12th Division and according to the divisional history were 'repulsed with tremendous losses'. See Edmonds (comp.), *Military Operations France & Belgium, 1915*, vol. 2, p. 372; E. Wyrall, *The History of the King's Regiment (Liverpool) 1914–1919. Volume I: 1914–1915* (London: Edward Arnold, 1928), p. 199; Sir A. Scott (ed.) & P. Middleton Brumwell (comp.), *History of the 12th (Eastern) Division in the Great War, 1914–1918* (London: Nisbet & Co, 1923), p. 17.
87 TNA: PRO WO 95/159, Robertson to Haig, 6 October 1915.
88 TNA: PRO WO 95/159, GHQ to Haig, 6 October 1915.
89 TNA: PRO WO 95/159, Haig to GHQ, 5 October 1915.
90 TNA: PRO WO 95/159, GHQ to Haig, 6 October 1915.
91 TNA: PRO WO 95/159, Haig to GHQ, 8 October 1915.
92 TNA: PRO WO 95/159, GHQ to Haig, 8 October 1915.
93 TNA: PRO WO 95/159, GHQ to Haig, 12 October 1915.
94 This reference to the 'salient' that Haig had 'created' perhaps betrays a certain frustration and disappointment that Sir John felt towards the results of Haig's attack on 25 September 1915.
95 TNA: PRO WO 95/159, Haig to GHQ, 12 October 1915.
96 Edmonds (comp.), *Military Operations France & Belgium, 1915*, vol. 2, p. 381.
97 Ibid., pp. 389–90.
98 NAM: Rawlinson Papers, 5301-33-25, Rawlinson Diary, 16 October 1915.
99 Edmonds (comp.), *Military Operations France & Belgium, 1915*, vol. 2, p. 388.
100 TNA: PRO WO 95/159, 'Scheme for the Attack by XI Corps on 13th October', p. 1. The document was original titled 'Scheme for the Attack by XI Corps on 12th October', but owing to the confusion over the exact date of attack, pencil marks have added '13 October' where necessary.
101 TNA: PRO WO 95/159, 'Notes of Conference Held at Advanced First Army Headquarters at Hinges at 6 pm on 6th October, 1915', p. 1.

102 Ibid., p. 1.

103 Ibid., p. 3.

104 TNA: PRO WO 95/159, 'Scheme for the Attack by XI Corps on 13th October', p. 7.

105 TNA: PRO WO 95/159, 'Artillery Support for the Attack of XI Corps on 13 October 1915', p. 4. It is not known whether any 18-pounders were actually used in this way on 13 October. For the effective use of guns positioned in the British front breastwork at Festubert see Edmonds (comp.), *Military Operations France & Belgium, 1915*, vol. 2, p. 59.

106 TNA: PRO WO 95/159, 'Notes of Conference Held at Advanced First Army Headquarters at Hinges at 6 pm on 6th October, 1915', pp. 1–2.

107 TNA: PRO WO 95/2662, 'Notes Made at a Visit by Lt. Col. Gathorne Hardy, GSO1, 7th Division to Divisional Headquarters, 7/10/15'.

108 TNA: PRO WO 95/2692, 'Information Supplied by an Officer Who Took Part in the Attack on Fosse 8'.

109 TNA: PRO WO 95/1846, 35 Brigade War Diary, 10 October 1915; and J.D. Hills, *The Fifth Leicestershire* (Loughborough: The Echo Press, 1919), pp. 74–5.

110 TNA: PRO WO 95/159, 'Notes of Conference Held at Advanced First Army Headquarters at Hinges at 6 pm on 6th October, 1915', p. 3.

111 TNA: PRO WO 95/159, 'Scheme for the Attack by XI Corps on 13th October', pp. 1–2. Haking probably meant 8 October as the date of the German counter-attack.

112 TNA: PRO WO 95/159, 'Artillery Support for the Attack of XI Corps on 13 October 1915', p. 1.

113 Ibid., p. 2.

114 TNA: PRO WO 95/159, 'Scheme for the Attack by XI Corps on 13th October', pp. 6–7.

115 TNA: PRO 95/WO 95/712, 'Telephone Conversations of Lieut-General Sir Henry Rawlinson, Bt., K.C.B., C.V.O., from the Commencement of the Attack', 28 September 1915.

116 TNA: PRO WO 95/159, 'Scheme for the Attack by XI Corps on 13th October', p. 7.

117 TNA: PRO WO 95/159, 'Notes of Conference Held at Advanced First Army Headquarters at Hinges at 6 pm on 6th October, 1915', p. 2. Emphasis added. Considering that the German troops on the northern sector of the battlefield had recently recaptured Fosse 8 and most of the Hohenzollern Redoubt, and had rarely 'ran away' during the entire battle, it is difficult to see on what grounds Haking was making such a statement.

118 For complaints about Montagu-Stuart-Wortley and his 'degumming' after 46th Division's abortive assault on Gommecourt on 1 July 1916 see T. Travers, *The Killing Ground: The British Army, the Western Front and the Emergence of Modern Warfare 1900–1918* (Barnsley: Pen & Sword, 2003; first published 1987), pp. 156–7. See also S. Robbins, *British Generalship on the Western Front 1914–18. Defeat into Victory* (London: Frank Cass, 2005), p. 22, 55, 64, 77.

119 TNA: PRO CAB 45/121, Lieutenant-General Hon. E.J. Montagu-Stuart-Wortley to Edmonds, 23 June 1926.

120 Ibid. Original emphasis.

121 See TNA: PRO CAB 45/121, Brigadier-General C.V. Wingfield-Stratford (CRE 46th Division) to Edmonds, 28 June 1926; and Colonel W.G. Neilson (Brigade Major 139 Brigade) to Edmonds, 26 June 1926. For Haking's optimism see Hills, *The Fifth Leicestershire*, p. 74.

122 See TNA: PRO WO 95/2674, IV (North Midland) Brigade RFA, 12, 13 October 1915.

123 For the gas operation on 13 October see D. Richter, *Chemical Soldiers. British Gas Warfare in World War One* (London: Leo Cooper, 1994), pp. 95–7.

124 Edmonds (comp.), *Military Operations France & Belgium, 1915*, vol. 2, p. 380, n. 3. Only 1,100 were discharged.

125 Ibid., p. 381.

126 C.H. Foulkes, *"GAS!" The Story of the Special Brigade* (London: Blackwood, 1934), pp. 88–9.

127 Richter, *Chemical Soldiers*, p. 97.

128 TNA: PRO CAB 45/120, Brigadier-General G.C. Kemp to Edmonds, 26 June 1926.

129 TNA: PRO WO 95/95/1846, 35 Brigade War Diary, 13 October 1915.

130 TNA: PRO WO 95/1858, 37 Brigade War Diary, 13 October 1915.

131 TNA: PRO WO 95/1860, 6/Buffs War Diary, 13 October 1915.

132 Hills, *The Fifth Leicestershire*, p. 76. Corporal J.L. Dawson of the Special Brigade won a Victoria Cross for his efforts to remove three leaking cylinders from the trenches.

133 IWM: 79/5/1, 'Attack by 46th Division Oct 13th 1915', by Lieutenant-Colonel G.J. Worthington (1/5th North Staffordshire), p. 5; 88/52/1, Account of F. Hunt (1/5th Lincolnshire, 138 Brigade).

134 IWM: P262, Account of J.W. Moore (1/6th South Staffordshire, 137 Brigade).

135 TNA: PRO WO 95/2662, 'Report on the Operations of the 46th Division. October 13th and 14th 1915', p. 5.

136 IWM: 79/5/1, 'Attack by 46th Division Oct 13th 1915', by Lieutenant-Colonel G.J. Worthington, p. 7; TNA: PRO WO 95/2662, 'Report on the Operations of the 46th Division. October 13th and 14th 1915', p. 2.

137 TNA: PRO WO 95/2683, '1/5th Battalion South Staffs Regt. Narrative of Events from 12 noon on 13th October 1915 to 3 a.m. 15th October 1915'.

138 See TNA: PRO CAB 45/121, Lieutenant-Colonel R.R. Raymer (CO 1/5th South Staffordshire, 137 Brigade) to Edmonds, 26 June 1926; PRO WO 95/2683, '1/6th Battalion North Staffs Regt. Narrative of Engagement – Fosse 8 – 13th October 1915'; 'Report of the Part Taken by the 1/6th Battalion South Staffs Regt in the Operations of the 46th Division on the 13th October 1915'.

139 TNA: PRO WO 95/95/1846, 35 Brigade War Diary, 13 October 1915; Scott (ed.) & Middleton Brumwell (comp.), *History of the 12th (Eastern) Division in the Great War, 1914–1918*, pp. 21–2; and TNA: PRO WO 95/1822, 12th Division War Diary, 13 October 1915. Captain Charles Hamilton Sorley, a young poet with 7/Suffolks, was killed in this assault. According to the battalion war diary, Sorley was 'killed whilst leading the attack'. TNA: PRO WO 95/1853, 7/Suffolk War Diary, 13 October 1915.

140 The attack of 6/Buffs (on the left of 37 Brigade's front) was a disaster. In a few minutes three companies were 'practically wiped out' and shellfire cut all the telephone wires to and from the battalion headquarters. TNA: PRO WO 95/1860, 6 Buffs War Diary, 13 October 1915.

141 At a 1 Brigade conference on 8 October 'It was stated frankly that the artillery had little hope of cutting the wire, but it was expected that the troops would be able to cut it for themselves under cover of a smoke cloud.' J.H. Lindsay, *The London Scottish in the Great War* (London: Regimental HQ, 1925), p. 84.

142 TNA: PRO WO 95/1264, 1/Cameron Highlanders War Diary, 13 October 1915.

143 TNA: PRO WO 95/1263, 1/Black Watch War Diary, 13 October 1915; WO 95/1265, 8/Royal Berkshire War Diary, 13 October 1915; 10/Gloucestershire War Diary, 13 October 1915; M. Lloyd, *The London Scottish in the Great War* (Barnsley: Leo Cooper, 2001), p. 66–7.

144 R. Prior & T. Wilson, *Command on the Western Front. The Military Career of Sir Henry Rawlinson 1914–18* (Oxford: Blackwell, 1992), p. 129.

145 Corporal J.D. Pollock (5/Cameron Highlanders, 26 Brigade), 27 September 1915; Corporal A.A. Bert (1/1st Hertfordshire, 6 Brigade), 27 September 1915; Second Lieutenant A.B. Turner (1/Royal Berkshire, 6 Brigade, attached to Carter's Force), 28 September 1915; Second Lieutenant A.J.T. Fleming-Sandes (2/East Surreys, 85 Brigade), 29 September; Private S. Harvey (1/York & Lancaster, 83 Brigade), 29 September 1915; Lance Sergeant O. Brooks (3/Coldstream Guards, 1 (Guards) Brigade), 8 October 1915; Acting Sergeant J.C. Raynes (LXXI Brigade RFA, 15th (Scottish) Division), 11 October 1915; Corporal J.L. Dawson (187 Field Company, Special Brigade), 13 October 1915; Captain C.G. Vickers (1/7th Sherwood Foresters, 139 Brigade), 14 October 1915.

146 Edmonds (comp.), *Military Operations France & Belgium, 1915*, vol. 2, p. 387.

147 Scott (ed.) & Middleton Brumwell (comp.), *History of the 12th (Eastern) Division in the Great War, 1914–1918*, p. 24.

148 Edmonds (comp.), *Military Operations France & Belgium, 1915*, vol. 2, p. 392.

149 See Appendix III: Senior British Officer Casualties.

150 IWM: 79/5/1, 'Attack by 46th Division Oct 13th 1915', by Lieutenant-Colonel G.J. Worthington, p. 2.

151 TNA: PRO WO 95/2691, 1/5th Lincolnshire War Diary, 8 October 1915.

152 TNA: PRO WO 95/1853, 7/Norfolk War Diary, 13 October 1915.

153 Hills, *The Fifth Leicestershire*, p. 84.

154 TNA: PRO WO 95/95/1846, 35 Brigade War Diary, 13 October 1915.

155 IWM: PP/MCR/104, Wedgwood Papers, Asquith to Wedgwood, 28 November 1915. Wedgwood's original letter to Asquith does not survive, but his report is included in Asquith's reply to Wedgwood. Asquith immediately sent the report to Sir Douglas Haig and his comments are contained in the same file, Haig to Asquith, 24 November 1915.

CONCLUSION: LOOS, THE BEF AND THE 'LEARNING CURVE'

1 For the dismissal of Sir John French see P. Bryant, 'The Recall of Sir John French', published in three parts in *Stand To! The Journal of the Western Front Association*, no. 22, 23 and 24 (1988); R. Holmes, *The Little Field Marshal. Sir John French* (London: Jonathan Cape, 1981), pp. 304–313; G.H. Cassar, *The Tragedy of Sir John French* (London: Associated University Presses, 1985), pp. 270–287.

2 TNA: PRO 30/57/53, Kitchener Papers, General Sir Douglas Haig to Lord Kitchener, 29 September 1915. Sir William Robertson (CGS GHS) and Sir Henry Rawlinson (GOC IV Corps) were also involved in undermining Sir John's authority.

3 See Sir J. French, 'Loos', 15 October 1915, in *Complete Despatches of Lord French, 1914–1916* (Uckfield: Naval & Military Press, 2001; first published 1916), pp. 391–413.

4 R. Prior & T. Wilson, *Command on the Western Front. The Military Career of Sir Henry Rawlinson 1914–18* (Oxford: Blackwell, 1992), passim.

5 To be fair to Rawlinson, his handling of Fourth Army between July and November 1918, particularly the battles of Hamel (4 July), Amiens (8–15 August) and the attack on the Hindenberg Line (29 September), proved that he had learnt something from his experiences in 1915–16. See Prior & Wilson, *Command on the Western Front*, part VI.

6 See Appendix II: Total Recorded British Deaths, 25 September 1915 and 1 July 1916.

7 These figures must, however, be used with some caution. The totals only show the number of soldiers who died on that day. It may also include soldiers who had died of wounds sustained from earlier actions, but it is not unreasonable to assume that most will have been killed in action that day.

8 TNA: PRO WO 95/1629, Lieutenant-General Sir W. Robertson to 7th Division, 3 October 1915.

9 For details of 'The Generals of Loos' see F. Davies & G. Maddocks, *Bloody Red Tabs. General Officer Casualties of the Great War 1914–1918* (London: Leo Cooper, 1995), pp. 30–5.

10 Sir J.E. Edmonds (comp.), *History of the Great War: Military Operations France & Belgium, 1916*, vol. 1, *Sir Douglas Haig's Command to the 1st July: Battle of the Somme* (London/Nashville: Imperial War Museum/Battery Press, 1993; first published 1932), p. 18.

11 Ibid., p. 24.

12 Ibid., p. 91.

13 G. Sheffield, *The Redcaps. A History of the Royal Military Police and its Antecedents from the Middle Ages to the Gulf War* (London: Brassey's, 1994), p. 62.

14 G. Sheffield, 'The Operational Role of British Military Police', in P. Griffith (ed.), *British Fighting Methods in the Great War* (London: Frank Cass, 1996), p. 82.

15 IWM: MISC 134 (2072), 'Administration Arrangements During the Battle of Loos', by Lieutenant-Colonel Hon. M.A. Wingfield, 4 January 1916.

16 Prior & Wilson, *Command on the Western Front*, pp. 163–70.

17 Prior & Wilson, *The Somme*, pp. 32–3.

18 Prior & Wilson, *Command on the Western Front*, p. 166.

19 Edmonds (comp.), *Military Operations France & Belgium, 1916*, vol. 1, p. 295.

20 P. Chasseaud, *Artillery's Astrologers. A History of British Survey and Mapping on the Western Front 1914–1918* (Lewes: Mapbooks, 1999), p. 115. See also C. Cole (ed.), *Royal Flying Corps Communiqués 1915–1916* (London: Tom Donovan, 1990; first published 1968), passim.

21 Edmonds (comp.), *Military Operations France & Belgium, 1916*, vol. 1, p. 85. See also D. Jordan, 'The Army Co-Operation Missions of the Royal Flying Corps/Royal Air Force 1914–1918', Ph.D., Birmingham, 1997.

22 Edmonds (comp.), *Military Operations France & Belgium, 1916*, vol. 1, p. 60.

23 Prior & Wilson, *Command on the Western Front*, p. 164. According to Brigadier-General E.W. Alexander (BGRA 15th Division), he had used a form of 'creeping barrage' at Loos, 'not in close conjunction with advancing infantry but to sweep the area behind the German front'. Cited in Bidwell & Graham, *Firepower*, p. 83.

24 S. Marble, *"The Infantry Cannot do with a Gun Less": The Place of the Artillery in the British Expeditionary Force, 1914–1918* <www.gutenberg-e.org>, Chapter 6, p. 6.

25 Sir M. Farndale, *History of the Royal Regiment of Artillery. Western Front 1914–18* (Woolwich: Royal Artillery Institution, 1986), p. 156.

26 P. Griffith, *Battle Tactics of the Western Front: The British Army's Art of Attack 1916–1918* (New Haven & London: Yale University Press, 1994), p. 61.

27 19 Brigade (2nd Division) was transferred to 33rd Division on 25 November 1915 and replaced by 99 Brigade (33rd Division). 21 Brigade (7th Division) was transferred to 30th Division on 19 December 1915 and was replaced by 91 Brigade (30th Division) the following day. 28 Brigade (9th Division) was broken up on 6 May 1916 and replaced by the South African Brigade, until 23 September 1918 when it joined 66th Division. 28 Brigade was reformed on 11 September 1918. 12th and 15th Divisions kept their original brigade structure throughout the war. 63 Brigade (21st Division) was transferred to 37th Division on 8 July 1916 and was replaced with 110 Brigade (37th Division) on 7 July 1916. 71 Brigade (24th Division) was transferred to 6th Division on 11 October 1915 and was replaced by 17 Brigade (6th Division) on 14 October 1915.

28 For raids see Griffith, *Battle Tactics of the Western Front*, pp. 61–2; and T. Ashworth, *Trench Warfare 1914–1918: The Live and Let Live System* (London: Macmillan, 1980), pp. 176–203.

29 'The Changes in the Composition of a British Division on the Western Front During the Great War, 1914–1918', Appendix 1, Major A.F. Becke, *Order of Battle of Divisions. Part I – The Regular British Divisions* (London: HMSO, 1935), pp. 126–7.

30 Edmonds (comp.), *Military Operations France & Belgium, 1916*, vol. 1, p. 289.

31 'Fourth Army Tactical Notes', Appendix 18, cited in Edmonds (comp.), *Military Operations France & Belgium, 1916*, vol. 1, pp. 131–47. Original emphasis.

32 J.P. Harris, 'The Rise of Armour', in Griffith (ed.), *British Fighting Methods in the Great War*, p. 115.

33 A. Palazzo, *Seeking Victory on the Western Front. The British Army and Chemical Warfare in World War I* (Lincoln & London: University of Nebraska Press, 2000), p. 79. For a description of the Livens projector see p. 103.

34 White Star was a mixture of chlorine and phosgene. Red Star contained only chlorine.

35 General Sir Douglas Haig, 'General Factors to be Weighed in Considering the Allied Plan of Campaign During the Next Few Months', 16 January 1916, cited in S. Marble, 'General Haig Dismisses Attritional Warfare, January 1916', *Journal of Military History*, vol. 65, no. 4 (October 2001), p. 1061. Original emphasis.

36 TNA: PRO 30/57/53, Kitchener Papers, Haig to Kitchener, 29 September 1915. Note the personalised reference to 'plucky fellows' again reflecting Haig's primarily human centred view of warfare.

37 Sir D. Haig, *The Haig Papers from the National Library of Scotland*, part 1, *Haig's Autograph Great War Diary* (Brighton: Harvester Press Microfilm, 1987), Haig to Lady Haig, 18 October 1915.

38 J. Terraine, *Douglas Haig. The Educated Soldier* (London: Cassell, 2000; first published 1963), p. 173.

39 Rawlinson to Kitchener, 28 September 1915, cited in Prior & Wilson, *Command on the Western Front*, p. 130.

40 Rawlinson Diary, 31 March 1916, cited in Prior & Wilson, *The Somme*, p. 41. Rawlinson also stated that had 15th Division been supported by 21st and 24th Divisions, 'I have no doubt whatever that we should have forced our way through the German third line and been able to release the cavalry against the enemy's lines of communication.' NAM: Rawlinson Papers, 5201-33-18, 'Letter Book Volume II, May 1915–Aug 1916', Rawlinson to Lord Stamfordham, 29 September 1915.

41 Brigadier-General C.E.D. Budworth cited in S. Bidwell & D. Graham, *Firepower: British Army Weapons and Theories of War, 1904–1945* (Boston: Allen Unwin, 1982), p. 79.

42 LHCMA: Montgomery-Massingberd Papers, 7/1, 'Lecture on Battle of Loos'. See also T. Travers, 'Learning and Decision-Making on the Western Front, 1915–1916: The British Example', *Journal of Canadian History*, vol. 18, no. 1 (April 1983), pp. 87–8.

43 Travers, 'Learning and Decision-Making on the Western Front, 1915–1916: The British Example', p. 96. Original emphasis.

44 See Prior & Wilson, *The Somme*, Chapters 5 & 6.

45 See Prior & Wilson, *Command on the Western Front*, Part IV.

46 Prior & Wilson, *The Somme*, p. 56.

47 TNA: PRO CAB 45/120, 'Comments on Loos', by Major R.B. Johnson (15/Durham Light Infantry, 64 Brigade), undated.

48 Prior & Wilson, *The Somme*, pp. 58–9.

49 A. Simpson, 'The Operational Role of British Corps Command on the Western Front, 1914–18', D.Phil., University College, London, 2003, passim.

50 See J. Lee, 'Some Lessons of the Somme: The British Infantry in 1917', in B. Bond (ed.), *'Look to your Front' Studies in the First World War by the British Commission for Military History* (Staplehurst: Spellmount, 1999), pp. 79–87.

51 See K. Grieves, 'The Transportation Mission to GHQ in 1916', in Ibid., pp. 63–78.

52 Prior & Wilson, *Command on the Western Front*, p. 305, 397. See also T. Travers, 'The Army and the Challenge of War 1914–1918', in D. Chandler & I.F.W. Beckett (eds.), *The Oxford History of the British Army* (Oxford: Oxford University Press, 2003; first published 1994), p. 232.

53 It is hoped that Nathan M. Greenfield's forthcoming *Baptism of Fire: The Canadians at Second Ypres 1915* will fill this gap in the historiography.

54 TNA: PRO CAB 45/120, General Sir H. Gough to Edmonds, 23 July 1926.

SELECT BIBLIOGRAPHY

PRIMARY SOURCES

ARCHIVE SOURCES

Bodleian Library, Oxford
H.H. Asquith papers

Imperial War Museum, London
Major-General R.H.K. Butler papers (69/10/1)
Lieutenant-Colonel B. Fitzgerald diaries and papers (PP/MCR/188)
Field-Marshal Sir J.D.P. French diaries, correspondence and papers
Lieutenant-Colonel A. de S Hadow papers (PP/MCR/185)
Major-General H.S. Horne papers
General Sir A.J. Murray diaries, correspondence and papers (79/48/4)
Brigadier-General Hon. J.F.H.S.F. Trefusis diary (82/30/1)
Major-General Sir H.H. Tudor diary (MISC 175 (2658)
Brigadier-General M.G. Wilkinson papers relating to command of 44 Brigade
Field-Marshal Sir H. Wilson diaries and correspondence
Lieutenant-Colonel G.J. Worthington papers (79/5/1)

Liddell Hart Centre for Military Archives, Kings College, London
General Sir J.T. Burnett-Stuart papers
Brigadier-General J. Charteris papers
Lieutenant-General Sir G.S. Clive diary
Brigadier-General Sir J.E. Edmonds papers
Major-General C.H. Foulkes diaries and papers

Brigadier-General P. Howell military correspondence and papers
Captain B. Liddell Hart correspondence and papers
Major-General Sir F. Maurice papers
Brigadier-General A.A. Montgomery-Massingberd papers
Field-Marshal Sir William Robertson correspondence and papers

National Army Museum, London
General Sir H.S. Rawlinson papers

The National Archives of the UK, Kew, London
Field-Marshal H.H. Kitchener papers
War Office Files (WO 95)
Cabinet Papers (CAB 45)

National Library of Scotland
Sir Douglas Haig, *The Haig Papers from the National Library of Scotland*, part 1, Haig's Autograph Great War Diary (Brighton: Harvester Press Microfilm, 1987).

Unpublished Letters and Memoirs in the Collections of the Imperial War Museum, London
Lieutenant J.H. Alcock (96/29/1); Lieutenant C.A. Ashley (85/22/1); Lieutenant-Colonel H. Bayley (86/9/1); Private F.W. Billman (76/210/1); Captain M.H. Carre (01/5/1); Captain Sir George Clark (88/52/1); W.H. Farmer (86/2/1); Lieutenant-Colonel V.M. Fergusson (PP/MCR/111); Lieutenant R.S. Flexen (01/51/1); Corporal R.E. Foulkes (94/11/1); Colonel Sir E. Gore-Brown (88/52/1); Major E.S.B. Hamilton (87/33/1); Lieutenant-Colonel K. Henderson (DS/MISC/2); Private F. Hunt (88/52/1); Major R.C. Ozanne (91/23/1); Reverend W.P.G. McCormick (03/30/1); Private J. McDaid (83/50/1); Lieutenant D. McDonald (01/29/1); Lieutenant A.H. Muggeridge (99/84/1); Private H. Panton (P262); Captain F.B. Parker (92/19/1); Major P.H. Pilditch (Con Shelf); Captain J.N. Pring (01/46/1); Rifleman W.J. Shewry (88/52/1); Rifleman F.A. Smith (94/22/1); L. Timpson (92/3/1); Private A.G.C. Townsend (86/65/1); Lieutenant C. Upcher (98/2/1); Sergeant B.W. Wollard (86/48/1); Rifleman Walter Young (88/57/1).

Unpublished Letters and Memoirs in the Liddle Collection at the Brotherton Library, Leeds
Lieutenant S. Burt (GS 0248); Private J. Campbell (GS 0262); General Sir P. Christison (GS 0309); Corporal G.A. Dawson (GS 0435); Captain E.C. Deane MC (GS 0439); Lieutenant H.L. Graham (GS 0650); Captain L. McNaught-Davis (POW 043); Private H. Old (GS 1201); Major-General R.H.D. Tompson (GS 1612).

OFFICIAL PUBLICATIONS

Field Service Regulations, Part I, Operations (London: HMSO, 1909; amended 1912).
Field Service Regulations, Part II, Organisation and Administration (London: HMSO, 1909; amended 1914).
Field Artillery Training 1914 (London: HMSO, 1914).

MEMOIRS AND PERSONAL ACCOUNTS

Asquith, H.H. *Memories & Reflections, 1852–1927* (2 vols., London: Cassell, 1928).
Bruce Lockhart, R.H. *Memoirs of a British Agent* (London: Pan, 2002; first published 1932).
Charteris, J. *At G.H.Q.* (London: Cassell, 1931).
Churchill, W.S. *The World Crisis, 1915* (London: Thornton Butterworth, 1923).
Dunn, J.C. (ed.) *The War The Infantry Knew 1914–1919* (London: Abacus, 2004; first published 1938).
Falkenhayn, E. *General Headquarters 1914–16 and its Critical Decisions* (London: Hutchinson, 1919).

Feilding, R. — *War Letters to a Wife*, ed. J. Walker (Staplehurst: Spellmount, 2001; first published 1929).

Foch, F. — *The Memoirs of Marshal Foch*, trans. T. Bentley Mott (London: William Heinemann, 1931).

French, J. Sir — *1914* (London: Constable, 1919).

Gough, H. — *The Fifth Army* (London: Hodder & Stoughton, 1931).

— — *Soldiering On* (London: Arthur Baker, 1954).

Graves, R. — *Goodbye To All That* (London: Penguin, 1960; first published 1929).

Grey, Viscount. — *Twenty-Five Years, 1892–1916* (2 vols., London: Hodder & Stoughton, 1925).

Hamilton, R.G.A. — *The War Diary of the Master of Belhaven 1914–1918* (Barnsley: Wharncliffe, 1990; first published 1924).

Hankey, M. — *The Supreme Command 1914–1918* (2 vols., London: George Allen & Unwin, 1961).

Hay, I. — *The First Hundred Thousand. Being The Unofficial Chronicle of a Unit of "K(I)"* (London: Blackwood, 1916).

Haig, D. — *War Diaries & Letters 1914–1918*, eds. G. Sheffield & J. Bourne (London: Weidenfeld & Nicolson, 2005).

Joffre, J.C. — *The Memoirs of Marshal Joffre*, trans. T. Bentley Mott (2 vols; London: Geoffrey Bles, 1932).

Lloyd George, D. — *War Memoirs* (2 vols., London: Nicholson & Watson, 1933).

MacGill, P. — *The Great Push* (London: Herbert Jenkins, 1916).

Macmillan, H. — *Winds of Change, 1914–1939* (London: Macmillan, 1966).

Maze, P. — *A Frenchman in Khaki* (Kingswood, Surrey: William Heinemann, 1934).

Stuart Dolden, A. — *Cannon Fodder. An Infantryman's Life on the Western Front, 1914–18* (Poole, Dorset: Blandford Press, 1980).

Talbot Kelly, R.B. — *A Subaltern's Odyssey. A Memoir of the Great War 1915–1917* (London: William Kimber, 1980).

SECONDARY SOURCES

OFFICIAL PUBLICATIONS

Becke, A.F. — *History of the Great War: Order of Battle, Part 4. The Army Council, G.H.Q.s, Armies and Corps 1914–1918* (London: HMSO, 1945).

— — *History of the Great War: Order of Battle of Divisions*. Parts 1, 3a & 3b (new edn., Newport: Ray Westlake, 1989).

Cole, C. (ed.) — *Royal Flying Corps Communiqués 1915–1916* (London: Tom Donovan, 1990; first published 1969).

Edmonds, J. (comp.) — *History of the Great War: Military Operations France & Belgium, 1915*, vol. 1, *Winter 1914–15! Battle of Neuve Chapelle: Battles of Ypres* (London: Macmillan, 1927).

Edmonds, J. (comp.) — *History of the Great War: Military Operations France & Belgium, 1915*, vol. 2, *Battles of Aubers Ridge, Festubert and Loos* (London/Nashville: Imperial War Museum/Battery Press, 1995; first published 1928).

French, J. Sir — *Complete Despatches of Lord French, 1914–1916* (Uckfield: Naval & Military Press, 2001; first published 1916).

Jones, H.A. — *History of the Great War: The War in the Air. Being the story of the part played the Great War by the Royal Air Force* (6 vols., Oxford: Clarendon Press, 1928).

Macpherson, W.G. — *History of the Great War: Medical Services General History*, vol. 2, *The Medical Services on the Western Front, and during the Operations in France and Belgium in 1914 and 1915* (London: HMSO, 1923).

Priestley, R.E. *The Signal Service in the European War of 1914 to 1918 (France)* (Chatham: W & J Mackay, 1921).

Reichsarchiv, *Der Weltkrieg 1914 bis 1918. Die Operationen Des Jahres 1915* (Berlin: E.S. Mittler & Sohn, 1933).

UNIT HISTORIES

Anonymous *The History of the Eighth Battalion the Queen's Own Royal West Kent Regiment 1914–1918* (London: Hazell, Watson & Viney, 1921).

Atkinson, C.T. *The Queen's Royal West Kent Regiment, 1914–1919* (London: Simpkin, Marshall, Hamilton, Kent & Co, 1924).

— *The Devonshire Regiment, 1914–1918* (London: Simpkin, Marshall, Hamilton, Kent & Co, 1926).

— *The Seventh Division, 1914–1918* (London: John Murray, 1927).

Buchan, J. & Stewart J. *The Fifteenth (Scottish) Division, 1914–1919* (Edinburgh & London: William Blackwood, 1926).

Dudley Ward, C.H. *History of the Welsh Guards* (London: John Murray, 1920).

Ewart, W. & Lowther, C. *The Scots Guards in the Great War, 1914–1918* (London: John Murray, 1925).

Ewing, J. *The History of the 9th (Scottish) Division* (London: John Murray, 1921).

— *The Royal Scots, 1914–1919* (London: Oliver & Boyd, 1929).

Farndale, M. *History of the Royal Regiment of Artillery. Western Front 1914–18* (Woolwich: Royal Artillery Institution, 1986).

Foulkes, C.H. *"GAS!" The Story of the Special Brigade* (London: Blackwood, 1934).

Gillon, S. *The K.O.S.B. in the Great War* (London: Thomas Nelson, 1930).

Headlam, C. *History of the Guards Division in the Great War, 1915–1918* (2 vols., London: John Murray, 1924).

Hills, J.D. *The Fifth Leicestershire* (Loughborough: The Echo Press, 1919).

Kipling, R. *The Irish Guards in the Great War* (2 vols., London: Macmillan, 1923).

Lindsay, J.H. *The London Scottish in the Great War* (London: Regimental HQ, 1925).

Lloyd, M. *The London Scottish in the Great War* (Barnsley: Leo Cooper, 2001).

Maude, A.H. *The History of the 47th (London) Division, 1914–1919* (Uckfield, East Sussex: Naval & Military Press, 2000; first published 1922).

Maurice, Sir F. *The History of the London Rifle Brigade, 1859–1919* (London: Constable, 1921).

Moody, R.S.H. *Historical Records of the Buffs East Kent Regiment (3rd Foot)* (London: The Medici Society, 1922).

Osswald, E.S. *Das Altenburger Regiment (8. Thuringisches Infanterie-Regiment Nr. 153) im Weltkrieg* (Oldenburg: Stalling, 1922).

Reichsarchiv, *Das Koniglich Sachsische 13. Infanterie-Regiment Nr. 178* (Dresden: Wilhelm und Bertha V. Baensch Stifung, 1935).

Sandilands, J.W. & Macleod, N. *The History of the 7th Battalion Queen's Own Cameron Highlanders* (Stirling: Eneas Mackay, 1922).

Scott, Sir A (ed.) & Brumwell, PM. *History of the 12th (Eastern) Division in the Great War, 1914–1918* (London: Nisbet & Co, 1923).

Simpson, C.R (ed.) *The History of the Lincolnshire Regiment, 1914–1918 Compiled from War Diaries, Despatches, Officers' Notes and Other Sources* (London: The Medici Society, 1931).

Tiede, V. *Das 4. Schlesische Infanterie-Regiment Nr. 157* (Oldenburg: Stalling, 1922).

Wauchope, A.G (ed.) *A History of the Black Watch (Royal Highlanders) in the Great War, 1914–1918* (3 vols., London: The Medici Society, 1925–6).

Wyrall, E. *The History of the 2nd Division, 1914–1918.* (Uckfield, East Sussex: Naval & Military Press, 2000; first published 1921).

— *The Die-Hards in the Great War* (London: Harrison & Sons, 1926).

— *The History of the King's Regiment (Liverpool) 1914–1919* (3 vols., London: Edward Arnold, 1928).

— *The East Yorkshire Regiment in the Great War, 1914–1918* (London: Harrison & Sons, 1928).

BIOGRAPHICAL SOURCES

Arthur, G.	*Life of Lord Kitchener* (3 vols., London: Macmillan, 1920).
Beckett, I.F.W.	*Johnnie Gough, V.C.* (London: Tom Donovan, 1989).
Blake, R. (ed.)	*The Private Papers of Douglas Haig, 1914–1919* (London: Eyre & Spottiswoode, 1952).
Bond, B. & Cave, N. (eds.)	*Haig A Reappraisal 70 Years On* (Barnsley: Leo Cooper, 1999).
Cassar, G.H.	*Kitchener. Architect of Victory* (London: William Kimber, 1977).
—	*The Tragedy of Sir John French* (London: Associated University Presses, 1985).
Charteris, J.	*Field-Marshal Earl Haig* (London: Cassell, 1929).
Collier, B.	*Brasshat. A Biography of Field-Marshal Sir Henry Wilson* (London: Seecker & Warburg, 1961).
Cooper, D.	*Haig* (London: Faber & Faber, 1985).
Davis, F. & Maddocks, G.	*Bloody Red Tabs* (Barnsley: Leo Cooper, 1995).
De Groot, G.J.	*Douglas Haig, 1861–1928* (London: Unwin Hyman, 1988).
Esher, Viscount	*The Tragedy of Lord Kitchener* (London: John Murray, 1921).
—	*Journals and Letters of Reginald Viscount Esher, Vol. 3, 1910–1915* (London: Ivor Nicholson & Watson, 1938).
Farrar, M.M.	*Principled Pragmatist. The Political Career of Alexandre Millerand* (New York: Berg, 1991).
Farrar-Hockley, A.	*Goughie: The Life of General Sir Hubert Gough* (London: Hart-Davis, MacGibbon, 1975).
French, G.	*The Life of Field-Marshal Sir John French. First Earl of Ypres* (London: Cassell, 1931).
Holmes, R.	*The Little Field Marshal. Sir John French* (London: Jonathan Cape, 1981).
Magnus, P.	*Kitchener. Portrait of an Imperialist* (London: John Murray, 1958).
Maurice, F.	*The Life of Lord Rawlinson of Trent* (London: Cassell, 1928).
Pollock, J.	*Kitchener, Comprising the Road to Omdurman and Saviour of the Nation* (London: Constable, 2001).
Prior, R. & Wilson, T.	*Command on the Western Front. The Military Career of Sir Henry Rawlinson 1914–18* (Oxford: Blackwell, 1992).
Recouly, R.	*Joffre* (London: D. Appleton & Company, 1931).
Royle, T.	*The Kitchener Enigma* (London: Michael Joseph, 1985).
Spender, J.A. & Asquith, C.	*Life of Herbert Henry Asquith, Lord Oxford and Asquith,* (2 vols., London: Hutchinson, 1932).
Terraine, J.	*Douglas Haig. The Educated Soldier* (London: Cassell, 2000; first published 1963).
Warner, P.	*Kitchener. The Man Behind the Legend* (London: Hamish Hamilton, 1985).
Woodward, D.R.	*Field-Marshal Sir William Robertson. Chief of the Imperial General Staff in the Great War* (Westport, CT: Praeger, 1998).

GENERAL WORKS

Adams, R.J.Q.	*Arms and the Wizard. Lloyd George and the Ministry of Munitions* (London: Cassell, 1978).
Ashworth, T.	*Trench Warfare 1914–1918: The Live and Let Live System* (London: Macmillan, 1980).
Batchelor, P.F. & Matson, C.	*VCs of the First World War. The Western Front 1915* (Stroud: Sutton, 1997).
Bernard, P. & Dubief, H.	*The Decline of the Third Republic, 1914–1938* (Cambridge: Cambridge University Press, 1985).
Bidwell, S. & Graham, D.	*Firepower: British Army Weapons and Theories of War, 1904–1945* (Boston: Allen Unwin, 1982).

Bond, B. (ed.) *The First World War and British Military History* (Oxford: Clarendon, 1991).

Bond, B. *The Victorian Army and the Staff College 1854–1914* (London: Eyre Methuen, 1972).

— *The Unquiet Western Front* (Cambridge: Cambridge University Press, 2002).

Bourne, J.M. *Britain and the Great War 1914–1918* (London: Edward Arnold, 1989).

Bristow, A. *A Serious Disappointment, The Battle of Aubers Ridge, 1915 and the Subsequent Munitions Scandal* (London: Leo Cooper, 1995).

Brose, E.D. *The Kaiser's Army. The Politics of Military Technology in Germany During the Machine Age, 1870–1918* (Oxford: Oxford University Press, 2001).

Brown, I.M. *British Logistics on the Western Front, 1914–1919* (Westport, CT: Praeger, 1998).

Chasseaud, P. *Artillery's Astrologers. A History of British Survey and Mapping on the Western Front 1914–1918* (Lewes: Mapbooks, 1999).

Cherry, N. *Most Unfavourable Ground. The Battle of Loos 1915* (Solihull: Helion & Company, 2005).

Chickering, R. *Imperial Germany and the Great War, 1914–1918* (Cambridge: Cambridge University Press, 1998).

Clark, A. *The Donkeys* (London: Pimlico, 1997; first published 1961).

Clayton, A. *Paths of Glory, The French Army 1914–1918* (London: Cassell, 2003).

Ferguson, N. *The Pity of War* (London: Allen Lane, 1998).

Foley, R.T. *German Strategy and the Path to Verdun. Erich von Falkenhayn and the Development of Attrition, 1870–1916* (Cambridge: Cambridge University Press, 2005).

French, D. *British Economic and Strategic Planning 1905–1915* (London: George Allen & Unwin, 1982).

— *British Strategy and War Aims 1914–1916* (London: Allen & Unwin, 1986).

Fussell, P. *The Great War and Modern Memory* (Oxford: Oxford University Press, 2000; first published 1975).

Gardner, N. *Trial by Fire. Command and the British Expeditionary Force in 1914* (Westport, CT: Praeger, 2003).

Gooch, J. *The Plans of War. The General Staff and British Military Strategy c. 1900–1916* (London: Routledge & Kegan Paul, 1974).

Green, A. *Writing the Great War. Sir James Edmonds and the Official Histories, 1915–1948* (London: Frank Cass, 2003).

Grieves, K. *The Politics of Manpower, 1914–18* (Manchester: Manchester University Press, 1988).

Griffith, P. *Battle Tactics of the Western Front: The British Army's Art of Attack 1916–1918* (New Haven & London: Yale University Press, 1994).

Guinn, P. *British Strategy and Politics, 1914 to 1918* (Oxford: Clarendon, 1965).

Herwig, H.H. *The First World War. Germany and Austria-Hungary 1914–1918* (London: Arnold, 1997).

Holt, T. & V. *My Boy Jack? The Search for Kipling's Only Son* (Barnsley: Leo Cooper, 1998).

Johnson, J.H. *Stalemate! Great Trench Warfare Battles* (London: Cassell, 1999; first published 1995).

Kennedy, P.M. (ed.) *The War Plans of the Great Powers, 1880–1914* (London: George Allen & Unwin, 1979).

Liddell Hart, B.H. *History of the First World War* (London: Pan, 1975; first published 1930).

Luvaas, J. *The Education of an Army, British Military Thought, 1815–1940* (London: Cassell, 1965).

Macdonald, L. *1915. The Death of Innocence* (London: Penguin, 1997).

Neilson, K. *Strategy and Supply. The Anglo-Russian Alliance, 1914–17* (London: George Allen & Unwin, 1984).

Palazzo, A. *Seeking Victory on the Western Front. The British Army and Chemical Warfare in World War I* (Lincoln & London: University of Nebraska Press, 2000).

Philpott, W.J. *Anglo-French Relations and Strategy on the Western Front, 1914–18* (London: Macmillan, 1996).

Porch, D. *The March to the Marne. The French Army 1871–1914* (Cambridge: Cambridge University Press, 1981).

Rawson, A. *Battleground Europe, Loos – Hill 70* (Barnsley: Leo Cooper, 2002).

— *Battleground Europe, Loos – Hohenzollern Redoubt* (Barnsley: Leo Cooper, 2003).

Richter, D. *Chemical Soldiers. British Gas Warfare in World War One* (London: Leo Cooper, 1994).

Robbins, S. British *Generalship on the Western Front 1914–18. Defeat into Victory* (London: Frank Cass, 2005).

Samuels, M. *Doctrine and Dogma. German and British Infantry Tactics in the First World War* (Westport, CT: Greenwood, 1992).

— *Command or Control? Command, Training and Tactics in the British and German Armies, 1888–1918* (London: Frank Cass, 1995).

Sheffield, G.D. *The Redcaps. A History of the Royal Military Police and its Antecedents from the Middle Ages to the Gulf War* (London: Brassey's, 1994).

— *Leadership in the Trenches* (London: Macmillan, 2000).

— *Forgotten Victory. The First World War: Myths and Realities* (London: Headline, 2001).

Sheffield, G. & Todman, D. (eds.) *Command and Control on the Western Front. The British Army's Experience 1914–1918* (Staplehurst: Spellmount, 2004).

Simkins, P. *Kitchener's Army. The Raising of the New Armies, 1914–16* (Manchester: Manchester University Press, 1988).

Stone, N. *The Eastern Front 1914–1917* (London: Hodder & Stoughton, 1975).

Strachan, H. *The First World War. Volume I, To Arms* (Oxford: Oxford University Press, 2001).

Terraine, J. *The Western Front* (London: Hutchinson, 1964).

Tooley, H. *The Western Front. Battle Ground and Home Front in the First World War* (Basingstoke: Palgrave Macmillan, 2003).

Travers, T. *The Killing Ground: The British Army, the Western Front and the Emergence of Modern Warfare 1900–1918* (Barnsley: Pen & Sword, 2003; first published 1987).

Warner, P. *The Battle of Loos* (Ware, Hertfordshire: Wordsworth, 2000; first published 1976).

Wynne, C.G. *If Germany Attacks. The Battle in Depth in the West* (Westport, CT: Greenwood, 1976; first published 1940).

ARTICLES

Bailey, J. 'The First World War and the Birth of the Modern Style of Warfare', *The Strategic & Combat Studies Institute*, The Occasional, 22 (1996).

Barnett, C. 'The Education of Military Elites', *Journal of Contemporary History*, vol. 2, no. 3 (July 1967), pp. 15–35.

— 'The Western Front Experience as Interpreted Through Literature', *R.U.S.I. Journal*, vol. 148, no. 6 (December 2003), pp. 50–6.

Beckett, I.F.W. 'Revisiting the Old Front Line. The Historiography of the Great War Since 1984', in *Stand To! The Journal of the Western Front Association*, no. 49 (April 1995), pp. 12–5.

— 'Haig and French', in B. Bond & N. Cave (eds.), *Haig. A Reappraisal 70 Years On* (Barnsley: Leo Cooper, 1999), pp. 51–63.

Bird, Sir W.D. 'Lost Opportunities in 1915?', *The Army Quarterly*, vol. 34 (April 1937 and July 1937), pp. 237–47.

— 'Lost Opportunities in 1915? Volume II', *The Army Quarterly*, vol. 35 (October 1937 and January 1938), pp. 37–49.

Bourne, J.M. 'Haig and the Historians', in B. Bond & N. Cave (eds.), *Haig. A Reappraisal 70 Years On* (Barnsley: Leo Cooper, 1999), pp. 1–11.

Crawshaw, M. 'The Impact of Technology on the BEF and its Commanders', in B. Bond and N. Cave (eds.), *Haig. A Reappraisal 70 Years On* (Barnsley: Leo Cooper, 1999), pp. 155–75.

Dawney, G.P. &Headlam, C (eds.) 'The Other Side of the Hill. The Fight for Hill 70: 25th–26th September 1915', *The Army Quarterly*, vol. 8 (April 1924 and July 1924), pp. 261–73.

— 'France & Belgium, 1915', *The Army Quarterly*, vol. 17 (October 1928 and January 1929), pp. 246–54.

— 'The Other Side of the Hill. Aubers Ridge: 9th May, 1915', *The Army Quarterly*, vol. 36 (April 1938 and July 1938), pp. 242–48.

— 'The Other Side of the Hill. Neuve Chapelle: 10th–12th March 1915', *The Army Quarterly*, vol. 37 (October 1938 and January 1939), pp. 30–46.

Echevarria II, A.J. 'The "Cult of the Offensive" Revisited: Confronting Technological Change Before the Great War', *Journal of Strategic Studies*, vol. 25, no. 1 (March 2002), pp. 199–214.

Edmonds, J.E. & Wynne, G.C. 'Military Operations: France & Belgium, 1915', *The Army Quarterly*, vol. 15 (October 1927 and January 1928), pp. 134–43.

Farrar, M.M. 'Politics Versus Patriotism: Alexandre Millerand as French Minister of War', *French Historical Studies*, vol. 11, no. 4 (Autumn 1980), pp. 577–609.

French, D. 'The Meaning of Attrition, 1914–1916', *English Historical Review*, vol. 103, no. 407 (April 1988), pp. 385–405.

Grieves, K. 'Making Sense of the Great War: Regimental Histories, 1918–23', *Journal of the Society for Army Historical Research*, vol. 69, no. 277 (1991), pp. 6–15.

Holmes, R. 'Sir John French and Lord Kitchener', in B. Bond (ed.), *The First World War and British Military History* (Oxford: Clarendon Press, 1991), pp. 113–39.

Howard, M. 'Men Against Fire: The Doctrine of the Offensive in 1914', in P. Paret (ed.), *Makers of Modern Strategy from Machiavelli to the Nuclear Age* (Oxford: Clarendon Press, 1986), pp. 510–26.

Hughes, M. "Revolution Was in the Air': British Officials in Russia During the First World War', *Journal of Contemporary History*, vol. 31, no. 1 (January 1996), pp. 75–97.

Marble, S. 'Artillery, Intelligence and Optimism. Wire-Cutting During the Somme Bombardment', *Stand To! The Journal of the Western Front Association*, no. 61 (April 2001), pp. 36–9.

Neilson, K. 'Kitchener: A Reputation Refurbished?', *Canadian Journal of History*, vol. 15, no. 2 (1980), pp. 207–27.

Porch, D. 'The French Army in the First World War', in A.R. Millett & W. Murray (eds.), *Military Effectiveness Volume I: The First World War* (London: Unwin Hyman, 1998), pp. 190–228.

Rothenberg, G.E. 'Moltke, Schlieffen, and the Doctrine of Strategic Envelopment', in P. Paret (ed.), *Makers of Modern Strategy from Machiavelli to the Nuclear Age* (Oxford: Clarendon Press, 1986), pp. 296–325.

Simkins, P. 'Everyman at War: Recent Interpretations of the Front Line Experience', in B. Bond (ed.), *The First World War and British Military History* (Oxford: Clarendon Press, 1991), pp. 289–313.

— 'Haig and his Army Commanders', in B. Bond & N. Cave (eds.), *Haig. A Reappraisal 70 Years On* (Barnsley: Leo Cooper, 1999), pp. 78–106.

Simpson, K. 'Capper and the Offensive Spirit', *R.U.S.I. Journal*, vol. 118, no. 2 (June 1973), pp. 51–6.

— 'The Reputation of Sir Douglas Haig', in B. Bond (ed.), *The First World War and British Military History* (Oxford: Clarendon Press, 1991), pp. 141–62.

Spiers, E.M. The Scottish Soldier at War' in H. Cecil & P.H. Liddle (eds.), *Facing Armageddon. The First World War Experienced* (London: Leo Cooper, 1996), pp. 314–35.

Travers, T. 'The Offensive and the Problem of Innovation in British Military Thought, 1870–1915', *Journal of Contemporary History*, vol. 13, no. 3 (July 1978), pp. 531–53.

— 'Technology, Tactics and Morale: Jean de Bloch, the Boer War, and British Military Theory, 1900–1914', *Journal of Modern History*, vol. 17, no. 3 (June 1979), pp. 264–86.

— 'The Hidden Army: Structural Problems in the British Officer Corps, 1900–1918', *Journal of Contemporary History*, vol. 17, no. 3 (July 1982), pp. 523–44.

— 'Learning and Decision-Making on the Western Front, 1915–1916: The British Example', *Journal of Canadian History*, vol. 18, no. 1 (April 1983), pp. 87–97.

— 'The Army and the Challenge of War 1914–1918', in D. Chandler & I.F.W. Beckett (eds.), *The Oxford History of the British Army* (Oxford: Oxford University Press, 2003; first published 1994), pp. 211–34.

Williams, R. 'Lord Kitchener and the Battle of Loos: French Politics and British Strategy in the Summer of 1915' in L. Freedman, P. Hayes & R. O'Neill (eds.), *War, Strategy and International Politics. Essays in Honour of Sir Michael Howard* (Oxford: Clarendon, 1992), pp. 117–32.

FICTIONAL WORKS

Buchan, J. *Greenmantle* (Ware: Wordsworth, 1994).

Masters, J. *Now, God be Thanked* (London: Sphere Books, 1979).

Romaines, J. *Verdun* (London: Prion Books, 2000; first published 1938).

Williamson, H. *A Fox Under My Cloak* (Stroud: Sutton, 1996; first published 1955).

UNPUBLISHED THESES

Jordan, D.J. 'The Army Co-Operation Missions of the Royal Flying Corps/Royal Air Force 1914–1918', Ph.D., Birmingham, 1997.

Simpson, A. 'The Operational Role of British Corps Command on the Western Front, 1914–18', D.Phil., University College, London, 2003.

APPENDIX I: ORDERS OF BATTLE

BRITISH ORDER OF BATTLE

GHQ

Field-Marshal Sir J.D.P. French
Lieutenant-General Sir W.R. Robertson (Chief of Staff)

FIRST ARMY

General Sir D. Haig

I CORPS

Lieutenant-General H de la P. Gough

2ND DIVISION

Major-General H.S. Horne

5 BRIGADE

Brigadier-General C.E. Corkran

1/Queen's
2/O&BLI
1/7th King's
2/Worcestershire
2/Highland Light Infantry
1/9th Highland Light Infantry

6 BRIGADE

Brigadier-General A.C. Daly

1/King's (Liverpool)
1/Royal Berkshire
1/5th King's
2/South Staffordshire
1/KRRC
1/5th Hertfordshire

19 BRIGADE

Brigadier-General P.R. Robertson

1/Middlesex
2/Royal Welsh Fusiliers
1/5th Scottish Rifles
2/Argyll & Sutherland Highlanders
1/Scottish Rifles

DIVISIONAL ARTILLERY

XXXIV Bde RFA
XLI Bde RFA
XXXVI Bde RFA
XLIV (H) Bde RFA

7TH DIVISION

Major-General Sir T. Capper[1]

20 BRIGADE

Brigadier-General Hon. J.F.H.S.F. Trefusis[2]

2/Border
8/Devonshire
1/6th Gordon Highlanders
2/Gordon Highlanders
9/Devonshire

21 BRIGADE

Brigadier-General H.E. Watts[3]
Brigadier-General R.A. Berners

2/Bedfordshire
2/Royal Scots Fusiliers
1/4th Cameron Highlanders
2/Yorkshire Regiment
2/Wiltshire

22 BRIGADE

Brigadier-General J.McC. Steele

2/Queen's
1/Royal Welsh Fusiliers
2/Royal Warwickshire
1/South Staffordshire

DIVISIONAL ARTILLERY

XIV Bde RHA
XXXV Bde RFA
XXII Bde RFA
XXXVII Bde RFA

9TH (SCOTTISH) DIVISION

Major-General G.H. Thesiger[4]
Major-General E.S. Bulfin[5]
Major-General W.T. Furse[6]

26 BRIGADE

Brigadier-General A.B. Ritchie

8/Black Watch
8/Gordon Highlanders
7/Seaforth Highlanders
5/Cameron Highlanders

27 BRIGADE

Brigadier-General C.D. Bruce[7]
Lieutenant-Colonel W.H. Walshe[8]
11/Royal Scots
12/Royal Scots
6/Royal Scots Fusiliers
10/Argyll & Sutherland Highlanders

28 BRIGADE

Brigadier-General S.W. Scrase Dickins
6/KOSB
9/Scottish Rifles
10/Highland Light Infantry
11/Highland Light Infantry

DIVISIONAL ARTILLERY

L Bde RFA
LI Bde RFA
LII Bde RFA
LIII Bde RFA

28TH DIVISION

Major-General E.S. Bulfin[9]
Major-General C.J. Briggs[10]

83 BRIGADE

Brigadier-General H.S.L. Ravenshaw
2/King's Own
2/East Yorkshire
1/KOYLI
1/York & Lancaster
1/5th King's Own

84 BRIGADE

Brigadier-General T.H.F. Pearse
2/Northumberland Fusiliers
1/Suffolk
2/Cheshire
1/Welsh
1/6th Welsh

85 BRIGADE

Brigadier-General C.E. Pereira[11]
Lieutenant-Colonel A.C. Roberts[12]
Brigadier-General B.C.M. Carter[13]
2/Buffs 3/Royal Fusiliers
2/East Surrey
3/Middlesex

DIVISIONAL ARTILLERY

III Bde RFA
XXXI Bde RFA
CXXX Bde RFA
CXLVI Bde RFA

IV CORPS

Lieutenant-General Sir H.S. Rawlinson

1ST DIVISION

Major-General A.E.A. Holland

1 BRIGADE
Brigadier-General A.J. Reddie
1/Black Watch
1/Cameron Highlanders
10/Gloucestershire
8/Royal Berkshire

2 BRIGADE
Brigadier-General J.H.W. Pollard[14]
Major R.J.A. Terry[15]
Brigadier-General H.F. Thuillier[16]
2/Royal Sussex
1/Northamptonshire
1/Loyal North Lancashire
2/ KRRC

3 BRIGADE
Brigadier-General H.R. Davies
1/South Wales Borderers
1/Gloucestershire
2/Welsh
2/Royal Munster Fusiliers

GREEN'S FORCE
Lieutenant-Colonel E.W.B. Green
1/14th London (London Scottish)
1/9th King's

DIVISIONAL ARTILLERY
XXV Bde RFA
XXVI Bde RFA
XXXIX Bde RFA
XLIII Bde RFA

15TH (SCOTTISH) DIVISION
Major-General F.W.N. McCracken

44 BRIGADE
Brigadier-General M.G. Wilkinson
9/Black Watch
8/Seaforth Highlanders
10/Gordon Highlanders
7/Cameron Highlanders

45 BRIGADE
Brigadier-General F.E. Wallerstein[17]
Brigadier-General E.W.B. Green
13/Royal Scots
7/Royal Scots Fusiliers
6/Cameron Highlanders
11/Argyll & Sutherland Highlanders

46 BRIGADE
Brigadier-General T.G. Matheson
7/KOSB
8/KOSB
10/Scottish Rifles
12/Highland Light Infantry

DIVISIONAL ARTILLERY
LXX Bde RFA
LXXI Bde RFA
LXXII Bde RFA
LXXIII Bde RFA

47TH (LONDON) DIVISION

Major-General C. St. L. Barter

140 (4/LONDON) BRIGADE

Brigadier-General G.J. Cuthbert

1/6th London
1/7th London
1/8th London (Post Office Rifles)
1/15th London (Civil Service) Rifles

141 (5/LONDON) BRIGADE

Brigadier-General W. Thwaites

1/17th London (Poplar & Stepney Rifles)
1/18th London (London Irish)
1/19th London (St Pancras)
1/20th London (Blackheath & Woolwich)

142 (6/LONDON) BRIGADE

Brigadier-General F.G. Lewis

1/21st London (1st Surrey Rifles)
1/22nd London (The Queen's)
1/23rd London
1/24th London (The Queen's)

DIVISIONAL ARTILLERY

V London Bde RFA
VI London Bde RFA
VII London Bde RFA
VIII London Bde RFA

XI CORPS

Lieutenant-General R.C.B. Haking

THE GUARDS DIVISION

Major-General the Earl of Cavan

1 (GUARDS) BRIGADE

Brigadier-General G.P.T. Feilding[18]

2/Grenadier Guards
2/Coldstream Guards
3/Coldstream Guards
1/Irish Guards

2 (GUARDS) BRIGADE

Brigadier-General J. Ponsonby

3/Grenadier Guards
1/Coldstream Guards
1/Scots Guards
2/Irish Guards

3 (GUARDS) BRIGADE

Brigadier-General F.J. Heyworth[19]

1/Grenadier Guards
4/Grenadier Guards
2/Scots Guards
1/Welsh Guards

DIVISIONAL ARTILLERY

LXXIV Bde RFA
LXXV Bde RFA
LXXVI Bde RFA
LXI Bde RFA

12TH (EASTERN) DIVISION

Major-General F.D.V. Wing[20]
Brigadier-General W.K. McLeod (acting)
Major-General A.B. Scott[21]

35 BRIGADE

Brigadier-General C.H. van Straubenzee[22]

7/Norfolk
9/Essex
7/Suffolk
5/Royal Berkshire

36 BRIGADE

Brigadier-General H.B. Borradaile

8/Royal Fusiliers
7/Royal Sussex
9/Royal Fusiliers
11/Middlesex

37 BRIGADE

Brigadier-General C.A. Fowler

6/Queen's
7/East Surrey
6/Buffs
6/Royal West Kent

DIVISIONAL ARTILLERY

LXII Bde RFA
LXIV Bde RFA
LXIII Bde RFA
LXV Bde RFA

21ST DIVISION

Major-General G.T. Forestier-Walker

62 BRIGADE

Brigadier-General E.B. Wilkinson

12/Northumberland Fusiliers
8/East Yorkshire
13/Northumberland Fusiliers
10/Yorkshire

63 BRIGADE

Brigadier-General N.T. Nickalls[23]
Lieutenant-Colonel E.R. Hill[24]

8/Lincolnshire
12/West Yorkshire
8/Somerset Light Infantry
10/York & Lancaster

64 BRIGADE

Brigadier-General G.M. Gloster

9/KOYLI
14/Durham Light Infantry
10/KOYLI
15/Durham Light Infantry

DIVISIONAL ARTILLERY

XCIV Bde RFA
XCVI Bde RFA
XCV Bde RFA
XCVII Bde RFA

24TH DIVISION
Major-General Sir J.G. Ramsay
Major-General J.E. Capper[25]

71 BRIGADE
Brigadier-General M.T. Shewen
9/Norfolk
8/Bedfordshire
9/Suffolk
11/Essex

72 BRIGADE
Brigadier-General B.R. Mitford
8/Queen's
9/East Surrey
8/Buffs
8/Royal West Kent

73 BRIGADE
Brigadier-General W.A. Oswald[26]
Brigadier-General R.G. Jelf[27]
12/Royal Fusiliers
7/Northamptonshire
9/Royal Sussex
13/Middlesex

DIVISIONAL ARTILLERY
CVI Bde RFA
CVIII Bde RFA
CVII Bde RFA
CIX Bde RFA

46TH (NORTH MIDLAND) DIVISION
Major-General Hon. E.J. Montagu-Stuart-Wortley

137 BRIGADE
Brigadier-General E. Feetham
1/5th South Staffordshire
1/5th North Staffordshire
1/6th South Staffordshire
1/6th North Staffordshire

138 BRIGADE
Brigadier-General G.C. Kemp
1/4th Lincolnshire
1/4th Leicestershire
1/1st Monmouthshire
1/5th Lincolnshire
1/5th Leicestershire

139 BRIGADE
Brigadier-General C.T. Shipley
1/5th Sherwood Foresters
1/7th Sherwood Foresters
1/6th Sherwood Foresters
1/8th Sherwood Foresters

DIVISIONAL ARTILLERY
I (N. Mid) Bde RFA
III (N. Mid) Bde RFA
II (N. Mid) Bde RFA
IV (N. Mid) Bde RFA

NOTES

1 Mortally wounded, 26 September 1915. Died of wounds, 27 September 1915.
2 KIA, 24 October 1915.
3 GOC 7th Division, 27 September 1915.
4 KIA, 27 September 1915.
5 Acting GOC 9th (Scottish) Division, 27 September 1915.
6 GOC 9th (Scottish) Division, 28 September 1915.
7 Taken prisoner, 25 September 1915.
8 GOC 27 Brigade, 26 September 1915.
9 Sick, 11 October 1915.
10 GOC 28th Division, 12 October 1915.
11 Wounded, 27 September 1915.
12 GOC 85 Brigade, 27 September 1915. Killed in action, 17 May 1917.
13 GOC 85 Brigade, 28 September 1915.
14 Wounded, 1 October 1915.
15 KIA, 28 September 1915.
16 GOC 2 Brigade, 28 September 1915.
17 Invalided home, 11 October 1915.
18 Wounded, 8 December 1915.
19 KIA, 9 May 1916.
20 KIA, 2 October 1915.
21 GOC 12th Division, 3 October 1915.
22 Sick, 25 October 1915.
23 KIA, 26 September 1915.
24 GOC 63 Brigade, 7 October 1915.
25 GOC 24th Division, 3 October 1915.
26 Relieved of command, 26 September 1915.
27 GOC 73 Brigade, 26 September 1915.

GERMAN ORDER OF BATTLE

OHL

General Erich von Falkenhayn

SIXTH ARMY

Crown Prince Rupprecht of Bavaria

IV CORPS

General Sixt von Armin

117TH DIVISION

22 Reserve Regiment
157 Regiment
11 Reserve Regiment

8TH DIVISION

72 Regiment
93 Regiment
153 Regiment
216 Regiment

7TH DIVISION

26 Reserve Regiment
27 Reserve Regiment

123RD (SAXON) DIVISION

106 Reserve Regiment
107 Reserve Regimen
178 Regiment
182 Regiment

VII CORPS

14TH DIVISION

16 Regiment (inc. 11/Jager Battalion)
56 Regiment
57 Regiment

X RESERVE CORPS

2ND GUARD RESERVE DIVISION

26 Reserve Brigade
38 Reserve Brigade

II BAVARIAN CORPS

9 Bavarian Regiment
17 Bavarian Regiment
18 Bavarian Regiment

THE GUARD CORPS

1ST GUARDS DIVISION

2ND GUARDS DIVISION

APPENDIX II: TOTAL RECORDED BRITISH DEATHS, 25 SEPTEMBER 1915 AND 1 JULY 1916*

TOTAL RECORDED DEATHS ON 25 SEPTEMBER 1915.

2nd Division	734
9th (Scottish) Division	1,171
7th Division	1,565
1st Division	872
15th (Scottish) Division	1,595
47th (London) Division	413
TOTAL	6,350
Average deaths per division	1,058

TOTAL RECORDED DEATHS ON 1 JULY 1916.

8th Division	1,668
34th Division	2,250
19th (Western) Division	20
4th Division	1,298
29th Division	1,251

31st Division	1,075
48th (South Midland) Division	395
32nd Division	1,238
36th (Ulster) Division	1,664
49th (West Riding) Division	24
18th (Eastern) Division	797
30th Division	625
7th Division	938
17th (Northern) Division	455
21st Division	835
46th (North Midland) Division	770
56th (London) Division	1,379
TOTAL	17,290
Average deaths per division	1,017

* Figures taken from *Soldiers Died in the Great War 1914–1919*, CD-ROM (Uckfield, East Sussex: Naval & Military Press).

APPENDIX III: SENIOR BRITISH OFFICER CASUALTIES

SENIOR OFFICERS KILLED IN ACTION OR MORTALLY WOUNDED BETWEEN 25 SEPTEMBER–15 OCTOBER 1915

Major-General Sir T. Capper (GOC 7th Division).
Major J.G. Collins (CO 8/Black Watch, 26 Brigade).
Lieutenant-Colonel H.D. Collison-Morley (CO 1/19th London, 141 Brigade).
Captain A.H. Connell (2/Royal Scots Fusiliers, 21 Brigade).
Major W.H. Dent (Acting CO 10/Yorkshire, 62 Brigade).
Lieutenant-Colonel A.F. Douglas-Hamilton (CO 6/Cameron Highlanders, 45 Brigade).
Lieutenant-Colonel R.C. Dundas (CO 11/Royal Scottish, 27 Brigade).
Lieutenant-Colonel A.G.E. Egerton (CO 1/Coldstream Guards, 1 (Guards) Brigade).
Lieutenant-Colonel F.H. Fairtlough (CO 8/Queens, 72 Brigade).
Lieutenant-Colonel G.H. Fowler (CO 1/8th Sherwood Foresters, 139 Brigade).
Lieutenant-Colonel W.T. Gaisford (CO 7/Seaforth Highlanders, 26 Brigade).
Major R.D. Garnons-Williams (CO 12/Royal Fusiliers, 73 Brigade).
Lieutenant-Colonel A.G.W. Grant (CO 8/Devonshire, 21 Brigade).
Lieutenant-Colonel A. de. S. Hadow (CO 10/Yorkshire, 62 Brigade).
Lieutenant-Colonel A.S. Hamilton (CO 14/Durham Light Infantry, 64 Brigade).
Lieutenant-Colonel M.G. Heath (CO 2/Queen's, 22 Brigade).
Major W.J.S Hosley (Acting CO 6/KOSB, 28 Brigade).
Lieutenant-Colonel J.H. Knight (CO 1/5th North Staffordshire, 137 Brigade).
Lieutenant-Colonel B.H. Leatham (CO 2/Wiltshire, 21 Brigade).
Lieutenant-Colonel B.P. Lefroy (CO 2/Royal Warwickshire, 22 Brigade).
Lieutenant-Colonel E.T. Logan (CO 15/Durham Light Infantry, 64 Brigade).
Lieutenant-Colonel G.H.C. Madden (CO 1/Irish Guards, 1 (Guards) Brigade).
Lieutenant-Colonel G.H. Neale (CO 3/Middlesex, 85 Brigade).

Brigadier-General N.T. Nickalls (GOC 63 Brigade).
Lieutenant-Colonel A. Parkin (CO 7/Northamptonshire, 73 Brigade).
Lieutenant-Colonel C.E. Radclyffe (CO 11/Essex, 71 Brigade).
Colonel R.C. Romer (CO 8/Buffs, 72 Brigade).
Lieutenant-Colonel J.R.E. Stansfeld (CO 2/Gordon Highlanders, 21 Brigade).
Major R.J.A. Terry (acting GOC 2 Brigade).
Major-General G.H. Thesiger (GOC 9th (Scottish) Division).
Lieutenant-Colonel G. de W. Verner (CO 7/KOSB, 46 Brigade).
Lieutenant-Colonel H.E. Walter (CO 8/Lincolnshire, 63 Brigade).
Major-General F.D.V. Wing (GOC 12th Division).
Lieutenant-Colonel C.A. Worthington (CO 2/Buffs, 85 Brigade).

SENIOR OFFICERS WOUNDED BETWEEN 25 SEPTEMBER–15 OCTOBER 1915:

Major L.W. Bird (CO 1/Royal Berkshire, Carter's Force).
Major R.V.G. Brettell (CO 9/Suffolk, 71 Brigade).
Brigadier-General C.D. Bruce (GOC 27 Brigade), captured.
Major C.G. Forsyth (Acting CO 2/Wiltshire, 21 Brigade).
Lieutenant-Colonel S.H. Godman (CO 1/Scots Guards, 2 (Guards) Brigade).
Lieutenant-Colonel J.C. Grahame (CO 10/Highland Light Infantry, 28 Brigade).
Major F.L. Grant (Acting CO 10/Scottish Rifles, 46 Brigade).
Lieutenant-Colonel G.C. Hamilton (CO 4/Grenadier Guards, 3 (Guards) Brigade).
Lieutenant-Colonel C.E. Heathcote (CO 1/4th Lincolnshire, 138 Brigade).
Lieutenant-Colonel G.B. Hinton (CO XXVI Brigade RFA).
Lieutenant-Colonel R.A.C.L. Leggett (CO 12/West Yorkshire, 63 Brigade).
Lieutenant-Colonel H.A.K. Livingstone (CRE, 9th Division).
Lieutenant-Colonel A.F. Mackenzie (CO 10/Argyll & Sutherland Highlanders, 27 Brigade).
Lieutenant-Colonel H.D.N. Maclean (CO 6/KOSB, 28 Brigade).
Lieutenant-Colonel R.E. Martin (CO 1/4th Leicestershire, 138 Brigade).
Lieutenant-Colonel H. McMicking (CO 6/Gordon Highlanders, 20 Brigade).
Lieutenant-Colonel A.C. Northey (CO 9/Scottish Rifles, 28 Brigade).
Lieutenant-Colonel C.C. Onslow (CO 2/Bedfordshire, 21 Brigade).
Brigadier-General C.E. Pereira (GOC 85 Brigade).
Brigadier-General J.H.W. Pollard (GOC 2 Brigade).
Lieutenant-Colonel G.K. Priaulx (CO 2/KRRC, 2 Brigade).
Lieutenant-Colonel A.G. Prothero (2/Welsh, 3 Brigade), captured.
Lieutenant-Colonel T.E. Sandall (CO 1/5th Lincolnshire, 138 Brigade).
Lieutenant-Colonel W.C. Sanderson (CO 1/Loyal North Lancashire, 2 Brigade).
Colonel Lord Sempill (CO 8/Black Watch, 26 Brigade).
Lieutenant-Colonel H.I. Storey (CO 9/Devonshire, 20 Brigade).
Lieutenant-Colonel N.A. Thompson (CO 8/Seaforth Highlanders, 44 Brigade).
Lieutenant-Colonel A.V. Ussher (CO 10/Scottish Rifles, 46 Brigade).
Lieutenant-Colonel J.E. Vanrenen (CRE the Guards Division), sick.
Colonel E. Vansittart (CO 9/Royal West Kent, 72 Brigade), captured.
Brigadier-General F.E. Wallerstein (GOC 45 Brigade), invalided home.
Lieutenant-Colonel H.B. Warwick (CO 12/Northumberland Fusiliers, 62 Brigade).
Lieutenant-Colonel B.I. Way (CO 8/East Yorkshire, 62 Brigade).
Lieutenant-Colonel O. de L. Williams (CO 2/Royal Welsh Fusiliers, 19 Brigade).

LIST OF ILLUSTRATIONS

Maps adapted from Sir J.E. Edmonds (comp.), *History of the Great War: Military Operations France & Belgium, 1915*, vol. 2, *Battles of Aubers Ridge, Festubert and Loos* (London/Nashville: Imperial War Museum/Battery Press, 1995; first published 1928), Map 6 & Map 9.

MAPS

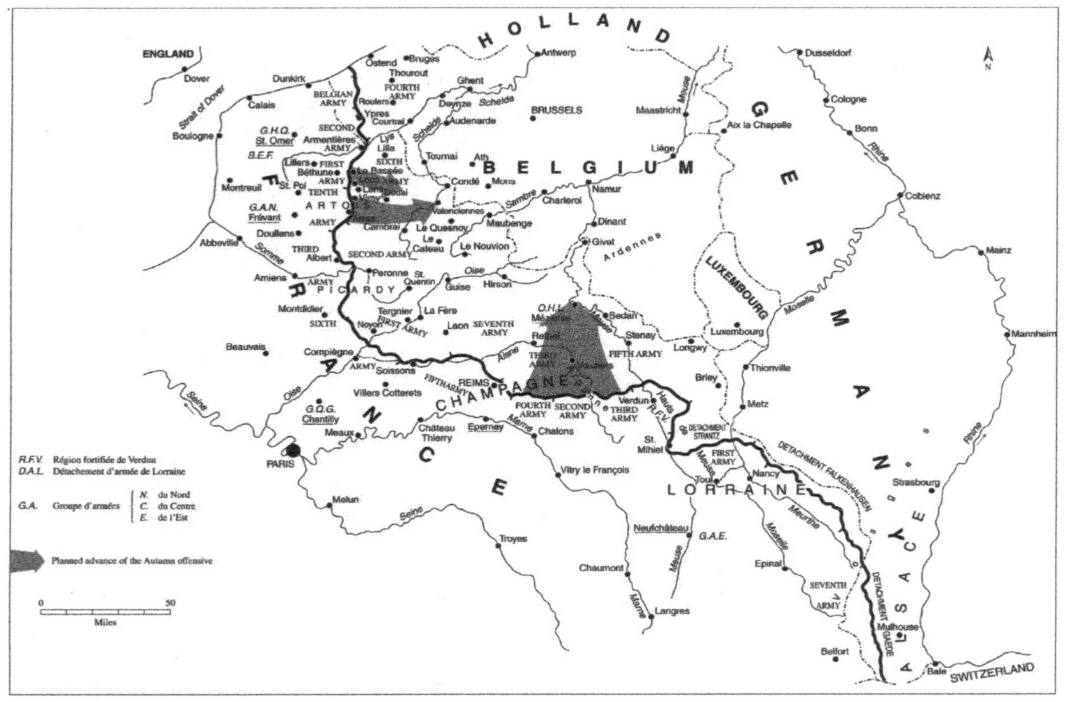

Situation on the Western Front in the Summer of 1915.

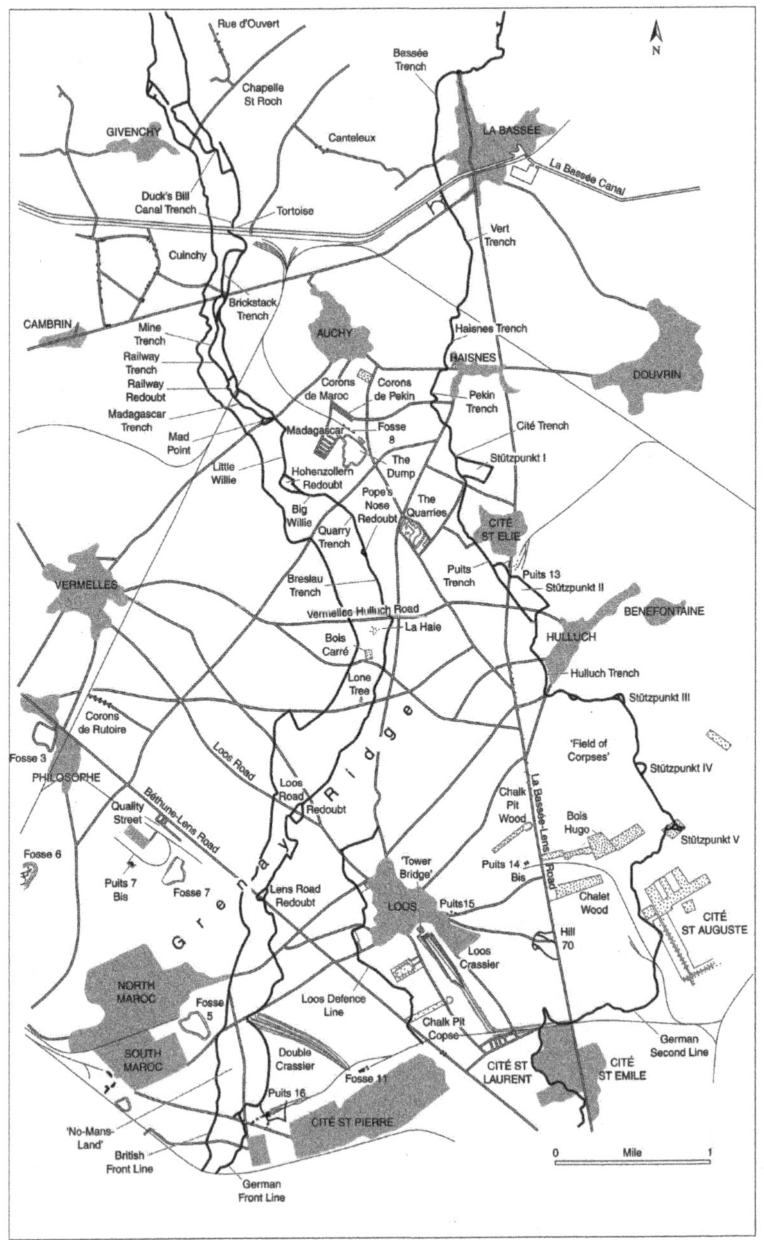

The Loos Battlefield.

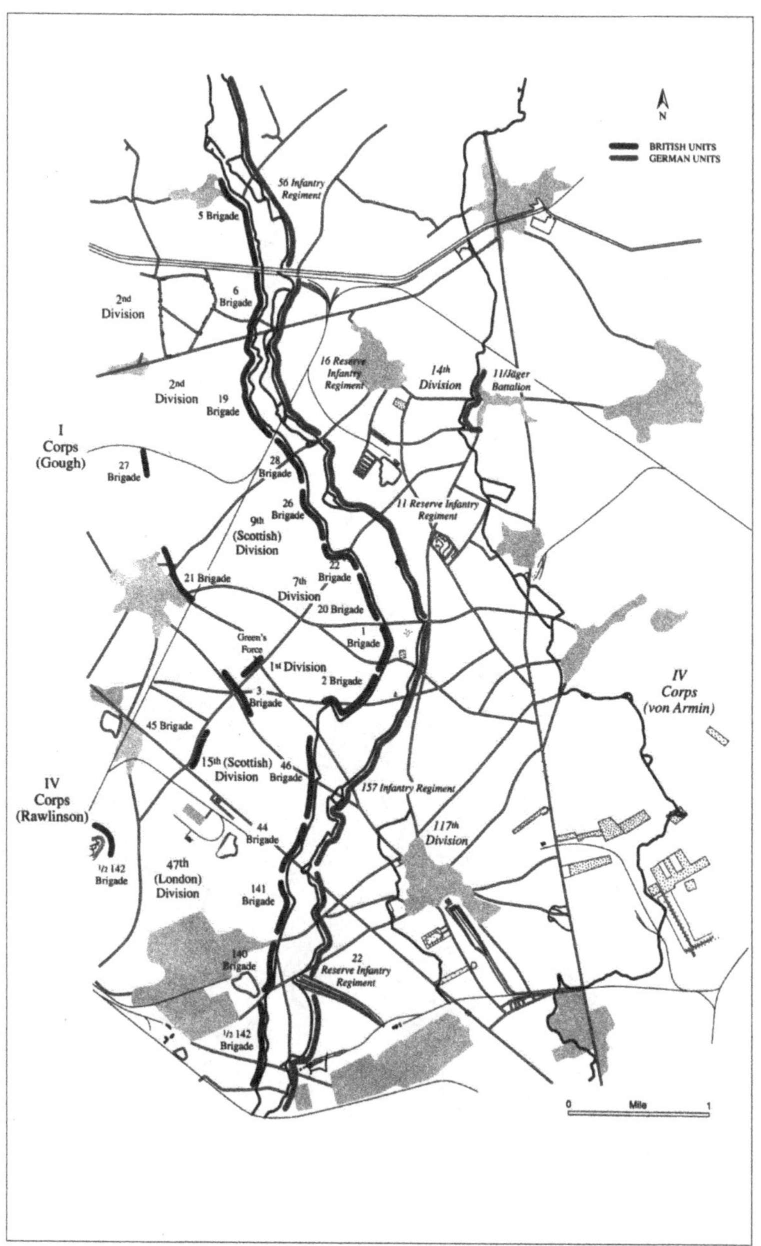

Dispositions: Zero Hour, 25 September 1915.

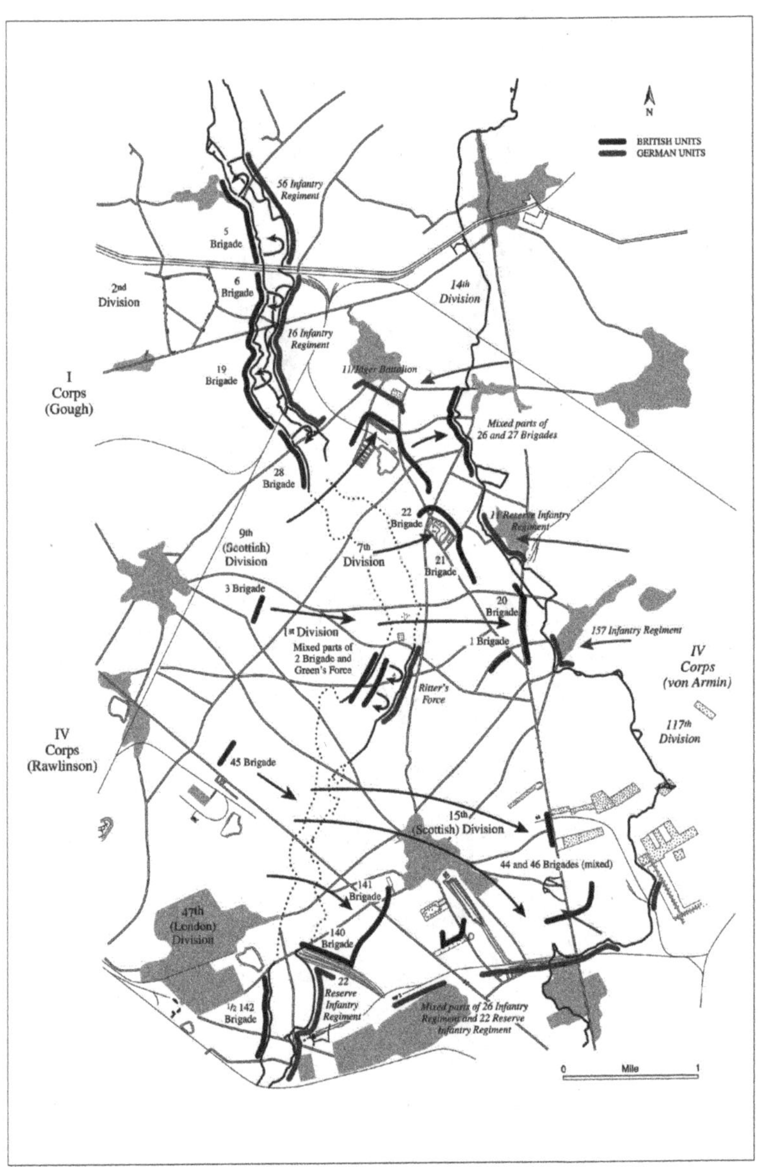

The Height of the British Advance, Mid-Morning, 25 September 1915.

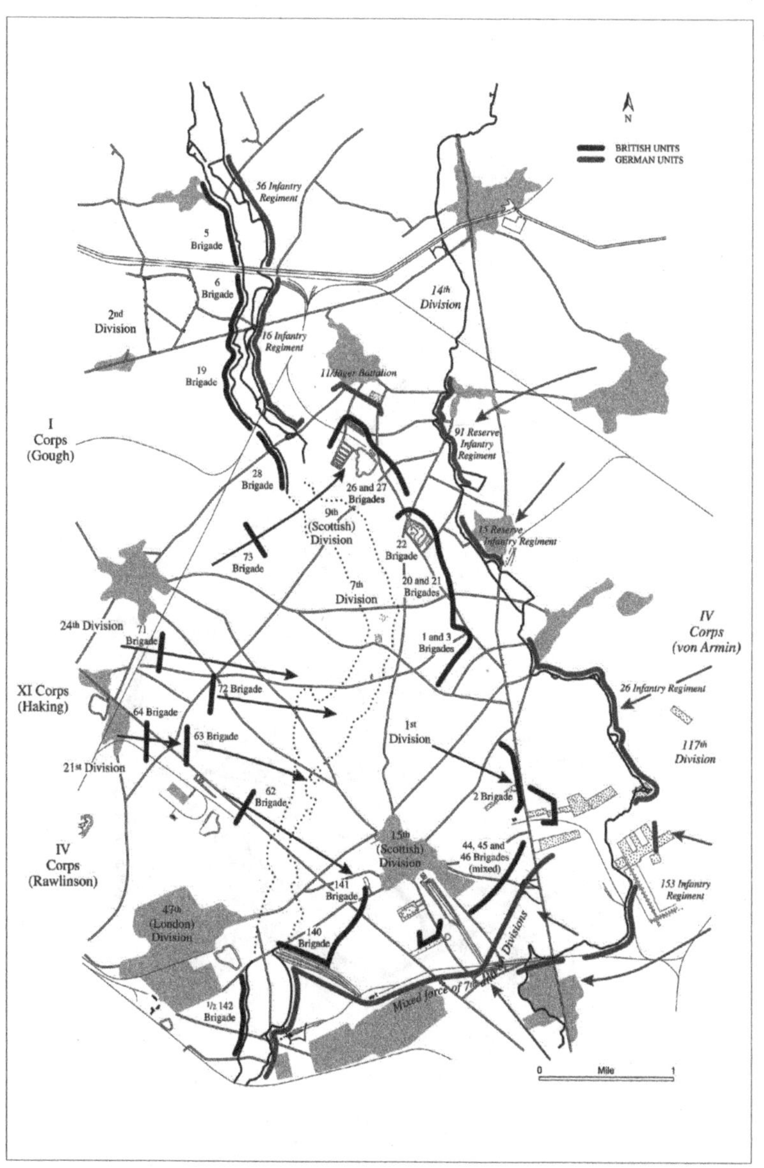

The End of the First Day, 25 September 1915.

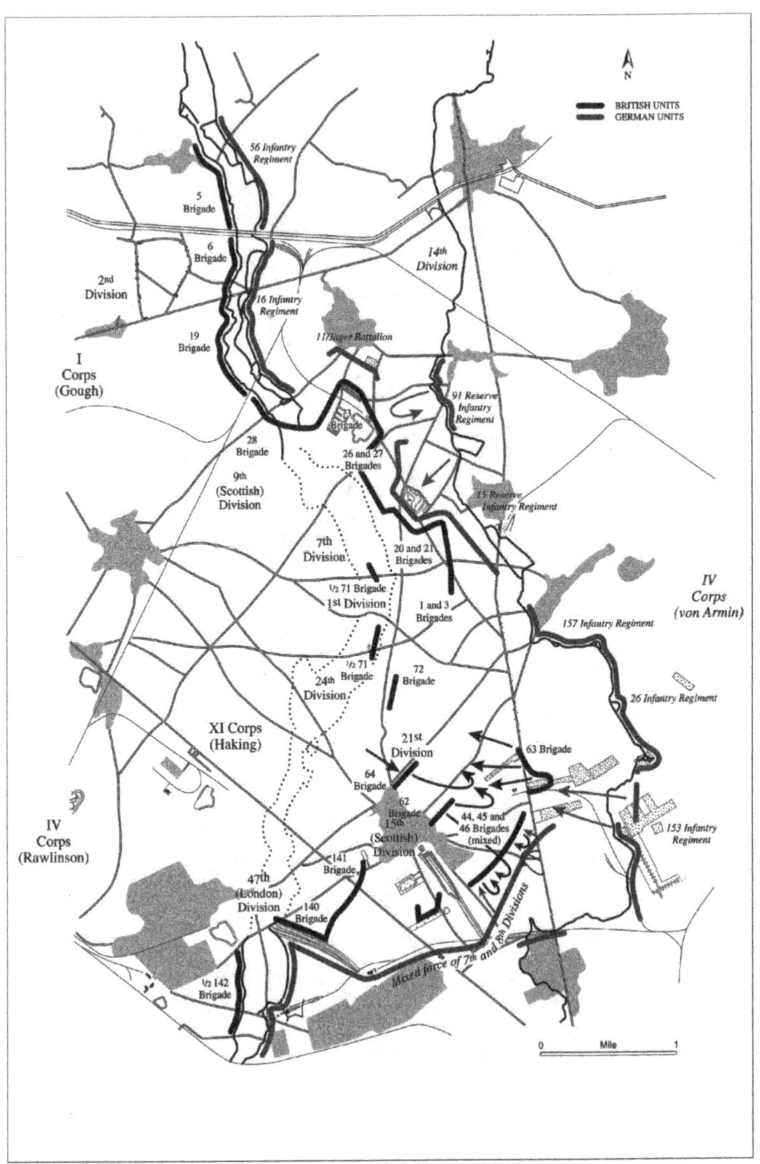

The Morning of the Second Day, 26 September 1915.

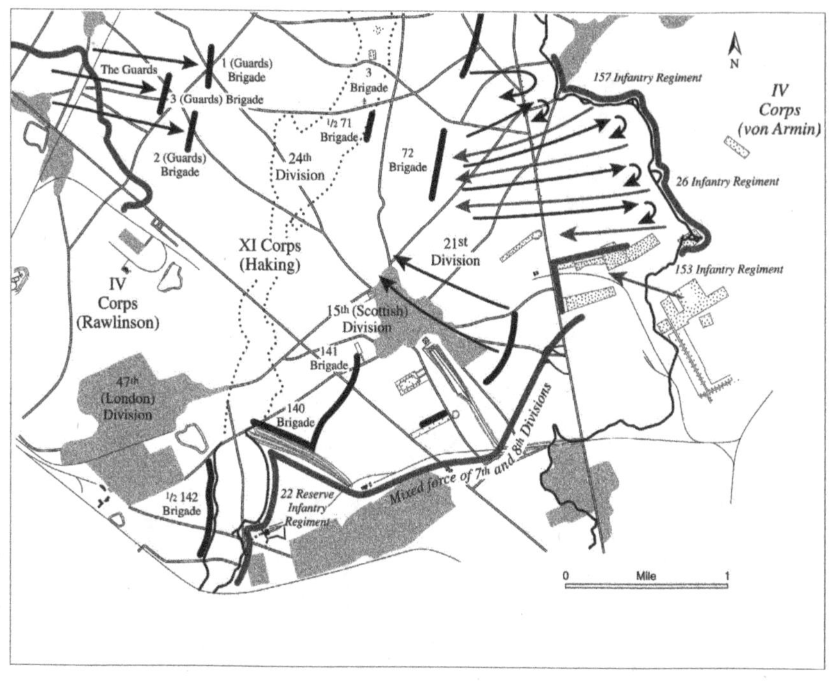

The Attack on the German Second Line, 26 September 1915.

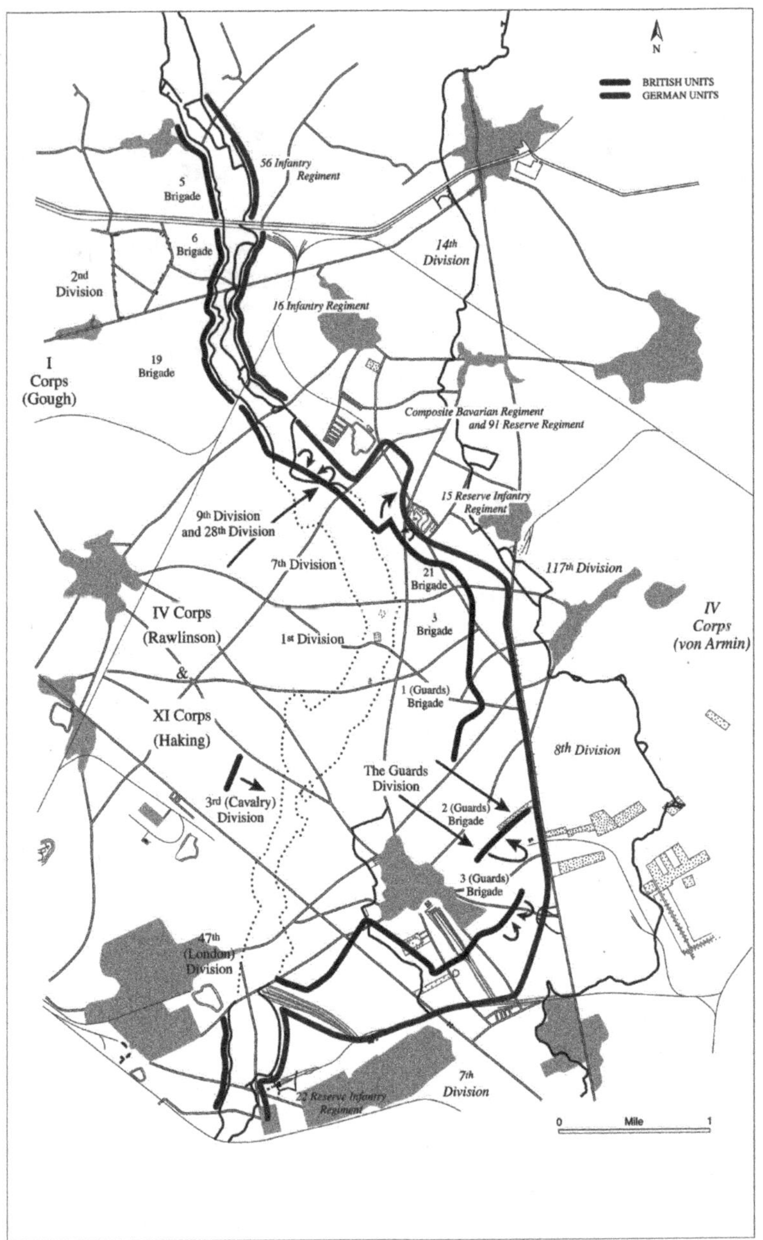

Continuing the Offensive, 27–28 September 1915.

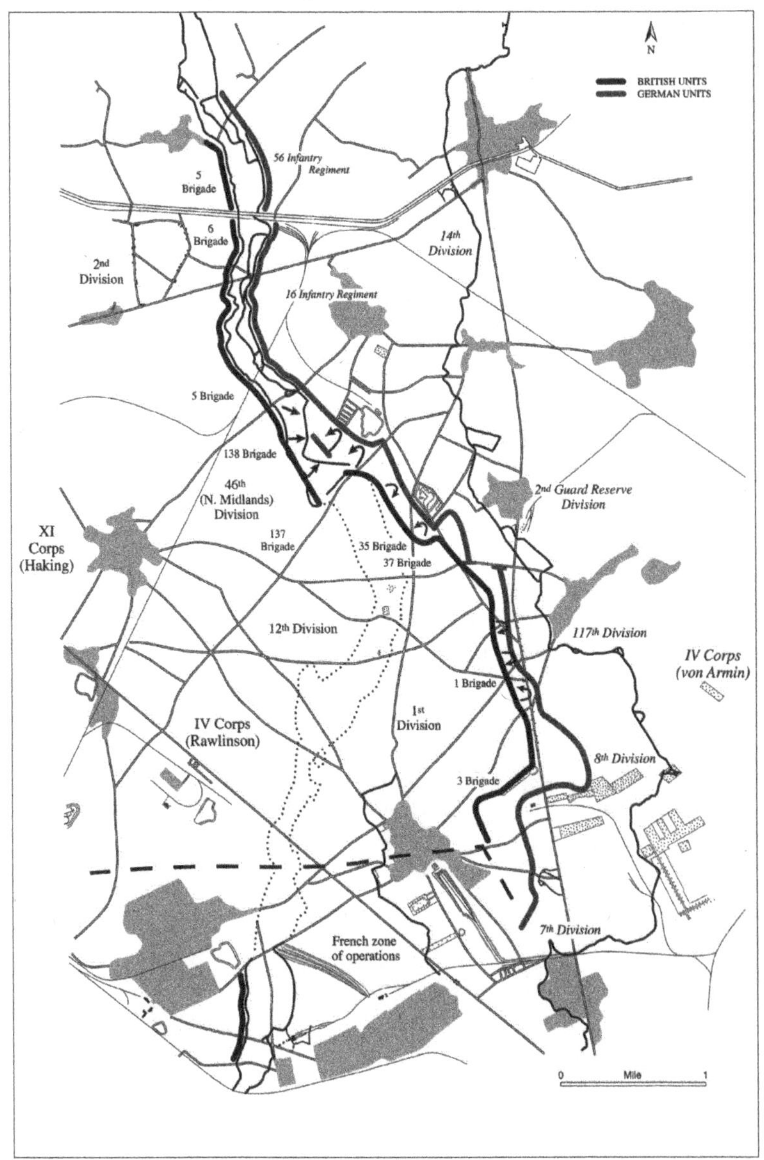

The Renewed Offensive, 13 October 1915.

INDEX

THE HISTORY PRESS

R.J.Mitchell
Schooldays to Spitfire
GORDON MITCHELL
'[A] readable and poignant story'
The Sunday Telegraph
£12.99 0 7524 3727 5

Forgotten Soldiers of the First World War
Lost Voices from the Middle Eastern Front
DAVID WOODWARD
'A brilliant new book of hitherto unheard voices from a haunting theatre of the First World War' ***Malcolm Brown***
£12.99 978 07524 4307 2

1690 Battle of the Boyne
PÁDRAIG LENIHAN
'An almost impeccably impartial account of the most controversial military engagement in British history' ***The Daily Mail***
£12.99 0 7524 3304 0

Hell at the Front
Combat Voices from the First World War
TOM DONOVAN
'Fifty powerful personal accounts, each vividly portraying the brutalising reality of the Great War... a remarkable book' ***Max Arthur***
£12.99 0 7524 3940 5

Amiens 1918
JAMES MCWILLIAMS & R. JAMES STEEL
'A masterly portrayal of this pivotal battle'
Soldier: The Magazine of the British Army
£25 0 7524 2860 8

Before Stalingrad
Hitler's Invasion of Russia 1941
DAVID GLANTZ
'Another fine addition to Hew Strachan's excellent *Battles and Campaigns* series'
BBC History Magazine
£9.99 0 7524 2692 3

The SS
A History 1919-45
ROBERT LEWIS KOEHL
'Reveals the role of the SS in the mass murder of the Jews, homosexuals and gypsies and its organisation of death squads throughout occupied Europe' ***The Sunday Telegraph***
£9.99 0 7524 2559 5

Arnhem 1944
WILLIAM BUCKINGHAM
'Reveals the real reason why the daring attack failed' ***The Daily Express***
£10.99 0 7524 3187 0

If you are interested in purchasing other books published by The History Press, or in case you have difficulty finding any History Press books in your local bookshop, you can also place orders directly through our website

www.thehistorypress.co.uk

THE HISTORY PRESS

The Wars of the Roses

The Soldiers' Experience

ANTHONY GOODMAN

'Sheds light on the lot of the common soldier as never before' ***Alison Weir***

'A meticulous work'
The Times Literary Supplement

£12.99 0 7524 3731 3

D-Day

The First 72 Hours

WILLIAM F. BUCKINGHAM

'A compelling narrative' ***The Observer***

A ***BBC History Magazine*** Book of the Year 2004

£9.99 0 7524 2842 2

English Battlefields

500 Battlefields that Shaped English History

MICHAEL RAYNER

'A painstaking survey of English battlefields... a first-rate book' ***Richard Holmes***

'A fascinating and, for all its factual tone, an atmospheric volume' ***The Sunday Telegraph***

£18.99 978 07524 4307 2

Trafalgar Captain Durham of the Defiance: The Man who refused to Miss Trafalgar

HILARY RUBINSTEIN

'A sparkling biography of Nelson's luckiest captain' ***Andrew Lambert***

£17.99 0 7524 3435 7

Battle of the Atlantic

MARC MILNER

'The most comprehensive short survey of the U-boat battles' ***Sir John Keegan***

'Some events are fortunate in their historian, none more so than the Battle of the Atlantic. Marc Milner is *the* historian of the Atlantic Campaign... a compelling narrative'
Andrew Lambert

£12.99 0 7524 3332 6

Okinawa 1945 The Stalingrad of the Pacific

GEORGE FEIFER

'A great book... Feifer's account of the three sides and their experiences far surpasses most books about war' ***Stephen Ambrose***

£17.99 0 7524 3324 5

Gallipoli 1915

TIM TRAVERS

'The most important new history of Gallipoli for forty years... groundbreaking' ***Hew Strachan***

'A book of the highest importance to all who would seek to understand the tragedy of the Gallipoli campaign' ***The Journal of Military History***

£13.99 0 7524 2972 8

Tommy Goes To War

MALCOLM BROWN

'A remarkably vivid and frank account of the British soldier in the trenches' ***Max Arthur***

'The fury, fear, mud, blood, boredom and bravery that made up life on the Western Front are vividly presented and illustrated' ***The Sunday Telegraph***

£12.99 0 7524 2980 9

If you are interested in purchasing other books published by The History Press, or in case you have difficulty finding any History Press books in your local bookshop, you can also place orders directly through our website

www.thehistorypress.co.uk

THE HISTORY PRESS

Private 12768 Memoir of a Tommy

JOHN JACKSON

'Unique... a beautifully written, strikingly honest account of a young man's experience of combat' ***Saul David***

'At last we have John Jackson's intensely personal and heartfelt little book to remind us there was a view of the Great War other than Wilfred Owen's' ***The Daily Mail***

£9.99 0 7524 3531 0

The German Offensives of 1918

MARTIN KITCHEN

'A lucid, powerfully driven narrative' ***Malcolm Brown***

'Comprehensive and authoritative... first class' ***Holger H. Herwig***

£13.99 0 7524 3527 2

Verdun 1916

MALCOLM BROWN

'A haunting book which gets closer than any other to that wasteland marked by death' ***Richard Holmes***

£9.99 0 7524 2599 4

The Forgotten Front

The East African Campaign 1914–1918

ROSS ANDERSON

'Excellent... fills a yawning gap in the historical record' ***The Times Literary Supplement***

'Compelling and authoritative' ***Hew Strachan***

£12.99 978 07524 4126 9

Agincourt

A New History

ANNE CURRY

'A highly distinguished and convincing account' ***Christopher Hibbert***

'A *tour de force*' ***Alison Weir***

'*The* book on the battle' ***Richard Holmes***

A ***BBC History Magazine*** Book of the Year 2005

£12.99 0 7524 3813 1

The Welsh Wars of Independence

DAVID MOORE

'Beautifully written, subtle and remarkably perceptive' ***John Davies***

£12.99 978 07524 4128 3

Bosworth 1485 Psychology of a Battle

MICHAEL K. JONES

'Most exciting... a remarkable tale' ***The Guardian***

'Insightful and rich study of the Battle of Bosworth... no longer need Richard play the villain' ***The Times Literary Supplement***

£12.99 0 7524 2594 3

The Battle of Hastings 1066

M.K. LAWSON

'Blows away many fundamental assumptions about the battle of Hastings... an exciting and indispensable read' ***David Bates***

A ***BBC History Magazine*** Book of the Year 2003

£12.99 978 07524 4177 1

If you are interested in purchasing other books published by The History Press, or in case you have difficulty finding any History Press books in your local bookshop, you can also place orders directly through our website

www.thehistorypress.co.uk